Crown under Law

Crown under Law

Richard Hooker, John Locke, and the Ascent of Modern Constitutionalism

Alexander S. Rosenthal

LEXINGTON BOOKS
A division of
ROWMAN & LITTLEFIELD PUBLISHERS, INC.
Lanham • Boulder • New York • Toronto • Plymouth, UK

JA
84
.G7
R67
2008

LEXINGTON BOOKS

A division of Rowman & Littlefield Publishers, Inc.
A wholly owned subsidary of The Rowman & Littlefield Publishing Group, Inc.
4501 Forbes Boulevard, Suite 200
Lanham, MD 20706

Estover Road
Plymouth PL6 7PY
United Kingdom

British Library Cataloguing in Publication Information Available

Library of Congress Cataloging-in-Publication Data
Rosenthal, Alexander S., 1969–
  Crown under law : Richard Hooker, John Locke, and the ascent of modern
constitutionalism / Alexander S. Rosenthal.
      p. cm.
  Includes bibliographical references and index.
  ISBN-13: 978-0-7391-2413-0 (cloth : alk. paper)
  ISBN-10: 0-7391-2413-7 (cloth : alk. paper)
  ISBN-13: 978-0-7391-2414-7 (pbk. : alk. paper)
  ISBN-10: 0-7391-2414-5 (pbk. : alk. paper)
  1. Political science—Great Britain—History—17th century. 2. Constitutional history—
Great Britain. 3. Locke, John, 1632–1704. 4. Hooker, Richard, 1553 or 4–1600—
Political and social views. I. Title.
  JA84.G7R67 2008
  321.8'7—dc22
                                                                                2008005844

Printed in the United States of America

∞™ The paper used in this publication meets the minimum requirements of American
National Standard for Information Sciences—Permanence of Paper for Printed Library
Materials, ANSI/NISO Z39.48-1992.

"Happier that people whose law is their King in the greatest things, than that whose King is himself the law."

Richard Hooker, *Laws of Ecclesiastical Polity, Book VIII*

This work is dedicated in loving memory of my father
Dr. Arthur Rosenthal, and my maternal grandmother
Elvira Martin Rodriguez

Et absterget Deus omnem lacrimam ab oculis eorum: et mors ultra non erit, neque luctus, neque clamor, neque dolor erit ultra, quia prima abierunt. - Apocalypsis 21:4

Contents

Acknowledgments

I would like to begin by thanking the editors of Lexington Books and particularly Mr. Patrick Dillon and Ms. Macduff Stewart for undertaking this project and guiding me along this process. I should also like to thank the anonymous reviewer with his very thorough and helpful comments. As this project was conceived during my doctoral years at the Higher Institute of Philosophy at the Katholieke Universisteit Leuven in Belgium I would certainly like to direct attention to my intellectual mentors. First, I'd thank my doctoral promoter Dr. Bart Raymaekers for his patient guidance, encouragement, and warm support for my project nourished by our discussions of political philosophy. It is thanks to Dr. Raymaekers, that I was able to find this new and for me felicitous direction for my academic pursuits, after the confusion and difficulty that followed the tragic death of my prospective promoter, Dr. Jos Decorte. I should also like to thank Dr. Martin Stone who went far beyond the call of duty to generously give of his time and of his extraordinary erudition in the field of medieval and renaissance philosophy to assist in this work. I would thank Ms. Kristina Pinto for her excellent work editing my introduction and conclusion, as well as Michael Funk Deckard for his assistance with the editing. The reader can be assured that whatever merits the formal aspect of this work has belongs to the editors, while any errors that remain are my responsibility alone. I would also like to thank my good friends David Pactwa and Biagio Tassone for very generous assistance provided at various point in my project. I should like to thank my parents, Arthur and Pili Rosenthal, for their constant love and support. Every son owes their parents an unpayable debt, but perhaps myself especially so, for all they have done for me in my life. I would like to thank my late, great aunt

Dorothy Halpern whose generosity helped to make the continuance of my academic pursuits possible. I would like to thank an old friend Richard Evans who was one of the first to suggest the importance of Hooker as a political thinker to me, many years ago.

List of Illustrations

The portrait of Richard Hooker on the cover is the frontispiece from Richard Hooker's *Of the Lawes of Ecclesiastical Politie.* (London: Andrew Crooke, 1666). This is copied from shelfmark Keynes T.17.13 with kind permission from Cambridge University Library, Cambridge University.

Fig 1. The illustration before Part I's opening page is from John Case's *Sphaera Civitatis* (Oxford: Iosephus Barnesius, 1588), page viii. Case was one of the most prominent figures among the Elizabethan Aristotelians. This is copied from shelfmark BYW. L4.6 with kind permission from Bodleian Library, University of Oxford.

Fig. 2. The illustration before Part II is from Edward Gee's *The Divine Right and Originall of the Civill Magistrate from God* (London: George Eversden, 1658). Gee was one the earliest significant opponents of Filmer's patriarchalist arguments, and he anticipated the Whig doctrines of Tyrrell, Sidney, and Locke. This is copied from shelfmark 8.119 Lin, with kind permission from Bodleian Library, University of Oxford.

Figs. 3–5. The illustrations before chapter V are from Locke's personal journal. The display is of Locke's notes on Hooker's theory of law. These are copied from Locke's unpublished journals with shelfmark Bodleian Oxford MS fol. 5. 69,74, 75 (1681), with kind permission from Bodleian Library, University of Oxford.

Biblical quotations on the dedication page are from the Clementine Vulgate Bible text from the following website vulsearch.sourceforge.net/gettext.html (last accessed 1/27/08).

Crown under Law:
A General Introduction

There is perhaps no idea in the history of political thought with greater centrality and influence than that of *constitutionalism*. Its roots can be traced back to the civilizations of antiquity and throughout the great signature events of political history. The great prophets of ancient Israel spoke of a divine law that not even kings could transgress without being called to account. Among the Greeks, Aristotle wrote in his *Politics* of the benefits of the rule of law over the rule of individuals. The Roman philosopher-statesman Cicero wrote of a law implanted in human nature and knowable by reason, arguing that the justice and injustice of earthly laws could be measured through this principle.[1] From the speeches of Pericles in ancient times, to the Magna Carta and the American Constitution, to contemporary developments in post-communist Europe after the fall of the Berlin Wall, constitutionalism has proven to be a subject of enduring interest and compelling practical importance across all ages and all over the world.

This study is intended as a contribution to answering the following question: what is the historical and theoretical origin of modern constitutionalism? In pursuing this question, my work focuses on two Englishmen central to the development of the modern form of the constitutional idea—Richard Hooker and John Locke. In undertaking this study, I am conscious of a certain asymmetry in recognition of these two figures. While Locke is already a canonical figure of the Western intellectual tradition, well known to Americans because of his direct influence on the founders, Hooker may be less familiar even to many educated modern readers. For that reason it is perhaps appropriate to begin by introducing him.[2]

Hooker lent his pen to prose during the full flower of the Elizabethan era in England—the very time and place where William Shakespeare, Edmund

Spenser, and Christopher Marlowe wrote their immortal works of poetry and drama. For a century after his death Hooker was seen as a preeminent authority invoked by the sundry factions in English political controversy to settle their conflicting claims. For Anglicans, Hooker was seen as a kind of doctor and patron saint; his status was so assured that without any hint of sarcasm a seventeenth century gentlemen like Sir Robert Filmer made parallel assertions about the authority of "Aristotle in natural philosophy . . . Hooker in divinity." Hooker was even widely respected and praised among non-Anglicans. In an era not known for ecumenical comity, Pope Clement VIII—regnant at the time of publication of Hooker's magnum opus *The Laws of Ecclesiastical Polity*—said of his work: "It has in it such seeds of eternity that it will abide until the last fire shall consume all learning."[3]

It is a mark of how much the situation has changed that the man now requires some introduction. Who was Richard Hooker? Born in Exeter in 1554,[4] he enrolled in Oxford as a young man with the generous support of one of the first great apologists for conformity to the Church of England, Bishop John Jewel. At Oxford, in 1568 he entered Corpus Christi College, where his tutor was John Rainolds, a figure of Calvinist theological leanings. After receiving his master's degree in 1577, Hooker became a professor of Hebrew at Oxford. In 1581, Hooker received Anglican orders, and four years later was appointed Master of the Temple, where his role was to serve as a spiritual guide to the Inns of Court. Hooker's involvement with the English legal community was to be of crucial importance in inspiring his interest in political and legal philosophy. At the Temple, he also became involved in his first major theological controversy on the issue of predestination with a stern Calvinist by the name of Walter Travers—an affair I shall investigate in more detail later. Hooker thereafter became a central figure in the controversy between Anglican conformists, who defended the Elizabethan settlement, and the nascent Puritan movement. In 1593 Hooker published the first book of his *Of the Laws of Ecclesiastical Polity*, in which he presented the most systematic defense of the theology and government of the Church of England up to that time. As we shall see, this work was also pregnant with important ideas in political philosophy.

While scholars of Richard Hooker generally agree on his importance in the history of religious and political thought, there seems to be little further concord among them. It is indeed striking to note the plethora of responses to Hooker's life and work. Up until the early twentieth century Hooker was widely regarded among English historians as a precursor to Locke and thus an early ancestor of modern liberal and contractarian theories of government.[5] A.P. d'Entreves, however, saw him as essentially a sixteenth-century Anglican example of seventeenth-century Catholic scholasticism.[6] Peter Munz, while broadly accepting a Thomistic core in his work, saw Hooker also as a disciple of Marsilius of Padua.[7] Others, however, reject the whole "Anglo-Catholic" interpretation, and see Hooker as very much in the mainstream of the magisterial Protestant and even anti-Romanist tradition.[8] The remarkable capacity of Richard Hooker to be "all things to all men" in the opinion of modern scholars echoes his reception in earlier periods.

Upon his death in 1600, Hooker left a long and distinguished legacy. All sides of religious and political controversy in seventeenth century England recognized Hooker as a major figure whose authority could be employed to settle difficult disputes about theology. During the Restoration era, Hooker was essentially canonized as an almost infallible saint and doctor of the Anglican Church. Meanwhile Whigs like Algernon Sidney, James Tyrrell, and especially John Locke turned to Hooker for their own, quite different, purposes. Hooker's status as a luminary of Anglican theology was more or less secure through the eighteenth and nineteenth centuries with Tractarians like John Keble (who guided a new publication of Hooker's works) and John Henry Newman celebrating Hooker as a proponent of the *Via Media* between Protestantism and Roman Catholicism. Meanwhile, Hooker's contribution to Whig constitutionalism was generally accepted (albeit in an often unreflective way) during this period.

It was not until the second half of the twentieth century that Hooker was largely neglected, and it is not immediately apparent why this occurred. If I might speculate, there are a number of reasons for the neglect of Hooker by contemporary scholarship. To some degree, the decline of interest in his work reflects the more general neglect of late scholasticism or early modern scholasticism represented by those great figures that carried forth the rich intellectual traditions of medieval scholasticism into what chronologists refer to as *modernity*. There is, on the one hand, the secularist prejudice stemming from the Enlightenment that sees the whole medieval period as barren of authentic learning and dominated by ignorance, religious fanaticism, and superstition. For those who accept this idea, it is more or less axiomatic that the great achievement of Western constitutional government was entirely the work of "enlightened" modern figures that at long last broke the chains of authoritarian kings and clerics. On the other hand, a number of contemporary trends in the academic world are essentially *anti-modernist* projects. These do little more to further the study of early modern scholasticism precisely because they are more interested in the *contrasts* between modern and premodern thought, rather then the *continuities*. In theology, for example, we might think of the anti-modernist polemic in *radical orthodoxy*, and in political philosophy we might think of the Straussian school with its hard and fast distinction between the "ancients" and the "moderns." Because of its wide influence, I have reserved a discussion of the Straussian reading.

None of these trends are highly conducive to an interest in Richard Hooker—a transitional figure whose work was deeply influenced by the medieval scholastic tradition represented by St. Thomas Aquinas, even while adapting this tradition to confront the new challenges of early modern political life. In the rich system that Hooker constructed from these resources, we find the great perennial questions of political philosophy addressed: How ought men to order their lives together? What are the moral goods at which political life should aim? How did human beings come to be subject to the authority of other human beings? Is man naturally a social animal? Is he naturally also a political animal? What is the origin of our political obligations? What principles render political action legitimate? What are the limits of the power to govern? From where does the source of the right to make laws that bind others descend? The answers that Hooker provided to these questions differ in many particulars from other thinkers who are more generally known and studied, and for this reason Hooker has his own intrinsic interest as a political thinker. However, Hooker is also of interest because of the influence he had on another thinker who is universally regarded as part of the Western canon.

HOOKER'S INFLUENCE ON JOHN LOCKE

John Locke is situated in popular consciousness as a progenitor of two of the most influential and characteristic ideas of modernity—empiricism and political liberalism. In the United States, Locke occupies a singular place because of the influence of his *Two Treatises of Government* on the language of the *Declaration of Independence* of 1776 and the more generalized importance many of the American founders attached to his formulations of natural law, natural rights, the separation of powers, government by consent, the right of resistance, and religious tolerance. The attentive reader of Locke's famous *Two Treatises of Government* might well be struck by the number of references to "The Judicious Hooker." Indeed, Richard Hooker is by far Locke's most quoted authority in this canonical work. Hooker is moreover invoked in reference to many of the most significant elements of Locke's political philosophy, including sovereignty, consent, the state of nature, and the social compact. Given the overwhelming presence of Hooker in Locke's texts, it is remarkable how little attention writers of the last thirty-five years have paid to Hooker's place in Locke's work. For example, a recent four-volume anthology of writings[9] on Locke's political philosophy included some two thousand pages of essays by the foremost Locke scholars in the world. Yet, not a single essay was devoted to the question of Hooker's influence on Locke. Ian

Harris's work *The Mind of John Locke* contains one of the more substantive discussions of Locke's natural law theory from the *Essays on the Law of Nature*. This theory refers to his idea that common consent to moral propositions is a sign that they form part of the natural law.

> Hooker had suggested a mode of apprehending natural law which did not use a theory of ideas in the Lockean sense. The view that the content of the law was disclosed through general agreement had a long lineage, being found in Aristotle. Hooker suggested that there were two ways to apprehend goodness, one through its causes, another through its signs and tokens. . . . he assumed that what was universal was natural and to be presumed to be God's work, so that the 'general and perpetual voice of men is as the sentence of God himself.'[10]

Harris notes that Locke's voluntarism is in part an effort to replace such a consent-based account with an emphasis on the primacy of the divine legislator: "Locke, as we shall see, wished to assert God's role as legislator, for he was keen to distinguish human opinion from divine authority. For him it made sense to close the avenue of consent."[11]

In *The Political Thought of John Locke* (1969), John Dunn includes some scant notes on Hooker[12] in which he echoes Strauss's position that Locke's use of Hooker was simply to provide a cover of respectability for Locke's radical ideas. James Tully's *A Discourse on Property: John Locke and his Adversaries* recognizes Hooker's importance for Locke, referring to him as "Locke's recommended authority and constant reference in the *Two Treatises*"[13], but he does not elaborate in detail. Ruth W. Grant, in *John Locke's Liberalism* (1987), makes a mention of Locke's use of Hooker in relation to the value of standing decrees, and John Simmons, in *The Lockean Theory of Rights* (1992), briefly references[14] Locke's use of Hooker in his discussion of whether egoism is the foundation of the Golden Rule. In *John Locke* (1994), John Marshall mentions Locke's use of Hooker in relation to the state of nature,[15] but he notes that the theories do not cohere because Hooker argued that unanimous consent would be needed to withdraw from the state, as well as because of the role of prescription and inheritance in Hooker's account. A few scholars have recognized the importance of the question but have declined to engage it in detail. Thus, Richard Ashcraft wrote in *Locke's Two Treatises of Government* (1989) that:

> There is . . . a need for a detailed examination of the relationship of Locke's ideas to those of Aristotle, Cicero, Hooker, and other thinkers from whom Locke drew inspiration. So little work has been done in this area, that I have chosen to leave the task to others.[16]

Similarly, in his introduction to Book I of Hooker's *Laws* in the Folger *Works of Richard Hooker*, Gibbs summarizes the debate up to the early 1960s by writing that "given the persistence of scholarly disagreement on this issue, there are grounds for taking a fresh look at the relation between the thought of Hooker and Locke."[17]

Given that one of the main purposes of the *Two Treatises of Government* was to elaborate the right of rebellion against unjust government, on the surface it would seem strange that Locke would turn to Hooker as one of his main authorities.[18] As we have seen, Hooker elaborates no explicit resistance theory whatsoever. In fact, the main purpose of his political philosophy was a conservative one: to defend the legitimate juridical authority of Crown and Parliament over the ecclesiastical and civil polity and to uphold the duty of conformity to the established Church against the potentially subversive exigencies of nascent Puritanism.

To understand the state of the scholarly appraisal of Hooker's relation to Locke, we need to turn to the debates of a somewhat earlier epoch. The picture of Hooker as an early "Whig constitutionalist" and a progenitor of Locke's ideas was a fairly standard one throughout the nineteenth century and was given weight when incorporated into the classic tome *The Constitutional History of England* by Henry Hallam, who wrote that "his theory coincides perfectly with that of Locke" and that "it will be obvious to the reader that their principles [Hooker's and Locke's] were the same.[19]

Even at the turn of the century, historical survey works in the English-speaking world generally presumed a fairly continuous relationship between Hooker and Locke and thus saw Hooker as the ancestor of liberal contractarianism. Thus, the *Cambridge Modern History* of 1904 remarked that Hooker "anticipated the great Whig doctrine of the seventeenth century, that government had its origin in a primary contract between the governor and the governed."[20] A number of more recent scholars defend his thesis of the basic continuity between Hooker and Locke. For example, in his essay on Locke's natural law theory, Raghuever Singh writes that "Extracts may be cited from almost all the major writings of Locke to prove that his conception of natural law is continuous with the classical Stoic and Christian tradition represented by Cicero and St. Thomas and coming down to Richard Hooker."[21] From this presumption of a continuous relationship between Hooker and Locke, some have drawn more general conclusions. For example, John S. Marshall draws a line of natural law theory from Aquinas through Hooker to the American founding fathers, going so far as to write, "for us Hooker is the true progenitor of the American Constitution."[22]

On the other hand, a number of significant scholars question the genuine continuity between the thought of Hooker and Locke and see Locke's use of Hooker as an effort to link his radical ideas on religion and politics to a figure of impeccable conservative credentials. One of the works that marked a turning point with regard to this interpretation was A. P. d'Entreves's 1939 work, *The Medieval Contribution to Political Thought: Thomas Aquinas, Marsilius of Padua and Richard Hooker.* For d'Entreves, Hooker's legal and political thought is essentially a continuation of that of Aquinas. As he writes, "I have tried to explain Hooker's attitude towards the idea of the law of nature, and the reasons which account for the fact that, as Dean Church remarked, the outlines of Hooker's theory of law and politics 'are to be found in the great work of Thomas Aquinas.'[23] For example, in dealing with his theory of law, d'Entreves believes Hooker held the intellectualist, rather then voluntarist, conception of law. Thus, d'Entreves writes that

> His definition of law echoes almost word for word the definition of Thomas Aquinas. Will and command are not to him the constituent elements of law. There is a close connection between law and reason: law is, as Aquinas had said, *aliquid rationis*. This idea has far reaching theological and philosophical implications. Through the definition of law, the idea of reason is introduced into the very concept of God's nature; and it is the principle of reason which in turn helps to bridge the gulf between man's limitation and God's infinity.[24]

For d'Entreves, Locke's agenda was to portray his radically contractarian theory as a mere continuation of the traditional Aristotelian and scholastic conception of Hooker. Thus, he writes,

> The interest of Locke's tendentious reading of Hooker lies not only in a comparison between Hooker's conception, and that of one of the most extreme and complete proponents of the idea of social contract, but in the particular value which Locke attributed to present his own theory as a vindication of the old and traditional doctrine concerning the origin and foundation of political society.[25]

D'Entreves is therefore concerned to show that Locke's reading of Hooker as a progenitor of his own contractarian theory is achieved on the basis of a kind of rhetorical slight of hand, whereby nominal similarities between Hooker's language and his own are exploited to make it seem as if there is conceptual contiguity. Thus, d'Entreves writes,

> The widely different implications and meanings of the apparently identical conceptions upon which Hooker's and Locke's political theories are based follow as a consequence of the radical divergence of the philosophical standpoints of their authors.[26]

D'Entreves acknowledges that Hooker has a notion of a pre-political state, which essentially corresponds to Locke's "state of nature" and that Hooker therefore does not accept the Aristotelian concept of natural inequality as an adequate account of the origins of political obligation. But, according to d'Entreves, "this refusal implies no assertion of 'natural rights' in the individual, prior to, and independent of the state."[27]

In this reading then, Locke's individualism is the signature difference between the two thinkers. For d'Entreves, Locke's social contract is a *pactum societatis* in which free individuals form a society by renouncing certain of their rights to a temporal prince commissioned to protect them. This type of individualism and rights-based theory is utterly foreign to Hooker. Thus, d'Entreves goes on to write that

> The contract which becomes in the seventeenth and eighteenth centuries the commonly accepted starting-point of political speculation and finds the complete development in Locke's political theory, is a contract between individuals, that is the social compact proper, or *pactum societatis.* . . . it may well be doubted, I think whether Hooker's words contain any assertion of that individualist' principle.[28]

While it is not self-evident that this reading of Locke as an advocate of the *pactum societatis* is entirely correct, other authors offer similar readings of the Locke/Hooker connection. For example, the Spanish scholar Angel Facio Moreno, writing in a 1961 article on the topic, concludes that while Hooker's theory is very close to the scholastic political philosophy of Suarez, Locke adapted Hooker to a somewhat different purpose and so misappropriated Hooker's original meaning.[29]

Those scholars who emphasize the discontinuity over the continuity between Hooker and Locke tend to turn with special attention to the question of natural law. For example, Peter Munz[30] does not deny that Hooker emphasizes a profound influence on Locke in the terms of the workings of a constitutional government:

> If one looks at the quotations [of Hooker by Locke], one will find that they are chiefly concerned with . . . what one might call the technology of constitutionalism. There is no doubt that in these points Hooker anticipated Locke; or rather that Hooker represents the link between St. Thomas and Locke. There are subtle differences between the constitutionalism of Hooker and that of Locke. But they are in agreement as to the spirit, if not as to the letter, of the basic principles of constitutional government.[31]

However, on questions of substance (as opposed to external form), Munz sees a wide variance between the fundamental conceptions of Hooker and Locke. One of these is that for Hooker there is an organic union between Church and State, and consequently the public polity is at once both ecclesiastical and civil. For Locke, the state is to a much greater degree a secular institution, and public laws are much more a domain where natural reason and morality are competent to judge. For Munz, the signal difference would be on the question of natural law, as he writes,

> The fundamental and far reaching difference between Hooker and Locke is reflected in their theories of natural law. Hooker, in fact, stood at a turning point in the history of natural law. He was the last great representative of the medieval natural-law school.[32]

This school was characterized by the view that "whatever man did because he was human he did as the analogy of God. His natural propensities were those divine propensities which God allowed man to exercise on His behalf."[33] It was the replacement of this theological horizon with that of empiricism that for Munz represents the decisive change between Hooker and Locke.

> When this [medieval] epistemological apparatus came to be discarded and human nature made the subject of a purely empirical study, its needs began to appear in a different light. Without the help of theology or revelation, one had to take human nature as one found it in every day experience: dominated by self-interest; ruled by worldly appetites; and here and there relieved by a sprinkling of rational enlightenment and brotherly affection. Hence the new law of nature laid down that men are working primarily for their own advantage.[34]

Munz therefore puts forth the opinion that in spite of their profound differences both Locke and Hobbes belong to the new empiricist vision that conditioned how they understood the grounds and manner of deriving natural law. In this they mark a profound departure from the medieval understanding that informed Hooker. He concludes that:

> Hooker stood at the turning point in the history of the theory of natural law. He was the last great representative of a theologically conditioned theory of natural law. The growth of an empirical outlook, and the consequent narrowing of the field over which reason could rule supreme, opened a new chapter in the history of natural law. Hooker would have been unable to understand the reasoning of Locke.[35]

We have a reading that focuses on the departures within Locke's idea of natural law, and thus views his use of Hooker as largely a polemical ploy to solicit a respected and traditional authority on behalf of a more radical and modernist agenda. The apotheosis of this kind of reading of Locke might be considered to be that of Leo Strauss. In his treatment of Locke in *Natural Right and History* and his earlier essay *Locke's Doctrine of Natural Law*,[36] Strauss sees an especially profound discontinuity between Locke's doctrine of natural law and that of the traditional natural law theory. Strauss's analysis rests on his distinction between the "ancients" and the "moderns." Strauss defines *classic natural right* as grounded in a teleological conception of nature having ends independent of the subject, and *modern natural right* as grounded in a notion of nature as an inert mechanism with rights being rooted in the assertions and exigencies of the subject.[37] Strauss's hermeneutics involves the presumption that there is an esoteric text that the overt terminology of the author aims to conceal. Thus, in the case of Locke, Strauss aims to expose how an esoteric doctrine of politics that is essentially Hobbesian lies concealed beneath certain of Locke's traditional language regarding natural law.

One of the interesting questions that Locke's relationship to Hooker addresses is how to understand the political philosophy that undergirds the American founding. Given the central importance of Locke in the political philosophy of the American founding, which is evinced in the very language of the *Declaration of Independence,* this conclusion would have considerable importance. For a certain breed of conservative, the "Jacobinism" that entered American political discourse in the 1960s (consisting of radical secularism, radical egalitarianism, and rejection of established authority) would be seen not as the subversion of the American order, but merely the historical working out of an ideological "infection" present in its very foundations. Indeed, this is roughly the train of thought that was put forth by Strauss's disciple, Allan Bloom. In his work, *The Closing of the American Mind*, he sees Locke as the theoretician behind the American Revolution and Rousseau as the leading figure behind the French. According to Bloom, Locke and Rousseau are essentially similar:

> What was acted out in the American and French revolutions, had been thought out beforehand in the writings of Locke and Rousseau, the scenarists for the drama of modern politics. These Columbuses of the mind . . . explored the newly discovered territory called the state of nature, where our forefathers all once dwelled, and brought the important news that by nature all men are free and equal, and that they have rights to life, liberty and the pursuit of property. This is the kind of information that causes revolutions because it pulls the magic carpet out from under the feet of kings and nobles. Locke and Rousseau agreed on the basics, which became the firm foundation of modern politics.[38]

For Bloom, therefore, Locke is part of the secularist Enlightenment ethos where human autonomy and self-sufficiency replace theological authority. No less than Rousseau and Hobbes. Locke is a quintessentially modern figure on this model in his emphasis on rights rather then duties. In his conception, the Lockean ideal is one where each person is left more or less free to pursue his private interests, in striking contrast to the classical (and medieval) conception where private interests are subordinated to the common good, and where the good itself is understood according to a universal, rather than an individual, concept. Thus, Bloom writes of the modern (and Lockean) framework that

> This scheme provides the structure for the key term of liberal democracy, the most successful and useful political notion of our world: *rights*. Government exists to protect the product of men's labor, their property, and therewith life and liberty. The notion that men possess inalienable natural rights, that they belong to him as an individual prior, both in time and in sanctity, to any civil order, and that civil rights exist for and acquire their legitimacy from ensuring those rights, is an invention of modern philosophy. Rights like the other terms discussed in this chapter, are new in modernity, not a product of the common sense language of politics, or of classical political philosophy. Hobbes initiated the notion of rights, and it was given its greatest respectability by Locke.[39]

For Bloom then, the American founding was predicated on an Enlightenment secularist ideology that on the one hand played down the existence of norms anterior to human subjectivity, and on the other hand asserted in a more forceful way the moral claims of subjectivity. Politically, this transformation is expressed in the shift from the classical and medieval language of natural law and natural virtue, to the modern language of natural rights. To no small degree, this reading of the American founding depends on the Straussian reading of Locke that I hope to demonstrate is fundamentally flawed. At the roots of the errors of the Straussian school is an anti-historicism and esotericism which leads Strauss and his followers to impute motives and intentions to Locke that cannot be found by a straightforward reading of either the text itself or the circumstances from which it arose. There are perhaps some merits to this kind of perrenialism—a great text will deal with ideas and issues that to some degree transcend the contingencies of time and place and, once understood, can be situated within a broader dialogue across the centuries.

At the same time, we cannot hope to understand a text—its problems, questions, and solutions—independent of history. In this respect, there is considerable value in the contributions of the Cambridge school represented by such thinkers as Quentin Skinner and J. P. A. Pocock, for whom the recovery of the original motives and intentions of the authors through attentiveness to historical context is essential. Following this line (broadly conceived) we hope to provide a more cogent explanation for the place of Hooker in Locke's writings by analyzing the role of Hooker's *Laws* in seventeenth century political thought. Because of the influence of the Straussian reading of Locke as one of the factors that led to the general neglect of Richard Hooker's contributions, I reserved an appendix to deal specifically with the important problems that he raises.

THE THEORY OF CONSTITUTIONALISM

Hooker's importance in the history of political thought rests largely on his centrality to seventeenth century political discourse—the matrix from which Lockean thought arose, with its broad influence on the Anglo-American world. Both Hooker and Locke can be regarded as important contributors to a distinctive tradition of political thought. In tracing this development of thought, this work is also intended as a contribution to the history of an idea—that of constitutionalism. Before moving on, it is apt to define what I mean by this term, which is no longer the dominant signifier in the rhetoric of contemporary political discourse. In this regard, I will remove ambiguity by first distinguishing constitutionalism from other ideas with which it is often associated, but which have no invariable or necessary connection with it.

Constitutionalism is first of all to be distinguished from *democracy*—a term that signifies rule by the people either directly or by chosen representatives. Although modern democracies typically strive to be constitutional democracies, it is perfectly possible to have a constitutional aristocracy or a constitutional monarchy. Even less is constitutionalism to be identified with *egalitarianism*. Constitutional government can easily coexist with institutions based upon social hierarchy and hereditary privilege.

Finally, it is necessary to distinguish constitutionalism from *liberalism*—an ambiguous term with a variety of meanings. Liberalism is sometimes used to refer to the "liberal state," meaning a state that guarantees certain basic freedoms, including freedom of speech, freedom of religion, and a freedom of the press. *Religious liberalism* is often taken to mean the view that privileges private judgment over structures of religious authority, or alternatively an *indifferentism* that views all doctrinal standpoints as of equal value and worth. *Economic liberalism* is generally understood to mean "classic liberalism," an approach that favors a minimum of state intervention in private economic decisions, including questions of taxation, regulation of businesses, markets, prices, and wages. In the U.S., classical liberals are usually called *Libertarians* to distinguish this position from those usually described as liberals in common speech.

Political liberalism can mean a doctrine that prioritizes the idea of personal rights, and sometimes is used to refer to an *individualism* that makes the autonomy of the individual the highest value; thus, it is often connected with what is sometimes (somewhat disparagingly) called "social atomism." In the American context, liberalism usually means a left of center political ideology favoring a more robust intervention of the state in society, particularly in order to create more equal conditions for those perceived to be disadvantaged by gender, race, economic status, and/or sexual orientation. Often, but not always, American liberalism is also combined with a *cultural liberalism*, which holds that many decisions should be based on personal choice rather then traditional concepts of morality, particularly in life issues (e.g., abortion, euthanasia, bioethics) and issues related to marriage, family, and sexuality. Cultural liberals also tend to be suspicious of the role of religion in public life, and thus they favor an expansive interpretation of the separation of church and state. Constitutionalism differs from all these forms of liberalism, although it does not necessarily contradict them. It is difficult, for example, to see how personal rights and freedoms could be guaranteed outside of a constitutional framework.

Having described several things that it is *not*, we can now turn to what I mean by using the term "constitutionalism." In essence, constitutionalism is the confluence of three ideas. First, it is a *theory of law*: constitutionalism favors a government limited by an order of law. The thinkers in the Western constitutional tradition who I will discuss (including Aquinas, Hooker, and Locke) see natural law as the foundation of the juridical order. There is, in other words, a moral order discernible by reason that is binding on all human beings and is anterior to the state. The decrees and enactments of governing institutions must conform to this natural moral law in order to be legitimate and binding in conscience. Thus, natural law represents an objective and independent standard by which the actions of the civil authority can be judged. Moreover, constitutional thinkers seek a government that is limited also by *positive law*, which is some order of either written or unwritten human law that defines the assigned powers of governments beyond which it possesses no licit authority. Constitutionalism, therefore, favors the rule of law and not of men. We may say then that the constitutionalist theory of law limits government both with reference to divine or natural law and with reference to the positive or civil law.

Secondly, constitutionalism is a *theory of sovereignty*. Much discussion in the history of political thought has focused on the question of *where* sovereignty resides. Some theorists, for instance Bodin Filmer, hold that sovereignty lies in the prerogative of a particular person, such as a king, since the essence of sovereignty is the power to command. On this thesis, the king is above the law, since it is his will that creates the law. Constitutionalism, however, holds that the *community* or the *body politic* is the original locus of sovereignty. In the constitutional theory then, the executive power (whether a king or president, etc.) holds authority as a delegated power from the community as a whole. Since the ruling authority receives his power as a trust from the community, he is also responsible to use it for the *common good* of the community, rather than his own private advantage. As Hooker and other constitutionalists would have it, the king is *singulis major; universis minor;*

that is, in political terms the king is the superior of each individual, while he is the subject of the community as a whole. According to Hooker, the king, therefore, is neither the ultimate source of the law, nor is he above the law.

Thirdly, and finally, constitutionalism signifies a *theory of political obligation*. Much discussion in the history of political philosophy centers on questions of why and how some human beings become the subjects of others. Depending on how this question is answered, there will be different notions of *why* and *when* and *under what circumstances* the obligation to obey those in authority comes into place. As we shall see, patriarchalists argued that the subjection of some to the authority of others has its origins in *nature*, which is to say that some are naturally subject to the authority of others. Constitutionalism, however, generally argues that political obligation has its origins in *consent* and that only governments based on consent have legitimacy. In many cases, the idea of consent is closely related to the notion of an original *compact* or agreement between the rulers and ruled, setting forth the particular form of government to be instituted and the limits of its assigned powers.

I will show from my study that Hooker was a central figure in the development of the constitutional idea, such that he is a mediating figure between medieval and modern political discourse. Hooker is on the one hand deeply informed by medieval scholastic thought—particularly that of St. Thomas Aquinas. On the other hand, he appears as a leading contributor to the modern constitutionalist tradition in the English-speaking world represented by Locke and others. There is a need to revise the Enlightenment mythos that sees the emergence of the modern constitutionalist state as simply a modern reaction against medieval autocratic notions regarding the divine right of kings. My study will present a much more complex picture in which constitutionalism represents an effort by early modern thinkers to harness elements of the medieval tradition in order to place limits on a peculiarly modern phenomenon—the centralized modern state and its pretension to absolute power in the person of the king.

THE PURPOSE AND PLAN OF THE WORK

The main purposes of this undertaking are to help illustrate the place of Richard Hooker in the history of Western political thought, to examine the relationship between Hooker and Locke, and finally to produce a better understanding of the ascent of modern constitutionalism particularly in the context of early modern England.

I have divided the work into two broad parts. Part I includes the first three chapters and is devoted primarily to Richard Hooker himself and to the Elizabethan world in which he wrote. In chapter one, I will examine first the historical context of sixteenth-century England and the great struggle between Calvinists and Anglican conformists to define the theology and government of both the church and the state in an era in which they were closely linked. This chapter will also examine the theology of Richard Hooker. Broadly speaking, I will defend the interpretation of Hooker as a *via media* figure who revived the medieval Roman Catholic scholastics in an effort to create a distinctive theology for Elizabethan Anglicanism, different from that of his Calvinist opponents. Chapter two will examine his approach to problems of grace and predestination, which Hooker grounds in notions of divine justice that underlie his concepts of law. I will show how Hooker defends an essentially Thomistic framework of eternal, natural, revealed, and positive law against the reduction by English Calvinists of all law to the single order of divine law revealed in Scripture. Hooker, however, develops Thomism in a quite particular and creative way, which is seen most clearly in his theory of political dominion, which will be the topic of chapter three. Skillfully exploiting ambiguities in the premises of Thomistic political theory, Hooker is able to develop an idea of sovereignty as belonging to the community and of authority as derived from the consent of the governed expressed though a compact from which the Crown receives its power. The fact that the ruling powers receive authority as a *delegated* power thus continues to impose ordinate norms on the legitimate use of government. The king is seen to be subordinate not only to the natural and divine law, but also to the positive or civil law. By showing the similarities between Hooker's thought and that of Roman Catholic thinkers like Francisco Suarez, I will show that those who reason from similar and basically Thomistic premises arrive at strikingly similar conclusions about the nature of government.

Part II of this book examines Hooker's relationship to seventeenth-century thought in general and to the writings of John Locke, specifically. This next unit in the work will examine Hooker's influence in seventeenth-century England. First, chapter four looks at how Hooker was a widely venerated authority used for quite opposite purposes by the two main contending factions in English political life: the Tories and the Whigs. During the Restoration period Hooker became a venerated figure because he had been the most sophisticated defender of Anglican conformity against nascent Puritanism, a faction that would later become the main enemy of English monarchism in the seventeenth century. At the same time, however, his constitutionalist theory of government was widely ignored by the Tories in favor of a rather new theory of patriarchalism, which defended monarchy through appeal to natural and divine right, rather than consent. The invocation of Hooker by these royal absolutists provides an opening for Whig theorists to reappropriate Hooker for their own political purposes and even to use Hooker's arguments as the basis for something he never intended—resistance.

For the transformation of some of the tenets of Hooker's political philosophy into an explicit authorization for resistance I turn to Locke in chapter five as the foremost Whig writer of the seventeenth century. Filmer's use of Hooker allows Locke to use Hooker as a way of arguing against the Tories from their own sources. In his *Two Treatises*, Locke repeatedly turns to Hooker to refute patriarchalism, to construct his account of the state of nature, to defend the sovereignty of the community, and to bolster his ideas of consent and compact as the legitimating origin of government. It is not too much to say that Hooker supplied Locke with many of the fundamental premises of his political theory. On the basis of these "Hookerian" premises, Locke reaches a radical conclusion that might have shocked Hooker and his conservative impulses: the lawfulness of overthrowing established authority when it refuses to govern consensually. It is this Whig theory that was to prove the most influential conduit through which the constitutional idea would impact the future history of Europe, America, and the world.

NOTES

1. For an interesting discussion of Cicero's contributions to the natural law tradition see John Fielding's article "Classical Natural Law: Cicero and the Stoics" in *The Christian Statesman* (May–June, 2004) – cf. http://www.natreformassn.org/statesman/04/cicero.html (accessed December 29, 2007)

2. This opening of the introduction is partially derived from my own unpublished prospectus on the work. I am grateful to Dr. Alan Stone for his helpful suggestions.

3. This statement is cited in Phillip Secor's work *Richard Hooker: Prophet of Anglicanism.* (Tunbridge Wells: Burns and Oats, 1999), p. 198. Secor notes that according to Izaak Walton, Hooker's seventeenth-century biographer, the Roman pontiff had read the first four books of Hooker's *Laws* and made this statement in 1597 in the presence of Cardinal William Allen.

4. For a short biography cf. http://www.luminarium.org/renlit/hookbio.htm

5. For a survey and discussion of this conception of Hooker as a precursor of Locke, see W.D.J. Cargill Thompson, "The Philosopher of the Politic Society," esp. pp. 133–134. In general terms some reputable 20th century sources regarding Hooker's specifically political ideas include F.J. Shirley's *Richard Hooker and Contemporary Political Ideas.* (London: SPCK 1949); Robert Faulkner's *Richard Hooker and the Politics of a Christian England* (Berkeley, CA: University of California, 1981.); E.T. Davies's *work The Political Ideas of Richard Hooker London: Society for Promoting Christian Knowledge* (London: Society for Promoting Christian Knowledge, 1946); and the chapter on Hooker (p. 177ff) in Christopher Morris's *Political Thought in England: Tyndale to Hooker* (Oxford: Oxford University, 1953). There is

a brief section on Hooker in J. W. Allen's *A History of Political Thought in the Sixteenth Century* (London: Methuen 1951) (p. 239ff), but it focuses rather narrowly on the issue of religious toleration.

6. Cf. A.P. d'Entreves, *The Medieval Contribution to Political Thought*. Another "Anglican Thomist" of Hooker is found in Marshall, *John S. Hooker and the Anglican Tradition* (London: Adam and Charles Black, 1963).

7. Peter Munz, *The Place of Hooker in the History of Thought*. Whether Hooker's theological politics holds together as a consistent system is one of the major debates in twentieth century scholarship. For Munz, the Erastian and Thomistic elements of Hooker's thought are in irresolvable tension. The thesis that Marsilius of Padua was a central influence on Hooker was broadly influential for a certain time. Thus the thesis was mentioned at the 1935 proceedings of the British Academy (cf. Previte, C.W. "Marsilius of Padua" Proceedings of the British Academy, 1935). Later H.F. Kearney influenced by Michael Oakshott argued that Hooker brings together two major strands of political philosophy—one based on reason and nature represented by Thomas Aquinas, and one based on will and artifice represented by Marsilius. See H.F. Kearney, "Richard Hooker: A Reconstruction" in *The Cambridge Journal*, Volume V, (Oct. 1951–Sept. 1952) pp. 300ff.

8. W.J. Torrance Kirby, *The Theology of Richard Hooker in the Context of the Magisterial Reformation.* (Princeton: Studies in Reformed Theology and History, Princeton Seminary Press, 1999) (also online).

9. See John Locke: *Critical Assessments*, ed. Richard Ashcraft (London: Routledge, 1991), 4 vols.

10. Ian Harris, *The Mind of John Locke.* (Cambridge: Cambridge University, 1994), p. 91.

11. *Ibid.*

12. See John Dunn, *The Political Thought of John Locke: An Historical Account of the Argument of the Two Treatises of Government* (Cambridge: Cambridge University Press, 1969), p. 169.

13. James Tully. *A Discourse on Property: John Locke and his Adversaries* (Cambridge: Cambridge University, 1980), p.38.

14. See Ruth W. Grant, *John Locke's Liberalism* (Chicago: University of Chicago Press, 1987), pp. 40–42.

15. See Alan John Simmons, *The Lockean Theory of Rights* (Princeton: Princeton University Press, 1992), p. 209 (note).

16. See Richard Ashcraft, *Locke's Two Treatises on Government* (London: Unwin Hyman, 1989), p. 11.

17. Cf. Richard Hooker, Folger Library Edition of *The Works of Richard Hooker*, ed. W. Speed Hill (Binghamton, New York, Center for Medieval and Early Renaissance Studies, 1993), Part One of Volume VI, pp. 112–113 (footnote). This text will hereafter be abbreviated as Folger.

18. As we have previously noted, Locke refers to Hooker frequently in the *Two Treatises* to bolster crucial points of his argument. Cf. Peter Laslett's introduction to John Locke, *The Two Treatises of Government* (Cambridge: Cambridge University Press, 1988), p. 57. Locke's treatment of Hooker in this text will be elaborated later.

19. Hallam, Henry, *The Constitutional History of England from the Accession of Henry VII to the Death of George II.* (London: Alex, Murray and Son, 1869), p. 163–164.

20. The contribution was made by Sir Sidney Lee in *Cambridge Modern History.* Volume III (Cambridge: Cambridge University, 1904), p. 348. It is mentioned also in the important essay by W.D.J. Cargill Thompson, "The Philosopher of the Politic Society," ed. C.W. Dugmore. *Studies in the Reformation: Tyndale to Hooker* (London: Athalone Press, 1980), pp. 133–134.

21. Raghuveer Singh, "John Locke and the Theory of Natural Law," *Political Studies* 9 (1961), p. 112.

22. John S. Marshall, "Origins of the Natural Law Tradition," p. 68, in *Origins of the Natural Law Tradition*, ed. Arthur L. Harding, (Dallas: Southern Methodist University Press, 1954). Another work which gives importance to Hooker in the American founding is Russell Kirk's *The Roots of the American Order* (Washington D.C., Regnery Gateway, 1991). While the cogency of the thesis would probably depend on what one makes of the influence of Hooker on Locke, certain of the more philosophically inclined of the founding fathers owed a direct debt to Richard Hooker. For example, James Wilson of Pennsylvania, in his "Of the General Principles of Law and Obligation," quotes extensively from Hooker's *Laws* and makes use of his division of law into eternal law, celestial law, divine law, natural law, and human law.

23. A.P. D'Entreves, *The Medieval Contribution to Political Thought: Thomas Aquinas, Marsilius of Padua, and Richard Hooker* (London: Humanities Press, 1959 – reprint of 1939 Oxford edition), p. 117. Interestingly, other scholars accept the image of Hooker as an Anglican Thomist and consequently reject his doctrine. Thus, Gunnar Hillerdal made the statement that "the whole conception [of Hooker] is philosophically untenable if one does not accept the basic metaphysics of Thomas Aquinas." Cf. Gunnar Hillerdal. "Reason and Revelation in Richard Hooker" in *Acta Universitatis Lundensis*, vol. 54 (1962), pp. 9–150.

24. *Ibid.*, 118.

25. *Ibid.*, pp. 125–126.

26. *Ibid.*, p. 127.

27. *Ibid.*, p. 128.

28. *Ibid.*, pp. 129–130.

29. See Angel Facio Moreno, *Dos Notas en Tornos A La idea De Derecho Natural En Locke* (Revista de Estudios Politicos, Madrid, 1961), who concludes that, "En Resumen puede afirmarse que del examen de las citas de Hooker por Locke en su Segundo Tratado se desprende un engarce poco afortunado, demasiado superficial, e impreciso. Se continuan las palabras, pero los conceptos tienen ya un signficado distincto,estan mas vacios, mas individualizados.' See also George Bull, "What did Locke borrow from Hooker?" *Thought* 7 (1932).

30. See Peter Munz, *The Place of Hooker in the History of Thought* (London: Routledge and Kegan Paul, 1952).

31. *Ibid.*, p. 205.

32. *Ibid.*, p. 206.

33. *Ibid.*, p. 207.

34. *Ibid*.

35. *Ibid*., p. 208.

36. Leo Strauss, "Locke's Doctrine of Natural Law," *American Political Science Review*, pp. 490–501.

37. For an interesting discussion of this topic see Neil G. Robertson, "The Closing of the Early Modern Mind: Leo Strauss and Early Modern Political Thought." http://www.mun.ca/animus/1998vol3/robert3.htm. (accessed 1/27/08)

38. Allan Bloom, *The Closing of the American Mind: How Higher Education has failed Democracy and Impoverished the Souls of Today's Students* (New York: Simon and Schuster, 1987), p. 162.

39. *Ibid*., p. 165.

PHILOSOPHORVM ΣΟΦΩΤΑΤΩ ÆSCVLAPIO SVO.

Vluere cui vires & robora fana dedifti
  Scribere ni vellem, næ robore durior effem.
Ergo mihi (qua priuato pertingere nulli
CASE datur) tecum fatis & fatis Aftra tueri eft.

SPHÆRA   CIVITATIS

Part I

RICHARD HOOKER AND THE THEOLOGICAL POLITICS OF ELIZABETHAN ENGLAND

Chapter One

The Historical and Theological Context of Richard Hooker's Laws

The constitutionalism of Richard Hooker set forth in *Of the Laws of Ecclesiastical Polity* must be understood in the context of the theological purpose that informs the whole work.[1] Hooker's main opposition was an influential circle of Calvinists who saw themselves as the vanguard of the *true* Reformation in England. Hooker's polemical purpose is laid out in the preface of Hooker's *Laws,* which lays out the principle points of controversy that divide him from these Calvinist opponents. The preface also provides a brief interpretation of the history that led to the conflict. There has been some discussion regarding the tenor as well as the content of Hooker's work. Given the *odium theologicum,* which was common in the sixteenth century, Hooker is notable for the irenic tone, which he often adopts. Thus, addressing his opponents he writes that:

> The wonderful zeal and fervour wherewith ye have withstood the received orders of the Church, was the first thing which caused me to enter into consideration, whether (as all your published books and writings peremptorily maintain) every Christian man, fearing God, stand bound to join you for the furtherance of that which ye term the *Lord's discipline*.[2] Wherein I must plainly confess unto you, that before I examined your sundry declarations in that behalf, it could not settle in my mind to think, but that undoubtedly such numbers of otherwise right well affected and most religiously inclined minds had some marvelous reasonable inducements, which led them with so great earnestness that way.[3]

This irenicism contributed to what critics called the "hagiographic" accounts of Hooker by Anglican authors.[4] Some modern scholars have labored to point out the hard edge beneath Hooker's apparently soft tones—thus Cargill Thompson notes, "While professing the greatest respect for Calvin as a person and as a theologian, Hooker in effect accuses him of being a pious

3

fraud . . . . Hooker adopts similar smear tactics to undermine the credit of the Puritans."[5] While these observations may serve as a worthy corrective to an excessively effusive approach to Hooker, the matter may not be so circumscribed. Hooker regards the contentions of the extreme Calvinist party as involving dangers of the utmost gravity. Hooker believes that the logic of his opponents will lead them inevitably to schism, separatism, and the overthrow of even the civil law of England. Thus, he writes that: "How just cause, there is to fear the manifold dangerous events likely to ensue upon this intended reformation, if it did take place."[6]

At the same time he strives on a principle of charity to distinguish between the error and the personal sincerity of those who err. Thus, he says of his chief opponent Thomas Cartwright,[7]

> Concerning the defender of the Admonitions, all that I mean to say is but this: *There will come a time when three words uttered with charity and meekness shall receive a far more blessed reward then three thousand volumes written with disdainful sharpness of wit.* But the manner of men's writing must not alienate our hearts from the truth, if it appear they have the truth; as the followers of the same defender do think he hath; and in that persuasion they follow him, no otherwise then himself, Calvin, Beza and the others, with the like persuasion that they in this cause had the truth. We being as fully persuaded otherwise, it resteth that some kind of trial be used to find out which part is in error.[8]

A fair approach would be to accept that Hooker does not endeavor to judge the motives and intentions of his opponents (whose earnestness he is prepared to concede), but finds that the issues, which divide them, are pregnant with profound implications for the theology and indeed the polity of the English church and commonwealth. In order to understand the conflict better, a brief background of the conflict's historical development would perhaps be helpful. The Reformation that occurred in England was quite distinct from the Lutheran and Calvinist revolts elsewhere. The continental Reformation began with primarily theological concerns regarding the doctrines of the Roman Catholic Church. Luther and Calvin broke from Rome in their affirmation of justification by faith alone, their conviction regarding the exclusive authority of the Bible, and their attack on the Roman Catholic hierarchical structure and sacramental system. As the theological controversy unfolded, the Continental Reformation *became* increasingly politicized. The Holy Roman Emperor, Charles V, viewed the juridical foundation of the imperial office as tied to the fate of catholic christendom, so logically he felt it necessary to suppress Lutheranism not only as a heretical but also as a politically subversive doctrine. Conversely, many of the German princes fearing the centralization of Imperial rule under the Hapsburgs embraced Luther's cause.

In England, however, the succession of events was quite the reverse—the break from Rome commenced with a *political act*, and only later did this act receive systematic theological defense and elaboration. Hooker's work is a crucial element of this period when a specifically Anglican theology emerges. When Henry VIII promulgated the Act of Royal Supremacy in 1534, thus severing England from communion with Rome, he had no intention of altering the Episcopal hierarchy, sacramental structure, or the fundamental dogmas of the Catholic Church. In 1539, King Henry VIII issued the first creedal statement of the now separated Church of England—the *Six Articles*. The articles re-affirmed against the Reformers such Catholic doctrines as the seven sacraments, the celibacy of the priesthood, the doctrine of purgatory, and auricular confession. There were, however, those in England who looked upon the break with Rome as the first stage toward a complete Reformation of the Christian Church along Calvinist lines. Many of these men such as John Hooper[9] were either imprisoned or forced into exile under King Henry's rule. In short, Henry VIII dealt with Protestant non-conformists with almost the same degree of rigor as recusant Catholics who refused to accept the Act of Supremacy.

Beginning with the reign of his son Edward VI (and owing largely to the influence of the reform minded Archbishop of Canterbury, Thomas Cranmer), Protestant and specifically Calvinist influences emanating from the continental Reformation became increasingly strong. English Reformers like Hooper were invited to return to England, and continental figures such as Martin Bucer were welcomed. It was under Edward VII that the first major liturgical reforms were initiated, particularly the introduction of a vernacular liturgy with the publication of the first Book of Common Prayer in 1549. Because the Book of Common Prayer was the uniform liturgical book of the nascent Church of England, changes in its many revisions constitute a historical guide to the shifting theological trends in England.

Since the 1549 Book of Common Prayer was largely an English translation of the Roman Catholic ordinary of the Mass, it aroused opposition from more radical Reformers. In 1552, a second Book of Common Prayer was authorized which made some concessions toward continental Protestantism. All references to the Mass as Sacrifice were suppressed, changes were introduced into the Ordinal for the consecration of priests, and the vow of clerical celibacy was abolished. However, the new liturgical forms were still regarded as too traditional by those such as John Hooper who in particular objected to the retention of clerical vestments, which were representative of the special ministerial role of the priesthood, and as such resonant with Catholicism.

In 1553, these emerging arguments were put off to a later date by the ascent of the Catholic Mary to the throne of England. Nonetheless, in the exiled

English churches, a significant internal dispute arose (e.g. in Frankfurt) with some that favored the form of worship authorized in King Edwards's Book of Common Prayer, and a group of reformers who favored the Calvinist liturgical discipline established at Geneva. Hooker mentions the issue between these two groups in exile when he states (with notable understatement) that a contention began between the two groups:

> And amongst ourselves, there was in King Edward's day some question moved by reason of a few men's scrupulosity touching certain things. And beyond seas, of them which fled in the days of Queen Mary, some contenting themselves abroad with the use of their own service-book at home authorized before their departure, others liking better the common prayer-book of the Church of Geneva translated those smaller contentions before begun were by this means somewhat increased.[10]

This conflict set the stage for a significant religious and political contest when Queen Elizabeth I arrived on the throne in 1558. Obviously the ascent of a non-Catholic monarch aroused the hopes of both groups of exiles, and both waited to see how the new Queen would address the question of religion in England. Thus in exile the stages were already set for a contest between those who favored the Edwardian *Book of Common Prayer*, and so called *disciplinarians* who favored the Calvinist discipline in liturgy and theology.

Some basic elements of the Elizabethan settlement began to emerge rather quickly. The central element of the 1559 parliament of course was the reinstatement of the Act of Supremacy. The act required an oath to the effect that:

> I A.B. do utterly testify and declare in my conscience that the Queen's highness is the only supreme governor of this realm, and of all her highness's dominion's and countries, as well in spiritual or ecclesiastical things or causes, as temporal, and that no foreign prince or potentate hath any jurisdiction, power, preeminence, or authority ecclesiastical or spiritual within this realm.

The act was meant primarily to seperate (for the second time) the ecclesiastical affairs of England from Papal jurisdiction. The Act returned matters to the *status quo ante* as it existed after Henry's 1534 act of supremacy that established the King as head of the Church—with one subtle difference. The new Act of Supremacy referred to Elizabeth not as supreme "head" of the Church but as supreme *governor.* This deceptively technical shift of language allowed later opponents of aspects of the English Church to claim that the Crown's role was that of a mere executive of the rules of the Church, not its head. At that same time it allowed conformists such as Hooker, to defend the settlement while in important ways circumscribing the licit powers of the Crown over church and commonwealth.

Early Elizabethan tracts defending the settlement were directed primarily against Roman Catholic arguments—among them was Bishop John Jewel's 1562 tract *Apologia Ecclesiae Anglicanae*,[11] which prior to Hooker was probably the most exceptional defense of the Elizabethan settlement. The rejection of papal primacy of jurisdiction would seem to place England once again in the camp of the Reformation kingdoms. Yet even among the non-Catholic of Elizabeth's supporters, there was still a faction that viewed the break with Rome as temporary and hoped for an ultimate reconciliation. They saw in the English form of Reformation, which preserved more traditional elements, the possibility of a form of religion which would ultimately prove acceptable to both Catholics and Protestants. This camp included Nicholas Throckmorton, and later Edward Cranmer.[12] The restoration of the Act of Supremacy defined what the Church of England was *not* (i.e. Catholic), but it remained unclear what the Church of England *was* in positive terms. Was it an adherent of the general magisterial Reformation as defined by Calvin and Luther, or was it something else?

As William Haugaard[13] notes, one of the peculiarities of the English Church lay in the fact that it relied for self-definition more on practical issues such as the liturgy, then on doctrinal confessions of faith as both continental Catholics and Protestants did. However there was an effort to give positive doctrinal definition to the emerging Anglican Church in 1563, when the convocation of Bishops promulgated the thirty-nine articles of faith, based essentially on Thomas Cranmer's forty-two articles of faith in 1552. While endeavoring to achieve some sort of *tertium quid* between Roman Catholicism and the proponents of the Reformation along continental lines it managed to be fully acceptable to neither side. But disputes between different ecclesial factions in the early period of Elizabeth's reign tended, one might say, to involve issues of *orthopraxy* more then orthodoxy.

The 1559 Parliament promulgated an Act of Uniformity[14] that required all worship in England to conform with a revised Book of Common Prayer. Moreover, the Court of High Commission was charged with enforcing the act by imposing legal penalties on those who refused to worship according to the rites of the Established Church. The 1559 Book of Common Prayer was on most points the same as the Edwardian text, but with some minor changes defined by the Queen's injunctions in a more conservative direction, and thus was on some points closer to the 1549 edition then to the aforementioned 1552 edition.[15]

Though in effect the Act of Uniformity banned the licit celebration of the Roman Catholic Mass even in private, the new Book of Common Prayer was regarded as insufficiently reformed by those who favored the Geneva discipline (many recently returning Marian exiles). These saw the Elizabethan settlement not as a final resting point, but only as the first step to a more "complete" Reformation along Calvinist lines. They wished in short to extirpate from England all the vestiges of Roman Catholicism ("Popery"). What particularly earned the ire of the Calvinists was that in the Book of Common Prayer the words of consecration from the Catholic Mass were essentially retained in the revised liturgy, and priests were required by law to wear vestments as specified also in the rubrics of the 1549 Edwardian prayer book. This latter enactment resulted in the so-called "Vestiarian controversy," which began in 1563 as a movement of civil disobedience by many of the clergy and learned theologians, and centered in the universities. Hooker refers to this controversy when he says that: "Under the Happy reign of her Majesty which now is, the greater matter a while contended for was by the wearing of the cap and surplice."[16]

Disciplinarians viewed priestly vestments as a hated symbol of Roman Catholicism, and they felt resistance to their introduction to be an obligation of conscience, even if it involved them in disobedience to the Crown. While the controversy involved a minority it included many of the kingdom's academic elite. Edwin Sandys, who would later become Archbishop of York, declared that no one could be obliged to obey the rubric on vestments. While initially the Queen and the Archbishop of Canterbury, Matthew Parker, were fairly indifferent to the matter, by 1564, the flouting of the rubrics began to result in disciplinary measures. The dean of Christ Church, Oxford Thomas Sampson, was deprived of his office, and in 1565 a general inquiry regarding dissent on the matters of vestments was inaugurated.

One of the leaders who first rose to prominence during the Vestiarian controversy was Thomas Cartwright who in 1569 was appointed Lady Margaret professor of divinity at Cambridge. There he engaged in bitter disputations with an ascendant divine, John Whitgift, who was later to become one of Hooker's chief supporters. In 1566, Archbishop Parker published his *Advertisements* clarifying the official position of the Church of England on the matter of vestments. Fierce pamphlets on both sides of the issue were published, and Calvinist disciplinarians appealed to their brethren in Switzerland for advice. As the controversy was heating up, one of the major figures of the Reformation, Henry Bullinger of Zurich, was consulted by English Calvinists— his counsel was obedience. By 1567 general conformity to the rubrics regarding vestments was effectively enforced and the first "test of wills" was resolved in favor of the Crown. For the moment it seemed that the Calvinist storm was calmed, but in fact it only temporarily abated. The disciplinarians had no intention of conceding permanent defeat, but viewed temporary obedience in the manner of a prudent general engaged in a tactical retreat. Lawrence Humphrey, dean of Magdalen College, Oxford and the ousted

Thomas Simpson writing to Bullinger said that "We must indeed submit *to* the time, but only *for* a time; so that we may always be making progress and never retreating."[17]

What the Vestiarian controversy did was highlight that the Elizabethan settlement of religion, rejected of course by Roman Catholics, was also strongly challenged from the other side by a stern brand of Calvinism. The level of frustration among the "Geneva men" may be ascertained by William Cole of (Hooker's own) Corpus Christi College's comment that: "If you wish to know what is the state of religion throughout all England, it is precisely the same as it has been from the beginning of the reign of our most gracious queen Elizabeth."[18]

The universities of England were, as we have seen, the central breeding ground of Calvinist dissent. At Oxford, Sampson and Humphreys carried wide followings and at Cambridge in addition to Cartwright, the master of Emmanuel seminary, Laurence Chaderton was sympathetic to strict Calvinism. Through their influence on university colleges and seminaries, Disciplinarian ideas became extended. Not a few nobles and high government officials were won over to the cause including the earls of Leicester, Warwick, and Bedford, and the privy counselor Walter Mildmay. Finally, among the common people in towns and parishes, various levels of resistance to the official religious norms occurred. Indeed networks of disciplinarians were established in which laity would meet with Calvinist clergy for "exercises" and "prophesying" in which instruction was given according to the doctrines of Geneva, and so one might say that a church *within* the church began to be formed.

When the Queen received word of these exercises, she insisted on their suppression and limited the right to preach to authorized clergy. However, this effort to enforce conformity suffered a blow when in 1575 the Archbishop Parker died, and Elizabeth chose for his successor Edmund Grindal in 1576. As it turned out, Grindal himself was sympathetic to the Calvinists, and refused her order to suppress the exercises. Another with impeccable conformist credentials promptly replaced him, Cartwright's opponent at Cambridge John Whitgift.

By the 1580s the stability of the Elizabethan settlement was felt to be increasingly insecure from both within and without. Already, in 1570, Pope Pius V[19] had in response to the Act of Uniformity suppressing Catholic rites, issued his famous Bull *Regnans in Excelsis* which absolved her subjects of allegiance to her, and called for loyal Catholics to remove her. The Queen was thus in a precarious position, and fears of plots and conspiracies abounded. While the majority of English Catholics at the time probably were interested only in being permitted to practice their faith without fear of the High Commission, in the period of 1569 to 1572, there were several failed efforts by those Catholics associated with the Duke of Norfolk, and the Earls of Northumberland and Westmoreland to depose Elizabeth.

Among those in England who still adhered to the Catholic faith and thus did not recognize the divorce, Elizabeth's childless status had raised the hope of a restoration of Roman Catholicism. These hopes largely rested on the claim of Elizabeth's Catholic cousin Mary Stuart to the throne of England. Ejected in 1568 from Scotland by the Calvinist rebellion of John Knox, Mary fled to England. Following her execution by Elizabeth's order in 1587, relations between Spain (then the major power of Europe) and England glided toward war. Relations between Spain and England had already sharply deteriorated when Elizabeth threw her support behind the Dutch revolt in the Spanish Netherlands, by sending Robert Dudley, Earl of Leicester on a military expedition to aid the rebels in 1585. The Spanish king, Phillip II, enraged by the Queen's support for Protestant rebels in the Spanish Netherlands, her approval of piratical activities against Spanish shipping, and motivated also by his zeal for the success of the persecuted Catholic cause in England, launched the famous Spanish Armada in 1588. The Armada's defeat proved (contrary to popular legend) to be only a temporary setback. One year after the Spanish Armada the English launched their own naval expedition led by Sir Francis Drake and Sir John Norris, 1589 to destroy the Spanish Atlantic fleet based in Portugal, Galicia, and Cadiz.[20] This expedition failed with great losses to England in blood and treasure. England later suffered a series of reverses in the 1590s culminating in the brief Spanish capture of Cornwall by Juan de Amesquita in 1595. Most Englishmen correctly saw the defeat of the Spanish Armada as only temporary and anticipated a long, drawn-out conflict on which the very future of religion in England depended.

As the long struggle with Spain dragged on amid the profound insecurities of the times, fear and loathing of the great Roman Catholic power in Europe waxed to a fever pitch. The war with Spain had two somewhat contradictory effects on England. On the one hand, it increased the anti-Catholic sentiments among all Protestants in England, and also the extremism of the Calvinist party. Catholicism was now associated with sympathy for England's foreign enemies, and anti-Romanism became a patriotic cause. In the 1589 parliament, Lord Christopher Hatton[21] spoke of the "unchristian fury, both of the Pope (that wolfish bloodsucker), and of the Spaniard (that insatiable tyrant)."[22] Thus when Travers and other opponents of Hooker would later accuse Hooker of docility toward Roman Catholicism, the accusation had an almost treasonous resonance.

A second, perhaps ironic effect of the war with Spain may have been to encourage greater rigor toward the extreme Protestant party. The Anglo-Spanish War placed the very survival of Elizabeth's regime in question, and her supporters closed ranks around her. Thus there was a determination to defend the Elizabethan settlement against any who would subvert it, whether they were followers of Rome or Geneva. The extremism of the Calvinists nonetheless gained strength in the 1580s when small numbers under leaders such as Robert Browne, Henry Barrow, and John Greenwood began to speak of separatism from the official Church.[23]

In 1586, Archbishop Whitgift convinced the Star Chamber to give him control over the Stationer's company, the printing presses, and broad powers of censorship. In 1588 and 1589, seven pamphlets written under the pseudonym of "Martin Marprelate" were published from secret presses and were widely distributed.[24] Written by Presbyterian opponents of the Episcopate, the tracts made Archbishop Whitgift and the Bishops into objects of satire and ridicule. In 1589, the efforts of the ecclesiastical high commission to investigate and suppress the Marprelate tracts uncovered evidence of a well-organized network of disciplinarian opponents of Episcopacy. In the atmosphere of the 1580s where fear of subversion was rife, these disclosures evoked an intense reaction in parliament. Lord Hatton addressing Parliament admonished it that: "You do not in this assembly so much as once meddle with any . . . matters or causes of religion, except it be to bridle all those, *whether papists or puritans*, which are . . . discontented."[25] The conformist case in the 1580s moreover received strong support from the writings of John Bridges, Richard Bancroft, and Hadrian Saravia all of whom were ready to defend the institution of the episcopacy—and not only on the basis of its institution in Apostolic times. [26]

It soon became clear that disciplinarian non-conformity was going to be one of the central subjects dealt with when the Parliament of 1593 opened under the leadership of the learned jurist Edward Coke. How this was going to occur was not immediately clear. The Queen's Attorney of the Court of Wards and Liveries, introduced bills to limit the power of the commissions against the militant reformers, those he termed "learned and godly ministers."[27] In this he followed a trend within the English legal profession to be uncomfortable with the accretion of judicial powers by the ecclesiastical commissions. Many of these powers seemed to James Morice to violate English common law—for example, in investigating breaches of Ecclesiastical order, the commissioners could require witnesses to testify against themselves under oath— that is *Ex Officio Mero*. Morice also objected to Whitgift's new articles of subscription directed again non-conformists. Sir Francis Knollys, a cousin of Elizabeth spoke eloquently in favor of the bill, criticizing Whitgift's ecclesiastical policies. He framed his argument in terms of the new powers of the commissioners being a play at limiting royal power in favor of ecclesiastical authority.

The Queen however intervened, ordaining that parliament should not meddle in ecclesiastical affairs, the bill was dropped, and Morice was summoned before the Privy Council. Miles Sandys, a leader of the conformist party in the commons parliament, called for the extension on penalties against Catholic recusants who refused to use the Book of Common Prayer, or attended the official services, to be extended to Calvinist dissenters. During this time the Commissioners had already been poised to vigorously repress the disciplinarians since the unauthorized publication of the Marprelate tracts. John Penry, one of the clergymen involved in the unauthorized publications, was executed for associating with separatists, which was considered treason. Other clerics (including Thomas Cartwright) went before the Star Chamber, and suffered penalties for refusing *Ex Officio More* oaths. After William Hacket, a Presbyterian rabble-rouser, called for the overthrow of the Queen, commissioners such as Richard Bancroft and Richard Cosin were able to point to the Puritans as a party with subversive and seditious intentions. Greenwood and Barrow, the two separatist leaders, were arrested and executed in 1593. In this year, it may be said that the cause of conformism had reached its apogee. And it was in that year that the first part of the most eloquent defense of the Elizabethan settlement was published—Richard Hooker's *Of the Laws of Ecclesiastical Polity.*

THE ADMONITION CONTROVERSY: CALVINISTS AND CONFORMISTS

Of special importance to understanding the ideas of Richard Hooker is the intense controversy between Calvinists and Anglican conformists over the structure and theology of the Church. The emergence of the Puritans as a dissenting sect distinct from Anglian conformists can be traced to a kind of pamphlet war touched off in 1572. Richard Hooker refers in his preface to the *Laws* to certain:

> Admonitions directed unto the high court of Parliament, by men who concealing their names thought it glory enough to discover their minds and affections, which now were universally bent against all orders and laws whrein this church is found unconformable to the platform of Geneva.[28]

This is a reference to the Admonition controversy, which was perhaps the most significant theological disputation between conformists and disciplinarians in the period before the *Laws,* and which profoundly influenced Hooker's exposition. In general, following the Vestiarian controversy, the disciplinarians endeavored to pursue their agenda through parliament. Bills demanding further reform of the Church of England continued to be introduced in Parliament until in 1572 Queen Elizabeth intervened by suppressing the introduction of any new bills regarding the ritual of the Church of England. The intervention of the Crown aroused deep frustration among the Calvinist party. Of particular importance for understanding the background to Hooker's *Laws* were the events which ensued from the publication in 1572 of an anonymous tract called *Admonition to Parliament*.[29] This tract systematically attacked as unbiblical and impious not only the rituals of the Church of England, but also its *government*, particularly the hierarchy of bishops and priests. The publication of this tract triggered the so-called "Admonition controversy" which centered around a five-year pamphlet war where the basic issues of the theological dispute between conformists to the Elizabethan settlement and supporters of the Geneva discipline were clearly elucidated. The contestants were Thomas Cartwright[30] of Cambridge University who defended the *Admonition* and called for a radical reform of the theology and liturgy along the lines of Calvin's discipline, and the new Archbishop of Canterbury, John Whitgift who defended the duty of conformity to the Act of Supremacy and the rites of the Book of Common Prayer.[31] One of the historical outcomes of the controversy was the increasingly wide use of the term "Puritan" to characterize the more radical Calvinist party. The term is referred to in the *Admonition* as a spurious term of abuse against disciplinarians. The *Admonition* complains of the slander that the supporters of the Geneva discipline are "charged with grievous faults, calling them *Puritans*, worse than the Donatists."[32] Whitgift initially attacked Cartwright and his group with the opprobrious term "Puritan" since he charged them with presuming to regard themselves as purer then others: "The name *Puritan* is very aptly given to these men; not because they be pure . . . but because they think themselves to be *mundiores ceteris* 'more pure than the others'"[33]

But Cartwright co-opts the concept with pride since he views his movement as attempting to "purify" the Church of ungodly practices, even though the "puritan" party makes no claim of being more righteous in works.

> The *pureness* that we boast of is the innocency of our Savior Christ; who shall cover all our *unpureness*, and not impute it unto us. And forasmuch as faith *purifieth the heart* the heart we doubt not but God of his goodness hath begun our sanctification, and hope that he shall make an end of it even until the day of our Lord Jesus. Albeit we hold divers points more *purely* than they do they who impugn them.[34]

From this point on, the somewhat formless and inchoate division within the Church of England becomes defined with increasing clarity as a contest between two broad theological camps. There was, on the one hand, a conformist party which defended the Act of Supremacy and Uniformity, and such things as ecclesial government by an episcopal hierarchy, clerical vestments, and the book of common prayer, and on the other side, there were the supporters of the Calvinist discipline—an emerging "Puritan" party, which viewed such practices as "Popish Remnants both in ceremonies and regiment" without any sanction in the Bible, and thus deeply repugnant to God.

In due course, the views of the two sides became sharply delineated and defined. For Cartwright the Bible contains all that is necessary and sufficient for the "edification" or building up of the Church of Christ, and anything done without the *explicit* authorization of Scripture is forbidden if not idolatrous. Thus, Whitgift is able to argue that in essence the Admonitioners contention is that "nothing is to be tolerated in the church of Christ, touching either doctrine, order, ceremonies, discipline or government, except it be expressed in the Word of God."[35]

In spite of a certain ambiguity,[36] Cartwright's main contention is that everything done in the Church whether in its government or ritual should have a divine command, and that anything else is forbidden. Thus, Cartwright says that:

> Forasmuch as the Lord God, determining to set before our eyes a perfect form of his Church, is able both to do it, and hath done it, a man may reason both ways necessarily: the Lord hath commanded it should be in his Church; therefore it must: and on the other side He hath not commanded, therefore it must not be.[37]

In the strict Calvinist view, for man to add to what is given in Scripture as regards the faith and government of God's Church is an impious and prideful rebellion against the Creator. Hooker summarizes their basic contention as follows: "That whatsoever the law of Christ commandeth not, thereof Antichrist is the author: and that whatsoever Antichrist and his adherents did in the world, the true professors of Christ are to undo."[38]

For Whitgift, the Admonition and its supporters like Cartwright represent a fanatical and potentially subversive current. Whitgift is prepared to concede to the Admonitioners that the Bible contains all that is *necessary* for salvation: "Nothing ought to be tolerated in the church *as necessary unto salvation, or as an article of faith*, except it be expressly contained in the word of God, or may manifestly be gathered."[39]

But the Archbishop is not prepared to concede that all that is not commanded in the Bible is therefore forbidden.

> Yet do I deny that the Scriptures do express particularly everything that is to be done in the church," since he denies that scripture "*doth set down any one cer-*

tain form and kind of government of the church to be perpetual for all time, persons and places without alteration.[40]

For Whitgift then there are "indifferent" areas, that is matters neither commanded nor forbidden by Scripture such as the external government and ritual of the Church. The distinction between "things necessary" for salvation and "things indifferent" is a fundamental one in the conformist polemic, and one that returns in Hooker's writing. The political implications of the polemic become plain once we realize what is at stake in the attack is not only such external practices as vestments and incense, but ultimately the Royal supremacy itself. In claiming the right of the Monarch to govern the Church, Anglican conformists implicitly affirmed that there were "things indifferent" in rites and doctrine that were matters of human discretion. The sixteenth century was an age in which theological controversy was often pregnant with direct and immediate political implications. Consider what is contained in the simple statement of Cartwright that "the word of God containeth the direction of all things pertaining to the church, yea, of *whatsoever things can fall into any part of man's life."*[41] If the Bible contains the *sole* law to govern all of human life, then the right of the sovereign to govern the Church is gravely in question. Thus, Whitgift says that if Cartwright is correct then *"every civil action*, every private action, *every civil kind of government* is expressed in the word."[42]

For Cartwright, indeed, the role of the sovereign is to *execute* the law of God but not to *promulgate* laws of his own:

> The prince and civil magistrate hath to see that the laws of God, touching his worship, and touching all matters and orders of the Church, be executed and duly observed . . . as for the making of ceremonies . . . so the civil magistrate has not to ordain ceremonies pertaining to the Church.[43]

During the Vestiarian controversy of 1566 an anonymous tract called *An Answere for the time* declared clearly that "Kings and Queens shold be nursies of the Church, but not Lordes of it."[44] Cartwright in similar language holds likewise that, in issues of the government and ritual of the church, the civil authority must be subordinate to the church:

> But it must be remembered that civil magistrates must govern according to the rules of God prescribed in his word, and that as nourises [nurses], so they must be servants unto the church, and as they rule in the church so they must remember to subject themselves unto the church, to submit their scepters, to throw down their crowns, before the church, yea as the prophet speaketh; to lick the dust of the feet of the church.[45]

For example, since the hierarchy of Bishops and priests is (for disciplinarians) without warrant in Scripture, the monarch has no mandate to permit them. But Cartwright's contention that the "the word of God containeth the direction of all things pertaining to the church, yea, of *whatsoever things can fall into any part of man's life*" has far more then ecclesiastical implications. In the conformist polemic, Cartwright's claim that all not found in the Scripture is forbidden would overturn not only the royal supremacy but also the civil and common law of England, since for Cartwright the Bible is the sole rule not only over Church government and ritual, but also over all of human life. What would this mean for the common law of England, which is not expressly on the judicial precepts found in Scripture?

This concern would stand later as one of the foremost issues for Hooker in his contention against the disciplinarians—namely, that the implications of their logic would lead to the overthrow of the English political and legal system, in favor of a form of government and law based directly upon the Bible. In that case the distinction between judges and presbyters would disappear:

> Your opinion concerning the law civil is that the knowledge thereof might be spared, as a thing which this land doth not need . . . The reasons wherewith ye would persuade that Scripture is the only rule to frame all our actions by, are in every respect as effectual for proof that the same is the only law whereby to determine all our civil controversies. And then what doth let, but that as those men may have their desire who frankly broach it already that the work of reformation will never be perfect, till the law of Jesus Christ be received alone; so pleaders and counselors may bring their books of the common law and bestow them as the students of curious and needless arts.[46]

Indeed, in the course of the admonition controversy, it becomes plain that for Cartwright the law that governs England must be directly based on the judicial precepts of the Old Testament. In the course of the debate, it is evident that for Cartwright the laws of the Old Testament are not only still valid but must be enforced literally and with utmost rigor.

> *It is not that the magistrate is simply bound unto the iudicial laws of Moses: but that he is bound to the equitie which/which I call also the substance and marrow off them.* In this regard/I affirmed that there are certain lawes amongst the Iudicalles/*which cannot be changed.* And hereof I gaue example/in the lawes which command/that a stubborn *idolater/blasphemers/murderer/incestuous person/and such like/should be put to death.*[47]

Cartwright is prepared to reinstate the broad use of the death penalty found in the Old Testament particularly for idolatry the concept now being extended even to Christians engaged in "unbiblical" practices, not attending public worship or "false" teaching. Cartwright proudly stands behind the full implications of this: "If this be *bloudie and extreme*: I am contented to be so counted / with the holie goste."[48]

This issue involved him in a dispute with Whitgift on the relation of the Old and New Testament. Whitgift maintains the traditional supercessionist position that the Old Law in its particular judicial and ceremonial precepts is superceded by the New. For Cartwright, on the other hand, the New Testament is an *addition* to the Old Testament, which does not supercede it.

For Whitgift, the argument of Cartwright would lead inevitably to the overthrow of the whole common law of England in favor of an Old Testament based theocracy:

> All the laws of this land, that be contrary to these judicial laws of Moses, must be abrogated: the prince must be abridged of that prerogative which she hath in pardoning such as by the law be condemned to die . . . to be short, all things must be transformed: lawyers must cast away their huge volumes and multitude of cases, and content themselves with the books of Moses: we of the clergy would be the best judges; and they must require the law at our hands.[49]

Cartwright's identification of the Church with ancient Israel provides another rationale for his invective against "Papist remnants." For Whitgift, a practice that is not found in Scripture and has it origins in Catholic traditions is not adequate grounds to reject the practice itself whether in ecclesiastical or in civil affairs. This would go for such practices as clerical vestments and the Episcopal government of the Church. The Calvinist party however saw themselves as the heirs of Israel, which consecrated itself to God by *separating* itself from the practices of the nations. For Cartwright, just as ancient Israel was forbidden to imitate the practices of the idolatrous nations, which surrounded it (even in matters not directly related to worship), so the purified Church is forbidden to imitate the Catholics who mix the scriptures with pagan idolatry. Indeed for Cartwright, Roman Catholics are not only not Christians, but the very worst of idolaters. Their apparent profession of the Gospel dissimulates their true nature: "The religion of God should not only in matter and substance, but also, as far as maybe, in form and fashion, differ from that of the idolaters, and *especially the papists*."[50] Indeed, Cartwright contends that it would be better to conform to the rites of the Turks then to those of the Roman Catholics since "there is less danger in following the example of "the Turks which are far off then . . . the papists which are so near."[51]

Cartwright's position then is that Catholicism is idolatry, and that the Church must keep itself "pure" by avoiding imitating them, just as Israel kept free from the practices of the pagans. For Whitgift, the analogy does not hold, because while he agrees that Roman Catholicism is false on many doctrinal points, he will not concede that it is simply an un-Christian religion.

> The Egyptian and idolatrous gentiles neither worshipped, nor pretended to wor-
> ship the God of Israel, and therefore no marvel though in rites and ceremonies
> they were utterly severed from them; but the papists either worship, or pretend
> to worship, the same God which we do; and *therefore there is no cause in all*
> *points of rites and ceremonies to differ from them.*[52]

For Cartwright, on the contrary, "whatsoever cometh from the Pope, which
is antichrist, cometh first from the devil."[53] The dispute on the status of
Catholicism is important also because Hooker was later involved in a similar
dispute with Travers over whether Catholics were Christians or idolaters. The
arguments of the two sides can now be fairly summarized. Cartwright's arguments for the Genevan discipline have essentially three planks. The first is
that Scripture *alone* contains all that is necessary for the edification of the
Church, if not indeed for the whole ordering of earthly affairs. The second is
that whatever is not positively commanded by God is *ipso facto* forbidden, so
the Church must be purified of whatever is not commended by the Bible. The
third is that the Church as the heir of Israel must not imitate the "idolaters"
which in the case of Elizabethan England meant primarily Roman Catholics.
That a practice is not found in Scripture might be adequate grounds in Whitgift's view to affirm that it is not required for eternal salvation. But this principle is not adequate grounds to make such a practice immoral or even im-
proper, whether in ecclesiastical or in civil affairs. This would go for such
practices as clerical vestments and the episcopal and hierarchical structure of
the Church. Whitgift's defense of the ecclesiastical order is therefore fundamentally based on the distinction between "things necessary" for salvation,
which is contained explicitly in Scripture and must be done, and "things indifferent" which the church is free to order as it elects. In general terms, the
question of whether there is a class of "indifferent" actions is one that has
long concerned moral philosophers, since it concerns the issue concerning
whether every human act has a moral quality. One finds for example in St.
Thomas Aquinas the discussion of whether every individual human act (i.e.
acts proceeding from reason and will) can be indifferent.[54] However, it is
Whitgift's assertion of a specifically theological concept of "things indifferent" (called also *adiaphora*) that invited Calvinist ire. The reason for this
finds its roots in Calvin's own theology.[55] One of Calvin's central points is
that Christ set man free from the yoke of the law with its many external prescriptions. In his *Institutes*, John Calvin charges the Roman Catholic Church
with offending against this Christian liberty by occupying Christians with external rituals and practices that have no discernible foundation in Scripture,
and serve only to trouble the Christian conscience with whether their external
works are rightly performed:

The third part of the liberty is, that we are not bound before God to any observance of external things *which are in themselves indifferent* . . . but that we are
now at full liberty either so to use or omit them. The knowledge of this liberty
is very necessary to us; where it is wanting our consciences will have no rest,
there will be no end of superstition. In the present day many think it absurd in
raising a question as to the free eating, the free use of dress and holidays, and
similar trifles . . . but they are of more importance then is commonly supposed.
For once the conscience is tangled in their net, it enters into a long and inextricable labyrinth, from which it afterwards is most difficult to escape.[56]

The basic problem for Calvin regarding things indifferent is that they snare
the soul in scruples regarding external works. Calvin's emphasis on the sovereignty of grace involves the notion that works are essentially profitless for
salvation, and consequently that the Christian saved by "grace working
through faith" need not be tormented by anxiety about externals:

It is, however, to be carefully observed that Christian liberty is in all its parts a
spiritual matter, the whole force of which consists in giving peace to trembling
consciences, whether they are anxious and disquieted as to the forgiveness of
sins, or as to whether their imperfect works, polluted by the infirmities of the
flesh, are pleasing to God, or are perplexed as to the use of things indifferent.[57]

Therefore, when Archbishop Whitgift spoke of "things indifferent," the
term already had for Calvinists a connotation of spiritual danger. The English
disciplinarians went even further however then Calvin himself in some respects. Calvin's main concern was to proscribe the use of the *adiaphora*, but
to warn his followers that a preoccupation with such matters is a threat to
Christian liberty. The English Calvinists tended, as we shall see, to be more
rigorous, asserting that "things indifferent" have no legitimate place in the
Church. One of the major reasons for this is almost certainly the fact that
those forms of Church government and ritual that Anglican conformists like
Whitgift and Hooker viewed as "indifferent" were for the most part derived
from Roman Catholic usage.

Archbishop Whitgift's distinction between "things necessary" and "things
indifferent" and his general project of defending the Elizabethan settlement is
also of crucial importance for Hooker. It is worthy of note that Hooker specifically thanks the Archbishop in Book V for his "long continued and more than
ordinary favour." In essence, Hooker's work is a continuation—in a more theologically robust register—of the Archbishop's defense of conformity against
Cartwright and other Calvinists. What Hooker takes to be the central plank of
Cartwright and his followers is that there is only one law, which ought to govern human acts, namely, the law which is found as positively revealed in

Scripture. Indeed, addressing himself to Cartwright, he says that "the very main pillar of your whole cause That scripture *'ought to be the only rule for all our actions'* and consequently that the church-orders which we observe not commanded in scripture are offensive and displeasant unto God,"[58] and that consequently, *"in Scripture there must of necessity be found some particular form of Polity Ecclesiastical, the laws whereof 'admit not any kind of alteration.'"*[59]

If indeed Scripture is the *sole* rule of human actions, and all rules not found in the Bible are illegitimate, then for example, Parliament has no lawful authority over the rites and government of the Church of England. The Acts of Supremacy and Uniformity could even have been seen as usurpations of the divine prerogative. Given the subversive implications of this doctrine in regards to the Anglican settlement, Hooker endeavors to challenge Cartwright's theory of law. Specifically, he proceeds to adapt the medieval (and specifically Thomistic) theory of law and political governance to the circumstance of an early modern national monarchy. In the Thomistic theory of law, man is not only under the divine positive law, but under a "three fold" subjection to the three orders of law—the divine positive law revealed in Scripture and known by the supernatural light of faith, the natural law discerned by reason and founded upon human nature itself, and finally the human positive law enacted by the civil authority. While the polemical purpose of the *Laws* is to defend the principle of conformity to the Church of England, in the course of this polemic an entire philosophy of law and model of government is sketched out. The polemic is in large part an effort to vindicate the authority of Parliament over the ritual and government of the Church. In the so-called Admonition controversy between Thomas Cartwright of Cambridge and Archbishop Whitgift, the lines of the emerging religious struggle for the Church of England were sketched out. For Cartwright, the Church (if not indeed civil society) should be guided by the sole rule of Scripture. If an ecclesiastical practice does not have explicit warrant in Scripture, then it should be excluded. Whitgift, on the other hand, argues that while in matters necessary for salvation the warrant of Scripture is required, in "things indifferent" which Scripture neither commends nor prescribes the civil authority may decide freely how such matters are to be adjudicated. Whitgift saw Cartwright's position of rule by Scripture alone as potentially subversive since it might ultimately call into question the legitimacy of the act of supremacy if not the entire structure of civil law. Hooker, taking up the conformist cause, sees in the strict Calvinism of Cartwright and his followers a potential subversive threat to the royal supremacy itself in both civil and ecclesiastical affairs.

HOOKER'S THEOLOGY

On the one hand Hooker is (as we have seen) immersed in the particular contemporary political conflicts of his day surrounding the Elizabethan settlement. Yet Hooker's philosophy of law and politics are inextricably tied to his broader theological concerns, complex theological concerns about divine justice, the relation of free will and grace, the problem of predestination, and justification.[60] This horizon places Hooker's thought within a great conversation among such Christian thinkers as St. Paul, St. Augustine, St. Thomas Aquinas and other scholastics, and Reformers like John Calvin. From an early period in his career, Hooker was concerned to defend the idea that God Himself in His dealings with mankind operates not arbitrarily, but according to a rule of justice, a type of "law" intrinsic to His very nature. This has clear political implications, both because the divine government of the world is a model for human government, but also because God's justice provides the foundation for the whole order of law, which he expounds in Book I of the *Laws*. The first clear articulations of Hooker's doctrine of divine justice and eternal law come in the context of his theological disputation with Walter Travers[61] (that we will shortly describe), and especially his elaboration on the questions emerging from these discussions in *A Learned Sermon on the Nature of Pride*. Hooker was to see a particular conception of divine justice as standing in opposition to the ascendant Calvinism of English theology in the late Elizabethan period. Very soon this concern to confront and refute the voluntarist tendencies of English Calvinism was to generate serious controversies. In the 1570s and 1580s one of the most important disputed questions concerned the issues of predestination and reprobation. In order to fully understand the nature of these controversies it is necessary to provide some background on the doctrine of predestination in Christian theology and the controversies it has occasioned.

PREDESTINATION IN PAUL AND AUGUSTINE

The issues arising from predestination are among the most perennial issues of debate within the Christian tradition, going back to the New Testament itself. Many of the controversies arose from the effort to understand Pauline doctrine on the gratuity of salvation. For the Apostle, no one is sufficiently righteous that he can claim salvation from God as the just desert for his good works: "for there is no distinction since all have sinned and fall short of the glory of God, they are justified by his grace as a gift, through the redemption which is in Christ Jesus." (Romans 3:22–23).[62] In the Pauline doctrine then, the source of salvation is in God's work rather than man's. Through the work of justification, God offers salvation as a free and unmerited gift in spite of man's sins: "For by grace you have been saved through faith; and this is not your own doing, it is the gift of God—not because of works lest any man should boast" (Ephesians 2:8–9).

Salvation is thus a consequence of God's free election to grace of which faith is the sign. Moreover, if we grant God's omniscience and provident governance of the world it would seem clear that God would foreknow those who He would elect to salvation, and who would not. In fact, given his provident governance of the world he does not merely foreknow who will respond to His grace, but positively and actively *predestines* those who will stand with the elect at the last judgment. This doctrine of predestination is found already in St. Paul's epistle to the Romans:

> For those whom he foreknew he also predestined to the image of the Son, in order that he might be the first-born among many brethren. And those who he predestined he also called; and those whom he called he also justified; and those whom he justified he also glorified (Romans 8:29–30).

Yet many other passages[63] in Scripture suggest the possibility that freely performed good works will merit a reward from God, while evil works will merit punishment. One clear example is found in Paul's own writing:

> *For he will render to every man according to his works*, to those who by patience seek for glory and honor and immortality he will give eternal life; but for those who are factious and do not obey the truth, but obey wickedness, there will be wrath and fury (Romans 2:6–8, italics added).

Moreover, if we suppose that salvation comes through God's predestination independently of any consideration of merits, the question then arises of whether the converse is also true for the reprobate—that is, are they condemned independently of God's foreknowledge of their faults? If so, this would seem to clash with the idea that God desires the salvation of all—an idea with Scriptural support: "This is good, and it is acceptable in the sight of God our Savior *who desires all men to be saved* and to come to the knowledge of the truth" (I Timothy 2:3–4, italics added).

In terms of the efforts of philosophical theology to resolve the questions regarding predestination, St. Augustine's writings in the context of the Pelagian controversy represent a *locus classicus*. The British or Irish monk Pelagius argues against the notion that the sin of Adam continued to affect his posterity except by way of bad example. For Pelagius and his followers (such as Celestius and Julian of Eclanum), it is possible then for man *by his own natural power* to live a life of moral virtue. By the undiminished power of free will, each person can choose either good or evil acts, and on the merit or demerit of these acts, he will be rewarded or punished. In this view, salvation is in fact earned by man's virtuous acts. Pelagianism would make each person the author of his or her own salvation, and on this account, predestination would be reduced to nothing more then God's foreknowledge of the merits or demerits of His rational creatures.

Against this position, St. Augustine directed several tracts including *De Natura et Gratia* in which he clearly articulates against Pelagianism the necessity and sovereignty of grace for salvation, merited not by naturally virtuous deeds but by grace of God won through the life, death, and resurrection of Jesus Christ. God not man is thus the author of salvation, and those who attain heavenly beatitude do so in virtue of God's sovereign act of election whereby he predestines them. As St. Augustine writes (alluding to St. Paul) in *De Dono Perseverantia*: "God so foreknew that he would grant to those whom he called, that he already gave them in predestination itself, as the Apostle declares without any ambiguity."[64]

Augustine's rejection of Pelagianism eventually became normative Christian doctrine though the question took a long time to definitively resolve. A Council of Carthage in 411 condemned Celestius as a major disciple of Pelagius, but the Council of Diospolis of 415 ruled that Pelagianism was compatible with the faith, and Pelagianism was adopted by major leaders in the Church including the Bishop of Jerusalem. At another Council of Carthage in 416 and at the Council of Milevis the same year (attended by Augustine) Pelagianism was again condemned, and the Bishops at Milevis requested that the Pope ratify its decision. In 417 Pope Innocent did so, occasioning Augustine's famous statement *"causa finite est, utinam aliquando finiatur error."*[65] Another Council of Carthage condemned Pelagius again, and its canons were ratified by Pope Zosimus who authored the *Epistola Tractoria* against the Pelagian error. Eighteen bishops however refused to sign the letter, the leader of which was Bishop Julian of Eclanum, against him Augustine directed a treatise. Though Pelagianism properly speaking was outside normative Christian teaching by the middle of the fifth century, associated controversies continued. Certain figures such as John Cassian, and St. Vincent of Lerin critiqued the Augustinian doctrine of grace, and developed alternative systems that have been described by many later writers as "Semi-Pelagian"— later a widespread term of abuse during the Reformation controversies. The positions of these authors were however much more attenuated then the pure naturalism of Pelagius himself and his followers. In 529, the local Council of Orange nonetheless condemned such positions as the following: that the first movements of faith and justification come from man's natural power, that man does not require divine assistance to attain final perseverance, or that the first grace can be merited.

The Pelagian controversy was important in that it traced the bounds of the discussion within which future controversies on grace would be circumscribed. Since that time Augustinianism in so far as it asserts the necessity of grace for salvation, has broadly informed the various systems of grace in Western theology. Most thinkers in the Latin Christian and the later Reformed traditions have broadly accepted that there is an eternal resolve in the will of God to accept some men into eternal beatitude (predestination), and an eternal resolve of the divine will to exclude others (reprobation). One central theological issue is whether God's reprobation is *conditional* on the foreseen demerits of the lost, or whether there is an unconditional predestination of the damned. In other words, does God positively ordain and predetermine some souls to eternal damnation?

To answer in the negative might seem to question God's providence over all events and omniscience, since God being omniscient would certainly foreknow from before the moment of their creation that some persons would be lost, and this event could be said to unfold in terms of His eternal plan of providence. But to answer yes might seem to call God's beneficence and justice into question, as well as God's desire to save all men, since it would seem that some persons are born with eternal damnation as their destiny, which they are incapable of altering. Thus, the central issue is whether there is a conditioned reprobation, in virtue of God's prevision of demerits (*post et propter praevisa demerita*), or an absolute reprobation before any consideration of demerits (*ante praevisa demerita*). It should be noted that St. Augustine himself did not argue for a *positive reprobation* whereby God ordains some persons to hell without consideration for their deeds—indeed, some passages suggest the opposite view. Thus, in his work *Contra Julian*, he writes: "God is good. God is just. He can deliver some men not meriting good, because he is good; but he cannot condemn any man not deserving evil, [because] he is just."[66]

ST. THOMAS AQUINAS

In the thirteenth century, the ascent of scholasticism lent a new rigor to the analysis of problems in philosophical theology including predestination. The foremost of the scholastics of this period, St. Thomas Aquinas addressed this difficult issue, and further developed St. Augustine's idea by making a distinction between the antecedent and consequent wills of God. *Antecedently,*

God wills all to be saved and provides sufficient grace to effect their salvation, but foreseeing that some would freely choose to reject His grace, he wills that the wicked suffer reprobation as a *consequence* of their foreseen demerits.

> Hence it may be said of a just judge, that antecedently he wishes all men to live; but consequently wills the murderer to be hanged. In the same way God antecedently wills all men to be saved, but consequently wills some to be damned, as His justice exacts.[67]

Aquinas is here stating the principle that divine justice except on account of evil works, condemns no one. Antecedently, there exists in God a universal salvific will toward all men, but in His justice He permits some in *consequence* of the evil deeds to fall away from grace and so lose salvation:

> Thus, as men are ordained to eternal life through the providence of God, it likewise is part of that providence to permit some to fall away from that end; this is called reprobation. Thus as predestination is a part of providence, in regard to those ordained to eternal salvation, so reprobation is a part of providence in regard to those who turn aside from that end . . . as predestination includes the will to confer grace and glory; so also reprobation includes the will to permit a person to fall into sin, and to impose the punishment of damnation on account of that sin.[68]

The Thomistic solution of the issue then rejects the notion of an absolute, unconditioned reprobation. It affirms that there is an antecedent universal will to save all men, that all receive *sufficient* grace to be saved, and that those who are lost do so on account of some fault. Reprobation is then a consequence of the free rejection of God's grace, and not of God's antecedent will for the reprobate. On the other hand, Aquinas does not hold that predestination to eternal life is conditional, but rather absolute, meaning that God's election of the predestined occurs without consideration of his foreknowledge of their merits (*ante praevisa merita*). The reason is that, for Aquinas, this would undermine the gratuity of salvation by making something within man (his merits) rather then God the author of salvation:

> The Apostle says . . . *Not by the works of justice which we have done, but according to His mercy He saved us*. But as He saved us, so He predestined that we should be saved. Therefore foreknowledge of merits is not the cause or reason of predestination.[69]

As a theory of predestination, St. Thomas's view has been called the "single particular election" thesis.[70] On this view, there is, on the one hand, an *absolute* predestination by God of the elect without respect to the divine fore-knowledge of their merits, and on the other hand, a *conditional* reprobation by God by which He resolves to deny eternal salvation to others in consideration of the divine foreknowledge of their demerits. It should be noted that the Thomistic approach to the problem, while broadly representative of what Halverson calls the "consensus view" of the thirteenth century, was soon challenged from various sides. Quite soon a plurality of approaches to predestination occupied Latin Christendom.

PETRUS AUREOLI AND GREGORY OF RIMINI

One significant if underappreciated figure, Petrus Aureoli, argued that the single particular election thesis does not sufficiently reconcile its doctrine of election with God's universal salvific will.[71] The problem that Aureoli perceived is that although the Thomistic position excludes a positive act of reprobation, nonetheless the reprobate do seem excluded from God's special act of predilection that is necessary for salvation. Thus, there is in St. Thomas a negative reprobation by which God excludes certain men and angels from the special unconditioned predestination of the elect, permitting them to fall into sin and suffer eternal damnation. If the individuals who belong to the elect are chosen by God's eternal will without regard to their merits, then in what sense was the grace received in earthly life by the reprobate (whom God did not so choose) truly sufficient for their salvation? In place of this doctrine, Aureoli instead taught a doctrine of "general election" that emphasized the general but conditional election of all men, the distinction between the elect and the reprobate resting solely on the question of whether or not they respond or impede the grace of God:

> But it remains that God is a universal agent from His goodness, willing grace and salvation to all rational creatures. For insofar as it is from Him, *He who makes the sun rise upon the good and the evil offers grace to all.* Therefore any who lack grace and salvation lack these things on account of their own impediment and obstacle that God perceives in him; but he who has grace and salvation lacks such an impediment. The former however is reprobate, and the latter is predestined. *Therefore the cause of the reprobation is the maintenance of an impediment forseen from eternity; but the cause of predestination is the foreknowledge and foresight of the absence of any impediment with respect to he who is called predestined.*[72]

Antecedently, no individuals belong either to the reprobate or the elect, but all are equally encompassed within God's general will of salvation. In this view, the predestination of the elect is not (contra Aquinas) absolute, but conditional on God's foreknowledge of their merits (*post et propter praevisa merita*), while the reprobate are denied salvation on account of God's foreknowledge of their rejection of grace (*post et propter praevisa demerita*).

Aureoli's thesis of general election proved to have a great influence on other luminaries of the fourteenth century including William of Ockham and Robert Holcot.[73] It is notable that in Petrus Aureoli's language there seems to be a cause of predestination in the elect themselves, namely, the absence of impediment to the salutary action of grace. Admittedly, for Aureoli, there is only a *negative* cause of predestination in the elect,[74] namely, the absence of an impediment to grace (*obex gratiae*). Yet, inevitably the attribution of any aspect of salvation to the merits of the elect was bound to raise again the specter of Pelagianism, since General election seemed to emphasize God's universal salvific will at the cost of the absolute gratuity of salvation. Aureoli's language made it seem to many as if predestination was virtually identical with God's foreknowledge of the merits and demerits of the elect and the reprobate, and to these critics "God was no longer the author, but merely the spectator of that which singles out the elect from the rest of mankind."[75] Moreover, some of Aureoli's followers and successors such as Thomas of Strasbourg were less circumspect than Petrus Aureoli, preaching not only a negative, but also a positive, cause of pre-destination, namely, the good direction of the will.[76]

One of the strongest reactions to Aureoli's thesis of general election is found in a remarkable series of lectures on Peter Lombard's *Sentences* given at Paris by Gregory of Rimini beginning in 1343. Here Gregory appears to argue that not only is the predestination of the elect not conditional on their merits, but even reprobation is not conditional on the demerits of the lost souls. Thus, he says of the blessed that:

> Whoever is predestined has been predestined by the mercy and graciousness of the divine work alone . . . and neither is anyone predestined on account of good works or the good use of free will, nor on account of a lack of sin or whatever else renders man unworthy of eternal life, which God foresaw as future; but rather these things follow from his predestination.[77]

In the same way, Gregory uses the authority of St. Paul in Romans who refers to God's election of Jacob and reprobation of Esau. From this passage, Gregory argues that not only are the elect not saved because of their foreseen good works, but neither is the reprobation of the evil a consequence of their foreseen sins:

> And this . . . is supported because the Apostle wishing to prove that [reprobation] is not from works, says these words [Romans 9:11]: 'For when they had not yet been born, or done anything good or evil.' Nor did he speak only of Ja-

cob, 'when he had not yet been born or done anything else good' in order to reveal that he is not yet predestined from future works., but having spoken in the plural the Apostle also mentions the doing of evil, in order similarly to declare that Esau was not reprobated from future evil works.[78]

We thus have perhaps for the first time in Latin theology, a theory of *double predestination* in which God positively, antecedently, and unconditionally wills both the salvation of the elect and the damnation of the reprobate without consideration of either their foreseen merits or demerits. In place of the Thomistic position of an absolute predestination (*ante praevisa merita*) and a conditioned negative reprobation (*post et propter praevsia demerita)*, we now have a symmetrical relationship between the elect and the reprobate.

On the one hand, Petrus Aureoli's thesis of general election in which both predestination and reprobation are conditional, and on the other hand the double predestination thesis of Gregory of Rimini in which there is both an absolute and unconditioned predestination of the elect and the reprobate. The general election thesis safeguards the universal salvific will of God and the efficacy of works, though arguably at some cost to the gratuity of salvation. The double predestination thesis, on the other hand, safeguards the gratuity of salvation but brings into question the universal salvific will of God, and the efficacy of free will. Other late medieval thinkers such as Marsilius of Inghen and Pierre d'Ailly took up Gregory of Rimini's thesis of double predestination.[79] Thus, the school of late medieval Catholic anti-Pelagianism exercised a profound influence on the Magisterial Reformation in its understanding of grace and predestination.[80]

Although hitherto much discussion has focused on the late medieval debates between the *Via Antiqua* (represented by the proponents of Thomas, Scotus, and Albertus Magnus among others) and the *Via Moderna* (associated especially with Ockhamism), scholars have recently focused more attention on the emergence of a distinctive Augustinian school in the fourteenth century, of which Gregory of Rimini is perhaps the most distinguished representative.[81] Because most of these tenets were later taken over by significant figures in the Reformation, in addition to its own intrinsic interest, this *Schola Augustiniana Moderna* seems to be an important link between late medieval and Reformation debates regarding grace, the efficacy of works, and predestination.

THE REFORMATION

One of the most brilliant of the Reformed theologians who exerted a particular influence on questions of soteriology was Peter Martyr Vermigli.[82] Vermigli in the early sixteenth century joined an Augustinian order in Northern Italy where it has by now been fairly well established that he was profoundly influenced by the thought of Gregory of Rimini.[83] Vermigli later became a convert to Protestantism, and in 1542 joined the circle of Martin Bucer in Strasbourg. Turning to his theology, we see that Vermigli explicitly takes up the theory of double predestination that we have seen previously in the writings of Rimini:

> He wants everyone to be subject to God so that salvation does not depend on their works, but upon divine predestination. For it would not happen if they were predestined and elected to salvation on the basis of forseen merits as these men pretend. Let us say then that we are predestined by the sheer mercy of God . . . thus as to why this person should be chosen individually by the Lord but another should be forsaken into depravity and cursing, no sort of explanation can be given other then the free purpose of God. However, we do not call into question the justice of this, but as far as we are concerned we have nothing that could compel God into such a plan of predestining us . . . indeed the human mind seems to bristle in astonishment at the fact that blessings are not given equally by God, yet we ought to accept it. All of us who are born children of Adam are admittedly equal in this condition, namely that nothing is owed to us except damnation. But God in his goodness wills to deliver some of us.[84]

Here we find all the major elements of the theory of double predestination: God's salvific will is not universal but selective in that those who are saved are the beneficiaries of an inscrutable divine predilection. The question of election and reprobation is entirely independent of God's foreseen knowledge of merits and demerits, and this for Peter Martyr Vermigli is what guarantees that salvation is based on God's grace and not on human works.

Another figure that likely came under the intellectual influence of Gregory of Rimini was John Calvin. In his youth Calvin was a student at the University of Paris at a time when the Augustinian school was a major influence. One of the most important doctors in Paris at or near the time Calvin was there was John Mair, who explicitly acknowledged the influence of Rimini.[85] It is however unclear whether Calvin ever actually attended Mair's lectures.[86] In the absence of explicit references to late medieval Catholic scholastics in Calvin, it is difficult to achieve certitude on the question, but the strongest evidence for such influence is the internal evidence of Calvin's own doctrine. Thus, McGrath writes:

> It is certainly that all the above six features [held by the Augustinian school] were also leading aspects of the thought of John Calvin . . . it is certainly therefore a remarkable coincidence, to say the least, that Calvin should reproduce the leading features of an academic Augustinianism which developed at the same

university as that which he himself attended, if he had not himself been familiar with such theological currents. Nor need he have encountered these views in lectures: Gregory [of Rimini]'s *Commentary* went through three editions at Paris.[87]

Given the fact that Hooker's primary opponents, Walter Travers and Thomas Cartwright, were strict adherents of Calvinism, it is perhaps useful to briefly discuss the architectonic of this theological system.[88] Calvin's doctrine rests on two major pillars—a doctrine about God, and a doctrine about man. As he writes "Our wisdom, in so far as it ought to be deemed true and solid Wisdom, consists almost entirely of two parts: the knowledge of God and of ourselves."[89] The principal focus of Calvin's doctrine of God, is the idea of His sovereign majesty, which inscrutably governs all things:

> [W]e hold that God is the disposer and ruler of all things—that from the remotest eternity, according to his own wisdom, he decreed what he was to do, and now by his power executes what he decreed. Hence we maintain, that by his providence, not heaven and earth and inanimate creatures only, but also the counsels and wills of men are so governed as to move exactly in the course which he has destined.[90]

For Aquinas, on the contrary, a certain *ratio* and the ends by which God acts must accord with His attributes of goodness and justice, which always govern the acts of God's will. For Calvin on the contrary, this way of speaking derogates from the absolute sovereignty of God—for it implies that the measure of goodness is something other then whatever God happens to will. There is clearly a strong relation between Calvin's system as expounded in the *Institutes of the Christian Religion* and theological voluntarism—the conception which gives a special priority to God's will which emerged in the fourteenth century with Franciscans such as William of Ockham. It is the height of insolence for man to ask why God should foreordain some to damnation without any forseen fault, since God's will itself is the measure of righteousness:

> Foolish men raise many grounds of quarrel with God, as if they held him subject to their accusations. First, they ask why God is offended with his creatures who have not provoked him by any previous offense; for to devote to destruction whomsoever he pleases, more resembles the caprice of a tyrant than the legal sentence of a judge; and, therefore, there is reason to expostulate with God, if at his mere pleasure men are, without any desert of their own, predestinated to eternal death. If at any time thoughts of this kind come into the minds of the pious, they will be sufficiently armed to repress them, by considering how sinful it is to insist on knowing the causes of the divine will, since it is itself, and justly ought to be, the cause of all that exists. For if his will has any cause, there

must be something antecedent to it, and to which it is annexed; this it were impious to imagine. The will of God is the supreme rule of righteousness, so that everything which he wills must be held to be righteous by the mere fact of his willing it. Therefore, when it is asked why the Lord did so, we must answer, Because he pleased.[91]

On the issue of reprobation, Calvin would say that if God has positively predestined some eternal damnation antecedent to their merits or demerits, there are no grounds by which man can question this inscrutable decree. Calvin indeed clearly holds that there is in God a positive decree of reprobation, and thus a double predestination:

> By predestination we mean the eternal decree of God, by which he determined with himself whatever he wished to happen with regard to every man. All are not created on equal terms, but some are preordained to eternal life, others to eternal damnation; and, accordingly, as each has been created for one or other of these ends, we say that he has been predestinated to life or to death.[92]

In this system, God absolutely and unconditionally elects some to receive the grace of salvation and be saved without any consideration of their merits (the whole idea of merit being excluded by Calvinism's doctrine of total depravity), and on the other side, God positively and absolutely predestines the reprobate before and without any consideration of their faults (*ante praevisa demerita*).

In a sense, Calvin's theory is a consistent working out of the logic of Luther's doctrine of *sola fide*.[93] Both Luther and Calvin shared a notion of the fall as not only disordering, but also destroying, the fundamental goodness and potencies of human nature. This is one of the points of greatest contrast with regards to the question of whether in the fallen state and without special grace man is able by his own free will to do *any* good. For Aquinas, the effects of the fall did not lead to the total corruption of man's natural powers:

> Yet because human nature is not altogether corrupted by sin, so as to be shorn of every natural good, it can by virtue of its natural endowments work some particular good . . . yet it cannot do all the good natural to it . . . just as a sick man can of himself make some movements, yet he cannot be perfectly moved with the movements of one in health, unless by the help of medicine he be cured.[94]

For Calvin, on the contrary, man in his fallen state is utterly powerless to work good deeds by his own natural power: "All this being admitted, it will be beyond dispute, that free will does not enable any man to perform good works, unless he is assisted by grace; indeed, the special grace which the elect alone receive through regeneration."[95] Salvation therefore is wholly God's work through the sovereign action of grace working through faith. If God chooses to elect a person for salvation in spite of his sins, then he is saved, and if God chooses not to provide grace then he is lost.

If as Luther (and Calvin) averred salvation is a gift of grace working through faith, in which human free will and good works are irrelevant or non-existent, then God would also foreknow and predestine from all eternity who He would elect to receive this grace independently of any human response. God would also foreknow those whom he did *not* elect for salvation (i.e. the reprobate) independent of their response. Thus, there is double predestination—some are predestined for salvation and others for damnation. It ought to be said that on both sides of the confessional divide the issues arising from the question of predestination continued to be debated in great detail.[96] A great Calvinist controversy concerned the Dutch Calvinist theologian Arminius from the University of Leyden who, beginning in the 1590s, held that it is possible to resist and fall away from grace, and conversely that no one is damned except through some voluntary fault.[97]

The internecine disputations concerning predestination within Roman Catholicism differed from those of Calvinism in that they generally accepted (at least prior to the ascent of Jansenism) that there is no absolute, unconditioned reprobation. They all agreed on Christ's antecedent universal salvific will. They differed however in whether God's predestination to salvation was absolute or conditional on the meritorious response to divine grace. To these differences corresponded the debate regarding the difference between the *sufficient grace* (which God offered all men in consequence of His universal salvific will), and the *efficient grace* that actually resulted in salvation.[98] Controversies concerning grace remained prominent in the Catholic world particularly with the Jansenists, who basing themselves on the *Augustinus* of Cornelius Jansen severely downplayed the efficacy of works in justification. Other systems of grace arose at various times to address the issues of grace, free will, and predestination.[99]

HOOKER AND THE CALVINISTS

It is not our purpose to investigate these complex systems in great detail, but merely to provide context about Hooker's world in which these debates on predestination had enormous importance in religious and even political terms. Given the peculiar nature of the English Reformation, it was far from clear which doctrine the emerging Anglican Church would adopt. As Calvinist influences came to England in the Elizabethan era, the issue of predestination became one of the most hotly disputed theological questions. How one answered the question of predestination was tied to one's whole view of salvation. A commitment to double predestination came to be seen as a test of fidelity to the doctrinal principles of the Reformation. Nowhere was this controversy more intense then in Temple Church in London.[100] In the 1570s, a Spanish émigré by the name of Antonio del Corro[101] (also known by his latinized name Coranus) lectured on the issue of predestination and was subsequently accused of Pelagianism. His successor was Walter Travers. Travers had already emerged during the Admonition controversy as one of the most important Puritan theologians, with his 1574 treatise *De Disciplina Ecclesiastica*[102] that outlined the tenets of the Presbyterian model of Church government. Unsurprisingly, Travers took a strict Calvinist understanding of the doctrine of predestination.

Richard Hooker was appointed Master of the Temple in 1586 and he did nothing to shy away from the controversy, becoming one of the central players in the so called "battle of the pulpit." Every Sunday morning Hooker would give a Sunday sermon on theological points, and in the afternoons Travers, now appointed Reader of the Temple, would rebut Hooker's arguments—clearly, a battle was underway. Walter Travers charged in a supplication to the Privy Council that Hooker "taught certain things concerning predestination, otherwise then the Word of God doth, as it is understood by all churches professing the gospel and not unlike that wherewith Coranus sometime troubled this Church."[103] Travers further attacked Hooker for his doctrine that Roman Catholics might be saved in spite of their doctrine that works are necessary also for salvation.

> So proceding he bestowed his whole time, in that discourse, confirming his former doctrine, and answering the places of Scripture in which I had alleged to prove that a man dying in the church of Rome is not to be judged by the Scriptures to be saved. In which long speech, and utterly impertinent to his text, under colour of answering for himself the true doctrine which I had delivered; and adding to his former points some others . . . . that they of the church of Rome may be saved by such a faith of Christ as they had, with a general repentance of all their errors, notwithstanding their opinion of justification in part by their 'works and merits.'[104]

Hooker began his reply in his *Answer to the Supplication*. In it, he argues against the theory of double predestination—that the reprobate are positively predestined to sin and damnation. Hooker argues that this view would make God the positive origin and author of sin:

> In the other conference he questioned about the matter of reprobation, misliking that I termed God a permissive, and no positive cause of the evil which the

schoolmen do call *malum culpae*; secondly that to their objection who say 'if I be elected, do what I will, I shall be saved,' I had answered, that the will of God in this thing is not absolute but conditional, to save the elect believing, fearing and obediently serving him; thirdly that to stop the mouths of such as grudge and repine against God for rejecting castaways, I had taught that they are not rejected no not in the purpose and counsel of God without *a foreseen worthiness of rejection* going through not in time yet in order before.[105]

In 1586, an anonymous tract attacked Hooker on precisely these points, particularly with the teaching "that the reprobate are not rejected but for the evil works which god did foresee they would commit." Hooker replied to the tract by admitting that, in his view, just as God's will to save the elect is not absolute but conditional upon their faith and obedience, so also no one is damned without "a forseen worthiness of rejection."[106]

At the core of Hooker's account is that, for God, to positively predestine anyone to damnation independently of their (forseen) demerits, is contrary to divine Justice. Hooker's most extensive treatment of the issue of predestination and its relation to the justice of God is in *A Learned Sermon on the Nature of Pride*. This treatise is important to Hooker's account of law because the eternal law by which God's purposes are ordered is what grounds the entire hierarchy of law discussed in Book I. Hooker discusses the issue of divine justice in relation to a broader treatment of the issue of justice. Hooker proposes to deal with the issue of justice in a three-fold manner: "the first thing to be inquired of is, the nature of justice in general: the second, that justice which is in God: the last, that whereby we ourselves being just."[107]

DIVINE JUSTICE AND HOOKER'S THEORY OF LAW

It is primarily the first and second question that concerns us here. Hooker's starting point is the notion that there is an order, to some degree intelligible within the visible universe. The creation for him is an inter-dependent whole and consequently that all things exist in relation to each other: "God hath created nothing simply for itself: but each thing in all things, and of every thing each part in other hath such interest, that in the whole world nothing is found whereunto anything created can say 'I need thee not.'"[108]

Since mankind is part of the created order it follows that he requires other created goods in order to attain the end for which he was created. Thus, Hooker goes on to argue that there is an objective order of communicable goods that correspond to the natural desires within human nature. For over there exists the possibility within the created order of fulfilling these natural inclinations: "Now forasmuch as God hath so furnished the world, that there is no good thing needful but the same is also possible to be had; justice is the virtue whereby that good which wanteth in ourselves we receive inoffensively at the hands of others."[109]

Certain goods therefore pertain to the fulfillment of human nature, but it does not follow that man may obtain these goods in any way he deems fit—the reason for the important qualification that we must receive goods "inoffensively." Justice, for Hooker, is therefore the rule that determines what goods may be pursued and how they may be pursued:

> If it be so, then must we find out some rule which determineth what everyone's due is, from whom, and how it may be had. For this cause justice is defined, a virtue whereby we have our own in such sort as law prescribeth.[110]

Law then is understood as a just relation that defines what is due between persons:

> So that neither God, nor angels, nor men, could in any sense be termed just, were it not for that which is due from one to another in regard of some received law between them some law either natural and immutable, or else subject unto change, otherwise called positive.[111]

Having defined to some degree justice and law, Hooker next devotes some time to explaining this difference between immutable and positive law. While the concept of natural law was far from absent among English Protestants, the meaning of the idea nonetheless seems to have been sufficiently obscure by the late sixteenth century that Hooker seems obliged to correct certain errors. Some, for example, were given to conclude that what makes a law immutable or positive is that the former is promulgated by divine, the latter by human authority. Hooker forcefully rejects the opinion: "The root of which error is a misconceit that all laws are positive which men establish, and all laws which God delivereth immutable. No it is not the author which maketh, but the matter upon whereon they are made, that causeth laws to be thus distinguished."[112]

As we have seen in Hooker's time, figures such as Cartwright contended that the judicial precepts of the Old Testament are still in force (including specifically the death penalty for idolatry). Hooker contends that this error is caused in part by the belief that the only distinction between immutable and positive law is the author, so that *whatever* laws are given by God are immutable. Hooker however contends that: "All those Jewish ordinances for civil punishment of malefactors 'that enticeth unto idolatry shall be slain' . . . though received from God himself, yet positive laws and therefore alterable."[113]

Hooker finds the point of difference between immutable and positive laws in the question of whether the obligation to obey the law is inherent in the moral order and thus immutable, or whether it arises from the promulgation of the law itself, in which case it can be later abrogated: "Herein therefore they differ: a positive law is that which bindeth them that receive it in such things as might before have been either done or not done without offence, but not after during the time it standeth in force."[114]

Hooker gives as an example of natural and immutable law the duty that is owed by children to their parents: "But there is no person whom, nor time, wherein a law natural does not bind. If God had never spoken word unto men concerning the duty which children owe unto their parents, yet from the first-born of Adam unto the last of us, 'Honour they father and mother' could not but have tied all. For this cause to dispense with the one can never possibly be justice; nor other than injustice sometimes not to dispense from the other."[115] While in Book I of the *Laws*, Hooker goes into far more detail concerning the relation of natural and positive law, in this third sermon in *Of Pride* his goal is primarily to elucidate the general concept of justice: "These things therefore justice evermore doth imply; first, some good thing which is due from one person due to another; secondly, a law either natural or positive which maketh it due; thirdly in him from whom it is due a right and constant will of doing what it as law prescribeth."[116]

Hooker's main point however is not in this work to focus on questions of law and justice in general, but to understand what justice means in relation to God. He addresses this topic in the third section of the third sermon. His goal is to show that justice is not a mere human concept that is applied to God, but is an essential attribute of the divine nature.[117] Hooker argues that if justice did not exist in God then his creatures would have a perfection that would be lacking in God: "Put therefore the case that angels and men were just, God not: should they not in this part of goodness excel God, and so be better then He to whom the title, as of 'greatest', so of 'best' is confessed due?"[118] Hooker's main argument (echoing Aquinas) is that since God is the cause of creatures, whatever perfections they possess must also pre-exist in God. Thus, if there is justice in men it must also exist in God.[119]

Hooker however raises some counter-objections to the conception of God's justice that he has sketched, in relation to the broader conception of justice in general. Namely, the general conception of justice involves due subjection to law. But can God be bound or subjected by any law? Is not God's will the absolutely free and sovereign source of law? If so, in what sense can God be said to work according to a law?

> We have already declared justice to be that virtue whereby we yield and receive good things in such sort as law prescribeth. Now God hath no superior; there is not that can lay commandment upon him; he is not subject; he standeth not bound to any higher authority and power. How then should there be any justice in his doing that which no superior's authority or law can bind him to do?[120]

Since God has no superiors are we to infer that His will is absolutely free and sovereign? This is precisely the voluntarist conception that influenced the Calvinist doctrine of predestination. God in this conception positively ordains or predestines some to damnation, not in virtue of their foreseen demerits, but as an inscrutable decree of his sovereign will. God's acts are not bound by any law, and thus there are no grounds from which His decrees may be questioned. This is precisely the point of view to which Hooker objects: "To this we could make no answer at all if we did hold to as they do which peremptorily avouch "that there is no answer" to be rendered of anything who God doth, but only this, *it was his absolute will to do*."[121] Hooker answers that this view of God's actions as utterly arbitrary is contrary to the genuine Christian understanding of God's nature as working toward ends that are both benevolent and in some manner and degree intelligible.[122] Because God's ends are always reasonable and good, Hooker argues that the Calvinist idea of a double predestination is contrary to the divine justice. Thus, in Hooker's conception, even God's own acts are not arbitrary but governed by a law, albeit one intrinsic to His own sublime and perfect nature. This law is not then something outside of God, but is nothing else than His own purposes and ends, which are always compatible with His perfect goodness. This law for Hooker is none other then the Eternal law, which becomes essential to his theory of law and politics since it grounds the whole hierarchy of law in Book I. One could also say that the model of God's lawful dominion over the world becomes a model for his idea of the just king as one ruled by law.

NOTES

1. The primary sources for the historical facts contained herein are found in D.J. McGinn, *The Admonition Controversy* (New Brunswick: Rutgers University press, 1949); and Folger, Vol VI, part one; specifically useful to me were the sections on the preface by William P. Haugaard, *Book I* by Lee W. Gibbs, and *Book VIII* by A.S. McGrade. For general background on the English Reformation see Diarmaid MacCulloch, *Thomans Cranmer: A Life* (New Haven, CT: Yale, 1996); Patrick Collinson, *The Elizabethan Puritan Movement* (London: Jonathan Cape, 1967); Peter Lake, *Anglicans and Puritans: Presbyterianism and English Conformism Thought from Whitgift to Hooker* (London: Allen & Unwin, 1988); McGrath, Patrick, *Papists and Puritans under Elizabeth.* (London: Blandford Press, 1967); Phillip Hughs, *The Reformation in England.* (London: Burns & Oats, 1963); A.G. Dickens, *The English Reformation.* (London: B.T. Batsford, 1964); and William Haugaard, *Elizabeth and the Reformation.* (London: Jonathan Cape, 1969).

2. The discipline here refers to the system of Church order which prevailed at Geneva under Calvinist auspices and which the English Calvinists wished to replace the "Popish remnants" still extant in the Edwardine and Elizabethan Church.

3. All quotations from Hooker unless otherwise indicated refer to *Of the Laws of Ecclesiastical Polity*, Hooker, Richard. "The Works of that Learned and Judicious Divine Mr. Richard Hooker" (Keble edition), Burt Franklin, New York (1970 reprint). It will henceforth be abbreviated "*Laws*," Preface i.2. Sometimes the conventional designation "K" will also appear before the book and chapter numbers, signifying the Keble edition.

4. The foremost example of this kind of "hagiographic" account might be *The Life of Mr. Richard Hooker* by Izaak Walton from 1664. This account was enormously influential well into the nineteenth century. A more critical approach to Walton's Hooker began to emerge in the mid-twentieth century with such historico-critical studies as David Novarr's The Making of Walton's Lives.(Binghampton: Cornell University Press, 1958) and C.J. Sisson's *The Judicious Marriage of Mr. Hooker and the Birth of the Laws of Ecclesiastical Polity.* (Cambridge: Cambridge University, 1940). More will be said about the Restoration politics involved in such accounts of Hooker's life and work in part II.

5. Cf. W.D.J. Cargill Thompson, "The Philosopher of the Politic Society," p. 142.

6. *Laws*, Preface viii.1

7. Cartwright was among the most notable Calvinist figures during the Admonition Controversy, hence Hooker's reference here to "the defender of the Admonitions." This controversy shall be discussed in more detail in the next chapter.

8. *Laws*, Preface ii.10

9. John Hooper, a devotee of the theology of continental reformers like Zwingli and Bullinger, was well known for his attacks on saints and vestments, and his adherence to the continental reformers on the doctrine of predestination. His Protestant zeal caught the attention of the Regius Professor of Divinity at Oxford, Dr. Richard Smith who wanted him tried under the heresy laws against contesting Henry VIII's six articles. After fleeing Oxford, Hooper was eventually tried, and forced into exile after his condemnation by the Bishop of Winchester, Stephen Gardiner. Hooper eventually returned to England, and was consecrated Bishop first of Gloucester and then of Worcester, under Archbishop Thomas Cranmer, during the reign of Edward VI, only to be executed under the Catholic Queen Mary I, in 1555. Cf. Newcombe, D.G. "John Hooper" in The Oxford Dictionary of National Biography. ed. H.C.G. Matthew and Brian Harrison. Volume 22, New York, 2004. Also see The Dictionary of National Biography, (New York: Oxford University Press, 1998), Volume IX.

10. *Laws*, Preface, ii.10

11. Bishop John Jewel's 1562 "*Apologia Ecclesiae Anglicanae*" together with its English language translation and his 1567 "Defence of the Apology" can be found in *The Works of John Jewel, Bishop of Salisbury.* ed. John Eyre. (Cambridge: Cambridge University, 1850). Jewel's apology unlike Hooker's is directed principally against Roman Catholicism as the conflict with Calvinist disciplinarians had not yet fully matured as of 1562, and Jewel was under the influence of Peter Martyr Vermigli. The slant of the *Apologia* is therefore toward am emphasis on the primacy of Scripture though the importance of tradition and the early church is not neglected. See McGrath, *Papists and Puritans*, p. 50–51.

12. Cf. Folger, Vol VI, Preface, pp. 4–5

13. William Haugaard is the contemporary scholar who wrote the commentary on the preface in Folger, Vol VI, and this is one of our primary sources of information.

14. Some historians have argued that the Act of Uniformity was undertaken only reluctantly by Elizabeth in response to the returning Marian exiles, who Bishop White of Winchester termed "the wolves of Geneva." Cf. Patrick McGrath, *Papists and Puritans under Elizabeth.* (London: Blandford Press, 1967).

15. *Ibid.*, pp. 9–10, as noted above, the 1552 edition made certain concessions to Reformation minded Protestants, like the removal of references to the Mass as a Sacrifice, and altering the form of the sacrament of Holy Orders accordingly.

16. *Laws*, Preface ii.10

17. Folger, pp. 12–13; another text consulted for this background was G.R. Elton, *England under the Tudors.* (London: Routledge, 1997 reprint, orig. published in 1960), particularly chapter VII: "The Tudor Revolution: Empire and Commonwealth."

18. Folger, p. 13.

19. Since the Act of Uniformity passed by Parliament in 1559 had essentially outlawed the Catholic Mass, an interesting historical question is why the Holy See's definitive response took over a decade. Two probable factors are that 1) Pope Pius IV believed that Elizabeth's anti-Catholic policy was a result of certain advisors, and he continued to correspond with her in hopes of reaching an accommodation and possibly reconciling England to the Roman Church. And 2) Phillip II of Spain still wanted to maintain cordial relations with England in the 1560's, so the Holy See was conscious that any move against Elizabeth would meet with a tepid response in Madrid. When Pope St. Pius V, ascended the throne of St. Peter, he proved to be a zealous pontiff with among other things, a markedly different attitude toward events in England. Cf. McGrath, *Papists and Puritans*, p. 67ff.

20. Ulm, Wes. "The Defeat of the English Armada and the 16th-Century Spanish Naval Resurgence," Harvard University personal website, URL: http://www.people.fas.harvard.edu/~ulm/history/sp_armada.htm, © 2004.

21. Lord Hatton interestingly also a kind of patron to Hooker's fellow Oxford Aristotelian John Case, to whom Case's work the *Sphaera Civitatis* was dedicated. Cf. Richard Tuck, *Philosophy and Government: 1572–1651* (Cambridge: Cambridge University Press, 1993). Paradoxically, Case was suspected of Roman Catholic sympathies.

22. Folger, p. 23

23. The danger of separatism and schism was one of the chief concerns of Hooker, and addressing himself to the Disciplinarians he blames them for the disturbances of separatism. Some might argue that Hooker was essentially smearing the whole Calvinist cause by associating it with the most radical elements. Thus, Haugaard writes that regarding Hooker's identification of the Calvinists in England with Anabaptist rebels on the continent that " Hooker used the excessive fanaticism of a radical fringe with the most radical elements . . . to characterize the whole movement." (Folger, Vol. VI, p. 49) Hooker's main point however would appear to be that the logic of the Disciplinarians—if followed consistently—leads inevitably to schism and separation. Thus, he says that: "The case so standing therefore, my brethren, as it"

doth, ye must not blame, in that they further also forecasting the manifold and strange innovations which are more then likely to follow . . . for that they already have seen some small beginnings of the fruits thereof, in them who concurring with you about the discipline, have adventured without more ado to separate themselves from the rest of the Church. (*Laws*, Preface viii.1) Hooker makes quite specific references to the logic tying discplinarianism to separatism when he discusses the specific separatist movements of Barrow and Brown: "Thus the foolish Barrowist deriveth his schism by way of conclusion, as to him it seemeth, directly and plainly out of your principles." Here he follows his advisor George Cranmer's reasoning when speaking of the separatist followers of Browne when he writes that, "If the positions of the Reformers be true, I cannot but see how the maine and generall conclusions of *Brownisme* should be false." (quoted in Folger, p. 48)

24. See *The Marprelate Tracts*: 1588–1589 (London: James Clarke & Co, 1911).

25. Quoted in *Folger*, p. 25—Haugaard's emphasis.

26. Among the important Elizabethan defenses of conformity include John Bridges, *A Defence of the Government Established in the Church of England*. (London: John Vindet for Thomas Chard., 1587), Matthew Suttcliffe, *A Treatise of Ecclesiastical Discipline*, (London: George Bishop and Ralph Newberrie, 1590), and Richard Bancroft, *A Survey of the Pretended Holy Discipline*. (Amsterdam: Theatrum Orbis Terravm, 1972).

Important for the idea that Anglican conformists did not view themselves as upholders of the magisterial reformation is the fact that these texts attack not only figures like Thomas Cartwright, but also leaders like Calvin and Beza. See for example Bancroft's *Survey*, p. 63 or p. 212, or Suttcliffe's *Treatise*, b4.

27. *Ibid.*, p. 28; cf. also p. 19.

28. *Laws*, Preface ii.10

29. The admonition is generally presumed to have been penned by two London clergymen, John Field and Thomas Wilcox.

30. For biographical information on Thomas Cartwright, see Scott Pearson, *Thomas Cartwright and Elizabethan Puritanism*. (Cambridge: Cambridge Press, 1925).

31. To follow the "paper trail," the controversy begins with the anonymous tract (probably written by John Field and Thomas Wilcox) entitled *An Admonition to Parliament* (Hemel Hemstead, J. Stroud, 1572). In response to the *Admonition*, Whitgift publishes his *Answere to a certen Libell instituled, An Admonition to the Parliament*. (London: Humfrey Toye, 1573). Cartwright responds in the spring of 1573 with his *Replye to an Answere made of M.Doctor Whitegifte Againste the Admonition to Parliament*.(Hemel Hemstead: J. Stroud, 1573) Whitgift responded in 1574 with his *Defense of the Aunsvvere to the Admonition against the Replie of T.C.* (London: Humfrey Toye, 1574). In 1575 and 1577 Cartwright published his second reply in two parts, *The Second Replie of Thomas Cartwright* (Heidelberg, Germany: Michael Schirat, 1575) and *The Rest of the Second Repie of Thomas Cartvuriht* (sic)(Basel: Thomas Guarinus, 1577). The use of foreign printing presses by Cartwright perhaps gives some indication of which way the prevailing political winds were favoring.

32. *Ibid.*, p. 26

33. *Ibid.*, p. 27, from the "*answere*."

34. *Ibid.*, p. 27, originally from *The Works of John Whitgift* ed. John Eyre (Cambridge: Cambridge University Press, 1851–1853), ed. John Ayre, pp. 171–172 (hereafter abbreviated W.W.).

35. *Ibid.*, p. 54, originally from W.W., p. 176.

36. Cartwright makes an obscure distinction between command and express mention, which Whitgift finds to be incoherent.

37. D. J. McGinn, *The Admonition of Controversy*, p. 54, from W.W., p. 176.

38. *Laws*, Preface viii.6.

39. D. J. McGinn, *The Admonition Controversy*, p. 55, from W.W., p. 180 (italics added).

40. *Ibid.*, p. 56, from W.W., p. 191.

41. *Ibid.*, p. 56, from W.W., p. 190.

42. *Ibid.*, p. 110.

43. *Ibid.*, pp. 114, 295–296.

44. Quoted in *ibid.*, p. 110.

45. Quoted on *ibid.*, p.115.

46. *Laws*, Preface viii.4.

47. D.J. McGinn, *The Admonition Controversy*, p. 118, from the "second replie," p. 117.

48. *Ibid.*, p. 118, from Second Replie, p. 115.

49. *Ibid.*, p. 120, from W.W., p. 273.

50. *Ibid.*, p. 127, from W.W., ii.440 (italics added by D.J. McGinn).

51. *Ibid.*, p. 127.

52. *Ibid.*, pp. 127–128, from W.W., ii.440 (italics added).

53. *Ibid.*, p. 129, from W.W., iii.499.

54. This discussion is found in a number of places in the Thomistic corpus including S.T. I-II, q.18, art. 8–9. Here Aquinas argues that an action can be indifferent in its species meaning that in itself it is neither good nor evil deriving its moral character from the particular circumstances. However, the concrete individual act for Aquinas is always either good or evil, depending on whether it can be ordered to a due end, apprehended by reason as a good. Acts however that do not involve the advertence of reason (e.g. scratching one's beard) can be indifferent, since they do not belong to the genus of moral actions.

55. Cf. the discussion of this question in Richard A. Muller. *The Unaccomodated Calvin: Studies in the Foundation of a Theological Tradition* (New York: Oxford University Press, 2000), pp. 84ff.

56. J. Calvin, *Institutes of the Christian Religion*, III, 19, p. 7, trans. Henry Beverage (italics added). Cf. http://www.ccel.org/c/calvin/institutes/institutes.html (henceforth abbreviated Institutes).

57. *Ibid.*, III.19.9.

58. *Laws*, Preface 7.3.

59. *Ibid.*, Preface 7.4.

60. A central reference for this segment is Alan Cromartie, "Theology and Politics in Richard Hooker's Political Thought," *History of Political Thought* XXI (2000): 41–66, which among other things strives to show "a very intimate connection

between his [Hooker's] teleological conception of law and his hostility towards conventional high Calvinist ideas about predestination." This article provides a lot of the background regarding Hooker's struggle with Calvinist opposition, and the importance of his conception of justice in *Of Pride* for understanding and grounding Hooker's concept of law. For more general background on Hooker's theology see Nigel Voak, *Richard Hooker and Reformed Theology* (Oxford: Oxford University Press, 2003). The idea of Hooker's thought as moving on two planes (the immediate discussion with the English Church, and the broader conversation with Paul, Augustine, and so forth was suggested to me by the anonymous reviewer.

61. Walter Travers would later write against another conformist theologian John Bridges to defend the Calvinist discipline in his *A Defense of the Ecclesiastical Discipline Ordayned of God in the Church* (Middleburg: Richard Schilders, 1588).

62. Biblical citations are from the RSV translation in the *New Oxford Annotated Bible*.

63. To provide some examples from the Gospels themselves: in Matt 5:12, Jesus Christ promises a reward for those who endure persecution for the sake of righteousness; in Matt 25, Jesus enumerates works of charity that will be eternally rewarded and, conversely, uncharitable deeds that will be eternally punished; and in Matthew 19:16ff, Jesus in response to the question of the rich boy who asks what he must do to attain eternal life, Jesus refers to the necessity of keeping the commandments.

64. Augustine, *Four Anti-Pelagian Writings*. trans. John A Mouran and William Collinge. (Washington D.C: Catholic University of America, 1986), 23:65, p. 333.

65. This information on the Pelagian controversy can be found in the preface to Augustine's, *Against Julian*. trans. Matthew Schumacher, (New York: Fathers of the Church, 1957).

66. *Ibid*, III.18.35, p. 140.

67. S.T. I, q.19, art. 7, part i.

68. S.T. I, q. 23, art. 4.

69. S.T. I, q. 23, art. 1.

70. Cf. James L. Halverson, *Peter Aureol on Predestination* (Leiden: Brill Press, 1998)—it is on this work that I rely for much of the following background on late medieval debates on predestination.

71. Expressed for example in St. Paul's epistle to Timothy 2:4, which speaks of God as He "who desires all men to be saved and to come to the knowledge of the truth" (RSV)—for Aureol's use of this Scriptural citation, see Halverson, *Peter Aureol on Predestination*, p. 102.

72. Petrus Aureoli is here quoted and translated by Halverson, *Peter Aureol on Predestination*, p. 105 (italics added)—from the *Scriptum super Primum Sentiarum*, p. 438ff. of the Vatican edition, MS Borghese 329.

73. Cf. Halverson, *Peter Aureol on Predestination*, pp. 111–129.

74. Cf. (http://plato.stanford.edu/entries/gregory-rimini/) Christopher Schabel, "Gregory of Rimini," in *Stanford Encyclopedia of Philosophy*.

75. Garrigou-Lagrange, *The One God*. trans. Dom. Bede. Rose (St. Louis / London, Herder Books, 1946), p. 664; his reference is to Semi-Pelagianism, but is a fitting description of what Aureoli's critics thought of him.

76. Cf. Halverson, *Peter Aureol on Predestination*, pp. 138–143, as well as the Schabel article cited above.

77. Translated by Halverson, *Peter Aureol on Predestination*, p. 153 from Gregory of Rimini's Lectura I, p. 345.

78. *Ibid.*, p. 154.

79. *Ibid.*

80. *Ibid.*, p. 6.

81. Alister McGrath sets forth six principles that characterized the *Schola Augustiniana Moderna* of Gregory: A strict epistemological 'nominalism' or 'terminism,' voluntarism, an emphasis on the anti-Pelgian works of Augustine, pessimism regarding original sin, the priority of grace over free will on the question of justification, and a radical doctrine of absolute double predestination. See Alister McGrath, *The Intellectual Origins of the Reformation* (Oxford: Blackwell, 1993), p. 104.

82. Peter Martyr Vermigli is also important to our story because in 1547, Peter Martyr Vermigli was invited to England by Archbishop Thomas Cranmer and became *Regius* Professor of Divinity at Oxford the next year. As an eminent theologian he was consulted on the changes in a reformed direction of the Edwardian Book of Common Prayer of 1552. Though forced to leave England for Switzerland during Queen Mary's reign, Peter Martyr continued an involvement in English affairs in later life, corresponding with Bishop John Jewel, the early Elizabethan apologist for Anglicanism. While Hooker and Vermigli never met, Hooker attended lectures by Vermigli's successor Lawrence Humphrey, and it is very likely Hooker was exposed to his thought through his tutor John Rainolds. Cf. the copy of the 1911 Encyclopedia Britannica article on Peter Martyr Vermigli here: http://en.wikipedia.org/wiki/Pietro_Martire_Vermigli and also Secor. *Prophet of Anglicanism*, 87 (et al.).

83. Cf. the article by Frank A James on Vermigli and Gregory of Rimini, "Via Augustini: Augustine in the Later Middle Ages, Renaissance, and Reformation," eds. Heiko Oberman and Frank A James (Leiden: Brill, 1991), pp. 157–188.

84. See *The Peter Martyr Vermigli Reader*, trans. John Donnelly and Joseph Mclelland (Kirksville, MO: Trueman State University, 1999), p. 178, from the commentary on Genesis.

85. See Alister McGrath, *The Intellectual Origins of the Reformation*, p. 105, based on the preface to John Mair's commentary on the Sentences.

86. Cf. David Steinmetz, "The Scholastic Calvin," in Carl R. Trueman and R. S. Clark, Protestant Scholasticism: Essays in Reassesment (Carlisle: Paternoster press, 1999), p. 17.

87. *Ibid.*, pp. 105–106.

88. For recent scholarship on the Calvinist system see Richard A. Muller. *The Unaccomodated Calvin.* (New York: Oxford, 2000). Muller contextualizes Calvin in terms of the late medieval scholastic debates showing areas of continuity as well as discontinuity (e.g. Calvin's critique of the Thomistic conception of faith as consisting principally in assent). Muller thus contributes to the growing awareness of the interplay between the scholasticism and the theological systems of the Protestant reformers.

89. Calvin, *Institutes* 1.1.
90. *Ibid.*, 1.16.8.
91. *Ibid.*, 3.23.2 (a number of references removed).
92. *Ibid.*, 3.21.5.
93. In other words, if, as Luther held, salvation is solely a result of faith, and if faith is solely a consequence of God's unmerited and irresistible gift of grace, then the human response is irrelevant to salvation. Since God in his omniscient and provident governance of the world would foreknow and predestine those who would receive or not receive the grace of faith and salvation, it would seem that the election to salvation or reprobation would take place without considering the issue of merits and demerits.
94. S.T. q. 109, art. 2, pt ii–ii.
95. *Institutes*, 2.2.6.
96. An early controversy in Geneva concerned Jerome Belsac, a former French Carmelite turned Protestant theologian. Belsac challenged Calvin's doctrine of predestination, for example, leading to a disputation that ended in 1551 when Belsac was tried and banished from Geneva. This controversy forms part of the context for the development of the prominent Calvinist Theodore Beza's formulating of his own doctrine of predestination in his *Tabula Praedestinationis* of 1555. Cf. Richard Muller's essay on the *Tabula* in Trueman and Clark, *Protestant Scholasticism*, pp. 33–60, and also *Catholic Encyclopedia* "Jerome Belsac" by N.A. Weber.
97. In the past Arminius has drawn attention particularly for his views on predestination. Richard A. Muller in his *God, Creation, and Providence in the Thought of Jacob Arminius* (Grand Rapids, MI: Baker Books, 1991), places Arminius's position on this subject of his broader theological system in such areas as the divine attributes, creation, God's knowledge and will, and providence. Muller argues that in these areas Arminius drew upon medieval sources such as Thomas Aquinas and Duns Scotus, as well as late Scholastics like Suarez and Molina. Muller thus shows that Arminius was in essence a Protestant scholastic. At all events the Arminian system stirred up intense opposition from Calvinist authorities, but also attracted a considerable following. In 1610, his followers drew up a Remonstrance to the States-General in Holland championing the idea that grace is resistable, which played into the political conflicts of the time between Johan van Oldenbarnevelt, defender of the Arminians, and Prince Maurits of Nassau, who had the support of the Calvinist party. Following Maurits's political victory in 1618, a Synod of Calvinist clergy and theologians from throughout Europe was convened at Dordt to decisively condemn Arminianism. The Council of Dordt proclaimed the five principles which then became the normative expression of Calvinism—the unconditional decree of election by God, that Christ died not for all but only for the elect (limited atonement), that the Fall led to mankind's total corruption, that grace is irresistible, and that the perseverance in grace of the elect is unalterable.
98. The two most important Roman Catholic systems of grace during this period were those of Banez and Molina. For Banez and his followers, there is an intrinsic difference between the two modes of grace—the efficacy of efficient grace lies in the nature of the grace itself which secures the free will of the elect to cooperate in their salvation. For Molina, the difference is only extrinsic—sufficient grace becomes

efficacious when the free will assents, and remains merely sufficient if the grace is resisted. The controversies regarding grace aroused by the contradiction between the two elaborated systems led to significant disputes between the Jesuit Molinists and Dominican Thomists. These were finally settled by the famous intervention of the Holy See which convened the *Congregatio de Auxillis* in 1598, at which leading Jesuit and Dominican theologians were present. The *De Auxillis* proceeding ended with neither system being condemned.

99. In addition to the Thomist and Molinist systems, various modifications of these systems have been constructed, including the Congruism of Suarez, Bellarmine, and Aquaviva, which added to Molinism the condition that the bestowal of grace was congruent with the particular conditions of the individual recipient. Various efforts to syncretize Thomism and Molinism occurred throughout the seventeenth century, as well as certain modifications of Thomism such as the Augustinian approach of Cardinal Heinirch Noris and Laurentius Berti. Cf. Ludwig Ott, *Fundamentals of Catholic Dogma*, (Rockford, IL: Tan Books and Publishers, 1974 reprint), pp. 248–249.

100. The Temple Church in London derives its name from its founding in the twelfth century by the Knights Templars. After the suppression of the Templars in the fourteenth century, two great societies of lawyers known as the Middle and Inner Temple used the building. During the reign of King Henry the Temple became a Crown property with a "Master of the Temple"—a cleric appointed by the King to minister to the community of jurists. Hooker's appointment as Master of the Temple is significant because it may be there that Hooker developed his understanding of the close connection between theology and law.

101. Antonio del Corro was a Spanish Protestant theologian of some note. A convert to Protestantism he fled Spain to avoid trial for heresy in 1558 and became a pastor in various parishes of Wallonia and Flanders. With the arrival of the Spanish army in 1567, Corro fled again to England where he became a leader of the exile community. Though too Protestant to remain in communion with Rome, he was regarded as insufficiently reformed in the English context. For suspicion of heterodoxy, he was suspended from his pastoral duties by the Archbishop Grindal in 1569, but later in 1571 received a prestigious appointment as Latin reader at the Temple. It was here especially that he acquired a reputation as a "Pelagian," and when Hooker took over his position three years leader, he was constantly associated by Calvinist detractors there with the Spaniard. Corro spent his later life as a scholar at Oxford, dying in 1591. Cf. Alexander Gordon and Rev. Jonathan L.Nelson, "Antonio del Corro," in the Oxford *Dictionary of National Biography*, Volume 13.

102. This treatise was translated and published the same year by Thomas Cartwright. As noted Travers also published an English language defense of the Discipline in 1588.

103. Travers, "Supplication," pp. 548–569, in Hooker, Richard, *The Works of that Learned and Judicious Divine Mr. Richard Hooker*, Keble edition, (New York: Burt Franklin, 1970). This will henceforth be abbreviated Works or where the reference is to the *Laws* will be abbreviated K (for Keble) followed by the book, chapter, and paragraph. Hooker's Answer to the Supplication follows immediately from pp. 570–596.

104. *Ibid*.

105. *Ibid*., p. 593 (italics added).

106. Cited in A. Cromartie, *Theology and Politics in Hooker's Thought*, p. 47ff.

107. *Works*, p. 617

108. *Ibid.*

109. *Ibid.*, p. 618, this echoes the Thomistic notion that no natural desire can be in vain, cf. for example S.T. I, q. 12, art 1, where Aquinas argues for the possibility that the created intellect can see God on the grounds that otherwise a "natural desire would remain void."

110. *Ibid.*

111. *Ibid.*

112. *Ibid.*, p. 619.

113. *Ibid.*

114. *Ibid.*

115. *Ibid.*

116. *Ibid.*, pp. 619–620.

117. "As we have spoken of the nature of justice in general, so now we must speak of the justice of God. Wherein lest any man should imagine that we term God just, not because he is so in Himself . . . it shall not be unexpedient, first to prove unto you that in God there is this divine virtue called Justice: secondly to show in what sort God doth exercise that virtue in the regiment of his creatures." in *ibid*, p. 623.

118. *Ibid.*, p. 624.

119. "Besides, God being the supreme cause which giveth being unto all things that are, and every effect resembling the cause whereof it cometh, that such as the one is the other cannot choose but be also; it follows that either men are not made righteous by him, or if they be then surely God himself is much more that which he maketh us; just a [He] be the author, fountain and cause of our justice." *Ibid.*, p. 624. This is similar to the Thomistic argument that the divine perfections are the source of perfections in created things—"Now since our intellect knows God from creatures, it knows Him as far as creatures represent Him. Now . . . God prepossess in Himself all the perfections of creatures, being Himself simply and universally perfect." ST I, q.13, art 2. From this St. Thomas Aquinas infers that it is possible to validly predicate perfections of God from concepts derived from creatures, though not the perfections as they exist in God transcend the form of our concepts. Thus he said " . . . the aforesaid names siginify the divine substance, but in an imperfect manner, even as creatures represent it imperfectly. So when we say God is good, the meaning is not God is the cause of goodness, or God is not evil; but the meaning is, whatever good we attribute to creatures, pre-exists in God." (cf. *ibid*).

120. Hooker, *ibid.*

121. *Ibid.*, pp. 624–625 (italics added).

122. "Thus seeing God doth work nothing but for some end, which end is the cause of all he doth, what letteth to conclude that God doth all things even in such sort as law prescribeth? Doth it not strictly require them to be such as always they are, so that if they be otherwise they could not be apt, correspondent and suitable unto their set and appointed end? There is it no impediment therefore but that we may set it down, God is truly and properly just," *ibid.*, p. 626.

Chapter Two

Hooker's Politics of Divine Law

Hooker's work is, on the one hand focused on a most pressing religious and political issue of his time—the defense of the Elizabethan settlement of the Anglican Church against the Puritans. Yet Hooker is also engaged in a much broader project of philosophical theology. While previous Anglican conformists like Whitgift saw the controversy with the Disciplinarians as focused on practical questions of liturgy and government (e.g. vestments and bishops), Hooker sees these things as merely symptoms of a far deeper problem—a diminished sense of the capacities of human nature in the Calvinist system, and its consequences for their notion of law. This concern leads Hooker to reappropriate Catholic thinkers such as Thomas Aquinas on questions of nature, grace, and law and to become in effect a mediator between the medieval Catholic tradition of scholasticism and the Protestant dominated world of early modern England. One of the central questions dividing Hooker and Calvin concerns the powers of human nature in its post-lapsarian state. For Calvin, the fall resulted in the nearly *total corruption* of human nature. Thus Calvin wrote that:

> It cannot be doubted that when Adam lost his first estate he became alienated from God. Wherefore, although we grant that the image of God was not utterly effaced and destroyed in him, it was, however, so corrupted, that any thing which remains is fearful deformity.[1]

With this conception of post-lapsarian man, it is not hard to imagine why the older conception of natural law—where man is able to discern certain ends within nature by his natural powers—comes under increasing skepticism among the Calvinists. It is not clear whether reason in its fallen condition is capable of guiding men in their religious and political life. The sole reliable light available to guide man is therefore the purity of God's Word. Scholars have noted[2] how this conception appears to be rooted precisely in the Calvinist anthropology. If human powers of reason and discernment have been radically blinded, if not vitiated, then one might logically infer that Scripture, revealed by God and so immune to human error is the only reliable rule for human government.

Hooker takes this to be the position of the Puritans, and expresses the distinction between their perspective and his own in this way:

> For whereas God hath left sundry kinds of laws unto men, and by all those laws the actions of men are in some sort directed; *they hold that only one law, the Scripture* must be the rule to direct, in all things, even so far as to the 'taking up of a rush or straw.'[3]

As we have seen, the position of Cartwright and other disciplinarians is that all actions are either commanded or prohibited by Scripture and nothing is indifferent. For Hooker this view is rooted in a profoundly pessimistic anthropology in which the natural power of reason is of no avail in governing men's actions, except perhaps in better discerning the meaning of Scripture. Of the Puritan contentions he says: "Let this be granted, and it shall plainly ensue either that the light of Scripture once shining in the world, all other light of Nature is therewith in some such drowned, that now we need it not; if it stand with us in any stead . . . our natural capacity and judgement must serve only for the right understanding of that which the sacred Scripture teacheth."[4]

Hooker argues on the contrary that Scripture is not the only or sole manner by which truth may be known: "For Scripture is not the only law whereby God hath opened his will touching all things that may be done, but there are other kinds of law which notify the will of God . . . nor is there any law of God, whereunto he doth not account our obedience his glory."[5]

The truths that God wishes to convey to man are mediated not solely by one source—the Scripture, but also by other forms of mediation:

> Whatsoever either men on earth or Angels in heaven do know, it is a drop of that unemptiable fountain of wisdom; which wisdom hath diversely imparted her treasures unto the world. As her ways are of sundry kinds, so her manner of teaching is not merely one and the same. Some things she openeth by the sacred books of Scripture; some things by the glorious works of Nature: with some things she inspireth them from above by spiritual influence; in some things she leadeth and traineth them by worldly experience and practice. We may not in any one special kind admire her, that we disgrace her in any other; but let her ways be according unto their place and degree adored.[6]

Thus, according to Hooker, the Scriptures do not exclude that in matters where it lays down no command, men should be permitted to discern what is to be done through the discretion of reason, which is also a divine gift:

> Nor let any man think that following the judgment of natural discretion in such cases we can have no assurance that we please God. For to the Author and God of our nature, how can any operation proceeding in natural sort be in that respect unacceptable? The nature which himself hath given to work by he cannot but be delighted with, when we exercise the same any way without commandment of his to the contrary.[7]

Indeed, Hooker will argue that Scripture itself appeals to the natural discretion of reason, and that the Fathers of the Church never held that whatever is not explicitly commanded in Scripture is therefore prohibited:

> Had the Prophets who succeeded Moses, or the blessed Apostles who followed them, been settled in this persuasion, never would they have taken so great pains in gathering together natural arguments, thereby to teach the faithful their duties . . . . St. Augustine was resolute in points of Christianity to credit none, how godly and learned so ever he were, unless he confirmed his sentence either on the Scriptures, *or by some reason not contrary to Scripture.*[8]

In the course of this argument regarding the role of nature and reason as well as Scripture, Hooker turns to the scholastics, in particular St. Thomas Aquinas, who taught that while human faculties of reason and will were weakened by the Fall they were not destroyed. We will argue in fact that Hooker becomes the most important mediator of the Thomistic /Aristotelian system to the political discourse of early modern England. A central Thomistic motif is that *gratia non tollit naturam, sed perfecit*—Grace strengthens and perfects nature but does not destroy it. The natural powers of human reason and will, though affected and disordered by the Fall, but still retain some of their natural potency and goodness. Man in Aquinas has two lights to guide him, the natural light of human reason, and the supernatural light of faith. Since the object of both is the same Truth there cannot be any contradiction between them, though some Truths known by faith are not demonstrable by natural reason.

Before moving on to discuss relevant elements of Thomistic political theory, it would do well to discuss why Aquinas forms so important a part in our analysis. Particularly since Hooker is relatively coy in his explicit references to Aquinas, it is necessary to provide an account of why Hooker can be said to be broadly speaking an "Anglican Thomist." One of the achievements of twentieth-century scholarship has been to dispel the myth that while Platonism and humanism flourished during the Renaissance, Christian Aristotelianism fell into abeyance as a relic of the Middle Ages.[9] In fact the egress of Byzantine scholars to Italy, and the consequent spread of interest in Greek encouraged by the humanists, led not only to the translation of Plato, but also of the Greek commentators on Aristotle.[10] Access to new commentaries stimulated the new and diverse approaches to Aristotle found in such writers as Vernia, Cremonini, Pompanazzi, and Zabaralla. The sixteenth century was also noteworthy for the great revival of interest in St. Thomas Aquinas that took place particularly in Spain where the *Summa Theologica* replaced Peter Lombard's *Sentences* as the main text of theological instruction—a fact that stimulated the "second scholasticism" of which Francisco Suarez, Luis de Molina, Domingo de Soto, and Francisco de Vitoria are outstanding examples. In this sense Thomism achieved a position during the Renaissance, which it had never achieved during the Middle Ages.[11]

In specific reference to the situation in sixteenth-century England, in spite of the fact that England broke from the Roman Catholic Church, the traditions that had made English universities centers of Christian Aristotelianism did not abruptly grind to a halt during the Elizabethan period.[12] For example at Oxford although many of the medieval commentators fell out of favour, Aristotle himself continued to be regarded as a major authority.[13] In particular in questions of logic, the Oxford faculty looked negatively on the new systems of logic developed by Peter Ramus in opposition to Aristotle, which won a large following in continental universities like Heidelberg.[14] Elizabethan Oxonians who commented on Aristotle also turned to the writings of medieval authors like St. Thomas Aquinas, as well as later scholastics.[15] Moreover, there is additional evidence that makes make it very likely that Hooker would have encountered certain Catholic scholastic influences.

Hooker's college, Corpus Christi, was a place of theological ferment in which prominent figures of Calvinist leanings (such as Hooker's own tutor John Rainolds) rubbed shoulders with other figures who kept alive the Catholic traditions. As Secor says "before Hooker arrived at Oxford all of Corpus Christi's presidents had decidedly Romanist leanings,"[16] and Hooker was surely exposed to this influence. Thomas Greneway who was president of Corpus Christi from 1561–1568 was accused of being a closet Roman Catholic.[17] Hooker would obviously have received knowledge of Calvinist and Reformed theology from his tutor Rainolds, and from attending the lectures of Lawrence Humphrey, the successor to Peter Martyr Vermigli as Regius Professor of Divinity.[18] Yet Hooker was probably also influenced by other figures at Corpus Christi like Antonio del Corro—who in his stress on free will and man's natural powers after the fall we have seen was later accused of Pelagianism by Walter Travers. Another figure that likely influenced him was Francesco Pucci, a kind of early latitudinarian.[19] Given the presence of both Calvinist and Catholic influences in Corpus Christi, Secor writes:

> With hindsight, a convincing case can be made that during this period Oxford was the seedbed for an emergent middle theological ground between Puritanism and Catholicism. Advanced forms of Calvinism provided the leaven which worked the old patristic system into a new synthesis. Richard Hooker, a son of Oxford, was to provide the most complete and influential formulation of that via media we call Anglicanism.[20]

Moreover, there is evidence that makes make it very likely that Hooker would have encountered the writings of St. Thomas Aquinas already in his early years as a student. The personal library of a student at Hooker's own college by the name of Richard Allen, included a text of Thomas Aquinas.[21] Perhaps most definitively, Hooker's tutor at Oxford, John Rainolds, was in spite of his Calvinist leanings apparently well acquainted with Thomas Aquinas (and other Catholic scholastics), as evidenced in a letter that he wrote to Hooker's close friend and fellow student at Corpus Christi, George Cranmer. Cranmer had apparently written to Rainolds a letter which included parallel quotations from Scotus and Aquinas, and Rainolds wrote back his opinion on their relative merits.[22] On the basis of such interchanges the eminent Renaissance scholar Charles Schmitt is able to say, "Both Thomas and Scotus were being read in the intellectual circle at Corpus Christi College, where Hooker spent his formative years."[23] Turning to Hooker himself it is apparent that he had read both Scotus and Aquinas, having a higher estimate of Scotus then his tutor apparently. Thus Hooker quotes Scotus[24] on the idea that God was not strictly bound to give man eternal salvation on account of virtue, even terming Scotus "the wittiest of the school-divines."[25]

Explicit references to Aquinas are even more common. Some of these may be outlined in brief. In Book I, he quotes Aquinas in a note in 3.2 on the subordination of all created things to the eternal law of God.[26] In 3.5,[27] he references Aquinas in regard to how God as the first mover is the principal of all motion in general. In 8.10,[28] he quotes Aquinas again in support of his contention that while in some sense every sin violates the natural law known by reason since it is contrary to the good in general which reason enjoins "yet we do not therefore so far extend the law of reason, as to contain in it all manner laws whereunto reasonable creatures are bound, but (as hath been shown) we restrain it to those only duties, which all men by force of natural wit either do or understand to be such duties as concern all men." In 11.4,[29] he cites Aquinas on the idea of the *desiderium naturale* for God within man; specifically that God would not create a natural desire, which was incapable of fulfillment. In 12.2,[30] he refers to Aquinas's contention that while the law of nature is in principle knowable by all, and none may be ignorant of its primary precepts, yet on account of the darkness of ignorance and concupiscence which are the legacy of original sin, it is possible for whole nations to be deceived in regards to its secondary precepts. In Book V, Hooker several times turns to Aquinas in reference to issues of sacramental theology as in 58.2,[31] where he shows his accord with the Thomistic principle that a sacrament is a sign which confers the very grace which its material element signifies, and again in 65.15[32] where Aquinas is cited in reference to the adoration of the Cross. In Book VIII in K 3.6, Hooker refers critically to a "little overflowing of wit in Thomas Aquinas" to use I Peter 2:9 to justify the supremacy of the sacerdotal over the regal authority.[33] In chapter 6.4 in Book VIII, Hooker refers to Aquinas[34] in his contention that while the natural and divine laws are sufficient to direct man toward his supernatural end, yet given the social and communal nature of human beings it is further necessary to have both positive political and ecclesiastical human laws for his due governance. As far as parallel passages are concerned, there are a wide number of passages in the laws that essentially paraphrase passages in the Thomistic corpus, particularly pertaining to the order of law and to issues of nature and grace.[35] The reasons for the relative reticence of Hooker to fully acknowledge his debt to Aquinas are easy to see. Hooker's patron and supporter Archbishop Whitgift was ambivalent at best about the growing popularity of "papist" literature among students and scholars. Whitgift wrote on this matter to the Vice-Chancellor of Cambridge in 1594. When reading Whitgift's words on the Scholastics, it would be well to recall Hooker's gratitude for Whitgift's "more then ordinary favour."[36]

> That in these times instead of Godly and sound writers, among their stationers, the new writers were very rarely bought: and that there were no books more ordinarily bought and sold then Popish writers . . . that upon the search that had been made by his Grace's appointment, many Divines' studies being searched, there were found in divers studies many Friar's, schoolmen's and Jesuit's writings, and of Protestants either few or none.[37]

Yet the very fact that Archbishop Whitgift felt it necessary to prohibit the reading of scholastic texts is external evidence that the study of Catholic scholastics was a not uncommon occurrence among scholars.

At the center of the issue between Hooker and Cartwright is whether there is a legitimate distinct sphere of nature and of reason, and whether nature and grace are harmonious categories.[38] For Hooker, as we have said, the pillar of the Disciplinarian argument is that there is *one order of law* which should govern all human affairs, namely, that which is revealed in Scripture. For

Aquinas, on whom Hooker depends for his fundamental standpoint on nature and grace, human reason is still able to certainly discern the ends and goods of nature. Thus, both Hooker and Aquinas can speak of other orders of law such as the natural law which reason is able to discern by reflection upon human nature, and the positive laws, which human authority is able to promulgate. For Hooker, the eternal law serves the central function of grounding even these orders of law in a transcendent source.[39]

As we have seen, one of the central points of contention was the Calvinist doctrine of predestination according to which God positively and absolutely ordains some to salvation and others to reprobation, independently of His foreknowledge of their actions. This too followed from their anthropology. Since the human will is utterly depraved, it is wholly reliant on divine grace for salvation. There is no merit or human cooperation in the process of justification. But since not all are saved, God must have selected before all time to whom He would give His Grace by a fiat of His inscrutable will. Thus, some are predestined to salvation and others to damnation.[40]

Richard Hooker in *A Learned Sermon of the Nature of Pride* undertook to refute the voluntarism behind the Puritan doctrine of predestination. There would be no reason for God to create a creature solely as vessel for damnation, and God never acts without purpose: "they err who think that of the will of God to do this or that there is no reason besides his will."[41] If we use the Thomistic distinction between the *potestas directiva* (the function of the law in directing man to the good), and the *potestas coactiva* (constraining or coercive function) we can say that while Hooker emphasizes the directive power of the law, the voluntarists (on whom Cartwright and Travers depended) emphasize its coercive power.[42] For them, the essence of law is something imposed on an inferior by the command of a superior. But in the case of God, there is no superior, and yet for Hooker his actions can be said to be lawful, because an eternal law governs His acts. Thus, the *essence* of law must be said to lie in its connection with rational purpose, and not *per se* with command.

For Hooker, even God's will is governed by a purpose that he understands as a law. It is not however a heteronymous law, but the divine reason itself governing the divine will. According to Hooker, God always acts for some good, principally the good of his creatures. While from a human standpoint, there is a mysterious aspect to the divine purpose that unfolds in creation and history; *that* God's acts are purposeful rather than arbitrary is not to be doubted. Hooker identifies this *telos* governing the divine will with the eternal law:

> Not that anything is made to be beneficial unto him, but all things for him to shew beneficence and grace in them. The particular drift of every act proceeding

eternally from God we are not able to discern, and therefore cannot give the proper and certain reason of his works. Howbeit undoubtedly there is a proper and certain reason there is of every finite work of God, *inasmuch as there is a law imposed upon it.*[43]

This doctrine of predestination in Hooker is closely correlated to his teleological definition of law as "that which enables a thing to attain some foreconceived end for which it worketh."[44] As with Aristotle and Aquinas, everything is working toward some end that will bring its potencies to full perfection, and the law is that rule by which beings are ordered to their proper end. He defines law in general as "that which doth assign unto each thing the kinde; that which doth moderate the force and power; that which doth appoint the measure of working."[45]

As Lee W. Gibbs points out,[46] Hooker is here attacking directly the voluntarist theory of law general among the Calvinists, which identifies law not so much with reason as with command. For Hooker even the divine will follows the divine reason, and since this eternal law in God is the ultimate foundation of all law; thus, all law is ultimately grounded in reason. God rules not according to His arbitrary will for he keeps to the immutable and benevolent purposes that govern His acts. For God to ordain the eternal reprobation of some regardless of their actions would make of God a lawless and arbitrary governor. For Hooker then, the just and lawful government of God becomes the model for earthly kingship: "Let no man doubt but that all is well done, because the world is ruled by so good a guide, *as transgresseth not his own law*: then which nothing can be more absolute, perfect and just."[47]

For Hooker that there is a law governing God's dominion does not make God less free, since the law is none other then the purposes that He Himself has chosen in accordance with His own eternal Wisdom and Justice. The foundation of all law is this "first" eternal law by which God orders his own acts. Hooker defines this as follows: "this law therefore we may name eternal being that order which God hath set down with himself for himself to do all things by."[48]

The *Lex Aeterna* is the divine wisdom that rules the universe and provides the ultimate and transcendent foundation of all law. How this law reflects itself in the creation is related to Hooker's ontology. Hooker's model of created being is one in which creatures are ordered in an ascending hierarchy according to their likeness to God, from inanimate beings, to irrational plants and animals, to man the rational animal, and finally to the angels.[49] Thus, to the hierarchy of being there must correspond a hierarchy of law. In essence, the eternal law is mediated and expressed through a hierarchy of laws.

The basic concept of the eternal law is derived from Thomas Aquinas. In the treatise on law in the *Summa* he defines the eternal law as "the type of Divine Wisdom, as directing all actions and movements."[51] For Aquinas, as for Hooker, the whole order of law—divine, natural, and human—is ultimately derived from the eternal law, which divine wisdom assigns all things their powers and their end:

> Since then the eternal law is the plan of government in the Chief governor, all the plans of government in the inferior government must be derived from the eternal law. But these plans of inferior governors are all other laws besides the eternal law. Therefore all laws insofar as they partake of right reason, are derived from the eternal law.[52]

Hooker here introduces an innovation in the typology of law. In essence, the eternal law has two moments, the *first law eternal* lies within the divine nature and is that by which God determines His purposes and binds Himself to them. The *second law eternal* consists in the eternal law as mirrored in the purposes of nature and mediated through the hierarchy of being. As by the first eternal law God orders His own acts in accordance with His wisdom, so by the second eternal law he orders the acts of creatures in accordance with His wisdom. It is this divine purpose as ordering all beings to their perfection that is the foundation of law.

Since God's purposes are inscribed in the creation, a law appropriate to each nature governs every type of creature and orders it so as it may attain the end for which it was created. As there is an eternal law within God, the celestial law governs the angels, and three orders of laws—the supernatural law revealed in Scripture, the natural law or law of reason governs man, and the positive law promulgated by human authority. Human beings are therefore governed by three orders of law in which the eternal law is mediated to man.

On the lowest rung there is the law guiding natural agents that attain to their end by the necessity of their natures, since they lack reason or will to guide them:

> Whereas therefore natural things are not in the number of voluntary agents . . . do so *necessarily observe their certain laws*, that as long as they keep those forms which give them their being, they cannot possibly be inclinable to do otherwise then what they do; seeing the kinds of their operations are both constantly and exactly framed according to the several ends for which they serve.[53]

Hooker here departs somewhat[54] from the Thomistic nomenclature, since the law of nature signifies not the participation of *rational* creatures in the eternal law, but the law by which irrational creatures "unwittingly" participate in the eternal law, by their necessary obedience to the law which governs their nature and guises them toward their ends. For Aquinas, irrational creatures can only by analogy be said to be subject to a law. The differences here between Aquinas and Hooker are primarily of a taxonomic kind. The substance of the Thomistic doctrine of natural law is called by Hooker "the Law of reason," while the term "law of nature" refers to the necessary order of the physical universe. This taxonomy appears in the English common law author Christopher of St. Germain. The meaning of the distinction between the "law of reason" and the "law of nature" is explicated in St. Germain's text *Doctor and Student*.[55] This remarkable work depicts a discussion between a scholastic doctor of theology and a law student desirous of understanding the foundations of the law. After explaining that the foundation of all law is the eternal law,[56] the doctor goes on to explain the distinction between the law of nature and the law of reason:

> The lawe of nature may be considered in twoo manners . . . when it is considered generallye, then it is referred to all creatures, as well reasonable and unreasonable, for al unreasonable creatures[are]under a certaine rule to them geuven ny nature, necessarie for them to the conseruacion of theire being.[57]

However, what was called the 'natural law' by St. Thomas Aquinas and other scholastics is for Christopher of St. Germain a *specification* of the natural law, namely the natural law as directing *rational* creatures. As the Doctor goes on to say that "The lawe of Nature specially considered: which is also called the lawe of reason, perteineth onelye to creatures reasonable . . . man which is create to the [image] of God."[58]

In the case of creatures such as angels and men, who are endowed with intellect and will, they are not directed to their end by necessity, but voluntarily. Nonetheless while man is not governed by necessity, Hooker conceives of man as being guided by natural *inclination*. It is here that Hooker assimilates the basic concepts of Aristotelian / Thomistic Eudemonism.[59] All human acts aim at attaining objective goods that perfect or fulfill human nature.[60] Most goods however aim at some further good; for example, the act of exercise aims at the health of the body, the act of labor aims at the acquisition of wealth, and so forth. But, says Hooker, there must be some highest good, which is desired for its own sake and not for the sake of some further good, and this highest good is that which all our acts ultimately aim at.

> And whatsoever such perfection there is which our nature may acquire, the same we properly term our Good; our Sovereign Good or Blessedness that wherein the highest degree of all our perfection consisteth, that being once attained unto there can rest nothing further to be desired; and therefore with it our souls are fully content and satisfied, in that they have they rejoice, and thirst no more.[61]

Along with Aristotle and Aquinas he affirms that this highest good must be one and universal to all men.

> These things are linked and as it were chained one to another: we labour to eat, and we eat to live, and we live to do good, and the good that we which is as seed sown with reference unto a future harvest: but we must come at the length to some pause. For every thing were to be desired for the sake of another without any stint, there could be no certain end proposed unto our actions, we should go on not whither; yea whatsoever we do we do in vain, or rather not at all were possible to be done. For as to take away the first efficient cause of our being were to annihilate utterly our persons, so we cannot remove the last final cause of our working, for we shall cause whatsoever we work to cease. Therefore something there must be desired for itself simply, and for no other.[62]

This *sumum bonum*, which is the end that all men universally desire for its own sake is happiness: "All men desire to live in this world an happy life. That life is led most happily wherein all virtue is exercised without impediment or let."[63] There is therefore no conflict between virtue and happiness since virtue in none other then the right ordering of desires so as to attain happiness. But since happiness consists in the possession of some good, we have yet to determine what is in fact the highest good in which happiness consists. For Hooker, as for Aquinas, this cannot be any finite good.

> Now that which man doth desire with reference to a further end, the same he desireth in such measure as is unto that end convenient; but what he coveteth as good in itself, toward that his desire is ever infinite. So that unless the last good of all, which is desired altogether for itself, be also infinite, we do evil in making it our end; even as they who placed their felicity in wealth, or honour, or pleasure or anything here attained; because in desiring anything as our final perfection, which is not so, we do amiss.[64]

There is therefore an objective, universal, and infinite good to which our inclination for happiness directs us. Since for Hooker the only supreme and infinite good is God, it is in God that man's final end and true happiness consists.

> No good is infinite but only God; therefore he our felicity and bliss . . . then are we happy therefore when fully we enjoy God, as an object wherein the powers of our souls are satisfied even with everlasting delight.[65]

Hooker is here assuming from Aquinas the idea of a *desiderium naturale*:[66] a natural desire for beatitiude — the vision of God — that requires grace for its fulfillment. Given that for Aquinas no desire can be vain (i.e. impossible of fulfillment) the status of the *desiderium naturale* was an object of delicate theological controversy among Thomistic scholastics. The main issue was whether the existence of a desire for the Beatific Vision in the order of nature exerted a claim on divine justice to grant the possibility of fulfillment to this desire, which in effect brings into question the theological gratuity of the vision. Spanish Thomists such as Cajetan, Banez, and de Soto extensively dealt in particular with these issues.

Hooker does not engage these debates in detail. For his purpose, what is important here is the contrast of (his understanding) of Thomistic anthropology with that of the English Calvinists. For the latter, man's nature is utterly depraved and turned away from God. Grace is manifested as God's act of forgiving this depravity. Justification is not so much the healing and perfecting of fallen nature by grace, but a forensic act by which sins are covered over by God's mercy revealed in Jesus Christ. For Hooker, as for Aquinas, postlapsarian human nature is not wholly turned away from God. There remains in man a natural desire—the *desiderium naturale*—for God that even after the fall continues to draw man to his supernatural end. The naturalness of this desire is shown by the universal desire for happiness that consists objectively in God: "Now if man had not naturally this desire to be happy, how were it possible that all men should have it? All men have. Therefore this desire in man is natural."[67]

Since the inclinations within man are oriented toward objective goods, man can discern the goods by reflecting upon the inclinations of human nature itself. Hooker categorizes these inclinations as a three-fold hierarchy—the sensual, the intellectual, and the spiritual. And just as there is a hierarchy of desires within human nature, so there is a hierarchy of goods to be sought.

> Man doth seek a triple perfection. First a sensual, consisting in those things which very life requireth either as necessary supplements, or as beauties and ornaments thereof; then an intellectual, consisting in those things which none underneath man either is capable or acquainted with; and lastly a spiritual and divine, consisting of those things whereunto we tend by supernatural means here, but cannot attain unto them.[68]

Hooker's schema assumes that the inclinations of human nature are directed to goods, that there is a hierarchy of inclinations, and that there correspondingly lies a hierarchy of goods, and that an analysis of these inclinations and goods enables reason to apprehend the precepts of the natural law closely approximates Aquinas, who says that:

> Wherefore according to the order of natural inclinations, is the order of the precepts of natural law. Because in man there is first of all an inclination to good in

accordance with the nature which he has in common with all substances, inasmuch as every substance seeks the preservation of its own being . . . [s]econdly, there is in man an inclination to things that pertain to him more specially, according to that nature which he has in common with other animals . . . those things are said to belong to the natural law, *which nature has taught to all animals*, such as sexual intercourse, education of offspring and so forth. Thirdly, there is an inclination to good, according to the nature of his reason, which nature is proper to him: thus man has a natural inclination to know the truth about God, and to live in society.[69]

In that latter case of the desire in man for God, supernatural helps are needed to bring this desire to fulfillment. But grace is here perfecting an inclination within nature, and not bringing salvation by fiat and in spite of nature, as in the Puritan conception. What is seen from this schema so far as the law is not something so much external to creatures, but is the means whereby they attain the fulfillment of their own *telos*. As such, all beings are drawn to their end by their inclinations immanent within their own nature.

Hooker thus accepts the central concepts of Aristotelian eudemonism in which all men desire happiness that consists in the attainment of the ends to which man is directed by inclinations immanent within human nature. These inclinations point man to the objective, universal goods that he needs to be fulfilled to attain happiness. Such beatitude consists in the knowledge and love of God, and in an ancillary way in all those lesser goods, which are required for this attainment, as he writes:

True it is that the kingdom of God must be the first thing in our purposes and desires. But inasmuch as righteous life, presupposeth life; inasmuch as to live virtuously it is impossible except we live; therefore the first impediment, which naturally we endeavor to remove, is penury, and want of things without which we cannot live.[70]

Virtue consists in ordering one's desires rightly so that the end for which we were created can be attained. Thus like Aristotle he sees virtue and happiness as harmonious if not identical strivings: "All men desire to live in this world an happy life. That life is led most happily wherein all virtue is exercised without impediment or let."[71]

Of course, what concerns Hooker most is the order of laws that are to govern man, which are the natural law or law of reason, the supernatural law given in Scripture, and the positive law promulgated by human government. As with Aquinas, for Hooker, God has given man two lights with which to discern the law. There is the supernatural light of faith by which man is able to see and accept the supernatural law revealed in Scripture, but also the natural light of reason by which man discerns the natural law. Central to this idea is the repudiation of the Puritan doctrine that man's faculties were totally corrupted by the fall.

Natural law is defined by Hooker as that part of the divine law which governs human action and which is discernible by natural reason:

> Law rational therefore which men commonly use to call the Law of Nature, meaning thereby the Law which human Nature knoweth itself in reason bound unto . . . this Law I say, comprehendeth all those things which men by the light of their natural understanding evidently know, or at leastwise may know, to be beseaming or unbeseaming, virtuous or vicious, good or evil for them to do.[72]

One of the most important scholarly contributions to the study of Hooker's work is that found in Cargill Thompson's landmark 1980 article, "The Philosopher of the Politic Society." Here Thompson identifies four fundamental characteristics of the natural law. First, that the natural law ultimately has a divine source, since God is the author of nature. The expression of this principle in Hooker is the dependency of the "second law eternal," which includes all laws that must be kept by creatures under the rubric of the first law eternal. Thus, he writes:

> For what good or evil there is under the sun, what action correspondent or repugnant unto the law which God hath imposed unto his creatures, but in or upon it God doth work according the law which himself hath eternally purposed to keep; that is to say the *first law eternal*.[73]

Second, there is the *universality* of the natural law—in other words, since all men share the same nature, and possess reason, the natural law is binding and knowable by all men, not specifically as Christians, but as rational animals. Thus Aquinas states[74] that the general principles of the natural law are the same in all men. Third, there is the fact that the natural law is apprehensible by the natural power of the human intellect, and does not require special revelation.[75] Fourth, there is the principle that the human law is derived from, and must cohere with, the natural law. Thus he says of humanly promulgated law that "human law that which *out of* the law either of reason or of God, men probably gathering it to be expedient, make into a law."[76] In all this Hooker follows Aquinas closely. In some of the particular questions regarding natural law however there are certain ambiguities.[77] For Aquinas, while it is possible to err in the application of general moral precepts of natural law to particular cases, it is impossible for the general precepts of the natural law themselves to be blotted out of the human heart.[78] For Hooker, the matter is less consistent. Sometimes he speaks of the fact that "Men do both as the Apostle teaches, yea, those men who have no written law . . . carry written in their hearts the universal law of mankind."[79] Yet earlier Hooker states that "The soul of man being therefore at the first as a book, wherein nothing is yet all things may be imprinted."[80]

Hooker seems to be dealing here with the tension between the conception that natural law is written on the heart and thus knowledge of its precepts is connatural to man, with the Aristotelian idea that all knowledge begins with sensation, and therefore ideas are not innate. As a result it is unclear whether knowledge of the precepts of natural law is innate or acquired. There are possible strategies for rendering the two notions consistent—for example, the idea that the natural law is grounded in human nature and in this sense the precepts are innate, but they are rendered intelligible by a process of reason. Hooker however does not engage these issues, so the matter is left unclear.

Another controversial issue is to what degree Hooker's natural law theory departs from that of the continental Protestant reformers. In this present exposition we have tended to emphasize the continuity of Hooker's concept of law with the Thomistic natural law theory, and see Hooker's thought on matters of law and politics in particular as following a trajectory not dissimilar from that of his Spanish scholastic contemporaries. But Cargill Thompson asserts that the idea that Hooker is simply retrieving a medieval natural law theory unknown to Protestants is untrue. As he writes: "The sixteenth-century reformers did not, as one school of modern historians has maintained, either reject or even substantially modify the traditional medieval concept of natural law."[81]

HOOKER AND THE MAGISTERIAL REFORMATION: THE QUESTION OF THE *VIA MEDIA*

The debate on the status of natural law in Hooker is tied to the ongoing debate about whether or not Hooker's theology coheres with that of the magisterial Reformation. At issue is whether Hooker is endeavoring to create an Anglican *via media* between Roman Catholicism and the continental Reformation, or is Hooker rather a reformed thinker in an English context. A school of recent authors has argued that Hooker's theology is essentially continuous with that of Luther, Calvin, and Melanchthon. The contemporary scholar who has galvanized the attack on the *via media* interpretation of Hooker's theology is W. J. Torrance Kirby[82] who has argued that the image of Hooker as a *via media* thinker is a myth created by nineteenth-century Anglo–Catholicism (represented by figures like John Keble and John Henry Newman). Thus he writes that:

> The classic nineteenth-century definition of the Anglican *via media* in theology was formulated, somewhat ironically by John Henry Newman . . . Newman's formulation of the *via media* myth has been assumed by many scholars in their interpretation of the latter's theology. John Keble, the great nineteenth century High Churchman and editor of Hooker's *Works*, portrayed Hooker as the originator of the *via media* theology. Ever since the influence of the anachronistic *via media* stereotype has been extraordinarily resilient.[83]

Kirby goes on to argue that "Anglicanism" as a distinct theological system did not exist in the sixteenth century, and thus Hooker's theology must be reinterpreted.[84] Once the central error of reading Hooker through an Anglo–Catholic lense is done away with, then for Kirby many of the central issues of Hooker scholarship can be exposed as pseudo-problems. Thus Kirby argues that reading Hooker as a late scholastic (as scholars like D'Entreves and Munz did) leads to the problem of how to render his work coherent since his Erastian political theory based on royal supremacy fits uneasily with a Thomistic ethic. Thus Kirby writes about Munz that

> his interpretation of Hooker according to the theological and metaphysical categories of Thomas Aquinas was extraordinarily superficial . . . such an assessment of Hooker as a 'belated medievalist' could only be argued by consistently ignoring Hooker's explicitly doctrinal statements. Thus our criticism of Munz's position is twofold: first, that he grossly over-estimates Hooker's debt to Aquinas and absurdly discounted Hooker's commitment to the theological principles of reformed doctrinal orthodoxy; and secondly that his main thesis of the logical inconstancy between Hooker's theories of law in Book I, and his defence of the 'practical reality' of the Royal Supremacy in Book VIII, rests on the same questionable hypothesis . . . we disagree . . . with his [Munz's] identification of Hooker's fundamental intellectual position with a scholastic metaphysic.[85]

If then the disputation between Hooker and the disciplinarians was not one between a *via media* position and a Reformed position then what was at issue? For Kirby, Hooker was *defending* the magisterial Reformed theology, against heterodox radical reformers. Thus he says that:

> The cornerstone of the reformed theology [for the disciplinarians] is identified as a vilification of reason, natural law, and 'the human' generally, in order to secure the rightful primacy of revelation, scriptural authority, and 'the divine' . . .

Hooker strongly resisted this simplistic dichotomizing which in his view was the hallmark of the Disciplinarian-Puritan divinity and contrary to the magisterial version of reformed orthodoxy.[86]

Turning to specific issues Kirby will argue that when Hooker attacks Disciplinarian Calvinists (like Cartwright) on issues like royal supremacy, Hooker is arguing from *within* the magisterial Reformation context, from which he considers Cartwright and others to have deviated.[87] The aim of Kirby and of others in the "anti-*via media*" school is to show how all of Hooker's theological positions are coherent with the magisterial Reformation. Thus other figures following Kirby like Nigel Atkinson have extended the debate into Hooker's views on scripture and tradition, endeavoring to show how Hooker's deference to tradition can be squared with allegiance to Reformation principles.[88] The issue of natural law is another crucial space for contention between opponents and proponents of the *via media* thesis. Natural law has been associated with the teaching of the Roman Catholic schoolmen, and thus seemed to be a clear example of an area in which Hooker drew upon pre-Reformation Catholic thought to argue against the disciplinarian Calvinists. It is thus crucial for those who wish to show the coherence of Hooker with the magisterial Reformers, to show that their views of natural law were consonant.

Kirby[89] indeed sees Hooker's natural law theory as fully consistent with Calvinism. At the core, Kirby argues against the view that Hooker represents a *Via Media* between Roman Catholicism and continental Protestantism and asserts on the contrary that:

> An alternative interpretation is here offered and is based on the proposal that Hooker shares considerable theological ground in his account of natural law with four leading representatives of the continental magisterial Reformation: Martin Luther, Phillip Melanchthon, John Calvin and Heinrich Bullinger.[90]

Kirby goes on to show how in fact contrary to a common impression, natural law occupies a significant position in the thought of these reformers. Kirby is on strong ground in this respect, as recent scholarship has reevaluated the facile claim that the major Protestant Reformers simply rejected the whole of the medieval scholastic tradition out of hand.[91] Kirby's contention is perhaps at its weakest in relation to Martin Luther. Kirby refers to Luther's remarks in his 1555 *Lecture on the Galatians*[92] as evidence that Luther was a proponent of natural law. While this passage proves that Luther believed in the reality of natural law, a close scrutiny of this entire passage reveals a profound ambivalence about man's power to keep or even *to understand* the precepts of natural law in his fallen condition:

All men have a certain natural knowledge implanted in their minds (Rom 2:14-15), by which they know naturally that one should do to others what he wants done to himself (Matt 7:12). This principle and others like it, *which we call the law of nature,* are the foundation of human law and of all good works. Nevertheless, human reason is so corrupted and blinded by the malice of the devil *that it does not understand this inborn knowledge*; or even if it has been admonished by the Word of God, it deliberately neglects and despises it.

This passage captures the duality which would mark Protestant reaction to natural law. On the one hand the Reformers generally accepted the reality of a moral law known independently of revelation, on the basis of St. Paul's words in the second chapter of Romans regarding the existence of a law written on the hearts of all men. On the other hand, there was some diffidence about any doctrine that seemed to emphasize man's natural powers of reason and will after the fall. A somewhat clearer doctrine of natural law[93] emerges in the writing of Luther's close collaborator Phillip Melanchthon. In his *Loci Communes,* Melanchthon remarks that the fall did not entirely extinguish the likeness to God in human nature. Evidence of this is shown in the natural capacity of man to distinguish between good and evil. This capacity is the divine gift or "light" that permits man to see and recognize the law of nature. Nonetheless, without the grace of God in Christ, the recognition of the law is of no advantage for salvation since man in his sinful state is unable to keep the law. Yet it still serves to educate the justified Christian in righteous works.[94]

For Heinrich Bullinger of Zurich, the law of nature is again that referred to by St. Paul in Romans 2:14–16:

When Gentiles who have not the law do by nature what the law requires, they are a law to themselves, even though they do not have the law. They show that what the law requires is written on the hearts, while their conscience also bears witness and their conflicting thoughts accuse or perhaps excuse them on that day when according to my gospel, God judges the secrets of men by Christ Jesus.

On the basis of this passage, Bullinger concludes that even without the written law given by God to the Jewish people, Gentiles were not left with no knowledge of good and evil. The law of God makes itself known in an unwritten manner, through the light of conscience.

The law of nature is an instruction of the conscience, and, as it were, a certain direction placed by God himself in the minds and hearts of men, to teach them what they have to do and what to eschew. And the conscience, verily, is the knowledge, judgement, and reason of a man . . . and this reason proceedeth from God. . . . Wherefore the law of nature [is so called] because God hath imprinted or engraven in our minds some knowledge, and certain general principles of re-

ligion, justice, and goodness, which, because they be grafted in us and born together with us, do therefore seem to be naturally in us . . . We understand that
the law of nature, not the written law, but that which is graffed in man, hath the
same office that the written law hath.[95]

In light of the evidence that natural law was a prominent feature of Reformed
thought, Hooker is reconstructed by Kirby not as a "belated Thomist,"[96] but
as a rather mainstream expositor of the magisterial Reformation in England.

Lee W. Gibbs, however, points out that the mere fact that the Reformers
used natural law theories misses the point. The real issue is not whether the
Reformers had a natural law theory, but what *kind* of natural law theory they
held.[97] Thompson himself acknowledges that the continental Reformers were
influenced by Ockham, and Gibbs says "the magisterial Protestant Reformation and their disciplinarian progeny stand squarely in the camp of medieval
voluntarists and nominalists." In other words, the foundation of the law is that
it is a command, which proceeds from God's will. Hooker[98] clearly takes the
intellectualist position of Aquinas. As we have seen in his debate with Travers, Hooker said that "They err therefore who think that of the will of God
to do this or that, there is no reason besides his will."[99] There must be a *ratio*,
which governs even the acts of God's will. Likewise, he says of the natural
law that:

> In cases therefore of such facility the Will doth yield her assent, as it were with
> a kind of silence, by not dissenting, in which respect her force is not so appar-
> ent as in express mandates and prohibitions, especially upon advice and consul-
> tation going before. Where understanding therefore needeth, in those things *rea-
> son is the director of man's Will by discovering in action what is good. For the
> Laws of well-doing are the dictates of right reason.*[100]

Gibbs goes on to point out that Hooker accepts the Aristotelian / Thomistic
principle that all things strive for their perfection, that is, those goods which
bring the potencies of a thing to actuality and fulfillment.[101]

> And for this cause there is in all things an appetite or desire, whereby they in-
> cline to something which they may be: and when they are it: and when they are
> it they shall be perfecter then now they are. All which perfections are contained
> under the general name of *Goodness*.[102]

Hooker further adds that in striving to attain their highest perfection, all creatures are wittingly or unwittingly striving toward God, from whence they came:

> Again since there can be no goodness desired which proceedeth not from God
> himself, as from the supreme cause of all things; and every effect doth after a

sort . . . at leastwise resemble the cause from which it procedeth: all things in
the world are said to seek the highest, and to covet more or less the participation
of God himself.[103]

This passage is an eloquent restatement of several Thomistic ideas. There is
the notion that whatever perfections are in the effect must preexist in the
cause. Thus Aquinas says that: "all created perfections are in God . . . because
whatever perfection exists in an effect must be found in the effective
cause."[104]

There is also the central notion of *redite* and *exitus*, creatures having their
origin in God and proceeding to God through their participation in the divine
likeness. Aquinas makes the central distinction, however, between rational
creatures which proceed to their end through knowledge of the intellect and
love of the will, and irrational creatures which attain their end solely through
unwitting participation.

For man and other rational creatures attain their end by knowing and loving
God, this is not possible to other rational creatures, which acquire their end, insofar as they share in the divine likeness, inasmuch as they are, or live, or even
know.[105]

Hooker also embraces this delineation through his distinction between the
law of nature and the law of reason. For Hooker, man shares with animals the
inclination to self-preservation, as well as the faculties of sense and fancy—
external sensation and inward imagination.[106] But what is particularly distinctive to man is his possession of reason, which is able to direct the will toward the good.

Hooker's analysis of natural law is, as we have seen, built up on an intellectualist (i.e. Aristotelian / Thomistic) framework; thus it is predicated on the
notion that the inclinations within human nature are directed towards ends
which consist in the possession of certain goods. In his emphasis on the idea
that even after the Fall man's desires retain an ultimate exigency toward the
divine, and his reason is competent within certain limits to discern the natural law, he is at odds with the Calvinist emphasis on the total vitiation of post-
lapsarian human nature.

In reply then to the formidable contention of Kirby that Hooker was
much more a Protestant in the continental magisterial tradition than an
"Anglican Thomist" in his use of natural law, we would make five replies.
First, in general terms Kirby's contention that Hooker is arguing on *behalf*
of the magisterial Reformation is highly dubious. If such were the case we
should have expected to see Hooker consistently arguing against
Cartwright using the authority of Calvin and other Reformers. Instead we

see Hooker attacking the disciplinarians for their excessive veneration of Calvin's authority:

> Of what account the Master of Sentences was in the church of Rome, the same and more amongst the preachers of reformed churches Calvin had purchased; so that the perfectest divines were judged they, which were skillfullest in Calvin's writings. His books became almost the very canon to judge both doctrine and discipline by.[107]

So far from Kirby's contention that Hooker saw the royal supremacy as consonant with the views of magisterial Reformers like Calvin, Hooker notes that for Calvin *himself* on account of the Anglican claim of royal supremacy "this realm is condemned of blasphemy.[108] Hooker attacks Calvin's view that the Reformed community ought not to receive in baptism the infants of Roman Catholics saying "the answer of Calvin unto Farel concerning the children of Popish parents doth seem crazed."[109] In his defense of the episcopate, he refers to Calvin as "an enemy unto regiment by bishops"[110] but uses him as a hostile witness, since even Calvin acknowledges that bishops were appointed in the post-Apostolic age. Finally, in his *Preface*, Hooker associates English defenders of discipline he is opposing, to the "Church of Geneva."[111] It is thus far from clear that Hooker is an uncritical admirer of the Calvinist system, and thus the argument that his use of natural law derives from the authority of the magisterial Reformers is questionable.

Secondly, the use of natural law by continental Reformers does not show that Hooker's doctrine of natural law does not stand in continuity with Aquinas. Rather, it indicates that in the earliest stages of the Reformation, the break with medieval thought on this point was not yet complete. Even if one accepts Thompson's and Kirby's argument, what is implied is continuity between early magisterial Protestant natural law theories and Medieval Scholastic ones, as we have already seen in Thompson. If that is the case, then Hooker is no less of a successor to the medieval natural law tradition on account of his ostensible kinship with continental reformers. Indeed an important trend in modern scholarship (Richard A. Muller, Heiko Oberman, Carl Trueman, Frank A. James, etc.) has been to posit the idea of a "Protestant scholasticism" or at least a Protestantism highly indebted to medieval Catholic modes of thought and argumentation. In addition to the aforementioned texts in Luther, Bullinger, and Melanchthon, Calvin himself has a doctrine of natural law which he identifies with the precepts of the Decalogue as they are written on man's heart: "Moreover, the very things contained in the two tables [of the Decalogue] are, in a manner, dictated to us by that internal law, which, as has been already said, is in a manner written and stamped on every heart."[112]

Due to the darkness of sin, however, the clear knowledge of the natural law has been obscured and requires revelation to make its precepts clear:

> Therefore, as a necessary remedy, both for our dullness and our contumacy, the Lord has given us his written Law, which, by its sure attestations, removes the obscurity of the law of nature, and also, by shaking off our lethargy, makes a more lively and permanent impression on our minds."[113]

It is true that for Calvin, while the light of nature has become very weak,[114] it yet remains clear that the natural law itself still exists, and is knowable by natural means through the voice of conscience:

> Conscience, instead of allowing us to stifle our perceptions, and sleep on without interruption, acts as an inward witness and monitor, reminds us of what we owe to God, points out the distinction between good and evil, and thereby convicts us of departure from duty.[115]

If we accept the idea of a fundamental continuity between, say, the Thomistic and magisterial Protestant versions of natural law, then there is no fundamental problem with continuing to interpret Hooker as a defender of the *via media*. The debate between Hooker as "magisterial Reformer" and Hooker as "Anglican *via media* proponent" in relation to natural law presumes, of course, that there is a fundamental opposition between Calvinism and Roman Catholic versions of natural law. Kirby is able to attack the *via media* hypothesis on the question of natural law, only by, in effect, presenting the Reformer's view of natural law as continuous with the medieval Catholic understanding of the matter. But if that is the case, then Hooker and the early Reformers would thus be read as simply continuing to hold to medieval natural law principles worked out by Catholic scholastics.

Thirdly, as a factual matter (as we have seen from Gibbs's argument), it is far from clear that Hooker's version of natural law and the version employed by the continental reformers were one and the same. The Protestant versions of natural law seem to have received a much stronger influence from nominalist and voluntarist conceptions of the Late Medieval period, while Hooker totally rejects voluntarism in favor of the intellectualist and teleological account of natural law, which he holds in common with Aquinas.

Fourthly, regardless of one's view of the status of natural law it seems unquestionable that *over time* the magisterial Protestant and especially Calvinist emphasis on the vitiation of man's natural powers by the Fall, would lead to a greater skepticism about the ability of human reason by its natural potency to discern the purposes immanent within nature, while magisterial Protestantism's unique emphasis on the authority of Scripture would render appeals to natural law more and more suspect. For Aquinas and Hooker, nature and grace remain fundamentally harmonious categories even after the fall. Grace heals and completes nature and brings its potencies to perfection and fulfillment. The Thomistic natural law theory involves reason discerning the goods to which human nature is directed. The trend within Calvinism was to take a far starker view of the degree to which the inclinations of fallen human nature remain oriented to good ends. It is easy therefore to see why Calvinists would tend to be increasingly mistrustful of the "natural light of human reason" as a guide to man in his post-lapsarian state.

Fifthly and perhaps most importantly, regardless of how the leaders of the continental Reformation felt about natural law, it seems to have played little role (except as an object of derision) among the English followers of Calvin that Hooker was addressing. Thus Kirby acknowledges that:

> It must nevertheless be acknowledged that there is a genuine dialectical difficulty in reconciling the authority of the natural law with the core assumptions of Reformation soteriology and scriptural hermeneutics. As we have already noted, Hooker's advocating of natural law to defend the constitution of the Elizabethan Church met with strong opposition from some of his contemporaries. To the anonymous authors of *A Christian Letter* he appeared to overthrow the very foundation of the doctrine of the reformed Church of England by setting a qualification on the perfect sufficiency of scriptural authority . . . in his debate with Archbishop John Whitgift earlier in the 1570s, Cartwright had argued that the dictum *sola scriptura* constituted a universal rule of human action and that whatever is not done in accord with God's revealed written word is sinful.[116]

Moreover, in 1599, there appeared an anonymous tract called *A Christian letter*[117] reproaching the theology of the *Laws* in the harshest terms for appealing to the authority of reason and thus reverting to the methods of Roman Catholic scholasticism:

> Yet in all your discourse, for the most parte, Aristotle the patriarch of Philosophers (with divers other human writers) and the ingenuous [sic!] schoolemen, almost in all pointes have some finger; Reason is highlie sett up against holie scripture, and reading against preaching; the church of Rome favourablie admitted to bee of the house of God; Calvin with the reformed churches full of faults; and most of all they which indevoured to be most removed from conformitie with the church of Rome;

> Almost all the principall pointes of our English creed, greatlie shaken and contradicted. . . Shall wee doe you wronge to suspect you as a privie and subtill enemie to the whole state of the Englishe Church, and that you would have men to deeme her Majestie to have done ill in abolishing the Romish religion, and

banishing the Popes authoritie; and that you would bee glad to see the back-
esliding of all reformed churches to bee made conformable to that wicked syn-
agogue of Rome . . . and that you esteeme . . . the bookes of holy scripture to
bee at the least of no greater moment then Aristotle and the Schoolemen: Or else
doe you meane to bring in a confusion of all thinges, to reconcile heaven and
earth, and to make all religions equall: Will you bring us to Atheisme, or to
Poperie?[118]

These statements are poignant examples of the rejection of any detente between Athens and Jerusalem by the more radical wing of the Reformation.
Roman Catholicism is here associated with the effort to achieve intellectual
harmony between the classical heritage of Greek philosophy and the Biblical
dispensation. These radical Calvinists thus charge Hooker with committing
an error they associate with medieval scholastic tradition of seeking harmony
between faith and philosophical reason. The effort is deemed blasphemous
because it sets up the work of merely human wisdom (represented by Aristotle) as an authority alongside the divine wisdom manifested in the Scripture.
Human powers are to too vitiated to place any great confidence in the specu-
lations of the pagan philosophers, and the effort to integrate Aristotelianism
into Christianity reveals a lack of confidence in the sufficiency of Scripture
to guide and direct human affairs.[119]

The question is however whether this attitude can be considered representative of English Calvinism. Kirby endeavors to depict the authors of the *Let-*
ter as radical reformers, and the magisterial Reformers as more amenable to
certain forms of rationalism and in particular the natural law tradition. But a
problem exists moreover in Kirby's effort to depict Cartwright and Travers as
radical reformers. Clearly, they saw themselves, and were seen by Hooker as
"Geneva men," not followers of for example Thomas Munzer. Thus even if we
accept the dubious idea that Calvin himself was a proponent of natural law in
the Thomistic / intellectualistic form that Hooker proposes it, it would have to
be acknowledged that by the end of the sixteenth century Calvinism—in its
English form at least—was more influenced by Calvin's pessimistic view on
man's natural powers after the Fall, and his negative views on the *adiaphora*,
then they were by his acceptance of natural law. English Calvinism had by
Hooker's time been set on a trajectory that would lead to the sidelining of natural law in favor of an exclusive emphasis on the revealed law of the scripture.

Thus, Hooker's specific opponents such as Cartwright and Travers make
little if any mention of natural law discoverable by reason. Such mention
would detract from their main point, which as Cartwright says, concerns the
sufficiency of Scripture to govern human affairs. Hooker's conception presupposes, in contrast to Cartwright, both that reason is still a fit guide for human conduct and that God's purposes, however dimly, are intelligible to hu-

man reason from nature: "By force of the light of Reason, wherewith God illuminateth everyone that comes into the world, men being able to know truth from falsehood, and good from evil, do thereby learn in many things what the will of God is."[120] Among the precepts of the natural law that Hooker regards as knowable without special revelation he says that: "Axioms less general, yet so manifest that they need no further proof are such as these: *God is to be worshipped, parents to be honoured, others to be used by us as we ourselves would by them.*"[121]

If the Puritans emphasized the transcendence of God and thus his radical otherness from the world of nature, Hooker emphasizes the manner is which God is reflected in His creatures. The natural creation can therefore mediate the Divine to man, "God being the author of nature, her voice is but his instrument."[122] But the Puritans might have countered that if the natural law is discernible by reason alone, why then is it necessary for God also to reveal the moral law (e.g. the Ten Commandments) in Scripture? Hooker provides several arguments. First, while some precepts of natural law are easily discoverable, others are more difficult, and therefore men would be liable to ignorance of their moral obligations.

> Neither is it vain that the Scripture aboundeth with so great stores of laws in this kind. For they are either such as we of ourselves could not easily have found out, and then the benefit is not small to have them readily set down to our hands.[123]

Secondly, man after the fall is wounded by the passions, which rebel against the law, and if they were not clearly and directly revealed by God these passions would lead men astray:

> so far has the natural understanding even of sundry whole nations been darkened, that they have not discerned no not gross iniquity to be sin. Again being prone as we are to fawn upon ourselves . . . how should our festered sores be cured, but that God hath delivered a law as sharp as the two edged sword, piercing the closest and most unsearchable corners of the heart, which the law of nature can hardly, human laws by no means possible reach unto?[124]

Finally, for Hooker, while man after the fall retains the natural desire for beatitude, because of the fall he cannot attain this end without supernatural helps added to the natural law, which the law of Scripture contains.

> We see that therefore that our sovereign good is desired naturally; that God the author of natural desire had appointed natural means whereby to fulfill it; that man having utterly disabled his nature unto those means hath had other revealed from God, and hath received from heaven a law to teach him how that which is desired naturally must now supernaturally be attained.[125]

Parenthetically, Hooker's statement that in the pre-lapsarian state, "the author of natural desire had appointed natural means whereby to fulfill," would seem to make Hooker even *more* optimistic in his anthropology then Aquinas. For Aquinas, it is connatural only to God to know His own essence, and consequently even in the condition of original justice man would require supernatural grace to attain the beatific vision. The consequence of original sin resulted therefore in the loss of a supernatural *gift* for Adam and his posterity, which would have allowed them to come to beatitude. For Hooker, on the contrary, it would seem that beatitude would have been attained by man's *natural power* had the fall not occurred. This distinction is somewhat academic since man exists in a post-lapsarian state, but it does show the lengths to which Hooker is willing to challenge the pessimism of Calvinist theological anthropology.

Having clarified and distinguished the relation and respective ends of the supernatural and natural law, it remains for Hooker to account for human law and its relationship to the divine and natural law. First of all, why is the human law necessary in addition to the natural law? Hooker states that the purpose of the human law is primarily *pedagogical* in its purpose to instruct men in the good, and secondarily *coercive* to constrain men from doing evil. "Laws do not only teach what is good but they enjoin it, they have in them a certain constraining force."[126] The natural law by itself prescribes no penalties, and without sanctions the majority of persons in the fallen state would be unable to keep the law.

> And because the greatest part of men are such as prefer their own private good before all things, even that good which is sensual before whatsoever is most divine . . . therefore unto laws that men do make for the benefit of men it hath seemed always needful to add rewards which may more allure unto good than any hardness deterreth from it, and punishments, which may more deter, then any sweetness thereto allureth.[127]

For Hooker, the positive law is founded upon the natural law, which it enforces. As an example, he says that "theft is naturally punishable, but the kind of punishment is positive, and such lawful as men shall think with discretion convenient by law to appoint. In laws that which is natural bindeth universally, that which is positive not so."[128] So for example, the punishment for theft can be changed from society to society or from one age to another, but the prohibition on theft itself is grounded in the natural law. Hooker refers to such laws as *mixedly* human, because the human law differs from the natural law on which it is based only in the manner it is enforced, and not in the conduct it enjoins. Since the civil law is not the origin of the obligation, in essence such laws have both a natural law and a positive law element:

Which law in this case we term *mixed,* because the matter whereunto it bindeth is the same which reason doth require at our hands, and from the Law of Reason it differeth in the manner of binding only. For whereas men before stood bound in conscience to do as the Law of Reason teacheth, they are now by virtue of human law become constrainable, and if they outwardly transgress, punishable.[129]

Other laws, however, Hooker says are *merely* or purely human, meaning that human law creates both the obligation and the sanction. He gives the example of laws of inheritance in regard to property:

Lands are by human law in some places after the owner's decease divided unto all his children, in some all descendeth unto the eldest son . . . now whichsoever be received there is no Law of Reason transgressed[130]

Hooker provides a third mode of law which he calls the law of nations, which consists in the human positive laws which govern not what occurs within the body politic, but between the body politic. The law of nations he further divides into primary laws, which govern peaceful commerce between the nations such as diplomatic exchanges, and the secondary precepts concerning the laws of arms, which regulate the conduct of war.[131]

This in outline is Hooker's hierarchy of law. At the summit, God Himself is governed by the eternal law that is nothing other than ends, which govern His acts. These ends are always to the benefit of His creatures since Hooker holds that God never acts except to diffuse his goodness to creatures. Founded on this eternal law, there is, on the one hand, the revealed law disclosed in Scripture and, on the other hand, there is the natural law discernible by natural reason, which orders all things to their proper end. In the case of inanimate or irrational creatures, the natural law guides them to their ends by necessity, while in the case of man the natural law must be freely obeyed. Finally there is the positive law, that is that law enacted by the civil authority. The positive law unlike the natural law is not immutable. Moreover it must conform to the natural law, and may not justly contravene it.

NOTES

1. *Institutes,* 1:15:4 (italics added)

2. Peter Munz, "The Place of Hooker in the History of Thought," see the introduction and the first chapter on Hooker and Aquinas, pp.1–67.

3. *Laws,* II.i.2, the mention of "taking up of a rush or straw" derives from the debates in the Admonition controversy in which Archbishop Whitgift uses these as examples of "indifferent matters" neither commanded nor prohibited by Scripture—a view Cartwright objected to (see the second reply, p. 60, quoted in note in Keble, p. 288).

4. *Laws*, II.iv.7.

5. *Ibid*. II.ii.2, Hooker says of the Calvinists that for them, ' . . . wheresoever faith is wanting, there is sin;' and 'in every action not commanded faith is wanting;' *ergo* in 'every action not commanded there is sin.' And Hooker also notes: 'I would demand of them first, forasmuch as the nature of things indifferent is neither to be commanded nor forbidden, but left free and arbitrary; how can there be anything left indifferent, if for want of faith sin be commited when any thing not commanded is done.'

6. *Ibid.*, II.i.4.

7. *Ibid.*, II.iv.5.

8. *Ibid.*, II.iv.7.

9. See for example Charles B. Schmitt, *Aristotle and the Renaissance*. (Cambridge, MA: Harvard University, 1983).

10. Among the important fifteenth-century translators of Aristotelian commentaries from Greek into Latin must be included Ermolao Barabaro (1454–1493), who also translated works of Themistius in the late fifteenth century, and Girolamo Donato who in 1495 translated the commentary of Alexander of Aphrodisias on the *De Anima* of Aristotle. See Jill Kraye for the influence of the new translations on Italian Aristotelianism, cf. "The Immortality of the Soul in the Renaissance: Between Natural Philosophy and Theology." In *Signatures*, Volume I (2000)—available online.

11. For an excellent overview see Paul Oskar Kristellar, *Renaissance Thought: The Classic, Scholastic, and Humanist Strains*. (New York: Harper Torch Books, 1961), especially pp. 24–47.

12. In fact, the English scholastic curriculum endured well into the seventeenth century. See William T. Costello, *The Scholastic Curriculum at Early Seventeenth Century Cambridge*. (Cambridge, MA: Harvard University Press, 1958). Costello points out that Henry VIII, even after his break from Rome, mandated that Aristotle remain the primary authority.

13. Cf. *The History of the University of Oxford*. Volume II, ed. James McConica, (Oxford: Clarendon Press, 1986), especially the article by J.M. Fletcher "The Faculty of the Arts," pp. 157–200. So great was the authority of Aristotle that Fletcher notes cases in 1562 and 1574 in which students and scholars were *compelled* to adhere to the opinions of Aristotle (cf. p.177).

14. *Ibid*, p. 177–178, Fletcher notes that Oxford Logicians like John Argall were notably favorable to Aristotle as against Ramus. This general attitude may help account for Hooker's clearly dismissive attitude toward "Ramistry" in relation to Aristotle—e.g. K I.6.4.

15. *Ibid.*, p. 711, James McConica in his article "The Collegiate Society" here refers to John Day of Oriel College who in his commentary on the physics "cited Franciscus Toletus, Beneto Pereira, and Pedro de Fonseca, as well as Aquinas, Buridan, and the Coimbra commentators . . . "

16. Cf. Phillip Secor, *Prophet of Anglicanism*, 85. Secor notes the strength of Catholic sympathies at Corpus Christi by noting that in King Edward's time, Thomas Morwent and two Corpus Christi fellows were imprisoned in 1551 for secretly using the Catholic rite. William Cheadsey who served from 1558–1559 was known as a pa-

pal sympathizer who attacked the views of Peter Martyr Vermigli when he taught at Oxford.

17. *Ibid*, p. 86, Hooker was at Oxford during William Cole's presidency of Corpus Christi, and was involved in some of the tumult there. When Cole was considering resignation a bitter campaign for his succession took place between Hooker's tutor Rainolds and John Barefoot, a Catholic-leaning candidate. Hooker supported his tutor, and as a result was briefly expelled together with Rainolds and a few other fellows, when Cole decided to stay on, and Barefoot attempted to remove Rainolds. Eventually both Rainolds and Barefoot left the college and the tumults died down, though Rainolds returned as president of Corpus Christi in 1598.

18. Cf. Secor, *Prophet of Anglicanism*, 87.

19. *Ibid*., p. 96.

20. *Ibid*., p. 97.

21. *Ibid*., p. 704, Allen died while a probationer fellow in 1569, and the inventory of his goods including his books is dated to that year. This indicates at a very minimum that other students at Hooker's own college were reading Aquinas at the same time Hooker was there—Hooker matriculated at Oxford in 1568.

22. Rainold's letter to Cranmer can be found recorded in Keble's *The Works of Richard Hooker* Vol. I, p. 106. The relevant section runs as follows: *"tamen in Scoto quam Aquinati non esse nihil quod inservire possit tuo studio promovendo, libens agnosco. Illid inter meum et tuum judicium discrminis intercedit. Quod tu de iis videris honorificentius sentire quam ego. Nam ego minus tribuo Scoto quam Aquinati, Aquinati quam Scaligero, immo vero pluris unum Scaligerum quam sexcentos Scotos et Aquinates facio."* Interestingly, Rainolds in spite of his apparent familiarity with Aquinas and Scotus, had somewhat Calvinistic tendencies and though he was Hooker's tutor, was censured by Archbishop Whitgift in 1586 for critiquing the Elizabethan discipline. cf. *Ibid*. p. 392 (which is in Jennifer Loaches's article in the Oxford History entitled "Reformation Controversies," (pp. 363–396).

23. Cf. Charles B. Schmitt, *John Case and Aristotelianism in Renaissance England* (Montreal: McGill-Queens University press, 1983), p. 64.

24. *Laws*, I. 11.5.

25. *Ibid*.

26. S.T. I-II, q.93, arts 4–6.

27. *Compendium of Theology*, ch. 3.

28. S.T. I-II, q.94, art. 3.

29. *Commentary on Metaphysics*, prologue 2.

30. S.T. I-II, q.94, art. 4–6.

31. Haugaard believes that the reference is simply from the index of the *Summa* with regard to the definition of *Sacramentum*—cf. Folger, p. 219. Haugaard points out several other passages in Book V where Aquinas is a direct influence without there necessarily being cited. For example, in 69.2, there is discussion of participation in which Aquinas's ideas are clearly borrowed and 64 includes a discussion of infant baptism, which is essentially paraphrased from Aquinas's (S.T. III, q.68, art. 9).

32. S.T. III. q. 25, art. 3.

33. In fact, the commentary on I Peter is not now attributed to Aquinas.

34. S.T. I-II, q.108, art. 9.

35. This feature of Hooker's thought has already been charted by scholars—for example, Peter Munz has an appendix with a large number of passages from the *Laws* and passages from the Thomistic side by side.

36. Cf. *Laws*, V. dedication.1.

37. Quoted in Schmitt, *John Case and Aristotelianism in Renaissance England*, p. 64.

38. Peter Munz, *The Place of Hooker in the History of Thought*.

39. *Ibid.*

40. Alan Cromartie, "The Theology and Politics of Richard Hooker."

41. *Laws*, I.2.5 (Italics added).

42. For this distinction, cf. Gibbs in Folger, Vol VI.

43. *Laws*, I.2.4.

44. *Ibid.*, I.ii.1.

45. *Ibid.*

46. Folger, VI, p. 97.

47. *Laws*, I.2.6.

48. *Ibid.*

49. Peter Lake, *Anglicans and Puritans*.

50. *Laws*, I.3.1.

51. S.T. I-II, q.93, art. 1.

52. S.T. I-II, q.93, art. 4.

53. *Laws*, I.3.4 (italics added).

54. Cf. Gibbs in Folger, p. 100.

55. Christopher of St. Germain, *Dialogues in English between a doctor of divinitye and a student in the lawes of England.* (London: Richard Totell, 1569). Often called *Doctor and Student* (a usage which we will adopt in further references) the text was first printed in Latin in 1523, and for the first time in English in 1530 or 1531. It seems to have been a fairly popular text throughout the sixteenth century as the prestigious printer of common law texts, Richard Totell issued another edition in the Elizabethan period to which we have referred.

56. The Doctor adopts the classic Thomistic view that the eternal law is the divine wisdom directing all things to their due end: "The wisedom of God mouinge all thinges by wisedom made to a good ende obtaineth the name and reason of law that is called the law eternall." This eternal law is the foundation of all other laws. "And this lawe eternall is called the first law, and it is well called the firste, it was before all other lawes and al other lawes be derived of it." (Cf. Christopher of St. Germain, *Doctor and Student*. fol.3; where the text was difficult to read, the probable words will be placed in brackets.)

57. *Ibid.* fol. 4.

58. *Ibid.* fol. 3.

59. The fundamental eudemonistic structure of human acts found in the first book of Aristotle's *Nicomachean Ethics* is taken over by St. Thomas Aquinas. All human acts are directed toward the possession of goods, but some acts are directed toward further goods (for example exercise is desired not for its own sake, but for health), thus the question becomes what is the *summum bonum* which is desired for its own

sake and not for the sake of some further good. For St. Thomas Aquinas as for Aristotle, happiness is the last end toward which all human actions are directed. "Man's last end is happiness; which all men desire." (ST I-II, q 1, art 8, *On the Contrary*), but what is the good in which happiness consists? For Aquinas the difference that emerges with Aristotle is that the *summum bonum* – that perfect, self-sufficient good desired for its own sake–is not any created good attainable by man's natural powers, but the vision of God according to His essence. Thus complex questions of nature and grace arise which were not issues for Aristotle.

60. As St. Thomas has it: "The will is a rational appetite. Now every appetite is only of something good. The reason of this is that the appetite is nothing else then an inclination of the person desirous of a thing towards that thing . . . since therefore everything insofar as it is being and substance is a good, it must needs be that every inclination is to something good. And hence it is that the philosopher says (ethic.i.1) that *the good is that which all desire*" (S.T. I-II, q.8, art 1).

61. *Laws*, I.11.1, as St. Thomas Aquinas holds "It is impossible for any created good to constitute man's happiness. For happiness is the perfect good, which lulls the appetite altogether; else it would not be the last end if something remained to be desired. Now the object of the will i.e. of man's appetite is the universal good; just as the object of the intellect is the universally true" (S.T. I-II, q.3, art. 1).

62. *Ibid.*, cf. Aquinas "So, then as to the aspect of all agree in desiring the last end: since all desire the fulfillment of their perfection, and it is precisely this fulfillment in which the last end consists...but as to the thing in which this aspect is realized , all men are not agreed as to their end: since some desire riches, as their consummate good; some pleasure, others something else...in like manner that good is most complete which the man with well disposed affections desires for his last end" (S.T. I-II, q.1, art. 7).

63. *Ibid.*

64. *Ibid.*, I.11.2. cf. Aquinas. "So, then, as to the aspect of last end all agree in desiring the last end: since all desire the fulfillment of perfection, and it is precisely this fulfillment in which the last consists . . . but as to the in which this aspect is realized, all men are not agreed as to their last end: since some desire riches, as their consummate good; some pleasure, others something else . . . that good is most complete in which the man with well disposed affections desires for his last end." And in the reply to the first objection "those who sin turn from that in which their last end consists: but they do not turn away from the intention of the last end which they mistakenly seek in other things" (S.T. I-II, a 1, art. 7).

65. *Ibid.*

66. The concept of the natural desire to see God is elaborated by St. Thomas Aquinas in S.T. I-II, q.3, art 8, which begins "Final and perfect happiness can consist in nothing else then the vision of the Divine Essence." Aquinas reasons that (as Aristotle held) since there is a natural desire in the intellect to know the essence of causes, and since it is possible for the intellect to acquire by its natural power the knowledge *that* there is a first cause, there is a natural desire in the intellect to know the first cause according to its essence, and thus perfect happiness cannot exist unless it is possible for man to attain to the knowledge of the divine essence, for otherwise there

would still be desire in the soul. However it is also the case that this desire cannot be satisfied within the order of nature, but only in the order of grace (cf. S.T. I, Q.12, art. I).

67. *Ibid.*, I.11.4.

68. *Ibid.*, it is perhaps instructive to compare Hooker's discussion of the hierarchy of desire and goods here, with that of St. Thomas Aquinas in S.T. I-II, q.94, art 2.

69. S.T. I-II, q. 94, art. 2.

70. *Laws*, I.10.2.

71. *Ibid.*

72. *Ibid.*, I.8.9.

73. *Ibid.*, I.3.1.

74. S.T. I-II, q. 94, art. 4.

75. *Ibid.*

76. *Ibid.*

77. Cargill Thompson, "The Philosopher of the Politic Society," p. 154.

78. S.T. I-II, q.95, art. 5 (*Repondeo*).

79. *Laws*, I.16.5.

80. *Ibid.*, I.6.1.

81. Thompson, "The Philosopher of the Politic Society," p. 156; J.W. Allen held a similar view.

82. Cf. W.J. Torrance Kirby, *Richard Hooker's Doctrine of the Royal Supremacy*. (Leiden and New York, Brill, 1990). I also had occasion at Oxford to see the unpublished dissertation on which this work was based William John Torrance Kirby, *The Doctrine of Royal Supremacy in the Thought of Richard Hooker*. Page numbers will refer to the published 1990 version.

83. Kirby, p. 36–37

84. Kirby, p. 36. In his contention regarding the non-existence of sixteenth-century Anglicanism, Kirby relies on Patrick Collinson, *The Religion of Protestants*. (Oxford: Oxford University 1984), ix. and Paul Christianson, "Reformers and the Church of England" J.E.H., 31 (1980). Kirby concludes on the basis of Christianson's and Collinson's scholarship that "now that the validity of the category 'Anglicanism' has been called into question it is inevitable that that the traditional interpretation of Hooker's theology . . . should itself be called into question."

85. Kirby, p. 15

86. Kirby, p. 37

87. So on the issue of royal supremacy, Kirby endeavors to show how reformers like Luther, Calvin, and Melanchthon held to a doctrine of two realms—an internal spiritual realm in which each Christian was subject to Jesus Christ, and an external realm in which each person was subject to the authority of the earthly prince. Kirby will argue on that basis that the two realms theory of the Reformers is the foundation of his defense of the royal supremacy and the duty to obey the magistrates in "external" matters of ritual and church government not pertaining to salvation.

88. Nigel Atkinson, *Richard Hooker and the Authority of Scripture, Tradition, and Reason*. (Carlisle: Paternoster, 1997). For a defence of the *via media* thesis against

Kirby and Atkinson see Lee W. Gibbs, "Richard Hooker's *Via Media* Doctrine of Scripture and Tradition," *Harvard Theological Review* (2002) 95, pp. 227–235. On the specific question of tradition, Gibbs refers to passages in Hooker's *Laws* in which Hooker appears to explicitly take a middle line between Rome that elevates Tradition to Scripture, and reformers who hold that Scripture is all sufficient. Hooker's position is that Scripture contains all that is necessary for salvation, but not all that is necessary for the organization of human life—for example "Two opinions therefore concerning sufficiency of Holy Scripture, each extremely opposite unto the other, and both repugnant to truth. The schools of Rome teach that Scripture to be so unsufficient, as if except traditions were added, it did not contain all revealed and supernatural truth, which absolutely is necessary for the children of men in this life to know that they may be saved in the next. Others justly condemning this opinion grow likewise unto a dangerous extremity, as if Scripture did not only contain all things in that kind necessary, but all things simply, and in such sort as to do anything according to any other law were not only unnecessary, but even opposite unto salvation, unlawful and sinful" (K.II.8.7).

89. W.J. Torrance Kirby, "Richard Hooker's Discourse on Natural Law in the context of the Magisterial Reformation," in *The Theology of Richard Hooker in the Context of the Magisterial Reformation* (Princeton, NJ: Studies in Reformed Theology and History, Princeton Seminary Press, 1999). The online version we used employs paragraph numbers rather than page numbers so that is what is referenced.

90. *Ibid.*

91. The simplistic assumption that the Reformers rejected the natural law theory out of hand, began to be questioned no later than the 1940s. An excellent overview of the views of Luther, Calvin, Zwingli, and Melanchthon on natural law can be seen in "John T.McNeil "Natural Law in the Teaching of the Reformers." *The Journal of Religion*, 26 (1946), p.168ff. McNeil argues that natural law was one area in which the reformers did not break sharply from the medieval scholastics—"There is no real discontinuity between the teaching of the Reformers, and that of their predecessors with respect to natural law" (p.168). With the partial exception of Ulrich Zwingli (cf. pp. 175–178), McNeil holds among the Reformers "they all express on occasion a quite ungrudging respect for the moral law naturally implanted in the human heart . . ." (p. 168). Another example from the mid twentieth century is seen in Emil Brunner's *Justice and the Social Order* (London: Lutterworth Press, 1949). Brunner claims that "For the unprejudiced reader, there can be no doubt of the absolutely fundamental significance of the *lex naturae* for Calvin" (p. 233). More recent scholarship has sought to elucidate the complex relationship between the reformers and medieval Roman Catholic scholasticism. For a good example of this type of approach see the anthology of essays in *Protestant Scholasticism: Essays in Reassesment*, ed. Carl Trueman (Carlisle: Paternoster press, 1999). Within this anthology, in "Luther and Scholasticism," D.V. N. Bagchi shows that in spite of the fact that Luther opposes the scholastic theology (*theologia scholastica*), in his own "theology of the cross" (*theologica crucis*) he continues to see value in many of the modes of scholastic argumentation (*modus loquendi scholasticus*). A similar equivocal attitude toward late medieval scholasticism is found in Calvin, Beza, and Peter Martyr Vermigli.

92. Cf. Kirby, p. 6, and 40 (footnote).

93. McNeil holds that Melanchthon's interest in natural law stems from his sympathy for Cicero and other classical writers—"Melanchthon's treatment of natural law is colored by his familiarity with classical authors and shows the influence of Cicero, to whose writings he pays tribute in voluminous commentaries." McNeil, p. 172.

94. '*Lumen divinum in mentibus non extinguendum est . . . ergo vera definitio legis naturae : legem naturae esse notitium legis divinae hominis insitam: ideo enim dicitur homo ad imaginem Dei conditus esse, quia in eo lucebat imago, hoc est notitia Dei, et similitudo quaedam mentis divinae, id est discrimen honestorum et turpium*' (cf. Melanchthon, *Locis Communi Theologici*, Erlangen (1828), quoted in Kirby, footnote 42).

95. This passage is found in Bullinger, Henry *The Decades of Henry Bullinger* (Cambridge: Cambridge University, 1849–1851), quoted in Kirby, paragraph 9.

96. A. Cromartie, "Theology and Politics of Richard Hooker," p. 41.

97. Another scholar who has done much to demonstrate that there was no single "medieval natural law theory" is Francis Oakley. In his article "Christian theology and the rise of the Concept of the Laws of Nature," (*Church History*, 30 (1961), Oakley demonstrates that fourteenth century medieval figures generally placed in the nominalist/voluntarist camp like William of Ockham, Pierre d'Ailly, and Gabriel Biel had their own versions of natural law quite distinct from Aquinas. For Aquinas the eternal law was the divine wisdom ordering all things in a rational and in some degree intelligible manner to their final end. The natural law was *aliquid rationis*—the created intellect is thus able to discern the law by which his acts ought to be ordered by right reason. Certain acts are evil in themselves (*per se malum*) because in their very essence they cannot be made to cohere with man's last end. For Ockham on the other hand the law receives its binding force from something external to the precept itself, namely the command of the divine will. God generally operates within the moral law by his ordained power (*potestas ordinata*), but God remains perfectly free to abrogate this law at any time by his absolute power (*potestas absoluta*). Since the precepts of the actually ordained moral order are discernible by natural reason, there is nonetheless for Ockham and the others a true law of nature. See also Oakley's article "Medieval Theories of Natural Law: William of Ockham and the significance of the Voluntarist Tradition." *Natural Law Forum*, 6 (1961), and also the discussions of nominalism and realism in relation to natural law in: Otto Gierke, *Political Theories of the Middle Age.* trans. Frederick Maitland, (Bristol: Thoemmes, 1996), and also A.P. d'Entreves, *Natural Law and Introduction to Legal Philosophy.* (London: Hutchinson University Library, 1970 repr.).

98. Cf. Gibbs, Folger VI, p. 104; for Gibb's detailed reply to Kirby, see his article "Richard Hooker's *Via Media* Doctrine of Scripture and Tradition," *Harvard Theological Review* (2002) 95, pp. 227–235.

99. *Laws*, I.2.5.

100. *Ibid.*, I.7.3–4 (italics added).

101. Folger (Part I of Vol. VI), pp. 104–105.

102. *Laws*, I.5.1.

103. *Ibid.*, I.5.2.

104. S.T. I, q.4, art. 2.

105. S.T. I-II, q.1, art. 8.

106. Cf. Gibbs, *Folger*, p. 105.

107. *Laws*, Preface. ii. 8.

108. *Laws*, VIII.iv.8; Hooker characteristically excuses Calvin's attack on the Anglican Church (found in his commentary on Amos vii.13) as a consequence of ignorance rather than malice.

109. *Laws*, III.i.12.

110. *Laws,* VII.vi.9.

111. Laws, Preface ii. 6ff.

112. Calvin, *Institutes,* 2.8.1; Henry Beveridge provides a translation on the following website: http://www.ccel.org/c/calvin/institutes/bookii/bookii10.htm.

113. *Ibid.*

114. "But man, being immured in the darkness of error, is scarcely able, by means of that natural law, to form any tolerable idea of the worship which is acceptable to God" (in *ibid.*).

115. *Ibid.*

116. W.J. Torrance Kirby, "Richard Hooker's Discourse on Natural Law in the context of the Magisterial Reformation," p. 3.

117. *A Christian Letter of Certaine English Protestants* (Middleburg: Richard Schilders, 1599). The tract may have been written by Andrew Willet.

118. *A Christian Letter* cited in Kirby in 24, (as *ACL* §20, Schoolemen, Philosophie, and Poperie. *FLE* 4:65.16– 68.19)—and can be found in *A Christian Letter,* p. 43.

119. Of the passionate opposition to Hooker's theology on the part of the English Calvinists, Kirby writes: "The authors of *A Christian Letter* interpret Hooker's theology openly to challenge to foundational teaching on the perfect sufficiency of the scripture (*sola scriptura*). His appeal to diversity of access to the divine wisdom is construed, as an affirmation that the "light of nature" teaches knowledge necessary to salvation and that scripture, therefore, is merely a supplement to the natural knowledge of God. The compatibility of natural law theory with such primary doctrines as justification by faith (*sola fides*) and salvation by Christ alone (*solus Christus*) is also called into question. Hooker's appeal to natural law tradition, the light of reason, the authority of philosophy in general and Aristotle in particular thought to pose such a serious breach with the *Articles of Religion* that, as the Letter puts it, "almost all the principall pointes of our English creed [are] greatlie shaken and contradicted." In short, against Hooker's protestations to the contrary, the authors of *A Christian Letter* regard the appeal to the authority of reason and natural law in theological discourse as simply irreconcilable with "all true christian doctrine."

120. *Laws*, I.8.3.

121. *Ibid.*, I.8.5 (italics added).

122. *Ibid.*, I.8.3.

123. *Ibid.*, I.12.1.

124. *Ibid.*, I.12.2.

125. *Ibid.*, I.12.3.

126. *Ibid.*, I.10.7.
127. *Ibid.*, I.10.6.
128. *Ibid.*, I.10.6-7.
129. *Ibid.*, I.10.10.
130. *Ibid.*
131. Cf. *ibid.* 1.10.13-14.

Chapter Three

Hooker's Theory of Political Dominion

The work of Richard Hooker occupies one of the most historically significant moments in the history of political thought. On the one hand, Hooker was working within the essentially medieval and specifically Thomistic framework of natural law; on the other hand, his development of the medieval tradition in terms of a consent theory of the origins of political obligation rendered his ideas useful to the polemics of seventeenth century political thinkers such as John Locke. We propose in fact that Hooker deserves recognition as one of the central figures in the history of English political philosophy. In the following pages it will be shown that Hooker provides one of the first major developed theories of *consent* as the origin of political obligation, with the corresponding notion of an *original compact* by which the community delegates its powers to govern to the ruling authorities. These ideas were to have a profound impact on Western political thought.

One of the most central contributions of Hooker is his clear delineation of the character of a specifically *political* society.[1] Hooker constructs a theory, which in many ways occupies the middle ground between two important and much commented upon theories in political thought. In any ordinary understanding of the *Aristotelian/Thomistic* framework (which informs most of his thought), the relationship between politics and society is a rather continuous one. Human beings are *naturally* social, and since society requires government to coordinate the activities of its parts, man is also naturally a *political* animal. In the Hobbesian conception, on the other hand, *both* the society/commonwealth and the state are *constituted* by human agreement through the instrument of a social compact. Much of the history of Western political thought has been presented as a kind of argument between the Aristotelian position that society and government are natural, but with the social contractarian position of Hobbes and his successors, these institutions are products of agreement and convention. Hooker's viewpoint occupies the middle ground. He asserts that we must carefully distinguish between the creation of *society,* which is the product of natural instinct, and the creation of a *political society*, which is the product of human artifice. In locating the roots of political society in "agreement" and "compact," Hooker opened the door to the consent theories of government that have played such an integral role in the political thought of seventeenth century English political thinkers like John Locke. Hooker deserves attention as an important and original political thinker in his own right, yet he also has importance for the way in which the lines of thought which he explored influenced other thinkers in the tradition of political philosophy. In this sense, we may say that Hooker not only made important and original contributions to Western political thought, but also acted as a crucial bridge between medieval and modern political theory.

At the outset it is unclear whether the Thomistic conception of society and the ideas of consent and social compact are harmonious. Hooker's intellectual creativity is nowhere more clearly manifested than in the effort to synthesize the Thomistic and consensual concepts of government. Both Aristotle and Aquinas seem to defend the idea of "the political man"—the idea that living under government pertains to human nature *as such*. Hooker's argument thus had to show the basic compatibility of his Thomistic/Aristotelian model of society with the artificial, consent-based compact theory he proposed. St. Thomas's political philosophy is expressed in a number of texts, but the two that we shall turn to are first the *Summa Theologiae*, particularly his treatise on Law in part I-II where his views on the relationship of natural to human law is explicated, and a more practical work the *De Regimine Principium* intended to the Latin king of Cyprus, King Hugh III, as a kind of guide to princes on rulership. This text's issues largely concern the forms of government specified by Aristotle—monarchy, aristocracy, democracy, and "mixed" government. In order to see how Hooker endeavored to develop the Thomistic theory of society in a manner which made room for the principles of consent and compact, we shall first explore the essentials of the Thomistic theory of community and politics.

One of the problems scholars of Hooker encounter is how to render his ethical and political theory coherent with each other. The ethics of Hooker and his theory of natural law falls broadly speaking into an Aristotelian/ Thomistic framework. However, it is unclear whether he accepts the principle clearly enunciated in Aristotle and Aquinas that not only society, but political government itself, is natural. Thus, Alan Cromartie writes that, "The most significant anomaly within his broadly Aristotelian world view was his belief that politics is nothing but a means to cope with sin."[2] Because Hooker attempts to work a new theory of political dominion based largely on premises supplied by the broader Christian intellectual tradition, we will begin with a brief examination of the ideas of political dominion in Augustine and especially in Thomas Aquinas, and then move to Hooker's own political theory.

AUGUSTINE

One of the most important debates in the history of Christian political theory is the question of whether government would have existed in the absence of the Fall. Put differently, the question is whether civil authority is only or principally a remedy for sin, or does it have its own intrinsic and natural value? The question dates back at least to St. Augustine. Although Augustine does not explicitly argue that government would not have existed without the Fall, he famously wrote in *Civitatis Dei* that the earthly city owes its origins to the murder of Abel by Cain. For Augustine, the archetype of Cain was replicated in the origins of the greatest temporal power of the time—Rome:

> Thus the founder of the earthly city was a fratricide. Overcome with envy, he slew his own brother a citizen of the earthly city, a sojourner on earth. So that we cannot be surprised that this first specimen, or as the Greeks say, archtype of crime, should long afterwards find a corresponding crime at the foundation of that city which was destined to reign over so many nations, and be the head of the earthly city of which we speak. For of that city also, as one of the poets has mentioned, 'the first walls were stained with a brother's blood' or, as Roman history records, Remus was slain by his brother Romulus.[3]

Yet while seemingly having its origins in blood lust and the desire for domination, even a pagan state like Rome serves a good function in the context of a sinful world. The good function specifically, of limiting and punishing the evil works of sinful men. Thus, Augustine acknowledges the right of the state to use the sword in order to repress and punish evildoers—a right that extends in the extreme case to the waging of just wars and the imposition of capital punishment:

> However there are some exceptions made by the divine authority to its own law that men may not be put to death . . . accordingly those who have waged war in obedience to the divine command, or in conformity with his laws, have represented in their persons the public justice and the wisdom of government, and in this capacity have put to death wicked men; such persons have by no means violated the commandment 'Thou shalt not kill.'[4]

The emphasis in Augustine however is on the *instrumental* good of government as an agent to repress forms of evil doing that make ordered life impossible, rather than on any *intrinsic* good of government. It is unclear whether for Augustine government would even be necessary if it were not for sin.

ST. THOMAS AQUINAS

For Aquinas, on the other hand, it is clear that government is a good that corresponds to man's social nature, and would have existed even without sin and the fall. Thus, Aquinas argues that:

> Man is master of a free subject by directing him either toward his proper welfare, or to the common good. Such a kind of mastership would have existed even in the state of innocence between man and man, for two reasons. First because man is naturally a social being and so in the state of innocence he would have led a social life. Now a social life cannot exist among a number of people unless under the presidency of one to look after the common good; for many as such seek many things, whereas one attends only to one . . . secondly if one man surpassed another in knowledge and virtue, this would not have been fitting unless these gifts conduced to the benefit of many.[5]

Aquinas follows Aristotle in seeing political life as following naturally from social life. Moreover, Aquinas like Aristotle sees the natural inequality of preeminence in politics as issuing from the natural inequality of gifts and talents. Since Hooker sees government as the product of consent and agreement, rather than nature the questions arises of whether his political thought is a kind of eclectic amalgam between a political theory based on notions of artifice, and a basically Aristotelian theory of nature and ethics. If this is the case, much of his political philosophy can be read out of the Thomistic/ Aristotelian framework in which, as we have so far argued, Hooker belongs. We will endeavor to show that the Thomistic political theory is not one that admits of a single self-evident interpretation, and that Hooker's political philosophy is not so much an eclectic combination of disparate elements, but a plausible though quite distinctive effort to develop a new political theory on Aristotelian/Thomistic foundations.

Hooker's work may in fact be best understood as part of the general revival of Aristotelian/Scholastic thought, which took place in late Elizabethan England. While in Medieval England universities such as Oxford were prominent centers of Scholasticism, by the first half of the sixteenth century under the dual influences of the Reformation and the new Humanism a rather marked reaction had set in. Such Protestant trends are seen for example in the Elizabethan statutes of 1564–1565 which call for the substitution of the study of the traditional medieval scholastic textbook—Peter Lombard's *Liber Sententitae*—with the direct study of Scripture.[6]

However, by the time Hooker arrived at Oxford he would have found the intellectual atmosphere there to be receptive to his interest in critical engagement with the texts of medieval scholastics. Documentary evidence indicates that by the 1580s English university libraries were making acquisitions of medieval scholastic texts.[7] At Corpus Christi College where Hooker studied, the texts of Aquinas and Scotus were present in the college library and apparently widely studied. In 1585, a new press was opened at Oxford, and through it John Case, a prominent scholar, published a widely read work on Aristotle's ethics entitled *Speculum Quaestionem Moralium*, which expounded the ethics of Aristotle, while in 1588 he wrote a political tract based on the *Politics* entitled *Sphaera Civitatis*.[8] Though the dominant chord in Case's treatment of Aristotle was humanist, Case evinces a respect for Catholic scholastics in works like the *Speculum*.[9] In the *Sphaera*, meanwhile, Case argues that while monarchy was according to Aristotle the best form of government, sovereignty in the best case at least partially belongs to the people, or "multitude," who mediate authority to the king. As we shall see, this type of Aristotelian constitutionalism was quite similar to the ideas expressed in the *Laws*.

Indeed, it is Hooker's own work that is the historically most significant product of what we may describe as an "Elizabethan scholastic revival." Hooker's debt was not so much to Aristotle directly as to the Christian Aristotelianism of St. Thomas Aquinas. The various elements derived from Aquinas present in Hooker will be discussed as they appear. However it may be important to have at least a preliminary clarity about what we mean when we say that "Thomism" is present in the work of Hooker. Some of these elements include: first, Hooker's acceptance of the basic schema of the hierarchy of law sketched in the *Summa Theologica* in terms of the orders of eternal, natural, divine, and human law; second, an acceptance of positions close to Aquinas on issues regarding nature and grace, which in relation to Calvinism are relatively optimistic; third, Hooker's acceptance of Thomas's views on the natural sociality of mankind; fourth, Hooker's acceptance of a teleological understanding of nature, and fifth, his stern rejection of theological voluntarism, in favor of an "intellectualist" doctrine of God.

But to focus solely on the most explicit references to Aquinas would be to dramatically undervalue the role of Aquinas[10] within Hooker's philosophical framework. The general architecture of Hooker's thought is in many ways fundamentally Thomistic. Hooker addressing the Disciplinarians sees as "the very main pillar of your whole cause, that *Scripture ought to be the only rule of all our actions*, and consequently that the Church orders which we have observed being not commanded in Scripture, are offensive and displeasent unto God."[11] As we saw during the Admonition controversy, Cartwright holds that at least the "substance and marrow" of the Biblical judicial precepts should be enforced in England, while the natural law theory receives little or no attention in the writings of the English Calvinists.

Thus we may say that in place of the threefold order of law found in Aquinas (defended by Hooker)—the revealed law of scripture, the natural law known by reason, and the human law promulgated the civil and ecclesiastical authority—Cartwright proposes that the positive enactments of Scripture alone should be the guide of all civil and ecclesiastical affairs and whatever is without explicit warrant in Scripture is without warrant at all. The subversive implications of this doctrine are clear when we see that this extreme principle would annul the civil and common law of England, much of which is not based directly upon the judicial precepts of the Bible. The issue is therefore ultimately not merely whether the ecclesiastical forms of England have a warrant, but whether the whole structure of the English political constitution must be reformed so as to conform to the explicit dictates of the Bible. Thus, Hooker says of the radical reformers that the logic behind their effort to amend the government and liturgy of the English Church will lead inevitably to political subversion. Taking the case of the Anabaptists on the continent as a salutary warning he remarks: "From this they proceeded unto public reformation, first ecclesiastical, and then civil."[12]

At the heart of Hooker's contention with disciplinarian Calvinists like Cartwright is the issue of nature and grace. Cartwright's argument seems to be underpinned by the notion that man is so radically fallen and blinded by ignorance and passion, that his natural power of reason is no longer competent to guide him. To accept that human reason after the fall can by its own light discern the moral order (the natural law), or is competent to frame and promulgate ordinances for the government of Church and state (positive law), is perhaps for Cartwright to assume too much about human powers after the fall.

The revealed law of Scripture therefore is the *sole* legitimate law and rule for all men's actions. Hooker, on the contrary, argues with Aquinas that grace does not overcome nature, but perfects what is present within nature, which must retain its fundamental ordination to the good. For example, man, though weakened by the fall, retains his *natural* desire for God, even if this natural desire can only be realized through the order of grace. Hooker moreover takes over the basic architecture of Aquinas's framework of law—man as subject not only to the revealed law of Scripture accepted through the supernatural light of faith, but also to the natural law knowable by the natural light of human reason, and to the human law of ecclesiastical and civil authority. Like Aquinas, he grounds all law ultimately in the *Lex Aeterna* of God, the divine wisdom guiding all things to their proper end. He inherits from Aquinas the basically teleological conception of the cosmos of all things moving toward some good, which perfects them. He also accepts the Thomistic/Aristotelian view that man's nature is intrinsically social and thus society has a natural foundation. Given the enormous debt of Hooker to Aquinas, it would be well to look at some specific aspects of the Thomistic political theory and legal theory.

Contrary to a popular misconception, the absolutist conception of government where the sovereign or king is both the source of law and above the law is much more a product of early modern thinkers (e.g. Bodin) than the medieval tradition.[13] The medieval political order rested on a delicate balance between kings, feudal princes, and the Roman Catholic Church, with the whole structure conceptualized as a loose unity under the Pope as spiritual head and the Emperor as temporal head. By the sixteenth century, the Royal authority tended to gain in relative position—the federation of Christendom was giving way to a Europe of nations ruled by kings. On the level of practical power, the consolidation of the national monarchy in, for example, Spain, France, and England undermined the older feudal structure with the rise of centralized professional bureaucracies and armies. In England, Scandinavia, and elsewhere we see also the effort to bring ecclesiastical affairs under royal jurisdiction. The new power of kings made an absolutist system a practical possibility in the early modern period.

We can define modern constitutionalism as the opposing principle that law must limit the sovereign's power. In the sixteenth century, constitutionalism emerged not as a reaction to medieval theory and practice, but as an effort to preserve elements of the medieval tradition from the new challenges posed by ascendant royal power. Chief among these elements was the natural law theory.[14] Simply stated, the theory proposed the existence of a moral law grounded in human nature and discoverable by reason to which the civil law promulgated by human authority must conform. The importance of natural law to constitutionalism can hardly be overstated. If there is a moral law anterior to civil authority then there is an external standard by which the positive laws promulgated by the sovereign can be judged. Aquinas addresses this question in the *Summa Theologica*, I-II, and Q. 96 art. 4:

> Laws framed by man are either just or unjust. If they are just they have the
> power of binding in conscience, from the eternal law from which they are

derived . . . on the other hand laws may be unjust in two ways. First by being contrary to human good, these like are acts of violence rather then laws, because as Augustine says "a law that is not just seems to be no law at all . . . Therefore such laws do not bind in conscience except perhaps to avoid some scandal or disturbance.[15]

Aquinas here states the very essence of constitutionalism—the idea that state power is not absolute or unlimited, but is subject to a rule of justice. Those who hold authority must do so with a sense of moral responsibility to the common good of their subjects. Aquinas even holds that under certain circumstances where this trust is grievously violated, the community may depose rulers. Aquinas views man as therefore subject to a *threefold order* which he must follow in order to fulfill the end for which he was created. There is the order of divine positive law revealed in Scripture, the natural law which is discerned by his own reason, but that is ultimately grounded in the eternal law of God, and finally, there is the human or positive law promulgated by human authority but grounded in the natural law whose precepts it applies:

There is a three fold order to be found in man. The first is that which derives from the rule of reason: insofar as all our actions and experiences should be commensurate with the guidance of reason. The second arises from comparison with the rule of divine law, which should be our guide in all things. And if man were a solitary animal, this double order would suffice: but because man is naturally a social and political animal, as is proved in *Politics,* chap 2; it is necessary that there should be a third order, regulating the conduct of man to his fellows with whom he has to live.[16]

But what is the principle by which human authority can legitimately make laws to begin with? Viewed from the standpoint of the subjects of this authority, the question can be framed in terms of trying to ascertain the origin of political obligation. There are statements in Aquinas that suggest that subjection to political rule is the *natural* condition of mankind. The background of the whole discussion is his position as a Christian Aristotelian that beings have their proper end in nature. The first guide which man has in attaining his end is the gift of reason.

Now every man is endowed with reason, and it is by the light of reason that his actions are directed to their end. So if it befitted man to live a solitary life, after the fashion of many other animals, he would need no other guide, under God, the King of kings, and would have the full ordering of his own actions by the light of God-given reason.[17]

But Aquinas goes on to argue that the guidance of his own reason by itself is insufficient for man to attain his end. Indeed rational reflection itself shows that man requires the assistance of a community in order to perfect and fulfill the potencies of his own nature. "When we consider all that is necessary to human life, however, it becomes clear that man is naturally a social and political animal, destined more than all other animals to live in community."[18] This natural communality of man can be discerned by reason in several ways. Thus, Aquinas observes that while other animals are given natural provision for the maintenance of their lives, human beings lack such natural defenses. To maintain their lives then human beings require the assistance of their fellows.

> Other animals have their food provided for them by nature and a natural coat of hair. They are also given the means of defense, be it teeth, horns, claws, or at least speed in flight. Man on the other hand, is not so provided, but having the power to reason must fashion such things for himself. Even so man alone would not be able to furnish himself with all that is necessary, for no one man's resources are adequate to the fullness of human life. For this reason the companionship of his fellows is naturally necessary to man.[19]

Aquinas further argues that since men must provide for the necessities of life through reason rather than by natural instinct, a division of labor is necessary, since all cannot be expert in every field required for human flourishing. For example, some are experts in medicine, others in agriculture, and others in carpentry. Through this cooperation in community, human beings can be provided with such goods as medicine, food, and shelter.

The third argument Aquinas deploys in defense of the thesis that human beings are social by nature is from the use of speech and language:

> This [social nature] is further evident from the fact that men alone have the power of speech which enables them to convey the full content of their thoughts to one another. Other animals show their feelings, it is true, but only in a general way, as when a dog betrays its anger by barking, and other animals in different ways. Man, then is more able to communicate with his kind than any other animal, even those which appear to be most gregarious.[20]

Indeed, if human beings were naturally solitary, it is difficult to account for the phenomena of language. But does it follow from the naturally *social* nature of man, that he is also naturally *political*?

Aquinas argues that indeed if human nature is social it must also be political: "The fellowship of society being thus natural and necessary to man, it follows with equal necessity that there must be some principle of government within the society."[21] Aquinas gives several reasons for this. First of all,

Aquinas reasons that just as with a natural body, if there were no controlling principle looking after the good of the whole by coordinating the activities of the members so the same is true of a social body:

> For if a great number of people were to live, each intent on his own interests, such a community would surely disintegrate unless there were one of its number looking after the common good: just as the body of a man or of any other animal would disintegrate were there not in the body itself a single controlling force, sustaining the general vitality of all the members.

Since there is no identity between the private interests of each member of the society and common interests of society as a whole, there must be a principle of government that assures the harmony of the individual elements. "So in addition to the motives of interest proper to each there must be some principle productive of the good of the many."[22]

One consequence of Aquinas's assertion that government is natural is the rejection of the basically Augustinian contention that government is primarily a remedy to restrain sin. Aquinas would not argue against the view that after the Fall the coercive power of government is also necessary to constrain evil. Thus, he writes that one of the main reasons why there must be a human law in addition to natural law is that while some are docile to the demands of the natural law "through a good natural disposition or upbringing," there are "others of evil disposition and prone to vice, who are not easily moved by words. These it is necessary to restrain from wrong doing by force and fear {*Vim et Metum*}."[23]

Nonetheless, the Thomistic assertion that government is made necessary by nature to *coordinate* the activities of the whole community implies that even without the fall, government would be a necessary good. Indeed, an argument occurs in the *Summa* to show that even in the state of innocence before the fall, subjection to political dominion would have existed:

> Such dominion would have been found between man and man in the state of innocence for two reasons. First because man is naturally a social animal; in consequence men would have lived in society even in the state of innocence. Now there could be no social life for many persons living together unless one of their number were set in authority to care for the common good. Many individuals are, as individuals, interested in a variety of ends. One person in interested in one end. So the Philosopher says (in the beginning of the *Politics*): 'Whenever a plurality is directed to one object there is always to be found one in authority giving direction.' Secondly if there were one man more wise and righteous than the rest, it would have been wrong if such gifts were not exercised on behalf of the rest.[24]

One of the elements in Thomistic thought that would later make Thomism amenable to a patriarchalist interpretation like that of Saravia is the fact that so far from seeing the natural, pre-lapsarian condition of man as one of equality, St. Thomas identifies natural hierarchy with due order. Thus, in addressing the issue of whether all men were equal in the state of nature, Aquinas argues that: "It is written *The things of God are well ordered* . . . but order consists chiefly in inequality . . . therefore in the primitive state which was most proper and orderly, inequality would have existed."[25]

Aquinas's view is predicated on a hierarchical account of dominion whereby natural relations of inequality are meant to serve the good of the whole. Thus, for example, those who are superior in wisdom are meant to use their wisdom to govern the less wise. These relations of hierarchy and governance would pertain even in the pre-lapsarian conditions, which excluded only modes of subjection, which do not benefit the subjects of dominion. Aquinas thus distinguishes two modes of political subjection—the just dominion of the wise which pertained to the state of original justice and worked to the benefit of both ruler and subject, and the servile dominion which emerged after original sin:

> There are two forms of subjection. The first is servile; in which case the master makes use of the servant for his own convenience and such subjection began as a consequence of sin. Then there is another form of subjection in virtue of which the master rules those who are subject to him for his own good and benefit. Such subjection already existed before sin: for it would argue a lack of reasonable order in human society if it were not regulated by those who are more wise.[26]

From Aquinas's position that subjection to political dominion is the *natural* condition of mankind, it is easy to see the exegetical difficulty Hooker had in trying to derive from fundamentally Thomistic premises a consent-based theory of the origins of political obligation. If the *natural* condition of man is subjection to political authority, then is it possible for government to be founded on the consent of the governed? Is the origin of government not then simply the natural disposition and right of some to rule over others?

SARAVIA AND THE PATRIARCHALIST ALTERNATIVE

That this was a possible reading of the Thomistic theory of political dominion can be shown by contrasting Hooker's reading of Aquinas with that of his friend and contemporary Hadrian Saravia. Saravia was one of the earliest expositors of the patriarchalist theory of government against which both Hooker and Locke strongly contended. Saravia's significance for our purpose is that he shows that Hooker's consent theory of the origin of government is not the only possible development from the premises of a basically Aristotelian/ Thomistic framework. Saravia, who was born in the Low Countries of a Spanish father and a mother from Artois, had been a Protestant pastor in Ghent before his taking up residence in Canterbury, England. Like Hooker, he became a strong defender of the Church of England and Royal authority against the Calvinist model of the Church, penning his *De Diversis Minis- tororum Evangelii Gradibus* to defend the authority of bishops. According to Izaak Walton's seventeenth-century biography of Hooker, Saravia and Hooker were friends, which is interesting because of the clear divergence in their political doctrines.[27] The extent of their friendship may have been some- what exaggerated by Walton since, as a Tory, he would have wanted to depict Hooker as close to a strong defender of royal authority like Saravia. At all events, both Hooker and Saravia begin from similar foundations, but arrive at quite different conclusions. Like Hooker, Saravia also built his political phi- losophy on Aristotelian and natural law foundations. Yet unlike Hooker, he developed this tradition in the direction of patriarchalism.[28] If man is natu- rally social and if society requires government, then the exercise of authority must be the exercise of a natural prerogative.

In his main political work *De Imperandi Authoritate*, Saravia likens the royal authority to the paternal authority. Within the family, children are not naturally free, and the father's rule is not legitimated by the consent of his children. Rather the children as soon as they are born are naturally subject to the father's rule. By analogy, Saravia contends that "men by nature are not born free," but are born into a natural subjection to the authority of kings. Sar- avia deploys Biblical arguments as well to the effect that Adam as the origi- nal father of the human race exercised royal/paternal sovereignty over the hu- man race. This authority was passed on by hereditary succession to kings. Saravia strongly opposed any notion of a "mixed" form of sovereignty where for example sovereign authority might be shared between a king and the peo- ple. For Saravia, the very nature of sovereignty requires that it has a single lo- cus. For him, "the nature of sovereignty is indivisible" since the sovereign is the principle of unity within a commonwealth. Like Bodin, Saravia defines sovereignty as the power to promulgate laws and, in this sense, the will of the sovereign is the sole source of the law—"That alone is law which pleases the sovereign."[29]

In the English context, for example, it is contradictory to suggest that sov- ereignty is shared between the king and parliament. Sovereignty is rather vested solely in the king, and parliament is merely an advisory body—"in Parliaments the estates command nothing with authority, but approach the king as supplicants, letting him know what should be done for the sake of himself and the kingdom."[30] Saravia's significance for our purpose is that he shows that Hooker's consent theory of the origin of government is not the only possible development from the premises of a basically Aristotelian/ Thomistic framework. A plausible reading would see the Thomistic theory of government as amenable to a patriarchalist interpretation. We have seen, for example, how Thomas shares Aristotle's conviction that man is by nature both social and *political*, and that subjection to political authority is for Aquinas the natural condition of mankind even in the state of innocence. Aquinas even compares the regal and paternal authority:

> Whoever then rules a perfect community, be it a city or province, is rightly called a king. The head of a household on the other hand, is not called king but father. Even so there is a certain similarity between the two cases, and kings are sometimes called the fathers of their people.[31]

Aquinas goes on to argue that monarchy is the best form of government, since "the welfare and prosperity of a community lies in the preservation of its unity."[32] But monarchy is more conducive to unity since

> That which is itself a unity can more easily produce a unity than that which is a plurality: just as that which is itself hot is best adapted to heating things. So government by one person is more likely to be successful than government by many.[33]

Aquinas even sees a certain affinity between the monarchical principle of government and the processes of nature:

> That is best which most nearly approaches a natural process, since nature always works in the best way. But in nature, government is always by one. Among members of the body there is one which moves all the rest namely the heart: in the soul there is one faculty which is pre-eminent, namely reason. The bees have one king, and in the whole universe there is one God, Creator and Lord of all. And this is according to reason: for all plurality derives from unity. So, since the product of art is but an imitation of the work of nature, and since a work of art is the better for being a faithful representation of its natural pattern, it follows of necessity that the best form of government in human society is that exercised by one person.

THOMISTIC CONSTITUTIONALISM?

There were however other aspects of the Thomistic theory of government which figures like Hooker were able to exploit. Indeed a closer reading of

Aquinas's texts would show that the matter of consent of the community is not quite as circumscribed as it might first appear from the aforesaid principles. Other passages in Aquinas stress that rulers are obligated to rule for the common good of the whole community. Should the ruler govern merely for his own private good, then the community would not commit sedition in deposing him. This suggests that, in a certain manner, sovereignty belongs to the community as a whole, rather than to an individual monarch. Thus, Aquinas writes that:

> A tyrannical government is not just because it is directed not to the common good, but to the private good of the ruler, as the philosopher states. Consequently there is no sedition in disturbing a government of this kind . . . indeed it is the tyrant rather that is guilty of sedition, since he encourages discord and sedition among his subjects.[34]

This would seem to suggest at the very least that sovereignty can never be vested in a single man in such a way as to give the community no recourse should he rule tyrannically. Government is properly directed to the good of the community. Certain passages in Aquinas indicate that the power of making laws is valid only insofar as they are made either by the community or by ruling representatives of the community:

> Law, strictly understood, has as its first and principal object the ordering of the common good. But to order affairs to the common good is the task either of the whole community, or of some person who represents it. Thus the promulgation of law is the business either of the whole community or of the political person whose duty is the care of the common good.[35]

This passage also shows that provided that government and law is directed to the common good and respects the moral law, there is no single mode of promulgating laws which is mandated by the Christian religion. In some cases (e.g. democracy), the laws are made directly by the whole community, which is governed, while in other cases (e.g. monarchy) they are made by a ruler on behalf of the community. As we have seen, although Aquinas tends to favor monarchy as the best safeguard for unity and peace, he is ready to acknowledge that in certain respects and in some circumstances a more democratic polity is more advantageous so as to prevent monarchy from becoming tyranny:

> Because both the best and worst is to be found in monarchy, or government by one man, many people knowing the evils of tyranny regard the very name of king with hate. For it sometimes happens that those who expect to be ruled by a king, fall instead under a savage tyranny, and too many rulers mask the injustice of their rule with the cloak of regal dignity.[36]

Aquinas moreover explains why a monarchy is sometimes more likely to fail to tend to the common good than rule by the many, namely, the tendency in some monarchies for the private good of the rulers to conflict with the public good of the community.[37] Moreover, because of the danger of the king becoming a tyrant, Aquinas asserts that even in a monarchy safeguards should be established to limit the power of the king:

> Since government by one person, being the best as we have shown, there is always a danger that it will develop into a tyranny which is the worst government, every precaution must be taken to provide the community with a ruler who will not become a tyrant . . . at the same time the kingly should be restricted so he could not easily turn to tyranny.[38]

In contrast to Saravia's insistence on the undivided sovereignty of the king, Aquinas sees in such absolutism the danger of tyranny. Thus, his preference seems to be for a *mixed* form of government, which keeps the advantage of unity and peace provided by monarchy with the limitations on power provided by aristocratic and democratic elements. Aquinas moreover considers some degree of popular participation as important in any good government.[39]

In sum, Aquinas indeed holds that subjection to political dominion is a natural condition. Nonetheless, he provides a highly circumscribed account of how the prerogative of rule should be exercised in practice. The laws enacted by the ruler may not contravene the natural moral law. The ruler must govern for the common good of the community. Human laws derive their legitimacy from the community or their representatives. Should the king rule unjustly or tyrannically for his private good, the community might justly depose him. Moreover, Aquinas seems to favor for pragmatic reasons a limited or mixed monarchy, in which royal authority is tempered by the place of delegated representatives of the community.

What is most important for this discussion is that while St. Thomas does say that man is naturally a "political animal" (*animal politicum*), his remarks on *political forms* seem to be of a highly pragmatic and prudential nature. While the divine and natural law ordains *that* there should be a government, it does not seem to state unambiguously *what* form this government should take. While in general he favors a monarchy, he sees that in certain respects and in certain historical circumstances the rule of the many is to be preferred. Thus, in contrast to Alan Cromartie's position that Hooker's theory of government is an Augustinian departure from the Thomistic tradition, we could say rather that Hooker is attempting to work through an ambiguity in the Thomistic political theory in order to develop it in a constitutionalist direction. Aquinas does not seem to elucidate unambiguously *how* and *by whom* the election of a particular form of government is to be made. It is within this space of ambiguity in the Thomistic tradition that Hooker will put forward his theory of consent and compact as the legitimating origin of political governance.

SOVEREIGNTY, CONSENT, AND COMPACT IN RICHARD HOOKER

While Hooker's moral and legal theory is fundamentally a reformulation of Thomist/Aristotelian principles, his political theory modifies the Aristotelian medieval framework by adding the crucial element of *consent.* The social contract theories of Locke and Hobbes have been extensively studied. Less explored, however, is Hooker's compact theory that preceded these latter theories and to a large degree influenced them. In what follows, we will present a summary of Hooker's theory of political dominion in which his views on sovereignty, consent, and compact may be clearly elucidated.

Some scholars have seen Hooker's model of government as constituting a kind of inconsistency in relation to the broadly Aristotelian (and Thomistic) structure of his work. Thus Cromartie writes that "examination of his argument reveals a genuine tension between an Aristotelian ethical theory, and a picture of political arrangements as nothing but a means to cope with sin."[40] The key point being that, if government is a matter of human arrangement, then how can it be natural?[41] It would seem that Hooker's view of politics might cohere better with the Augustinian theory according to which government emerged only after the Fall as both consequence and remedy of sin, than with the Aristotelian-Thomistic theory which sees man as a "political animal" in the very texture of his being. Hooker's political philosophy then could be seen as a kind of eclectic hybrid between an Aristotelian/Thomistic ethical system, upon which is erected a kind of Augustinian political theory emphasizing government as merely an artificial instrument to constrain sin.[42] But this is to presume that the Thomistic political doctrine can be easily, unequivocally, and unambiguously construed in only one way. The primary text in which Hooker's specifically political theory is set forth is Book VIII of the *Laws.* First printed in 1648 during the English civil war, it was to become a major source for seventeenth-century political theorists of various shades of opinion regarding the issue of monarchical powers.[43] The primary assertion the text endeavors to refute regards the Act of Supremacy, which made the monarch supreme in ecclesiastical affairs; namely, it held: "That unto no civil prince or governor there may be given such power of Ecclesiastical dominion as by the laws of this Land belongeth unto the supreme regent thereof."[44]

CHURCH AND COMMONWEALTH

For various reasons, this formulation was contested both by Roman Catholic polemicists such as Thomas Stapleton[45] (who naturally upheld the primacy of the Roman pontiff over the ecclesiastical order) and by disciplinarian reformers such as Thomas Cartwright, who contested the right of the monarch to direct the internal government of the Christian Church, such matters being set down in Scripture as interpreted by the Geneva discipline. Both Roman Catholics and Disciplinarians affirmed that the Church is a society set apart from the political commonwealth with its own proper mode of governance. Thus, Hooker's defense of conformity to the Act of Supremacy would be hotly contested by both Roman Catholics and Calvinist Disciplinarians, who (despite their opposed theological visions) shared a conviction regarding the autonomy of the Church founded by Jesus Christ from all earthly and civil jurisdictions. What is at issue, then, is whether the situation in which "the like power in causes *Ecclesiastical* is by the laws of the Realm annexed unto the *Crown*" is acceptable from a theological standpoint. Moreover, given the fact that Hooker's work in Book I emphasizes the subordination of the order of human law to the orders of eternal, divine, and natural law, his assertion in Book VIII that the secular prince has lawful jurisdiction over the Church raises issues regarding the internal coherence of his work. If, in Book I, he seems to be an Anglican Thomist, some see the Hooker of Book VIII as more a disciple of the fourteenth-century political philosopher Marsilius of Padua (d.1342).[46]

Marsilius's seminal text *Defensor Pacis* has as its central purpose the assertion of the sovereignty and autonomy of the secular ruler—specifically the Holy Roman Emperor Louis Bavaria—against papal political claims, specifically those of Pope John XXII. Several facts could be used to defend the interpretation that Marsilius may have been an influence on Hooker. In 1535, one William Marshall translated the majority of *Defensor Pacis* into English for the first time; thus it was clear that defenders of the nascent Church of England were almost certainly interested in Marsilius—because of his attacks on the claim of papal jurisdiction. Like Marsilius, Hooker markedly subordinates the Church—at least in issues regarded as "indifferent matters"—to the secular authority, in this case Crown and Parliament. Marsilius also shared with Hooker a conviction regarding the importance of consent as what makes law and rule legitimate.[47] It is certainly not impossible that *Defensor Pacis* in some way influenced Hooker's thought. Hooker had clearly read Marsilius, since he quotes him in Book VII of the *Laws*, which is concerned with the authority of the bishops.[48] Yet this quote is taken as an example of the view Hooker strenuously opposes—namely "that the inequality of pastors in the

Church is a mere human invention, a thing not found in the word of God."[49] Indeed, Hooker proceeds to systematically refute Marsilius's position on the authority of bishops[50]—a view that would if accepted give standing to Presbyterian claims against the Anglican episcopacy. Other then this attack on Marsilius in Book VII, *Defensor Pacis* is not referenced by Hooker in relation to any of the key themes of Hooker's political philosophy. Thus, we must regard the idea that Hooker had taken central elements directly from Marsilius as at best speculative. There are after all other closer sources for such views. The subordination of Church to Parliament in "indifferent matters" was a major theme of Hooker's close ally Archbishop Whitgift. Moreover, the defense of the royal supremacy and the idea of the unity of Church and Commonwealth is integral to Anglican apologetical texts like Bishop Stephen Gardiner's *De Vera Obedientia*.[51] There is therefore no reason to postulate the special, direct influence of Marsilius when the advocacy of Erastianism in Ecclesiastical matters was commonplace in the conformist circles of Tudor England in which Hooker moved.

Hooker's polemic indeed aims at calling into question the idea of the autonomy of the Church from the "political society." But we must remember that his view on such matters takes its start from Whitgift's distinction between "things necessary" for salvation, and over such essentials it is God alone who is sovereign, and "things indifferent" such as vestments, forms of liturgy, and so forth. Hooker holds that in these latter *external* matters church and Commonwealth are united forming a single society under the civil authority. Hooker grants that in a sense the Church and the Commonwealth are formally distinct:

> To lurk under shifting ambiguities and equivocations of words in matters of principal weight is childish. A *Church* and a *commonwealth* we grant are things in nature, the one distinguished from the others.[52]

In a situation such as where the Christian Church is subject to non-Christian political dominion, this separation is both formal and practical. Thus, before the conversion of the Romans to the Christian religion, "we say as much and grant that the *Commonwealth of Rome* was one society, and the *Church of Rome* was another, in such sort as there was between them no mutual dependency."[53] But what is the proper relationship between Church and Commonwealth when the commonwealth embraces the Christian religion?

> For whether a church and a commonwealth do differ is not the question we strive for; but our controversy is concerning the kind of distinction, whereby they are severed the one from the other; as under *Heathen* kings, the Church did deal with her own affairs within . . . herself without depending at all upon any in civil authority.[54]

The question then is whether "so it ought to continue still even in such *Commonwealths* as have now publicly embraced the truth of the *Christian religion*, whether they ought to be evermore two societies in such sort several and distinct."[55]

The idea of "the Commonwealth" and its specific relation to the Church in England was one of particular importance since the beginning of Henry's assumption of Royal jurisdiction over the Church. In the time of Henry and Edward there was a popular, vernacular circle of pamphleteers known as "the Commonwealth men" which included such figures as Thomas Starkey, Richard Morrison, and Richard Taverner who wrote on behalf of Richard Cromwell's theory of the state.[56]

In the aforementioned work by Gardiner, *De Vera Obedientia*, we find the precise view that Hooker defends—that in a Christian Kingdom, the Church and Commonwealth are inextricable because of their identical membership.[57] Following Gardiner, Hooker opines that where the members of the Commonwealth and its governors are Christian, the condition of absolute autonomy of the Church from the civil authority no longer obtains. In short, there is a *personal* identity between the members of the Church and those of the Commonwealth, in spite of the fact that they are subject in different ways to the Church and the political authority.

> How should the Church remain by personal subsistency divided from the *Commonwealth*, when the whole *Commonwealth* doth believe? The Church and the Commonwealth are in this case personally one society, which society being termed a *Commonwealth* as it liveth under whatsoever form of secular law and regiment, a *Church* as it hath the *Spiritual* law of Jesus Christ.[58]

What he objects to then is not the effort to *theoretically* separate the formal functions of church and commonwealth. His point is that where the members of the political commonwealth are also all members of the church, there are no longer for practical purposes two separate societies, but a single society considered in two different ways. Thus he says that:

> We hold seeing that there is not any man of the Church of England, but the same man is not also a member of the Commonwealth, nor any man a member of the commonwealth which is not also of the Church of England. And therefore as in a figure triangular the base doth differ from the sides thereof, and yet one and the selfsame line is both a base and also a side, a side simply, a base if it chance to be the bottom and underlie the rest: so albeit properties and actions of one kind do cause the name of commonwealth, qualities and functions of another sort the name of Church to be given unto a multitude, yet one and the selfsame multitude may in such sort be both.[59]

Besides there is the fact that in a Christian kingdom the members of Church and Commonwealth are *personally* identical meaning that the same persons that make up the commonwealth of England also make up the Church of England. The distinction in England between Church and Commonwealth is then one of function. Moreover, for Hooker, there is also an identity of *end.* The end of the civil authority is the public good of the Commonwealth. "The end whereunto all government was instituted was *bonum publicum*, the universal or common good."[60]

But this good is not to be understood simply as the temporal or material well being of the subjects. Just as there is a hierarchy in the order of human ends, with the spiritual and eternal good of the soul taking precedence over the temporal goods of the body, so for Hooker the goods of religion ought to be the highest care of any civil authority.

> A gross error it is to think that regal power ought to serve for the good of the body, and not of the soul, for men's temporal peace, and not their eternal safety, as if God had ordained *Kings* for no other end and purpose but only to fat men up like hogs, and to see that they have their mash?[61]

In so far as communities embrace the Christian religion they are also designated churches. As Hooker notes:

> We say that the care of religion being common unto all societies politic, such societies as do embrace the true religion, have the name of the Church given unto every of them for distinction from the rest . . . truth of religion is that proper difference, whereby a Church is distinguished from other politic societies of men.[62]

Since the care of religion for Hooker is an essential role for any form of society, seeing as the end of society is conceived of as the fostering of virtue, so also for Hooker is the Church defined as that mode of polity which embraces the true religion—in other words, Christianity. For Hooker, a Christian society is an integrated ecclesiastical polity where the civil authority also has care for the good of religion and is not severed from the Church, while he characterizes his opponents as holding to the view that the Church and Commonwealth are two utterly distinct and self-subsistent orders.[63] For Hooker then, since the Church and Commonwealth share the same end and membership the civil authority cannot avoid concerning itself with the care of religion. On the duty of the civil authority to promote and foster the highest goods of the soul is grounded the extension of the royal supremacy not only over civil but also ecclesiastical affairs.[64] It is on the ground of this "Erastian" understanding of Church/State relations that some scholars have argued that Hooker "lapses into the very authoritarianism that he hoped to avoid."[65]

We must however carefully distinguish between constitutionalism which argues for a limitation of government through law, and the modern liberal doctrine of individual rights which had little currency before the late seventeenth century. Nothing in Hooker's teachings suggests there is an individual right to disobey the ecclesiastical and civil authority—at least where their ordinances evince no contradiction with divine or natural law. Hooker is not a modern liberal—but he is a constitutionalist. He argues against an absolutist conception of government in favor of one limited by law and based on consent of the governed.

THE LOCUS AND LIMITS OF SOVEREIGNTY

Hooker's position stands in marked contrast to defenders of royal absolutism represented by patriarchalists like his friend Hadrian Saravia, as well as the works of the most prominent sixteenth-century absolutist Jean Bodin. It is in their respective doctrines of sovereignty that we find the greatest contrast between Hooker and Bodin. For Bodin, sovereignty is invested exclusively in the sovereign authority of the king. The marks of the king's sovereignty are principally twofold. First, the king if he is sovereign is the sole *source* of the law:

> We may thus conclude that the first prerogative *(Marque)* of the sovereign prince is to give law to all in general and each in particular. But this is not sufficient. We have to add 'without the consent of any other whether greater, equal, or below him.' For if the prince is obligated to make no law without the consent of a superior, he is clearly a subject; if of an equal he has an associate; if of subjects, such as the senate or the people, he is not sovereign.[66]

The second mark of sovereignty for Bodin is the Roman law principle of *Princeps Legibus Solutus*, that the one who possesses sovereign power (in this case a king) is absolutely absolved from any duty to obey the law himself, the king being above the law.

> Persons who are sovereign must not be subject in any way to the commands of someone else and must be able to give the law to subjects, and to suppress or repeal disadvantageous laws and replace them with others—which cannot be done by someone who is subject to the laws or to persons having power of command over them. That is why the law says that the prince is not subject to the law; and in fact the very word 'law' in Latin, implies the command of him who has sovereignty.[67]

Or later Bodin asserts that:

> If the sovereign prince is exempt from the laws of his predecessors, much less
> is he bound by laws and ordinances that he has made himself. For although one
> can receive law from someone else, it is impossible by nature to give one's self
> a law as it is to command one's self to do something that depends on one's own
> will.[68]

Hooker[69] quotes Bodin with respect to the Christian duty to submit to the
civil authority. Yet the trajectory of his argument regarding sovereignty runs
diametrically counter to the position sketched by Hooker. If for Bodin the
king is both the source of law and above the law, for Hooker the king is *neither* the sovereign source of law, and is himself under the law. While his main
concern throughout the *Laws* is the defense of a particular model of ecclesiastical order, Hooker clearly has a strong subsidiary concern to establish the
consensual basis of monarchical authority, and to subordinate the king to divine, natural, and positive law. His purpose is not here to provide a justification for rebellion or resistance against the monarch.

LEGITIMACY AND CONSENT IN THE ENGLISH TRADITION

Rather, Hooker belongs to a tradition in English political thought that praised
the distinctive and unique wisdom of the English constitution. As Robert Eccleshall[70] puts it:

> Hooker sought, then, to refine the patriotic doctrine of the English constitution that
> ran from Bracton(whom he cited several times)through Fortescue and Reformation
> writers. Long ago the English had sensibly agreed to establish a limited monarchy
> 'for their own most behoof and security' in which the king was *major singulis, uni-
> versis minor* and where, consequently, arbitrary power was excluded by the rule
> (VIII.vi.7; VIII.ii.13). The result was that the monarch could make statutes only
> with the approval of the body politic assembled in parliament. The ancestral be-
> queathal of procedures to mobilize consent provided the assurance that nothing was
> done in English public life to infringe the divine order.

Eccleshall also notes that the foundation of this tradition is a confidence in
two particularly English institutions—the Parliament and the common law.[71]
The lawyers of England were perhaps the most important transmitters of the
belief in the essential harmony between the eternal and unchanging precepts
of natural law with the English system of government and jurisprudence. The
concern of English lawyers was in part defensive and polemical. Certain detractors argued that the Roman law, with its clearly ordered and enunciated
divisions of local law (*ius civile*) and the law of nations (*ius gentium*), was the

only proper human application of the natural law (*ius naturale*).[72] The advocates of Roman law tended to point to its universality, which corresponded in
a sense to the universality of the natural law itself.[73] Because English law relied so much on custom, a particular apologetic problem was how to reconcile the particular and local usages of the English common law which can be
considered an expression of the universal and unchanging precepts of the natural law. One thing that came out of the effort to show the consonance between natural law, as taught by the theologians, and common law, as taught
by the lawyers, was to promote an intense interest in the scholastic doctrine
of law among scholars of jurisprudence.[74] Even into the sixteenth century it
appears that the English schools of jurisprudence continued to transmit the
Catholic scholastic doctrines of law. In this regard it is not improbable that
Hooker imbibed the Thomistic schema of eternal, divine, natural, and human
law, during his time as Master of the Temple.

What the lawyers were endeavoring to defend was the notion that custom
(on which the English common law is based) is a legitimate and even superior means of applying the precepts of natural law to the concrete case of a
particular nation, because unlike statutes, customs are flexible and adapted to
the local conditions and habits. Moreover custom receives its authority from
the corporate consent of the community, rather than simply the will or command of a superior. This juristic tradition can be traced at least to the thirteenth century. The jurist lawyer Henry Bracton (d. 1268) authored an exposition and defense of English laws in his *De Legibus et Consuetudinibus
Angliae* written during the reign of Henry III. Bracton makes a plea for the
uniqueness and distinction of English common law on the grounds that English law rests not only or primarily on statutes but on unwritten customs.
These are nonetheless true laws because they involve the consent of the commonwealth and the approbation of the monarch:

> Though in almost all lands use is made of the *leges* and the *jus scriptum*, Eng-
> land alone uses unwritten law and custom. There law derives from nothing writ-
> ten [but] from what usage has approved. Nevertheless, it will not be absurd to
> call English laws *leges*, though they are unwritten, since whatever has been
> rightly decided and approved with the counsel and consent of the magnates and
> the general agreement of the *res publica*, the authority of the king or prince hav-
> ing first been added thereto, has the force of law.[75]

Later also, he lays down principles of constitutionalism, which were often
quoted by later authors, including Hooker[76]—namely, the subordination of
the king to the law:

> The king must not be under man but under God and under the law, because law
> makes the king. Let him therefore bestow upon the law what the law bestows

upon him, namely, rule and power. [for there is no *rex* where will rules rather than *lex*].[77]

Perhaps the most important figure in this tradition was Sir John Fortescue (1394-1476) who had served as chief justice of the King's Bench for nearly twenty years, until his exile by the Yorkist side during the War of the Roses. While in exile in France, Fortescue wrote one of his most important works, the *De Laudibus Legum Anglie*. Here he praises the wisdom of the English system of governance for setting up a monarchy limited by law, as opposed to the more autocratic system of more benighted nations like France. Fortescue quotes frequently from Thomas Aquinas in his endeavor to demonstrate the special consonance of the English form of law and government with the eternal precepts of the divine and natural law. A central feature of Fortescue's analysis is his understanding of the different types of dominion. In his work *De Natura Legis Natura*,[78] Fortescue relying on the *De Regimine Principium* of both St.Thomas Aquinas[79] and Giles of Rome distinguishes between a *dominium regale* in which the king's will is the law, and the *dominium politicum* in which the laws are made by the people. England, however, is unique in that its constitution is a *dominium regale et politicum* combining the best of both systems of government. As he puts it in *De Laudibius*:

> For the King of England is not able to change the laws of his kingdom at plea-sure, for he rules his people with a government not only royal but also political. If he were to rule over them with a power only royal, he would be able to change the laws of the realm, and also impose on them tallages and other burdens with-out consulting them; this is the sort of dominion which the civil laws indicate when they state that 'What pleased the prince has the force of law.' But it is far otherwise with the king ruling his people politically, because he is not himself . . . able to change the laws without the assent of his subjects nor to burden an unwilling people with strange impositions, so that, ruled by laws that they them-selves desire, they freely enjoy their goods, and are despoiled neither by their own king nor any other.[80]

In this system, the law to be valid requires the consent of both the community *and* the king. In *De Natura Legis Naturae*, the importance of consent is made manifest:

> For in the kingdom of England the king make not laws, nor impose subsidies on their subjects, without the consent of the Three Estates of the realm; and even the judges are all bound by their oaths not to render judgement against the laws of the land (*leges terrae*) even if they should have the command of the prince to the contrary. May not, then, this dominion be called political, that is to say, reg-ulated by the administration of many, and may it not also deserve to be named

royal dominion, seeing that the subjects themselves cannot make laws without the authority of the king, and the kingdom being subject to the king's dignity, is possessed by kings and their heirs successively by hereditary right, in such matter as no dominions are possessed which are only politically regulated.[81]

This emphasis on communal approbation as legitimating laws remained important in English political thought of the sixteenth century. Sir Thomas Smith elaborated the place of Parliament as the locus of consent in the early sixteenth century. Smith, a Cambridge humanist, who served Queen Elizabeth as an ambassador to France, wrote his *De Republica Anglorum* to explain the workings of the English form of government. Interestingly Smith was a strong advocate of Roman as opposed to common law. His importance for our discussion is his conception of the place of Parliament:

> The most high and absolute power of the realme of England consisteth in the Parliament . . . that which is done by this consent is called firme, stable, and *sanctum* and is taken for lawe. The Parliament abrogateth old lawes, maketh newe, giveth orders for thinges past, and for thinges hereafter to be followed . . . for every Englisheman is extended to bee there present, either in person or by procuration and attornies . . . from the Prince (be he King or Queene) to the lowest person of Englande. And the consent of the Parliament is taken to be everie mans consent.[82]

Another central figure in this regard is the aforementioned jurist, Christopher of St. Germain. Given that Hooker and St. Germain used a very similar taxonomy of law, it is not unlikely that Hooker had been exposed to his work. In his discussion of the grounds or foundation of the laws of England, Christopher of St. Germain lists five that come before statutes—the law of reason (natural law), the law of God (revealed law), general customs, particular customs, and what he calls *laws maxims*.[83] What this refers to are things which have always been taken for law. The assumption is that—provided there is no contradiction with the law of reason or God—we should presume that something which has been received as law without change for centuries is more likely to promote the good, then what is innovated by the mind of the lawgiver. This principle of prescription was very important for Hooker, and of course for later figures like Burke.

Like these predecessors, the basis of Hooker's approach to the theory of government is the question of *legitimacy*. Though in some degree the question of legitimacy has always been integral to political philosophy, the question "what conditions make the power to rule legitimate?" became particularly important in the sixteenth and seventeenth centuries. This was in part because during this period kings were centralizing and consolidating their power in new ways, and this very expansion of royal power generated a desire to delineate the limits of this power. In its assumption that power must legitimate itself, Hooker stands firmly in the tradition of natural law constitutionalism.[84] The conditions of legitimacy are thus also *principles of limitation* in the manner that power can be lawfully and morally used.

Specifically two modes of limitation are placed upon government prerogatives—first, there is a rearticulation of the natural law theory; we may call this a *limitation from above*. The natural moral law is ultimately grounded in the eternal law of God and so the *divine* sovereignty ultimately imposes a limit on *human* authority. The civil law promulgated by human authority must conform to, or at least not contravene, the moral law grounded in God and nature. The second mode of limitation we may call *limitation from below*. For Hooker the king's authority to govern is limited by the principle that sovereignty belongs to the community as a whole and not to the king alone. Presupposed in this view is the idea that the king rules as part of a *body politic*. The king is indeed the head of the body, but is ultimately at the service of the community as a whole. [85]

Another way to conceptualize these limitations is to see the qualification of royal power from God and from the community as *modalities*, which express the supremacy of law over the king. After all, the law, which circumscribes the king's power and subjects the king to itself invariably, has its source either from God or from the community. The limitation of the royal supremacy with respect to God is for Hooker a clear and obvious point. As he writes: "But withal it must be noted we must likewise note that, that their power is termed supremacy as being the highest not simply without exception of anything. For what man is not so brainsick as not to except in such speeches *God* himself the King of all the kings of the earth? Besides where the law doth give dominion, who doubteth that the King who receiveth it must hold it of and under the law."[86] Hooker spends much time showing how distinct in order, degree, and kind is the headship of the king from the headship of Christ. "The power which we signify by that name differeth in three things plainly from what Christ doth challenge. It differeth in order, measure and in kind."[87]

The kingly power of Christ differs from earthly kings in *order* because God *directly* gave to Christ the kingship over the church, while "the powers others have is subordinated unto him"; it differs in *degree* because unlike earthly kings, God's dominion is not limited in time, place, or measure—"nor is there any king of law which teeth him but his own proper will and wisdom, his power is absolute." On the other hand this is not the case with earthly kings: "Not so the power of any other *Headship*. How Kings are restrained and in what sort their authority is limited we have showed before."[88] Finally, there is the very supernal nature or "kind" of the headship of God, which is superior to the dominion which kings exercise which he calls "the last and weightiest difference" that Christ rules inwardly and spiritually by grace and is the source and end of all the Church's activities, while the king acts only over externals and even there only as an instrument of Christ's headship.

In developing his understanding of human law and its relationship to divine and natural law, Hooker turns explicitly and indeed reverently to the authority of St. Thomas. The principal point here is that the application of general principles to the particular cases and circumstances belongs to the competence of human reason, applied according to the prudential judgment of the human legislator:

> The greatest amongst the school-divines[i.e. Thomas Aquinas] studying how to set down by exact definition the nature of an human law . . . found not which way better to do it than in these words 'out of the precepts of law of nature, as out of certain common and undemonstrable principles, man's reason doth necessarily proceed unto more particular determinations; which particular determinations being found out according unto the reason of man, they have the name of human laws, so that such conditions may be kept as the making of laws doth require,' that is if they whose authority is therefore required do establish and publish them as laws.[89]

However, for Hooker as for St. Thomas, one consequence of dominion of God over kings is that the civil law promulgated by royal authority may never contravene the law of God, known either through revelation or through reason. The law of God thus serves as a measure whereby the actions of the civil authority can be evaluated.

> The same Thomas therefore whose definition of human laws we mentioned before, doth add thereunto this caution concerning the rule and canon whereby to make them: *human laws are measures* in respect of men whose actions they must direct; howbeit such measures they are, as have also their higher rules to be measured by, *which rules are two the law of God and the law of nature.* So that laws human must be made according to the general laws of nature and without contradiction unto any positive law in Scripture.[90]

With respect to the qualification of the royal sovereignty by the community it is clear that Hooker rejects the notion that the authority of king's is legitimated by a *jure divino* where God directly grants dominion to the king. Royal authority for Hooker is as a rule neither natural nor divinely ordained — Hooker rejects both the view that Kings govern by *jure Divino*, and the view that the exercise of government arises from natural prerogative of some to rule over others, for "that the *Christian* world should be ordered by Kingly regiment the law of God doth not anywhere command."[91] But if not by direct divine command, how does the authority of kings to rule arise?

Hooker agrees with Aristotle and St. Thomas that human beings are naturally social since they depend upon others for the fulfillment of their needs. But there is a point of difference for in the Aristotelian conception, the exercise of rulership is a natural prerogative deriving from the exigencies of man's social nature. The coordination of the activities of a community requires authority, and some are naturally fitted to rule. Hooker, however, makes a vital distinction between *society*, which is indeed natural, and *political society*, which is constructed by human agreement. For Hooker, the existence of a social instinct is by itself an insufficient foundation for the origin of political obligation. Nature and *agreement* together constitute the two foundations on which political society rests:

> Two foundations there are which bear up public societies, the one a natural inclination, the other an order expressly or secretly agreed upon, touching the manner of their union together. The latter is that which we call the law of a commonweal, the very soul of a politic body, the parts whereof are by law animated, and set on work as the common good requireth.[92]

Hooker's contention is that government is not natural but a product of artifice. This is a significant modification of the Aristotelian theory according to which man is naturally political. If political community is natural, it might by extension be argued that there is a natural right in some to govern others. One influential elaboration of this theory is patriarchalism, which conceives of political rule on the analogy of the rule of fathers over their children. Just as children are *naturally* subject to their fathers, so are persons *naturally* subject to the authority of kings. Because of the patriarchalist theory on the origins of political authority, the relationship between the authority of fathers and the authority of kings was one of the most significant discussions of the late sixteenth and seventeenth centuries. Many of the sixteenth-century Catholic scholastics in contrast to the patriarchalists, developed theories which saw the origin of political obligation not in nature, but in consent. As we have already seen, Hooker's friend and contemporary Saravia provided one of the most extensive defenses of the patriarchalist thesis up to that time.[93]

Though Hooker works within the context of Canterbury, rather then Rome, the trajectory of his arguments follows a similar trajectory to those of the Spanish scholastics.[94] The so-called "school of Salamanca" represented by such Thomistic commentators as Francisco Suarez, Thomas de Vitoria, Luis de Molina, and Domingo de Soto brought a second phase of early modern scholasticism to its highest point. Like Hooker they were concerned about the new powers claimed for kings in the early modern epoch[95] and used the resources of medieval scholasticism to argue for a constitutional model of government. In what follows, we shall provide some context by sketching out some of the arguments of the main doctrine opposing constitutionalism at this time—the nascent patriarchalism represented by Saravia, and contrast it with Hooker's constitutionalism. In the process we will show how Catholic scholastics working within a Thomistic tradition similar to Hooker's followed a remarkably parallel line of reasoning in spite of the confessional and political gulf separating Anglican England from the Catholic world.

SARAVIA REVISITED

While patriarchalism may strike many of us in the modern world as preposterous, it should be noted that its sixteenth-century articulation was able to draw upon a long lineage in the philosophical tradition. Thus, Aristotle forms certain analogies between royal government over subjects and paternal government within a household, as when he says that: "the rule of a father over his children is royal, for he receives both love and respect due to age, exercising a kind of royal power."[96]

Expanding upon this tradition, Saravia argues for a fundamental equation of fatherly with kingly rule. As the life of the family shows, the natural condition of mankind is one of subjection, since the child is born under the authority of the father (*naturae lege filiusfamilas in patris est potestate*).[97] In no sense is the father's authority grounded in the consent of his children to his rule. Rather, God appoints fathers through natural law to rule over their families. Thus, Saravia rejects the idea that men are born free—rather their natural condition is one of subjection to a superior (*homines natura non nascuntur liberi*).[98] Indeed, Saravia regards as "beastly" the theory that there was once a time when men were under neither king nor law—since that would make the human condition similar to the animals.[99] Saravia turning to the scriptures finds that fathers and kings were essentially identical in sacred history. Adam, the father of the human race, was also its first ruler, and for Saravia those who are attentive to the Scriptures see that the first fathers of mankind were also their kings.[100]

For Saravia, fathers indeed had a *supreme power* since Genesis makes Adam the first man also the supreme ruler (*ex Genesi notum est, summam potestam cum ipsis simul hominibus incepisse*).[101] Saravia then goes on to argue that the plenitude of kingly authority possessed by Adam devolved by natural generation to his descendents in the ordinary course of things by primogeniture to the first born, though this could be altered by the will of the father—"*primogeniturae praerogatiua principatum cum sacerdotio coniunctum dabat maximo natu, nisi parens, penens, quem summa erat potestas, aliud statuisset.*"[102]

God confirms once again the prerogative rule of fathers, when after the flood, Noah becomes prince of the world *(princeps totius orbis Noah fuit),*[103] and his three sons divide the world between them with the eldest son having the largest share (*in tres partes inaequales vniuersum mundum diuisit*).[104] Saravia thus concludes that the Scriptures support the identification of paternal authority with supreme kingship, since at all points in the Biblical account, fathers had the power of kings: *"Hoc igitur certo tenendum est, patriam potestatem regiam,hoc est, summam fuisse apud primos humani generic authores."*[105] Though the natural inheritance of supreme power could be altered by the fiat of the father himself, by conquest, or by God Himself—contemporary kings needn't have received their power by right of primogeniture from Adam—the supreme and unlimited power included in the original grant of authority by God to Adam belong also to kings. At all points in history, kings have been received and not chosen (*accepisse Principes non elegisse*).[106]

For a stark contrast to Saravia's views, we need to turn to the Spanish scholastic Francisco Suarez. Suarez takes acute notice of the patriarchal theory of the origin of political rule, which he identifies with St. John Chrysostom. Thus, he writes in the *Tractatus de Legibus* about the theory that Adam from the time of creation had a special primacy as the father of the human race, and consequently a sovereign rulership over all men.[107]

From this, the argument follows that by the natural order of primogeniture (or by the special will of Adam) this authority was transmitted to his descendents. So just as a single Adam procreated all men, so men are born into subjection to a single sovereign power—or as he puts it— *"Et ita potuisse ab illo derivari, vel per naturalem primogenitorum, vel pro voluntate ipsius Adae . . . ex uno Adamo omnes homines formatos et procreatos, ut significaretur subordinatio ad unum principem."*[108]

Against this view, Suarez argues that the condition of political subjection did not commence with Adam, and therefore it is impossible to locate political primacy in him as an individual.[109] Suarez concedes that as a father, Adam had a certain dominion over his family. But he does not accept the patriarchalist position of identifying the *pater potestas* with the *regia potestas*. He answers this theory by distinguishing between the "economical" power, which Adam indeed exercised over his domestic household, and political power properly speaking, which is exercised over a society. Thus he emphasizes that Adam's authority was merely domestic or "economic" and not political.[110]

The distinction for Suarez between political and economic powers has some support in Aristotle's *Politics*. In Book I, Aristotle argued against the analogy between rule in a family and rule in a state: "there is an erroneous opinion that the statesmen, king, householder, and master are the same, and differ not in kind but only in the number of their subjects."[111] His treatise goes on to enumerate the distinctions between domestic and political rule.[112] Hooker, in a very similar vein to Suarez, also argues that there is no analogy between regal and paternal authority, because the authority of fathers is based on the dependency of their children on them, while there is no natural condition of dependency between equal men:

> To fathers within their private families nature hath given a supreme power . . . . howbeit over a grand multitude having no such dependency upon anyone . . . impossible it is that any should have complete lawful power but by consent of men, or immediate appointment of God; because not having the natural superiority of fathers their power must needs be either usurped, and then unlawful; or if lawful then granted or consented by them over whom they exercise the same.[113]

LIBERTY AND SOCIALITY: THE PRE-POLITICAL CONDITION IN HOOKER (AND SUAREZ)

If Adam's authority was merely domestic rather than also political, then when and how did political authority first arise? If political structures of authority were not natural and coeval with the human race itself, it would seem necessary to posit some pre-political state or condition of man. Indeed, Hooker is able to conceive of the possibility that, without the Fall, government would be unnecessary: "there being no impossibility considered by itself, but that men might have lived without public regiment."[114]

What would make Hooker useful for later thinkers with different purposes (such as John Locke) is his theory of a pre-political condition before government comes into being. In what follows, we will attempt to show how Hooker is able to construct the notion of a pre-political "state of nature" upon foundations essentially derived from Thomas Aquinas. The space for such a theory opens because of Hooker's view that the condition of subjection to political authority is the product of deliberate artifice rather than nature. This belief leads him to attempt to reconstruct the conditions leading to the establishment of government to begin with.

While Hooker does not use the term "state of nature," postulations about the natural state of man prior to the creation of political authority and obligations abound in his writings (as they did also in the writing of the sixteenth-century Catholic scholastics). For example, Skinner remarks that Luis de Molina refers explicitly to the idea of a "state of nature," which contains no inherent right of political rule of one over others. However, Skinner's equation of Molina's use with later utilization of the term could be questioned.[115] It might be anachronistic to assume a simplistic univocity between Molina's term state of nature, and the concept as it came to be employed in the seventeenth century. For one thing, in Molina, its theological import is probably primary—it refers to the condition of man after the Fall when God has withdrawn the supernatural gift of grace in consequence of original sin, and thus man is in the state of nature alone—albeit fallen. Nonetheless, it must be emphasized that Locke was not innovating, but drawing upon an existing tradition—mediated largely through Hooker—when he argues against patriarchal theories of prerogative government, and speculates on what would be the state or condition of man before government. In the older tradition, the focus would be on the attributes of man in the state of the posterity of Adam deprived of sanctifying grace. Man, bereft of the grace which is superadded to him, is thus in the "state of nature" in that he has only his natural endowments and powers—however disordered by the Fall—to guide him. For Locke (and especially Hobbes), this specific theological context is secondary to the political question of what conditions were like prior to the existence of political obligation. Thus, speculation on the characteristics of man in his social, but pre-political—and thus "natural"—condition, was already a central aspect of sixteenth century scholastic speculation. Their description of this natural condition centers around three broad notions: 1) sociality, 2) freedom, and 3) equality.

Hooker (like the Iberian scholastics) does not believe that because the natural condition of man is *pre-political* it would therefore be *pre-social*. Thus, he writes that:

> But forasmuch as we are not by ourselves sufficient to furnish ourselves with competent store of things needful of such a life as our nature doth desire, a life fit for the dignity of man; therefore to supply those defects and imperfections which are in us living single and solely by ourselves, we are naturally induced to seek communion and fellowship with others.[116]

Thus far Hooker closely follows the Aristotelian/Thomistic position that man is not a solitary but a social animal by nature. This position is then taken up by all the Iberians. Thus, Vitoria writes that it belongs to human nature,

> But to mankind Nature gave 'only reason and virtue,' leaving him otherwise frail, weak, helpless and vulnerable, destitute in all defense, and lacking in all things . . . So that in order to make up for these natural deficiencies, mankind was obliged to abandon the solitary nomadic life of animals, and to live life in partnerships (*societates*) each supporting the other.[117]

Suarez likewise writes that man is a social animal; it belongs to his nature to desire to live in community with other men.[118] Since there is no natural dominion of some to rule over others, writers like Suarez argue that political primacy was originally vested in the whole community and not under any individual: *Dicendum ergo est hanc potestatem ex sola rei natura in nullo singulari homine existere sed in hominum collectione.*[119] This, for Suarez, means that the original locus of supreme authority is the community (*potestas ex natura rei est immediate in communitate*).[120] Hooker makes an essentially identical argument: "It seemeth almost out of doubt and controversy that every independent multitude before any certain regiment established hath under God's supreme authority full dominion over itself."[121]

Thus far, a basic picture of the pre-political condition of man is beginning to emerge. In such a condition, man is under divine and natural law and naturally forms his mode of life in community and fellowship with other men. These two aspects are the most important qualifications to the other features of the pre-political condition—freedom and equality. If man is not born naturally under political subjection, then he is by nature free and holds an equal station with other men. This freedom of the natural, pre-political state *vis à vis* other men, is an inference from the rejection of the patriarchal theory of government. If political authority arises from human artifice, it follows that in his natural condition man is free from subjection to other men, and from the requirements of human or positive law at least in his social as opposed to domestic life. This implies evidently that in political terms—if not in natural endowments—men enjoyed an equal station. Suarez writes that all men are born free by nature, and thus no one has natural political dominion over others (*ex natura rei omnes homines nascuntur liberi, et ideo nullus habet iurisdictioonem politicum in alium, sicut nec dominium*).[122] Suarez then argues that the natural condition of man is, hence, not one of subjection to the authority of another superior man, but a state where there is no reason for one to be favored over the others since there are no superiors by nature (*quia neque omnes sunt aliorum superiores, neque ex natura rei aliqui habent potestatem magis quam allii*).[123]

Likewise, de Soto states that "All men are born free by nature."[124] Vitoria expresses it in terms of the fact that prior to the creation of commonwealths, "no man was the superior of all the others."[125] Thus, the question arises of what are the sources, origin, and legitimation of political obligation—the right of one to rule and the other to obey? Nearly all of the major sixteenth-century scholastics that address the issue lean toward some idea of consent. They believe it follows that, if political authority does not follow from the nature of things or from direct divine appointment, then it must arise rather by the will of the community. Suarez, for example, argues that the only way in which the authority of one to rule over others can be justified is by way of the consent of the members of the community to be ruled.[126]

Molina likewise seems to put forward the idea that the power of rulers derives from the will and good pleasure of the republic which is ruled.[127] Suarez
would argue that the natural condition of man is not one of subjection to the
authority of another superior man, but a state where there is no reason for one
to be favored over the others since there are no superiors by nature (*quia
neque omnes sunt aliorum superiors, neque ex natura rei aliqui habent potestatem magis quam allii*).[128] This condition furthermore would be a state of
freedom since no one is yet subject to the authority of another. If for Saravia
men are not naturally free (*homines natura non nascuntur liberi*), for Suarez
it is quite the reverse: *Ratio prioris parties evidens est quae in principio est
tacta, quia ex natura rei omnes homines nascuntur liberi, et ideo nullus habet iurisdictionem politicam in alium*.[129]

If political subjection is not natural, then from where does political obligation first arise? Most of the early modern scholastics argue that if political authority does not follow from the nature of things, or from direct divine appointment then it must arise but rather by the consent of the community
which is the original locus of sovereignty (under God of course). Thus,
Suarez writes that the community, not an individual like Adam, is the original locus of sovereignty.[130]

Here again Hooker follows nearly the same line of reasoning. For him the
principle which legitimates political authority is the consent to be governed.
Hooker interestingly agrees with the Aristotelian/Thomistic doctrine we have
seen regarding the natural inequality of gifts in nature. Hooker's argument for
consent appears to be a somewhat pragmatic one: there is no way to convert
the natural superiority of the more wise or the more virtuous into a right to
rule that will be generally accepted as reasonable, unless those who will be
governed consent to such rule:

> There were no reason, that one should take upon him to be Lord or Judge over
> another; because although there be according to some very great and judicious
> men a kind of natural right in the wise, the noble and virtuous to govern them
> that are of servile disposition, nevertheless for manifestation of this right, and
> men's more peaceful contentment on both sides, *the assent of them who are to
> be governed seemeth necessary*.[131]

A further question of the theory sketched out by Hooker (as well as Suarez,
etc.) is not only *how* political subjection first arose, but *why*, if men began in
a state of freedom and equality, would they *choose* subjection to other men
over this original state of freedom? They generally reply by referring to the
fact that at least for post-lapsarian man, human selfishness would inevitably
lead to conflicts which would make a community life difficult if not impossible. Suarez, for example, writes that in such a condition peace between men

cannot be preserved, nor injuries effectively adjudicated and punished: "*vix posset pax inter homines conservari neque iniuria possent ordinate propulsari, aut vindicare.*"[132]

Hooker in a similar way argues that, in the fallen state at least, government is necessary to restrain sin:

> To take away all such mutual grievances, injuries and wrongs, there was no way but only by growing unto composition and agreement amongst themselves, by ordaining some kind of government public, and by yielding themselves subject thereunto, that unto whom they granted authority to rule and govern, by them the peace, tranquility and happy estate of the rest might be procured.[133]

Moreover, in a purely natural, pre-political condition, while the right of self-defense would exist without arbitration, people would be partial to themselves and this would give rise to great inconveniences "inasmuch as every man is toward himself and those he greatly affecteth partial."[134] Yet while (because of the fallen state of human nature) the natural law ordains the necessity of government to restrain sin, it does not ordain any particular political form: "the case of man's nature standing as it doth some of kind of regiment the law of nature doth require; yet the kinds thereof being many, nature tieth not any to one, but leaveth the choice a thing arbitrary."[135]

Much of Book VIII is an exploration of the nature and extent of royal supremacy over both the church and the commonwealth, that is: "By what right, after what sort, in what measure, with that conveniency, and according to what example, Christian Kings may have it. In a word their manner of holding dominion." Hooker grants to the king a certain preeminence over both civil and ecclesiastical affairs, but he is also concerned to show the qualification and limits of royal prerogatives in both civil and ecclesiastical affairs. In this respect, his argument seems to be developed consciously in contrast to the arguments of absolutist writers on royal authority.

For Hooker, then, there are two stages in the origins of political society. In the first stage, the community exists in the natural condition of self-dominion with no one in authority. This condition is thus social, but not yet political. The pre-political condition of man is thus understood in similar terms by Hooker and by the sixteenth-century Catholic scholastics. It is a condition of freedom from subjection to human authority, where man would be governed solely by the divine and natural law of God. In this state, a community of men would exist, but all would be equal and no one would have a manifest right to rule over others. For political society to emerge, then, there must be some act of the community whereby consent is given to some to rule over the whole. This natural condition of community is one where man would be only under the divine and natural law, and the formation of any government, which would necessarily result from common agreement by the members of the community: "So that in a word all public regiment of any kind soever seemeth to have arisen from deliberate advice, consultation and composition among men, judging it convenient and behoovful."

Admittedly, Hooker is able to conceive of two exceptional situations in which government can be legitimate without consent: first, there God directly appoints the king and establishes his dominion, in which case God alone sets the limits whereby this dominion may be exercised, and second, where the Royal power is due to conquest. In the first case, God always has supreme dominion over every form of government but usually this dominion is expressed through the mediation of the community and its consent, since in general there is no natural condition of subjection of one man to another. Thus he says that: "God creating mankind did naturally endow it with full power to guide itself in what kind of societies soever it should choose to live."[136] But on rare occasions God can reserve the power to directly appoint kings:

> Sometimes it pleaseth God himself by special appointment to choose out and nominate such as to whom *Dominion* shall be given, which thing he did often in the *Commonwealth of Israel.* They who in this sort receive power have it immediately from God by divine right.[137]

The effect of this qualification is actually to reenforce the doctrine of consent, since his characterization of such cases as exceptional undermines the arguments of patriarchalists and absolutists that the Biblical cases of special divine appointment can be deployed to defend a contemporary *jure divino*. The second case is when the right of conquest legitimates rulership: "*Conquerors* by just and lawful wars do hold their power over such multitudes as a thing descending unto them, divine providence itself so disposing. For it is God who giveth victory in the day of war."[138]

We might add that this exception had an important political dimension, since the kings of England traced their throne to the Norman conquest of 1066, whose consensual basis was contestable. Yet these exceptions do not mark a significant departure from Hooker's general theory of consent, because the first case of God's special appointment is deemed to be an extraordinary exception that would require an authentic prophet such as those of the Biblical era. The second case of the right of conquest is tempered by the fact that not only must the conquest be just and lawful but the conqueror is still bound by divine and natural law and, moreover, with the passage of time government based on conquest is often moderated by a kind of *ex post facto* contract into government by law and consent.

> By means of after agreement it cometh many times to pass in kingdoms, that they whose predecessors by violence and force made subject do grow even lit-

tle by little into that most sweet form of kingly government which *Philosophers* define to be regency, willingly sustained and endowed.[139]

Regency here means a government where the king is *under* the law; rather then where the king *is* the law.

TWO KINDS OF COMPACT

Since Hooker argues, however, that as the rulership of kings is founded on the consent of those they govern, the king is not the original source of the law. As we have seen, original sovereignty is vested in the whole body of the community. Since every body politic is originally sovereign over itself, the power of law belongs originally to the whole community and not only to the king.

> The lawful power of making laws to command whole political societies of men belongeth so properly unto the same entire societies, that For any Prince or potentate of whatsoever kind to exercise the same of himself, and not either by express commission of God, or else by authority derived at the first from their consent upon those persons they impose laws, it is no better then tyranny.[140]

It might be useful to compare for a moment Hooker's account of social compact with that of Hobbes. For Hobbes, first of all, the natural condition of man is not merely pre-political, but pre-*social*. Hobbes famously described the condition before the establishment of a political power in the starkest of terms: "Hereby it is manifest, that during the time men live without a common power to keep them all in awe, they are in that condition which is called war; and such a war as is of every man, against every other man."[141]

For Hobbes, there is not only a need for a compact that establishes political objection (*pactum subjectionis*), but also a need for a compact to establish society itself *(pactum societatis)*. This distinction is of the utmost importance. The idea of a *pactum subjectionis* by which king's derive their power to rule by consent of the people existed already in the Middle Ages. Perhaps the earliest explicit invocation of the idea of a *pactum* between the ruler and the ruled is found in Manegold of Lautenbach. Manegold was writing in the context of the famous Investiture controversy of the eleventh century between Pope Gregory VIII and the Holy Roman Emperor, Henry IV.[142] Manegold argued that not only may a pope declare a tyrannical ruler worthy of being deposed, but the people themselves are *ipso facto* absolved of their duty of obedience by the very fact that their ruler has become tyrannical. This is because the right to rule is dependent upon a two way agreement between the people and the ruler, whereby the people agree to be subject to his rule, and the ruler agrees to rule justly and within due limits. As Manegold writes:

> No man can make himself Emperor or King; a people sets a man over it to the end that he may rule justly, giving to each man his own, aiding good men and coercing bad . . . if he then violates the agreement [*pactum*] according to which he was chosen, disturbing and confounding the very things which he was meant to put in order, reason dictates that he absolves the people from their obedience.[143]

This tradition that kings rule by the agreement and consent of those who are ruled is found also in later writers. Giles of Rome in the thirteenth century argued that kings ruled consensually by the assent (*consensum*) of their people, and should they betray this trust by ruling in a tyrannical and unjust manner, the people may withdraw their consent to be subject to his rule.[144] The general concept of the right to depose unjust rulers is found in the aforementioned texts of Thomas Aquinas, and in other works of medieval political philosophy such as the *Policraticus* of John of Salisbury.[145] This notion of a pact between ruler and people by which they consent to his rule over them was, as we have seen, further developed by sixteenth-century writers in the Aristotelian/Thomistic tradition such as Suarez and Hooker, and so was seen as at least consistent with the traditional view that society is natural and natural law was operative even prior to the emergence of political governance.

In contrast, the *pactum societatis* of Hobbes marks a radical departure from this tradition. In this framework the covenant which establishes the commonwealth involves not only the intention of establishing an authority, but to do so for the purpose of ending the natural state of war and so as to foster the stable conditions which allow society to emerge. Thus, he says that government is instituted "to the end to live peaceably amongst themselves, and be protected against other men."[146] This theory by which *society itself* is established by an artificial contract may be described as contractualism proper. Indeed for Hobbes even the paternal authority has its foundation in contract.[147]

Thus for Hobbes it is clear that man is *neither* political nor social by nature and these things are purely the product of convention:

> It is true, that certain living creatures as Bees and Ants live sociably one with another (and are therefore by *Aristotle* numbred amongst Politicall creatures . . . the agreement of these creatures is Naturall; that of men by Covenant only, which is Artificiall: and therefore it is no wonder that there be somewhat else required (besides Covenant) to make their agreement constant and lasting; which is a Common Power to keep them in awe.[148]

Hooker, of course, rejects the view that there was no community before the erection of political societies. He follows in this the position of Aristotle and

St. Thomas that man is social by nature, and so no special artifice is necessary to bring society into existence. Another fundamental distinction of Hooker's account of the natural state before government is the fact that, for Hobbes, this pre-political state is also *pre-moral*. Justice is what is created and imposed by the civil power. Thus Hobbes writes:

> To this warre of every man against every man, this also is consequent; that nothing can be unjust. The notions of Right and Wrong, Justice and Injustice have no place. Where there is no common Power there is no Law: and where no Law, no Injustice.[149]

For Hooker, as we have seen, even before government the members of the community are subject to the natural law. Thus, the moral law precedes the emergence of civil society. As Hooker writes:

> That which hitherto we have set down, is (I hope), sufficient to show their brutishness, which imagine that religion and virtue are only as men will account of them . . . we see then how nature itself teacheth laws and statutes to live by. The laws which have hitherto been mentioned do bind men absolutely even as they are men, although they have never any settled fellowship, never any solemn agreement among themselves what to do, or not to do.[150]

The "articles of compact" which Hooker mentions, relate only to the delegation of some to rule by the community. Thus, we may legitimately say that in Hooker there is a *pactum subjectionis*. But even here there is a stark difference between Hobbes and Hooker. For Hobbes says that in the compact the members of the community agree "in such manner as if every man should say to every man, *I Authorize and give up my Right of Governing my selfe, to this Man, or to this Assembly of men*."[151]

We see then that, whereas in the *pactum subjectionis* of Hobbes the power of the community to govern itself is *transferred* to the king or sovereign, in Hooker this power is merely *delegated*. This has great significance in terms of understanding the *present* relation of the king to the community. On this point there is some ambiguity about whether the doctrines of Hooker and Suarez are in accord. Thus, Suarez seems at points to argue that the pact between the king and the community is transference rather then a delegation. He writes that:

> once power has been transferred to the king, he is at once the *vicar of God* and by natural law must be obeyed . . . he is by that very power made superior even to the kingdom which granted it for in giving it the kingdom subjected itself and deprived itself of its former liberty . . . the transference from the community to the prince is not a delegation but almost an abrogation i.e. a total grant of all power which was formerly in the community.[152]

But the difference between them may be more apparent then real. Suarez seems to be speaking of the case where the community and its compact establish a *pure* monarchy. The community may not take back powers which it consented freely to give away. However, Suarez (like Aquinas) does not necessarily recommend a pure monarchy, and in fact seems to warn against it:

> Monarchy is found in many places but rarely in pure form, because—since men are frail, ignorant and wicked—it is generally expedient to add something of common government (executed by several people) which may be more or less according to different customs and the judgment of men.[153]

Thus, in practice "the power of the king is more or less according to the pact or agreement between him and his people."[154] This is, as we shall see, the view of Hooker, who regards the limit and extent of the king's authority as determined by the compact. For Hooker, kings receive their authority by an "original conveyance" by which their powers were delegated by the community. The king therefore is in his words *"major singulis, universis minor,"*[155] meaning that while every member of the community is his subject, the king is himself the subject of the whole community. This is because his authority is dependent on the sovereign power of the community as a whole—"Original influence of power from the body to the king *is cause of the king's dependency in power upon the body.* By dependency we mean subordination and subjection."[156]

Thus nothing is a law without the consent of the governed—"Laws they are not which public approbation hath not made so."[157] But such consent need not be personal, direct, or explicit. It can be shown first of all through *representation* as in Parliament—"As in Parliaments, councils and the like, although we be not personally present, notwithstanding our assent is by reason of others agents there in our behalf."[158] Secondly, such consent can be shown through *prescription*—that is through the traditions and customs which were assented to past times and which are received as an inheritance. In a phrase similar to Burke, he writes that:

> Wherefore as any man's past deed is good as long as he himself continueth: so the act of a public society of men done five hundred years since standeth as theirs, who presently are of the same societies, because corporations are immortal: we were alive in our predecessors and they in their successors do live still.[159]

From the idea that each community is free to determine what political forms are to govern it, Hooker supposes then that there is some distant past historical time within every society a "compact" whereby the people agreed among themselves who would hold authority and what powers the authority would wield. The customs and traditions, which govern nations, give witness to the original compact:

> Touching Kings which were instituted by agreement and composition made with them over whom they reign how far their power may lawfully extend, the articles of compact between them must show, not only the articles of compact at the first beginning which for the most part are worn clean out of knowledge . . . but whatsoever hath been after in free and voluntary manner condescended whether by express consent, whereof positive laws are witnesses, or lese by silent allowance famously notified through custom reaching beyond the memory of man.[160]

According to Hooker, sovereignty belongs originally to the people as a whole, as he says:

> it seemeth almost out of doubt and controversy, that every independent multitude, before any certain regiment established, hath, under God's supreme authority, full dominion over itself, even as a man not tied by the bond of subjection as yet unto any other, hath over himself the like power. God creating mankind did endue it naturally with full power to guide itself, in kind of societies soever it should choose to live.[161]

From the principle of an original sovereignty of the people, Hooker argues that the government derives its powers from the consent of the commonwealth. Hooker posits an "original compact" whereby the king receives his powers to rule from the agreement of the whole body. While all kings are bound to obey the divine and natural laws of God, the specific powers of the king may be more or less expansive depending on the specific terms of this original compact. If the compact specifies that the king is the supreme authority and that he be above the civil laws then like Suarez, Hooker would argue that the terms of the compact must be thenceforth honored. In other words, the people are free to choose any form of government they wish, including a more or less absolute monarchy. However, in England the Crown is also bound by the particular "articles of compact" of the English constitution to obey the positive laws of the realm.

HOOKER AND THE QUESTION OF RESISTANCE

Since John Locke and other Whig thinkers would later use Hooker's presuppositions to construct a theory of resistance, Hooker's own attitude to resistance theories is important to consider. We have already seen that according to

Hooker, kings received their right to rule from the community—does it follow that they may be deposed by the same? Hooker is apparently wary of this
conclusion:

> May then a body politic withdraw in whole or in part that influence of domin-
> ion which passeth from it, if inconvenience doth grow thereby? It must be as-
> sumed that supreme governors will not in such case oppose themselves and be
> stiff in detaining that, the use whereof is with public detriment. But surely with-
> out their consent I see not how the body should be able by any just means to help
> itself, saving when Dominion doth escheat. Such things must be thought upon
> beforehand, that power may be limited ere it be granted.[162]

In other words, once power is contractually delegated to the king it would be
in bad faith for the community to try to reserve the powers it granted. Thus
Hooker regards it as better for the community to consider that before grant-
ing unchecked power to the king "Such things must be thought upon before
hand, that power may be limited ere it be granted."[163]

Since Hooker's main aim is to defend the Elizabethan settlement, Hooker
is concerned here about the Calvinist resistance theories put forth for example in the pamphlet *De Vindiciae Contra Tyrannos* attributed to the French
Huguenot Philippe du Plessis Mornay. The pamphlet includes the preference
for a "free" or elective monarchy over hereditary monarchy, and the permis-
sibility of tyrannicide. Given that the legitimacy of Elizabeth's reign was
called into question explicitly by many Roman Catholics who regarded Henry
VIII's divorce as illegitimate, and (if more implicitly) by Puritan doctrines,
the issue of rebellion and tyrannicide was highly sensitive in the context of
sixteenth-century England. Hooker refers to these "strange and unnatural
conceits set abroad by seedsmen of rebellion, only to animate unquiet spirits."[164] Interestingly, however, he does not answer the partisans of rebellion
and regicide by asserting that hereditary monarchy is a natural or divinely ordained mode of governance, but solely on the grounds that if by the terms of
the compact a hereditary monarchy was decided upon, then that is how rulership is conveyed "in Kingdom's hereditary birth giveth right unto supreme
dominion."[165]

What is unclear in Hooker is what happens when the king tries to usurp
more power then the compact allows, or when the king violates natural and
divine law. While the medieval Thomistic theory allowed for the deposition
of the tyrant in such cases, Hooker seems reticent to support this view—at
least overtly. It is an unclear point among Hooker scholars whether his theory
rules out resistance altogether. Cargill Thompson regards the "compact" theory of Hooker as essentially different from the contractualism of Locke in ruling out resistance once the compact is established—Hooker's theory is prin-

cipally then about the origins of government and not about the present relationship of the regime to the community. For Thompson, the "compact" theory of Hooker is of a wholly different order than the "contract" theories of the seventeenth century, in part precisely because the latter were primarily interested in articulating a right of resistance.[166] On the other hand, J.P. Sommerville[167] holds that the logic of Hooker's constitutionalism and its continuity with the medieval tradition do not altogether rule out resistance to tyrannical rule.

The simple fact is that Hooker never addresses the question of what to do about a tyrant king who strives to *annul* the original compact which requires him to obey the positive law, or who goes even beyond that and acts against the natural and divine law. We can agree with Thompson that Hooker has no interest in elaborating on the conditions under which resistance to a ruler can be justified. One must remember that Hooker's polemical objective is the defense of conformity to the Elizabethan settlement, which includes the Act of Supremacy. It would be unrealistic perhaps to imagine him hypothesizing about the circumstances which justify legitimate rebellion. But neither is Hooker willing to defend conformity by appealing to the natural or divine origins of kingship, as was increasingly the practice of Anglicans. His approach was therefore to defend conformity by appeal to the consensual origins of the English constitution and the authority of parliament over "indifferent" matters on which the divine and natural law are silent. Thompson goes too far if he is saying that Hooker is interested *only* in the origins of government as if this historical dependency has no relation to the present political relationship between the king as head to the whole body of the community. As we have seen, the origin of rulership in the delegation of powers by the sovereign community is the reason why the king continues to be the subject of the whole community: "Original influence of power from the body to the king is cause of the king's dependency in power upon the body. By dependency we mean subordination and subjection."[168]

Hooker does not say what this seems to imply, for if the body politic rather then the king is the ultimate locus of sovereignty, it would seem possible that the people as sovereign could in extreme cases depose its subject the king should he exceed his assigned powers. What we seem to have is a kind of "strategic ambiguity" in the text, resulting from the fact that Hooker does not want to sanction either an absolutist theory such as that of the *jure divino* while, at the same time, he wishes to respect the sensitivities of the historical situation by not elaborating a theory of resistance. Thus, what he does is argue against the *specific* resistance theories extant (such as that of Mornay) without addressing the general issue of whether resistance as such can ever be just. Just as Hooker was able to develop upon the ambiguities in the

Thomistic understanding of politics in order to elaborate a consensual theory of the origins of government, so was Locke later able to exploit the ambiguities of Hooker's theory of the political society in order to develop a theory of resistance. However in his own time Hooker staked a position between absolutists like Saravia and Bodin on the one side, and revolutionaries like the French Calvinist Monarchomachs on the other.

A CROWN UNDER LAW

What *is* clear is Hooker's belief that when kings are unrestrained by law, monarchy degenerates into tyranny: "They saw that to live by the rule of one man's will, became the cause of all men's misery."[169] Thus he regards it as far more preferable for the king to be under not only the natural law but also the *positive law*. In one of the most significant passages in the whole of his work, Hooker attests to the prudence of subordinating the king, not merely to the divine and natural law, but also to the positive or human laws of the realm:

> I mean not of the law not only of nature and of *God*, but every national or municipal law consonant thereunto. Happier that people whose law is their *King* in the greatest things, then that whose *King* is himself the law. Where the *King* doth guide the state, and law the *King*, that commonwealth is like an harp or melodious instrument, the strings whereof are tuned and handled all by one hand, following as laws the rules and canons of musical science.[170]

Hooker therefore praises the English Constitution in particular for placing the crown under the laws of the realm. On these points Hooker echoes the Bractonian dictum that the king is *sub Deo et Lege*.

> I cannot but choose to commend highly their wisdom by whom the foundations of this Commonwealth have been laid, wherein though no manner person or cause be unsubject to the *King's* power, yet so is the power of the *King* over all and in all limited that unto all his proceedings the law itself is the rule.[171]

Hooker distinguishes between the king's supreme and limited powers. But even in those matters where the king of England has full authority it is because he is allowed such under the law.

> It hath been declared already how the best established dominion is, where the law doth most rule the *King,* the true effect is found as well in *Ecclesiastical* as in *civil* affairs. In these the *Kings* through his supreme power may do sundry great things himself both appertaining unto peace and war both at home by commandment and by commerce with states *because so much the law doth permit*.[172]

On the other hand, Hooker makes it clear that the king's authority is sharply limited, and not only by the natural law but also by the positive law:

> Some things on the other side the *King* alone hath no power to do without the consent of the *Lords* and *Commons* assembled in *Parliament*. The *King* of himself cannot change the nature of pleas and courts, nor do so much as restore blood, because the law is a bar to him, not any law divine or natural, for against neither it were though the *Kings* themselves might do both, but the positive laws of the realm have abridged therein, and restrained the *King's* power.[173]

Against the absolutist concept that the sovereign Crown alone is the source of law,[174] Hooker instead asserts the same point made by Sir Thomas Smith. In England it is Parliament that is the source of the law in which the whole realm is represented—the Lords spiritual, the Lords temporal, and the Commons. "The *Parliament* of England together with the *Convocation* annexed thereunto is that whereupon the very essence of all government within this Kingdom doth depend."[175]

Indeed, the power of the king over the law is limited to vetoing the acts of Parliament, thus there is no *positive* power for the Crown to enact laws: "Touching the supremacy of power which our *Kings* have in this case of making laws it resteth principally in the strength of a negative voice."[176] The original sovereignty of the people is therefore not simply a remote historical event for Hooker, but that which conditions the present relation of the monarch to the community. The authority to rule originally proceeds from the commonwealth, and therefore the king is in essence a subject of the people. The continuing consent of the people to the king's rule is shown both prescriptively in the assent of the people to the traditional laws and customs of the kingdom, and also (in the case of England) to the assent of Parliament where the whole body of the people is represented, from the Commons to the Lords spiritual and temporal. Indeed Hooker argues that it is not the Crown that legitimates the acts of Parliament but Parliament which legitimates the acts of the Crown, Indeed, Hooker is clear that the Crown's power over laws is confined to "the negative voice." Thus while the assent of the Crown is necessary for law, the Crown is neither the source of the law, nor above the law.

Much of the remainder of Book VIII is devoted to a discussion of the particular prerogatives of royal supremacy showing their extent and limits, which will not long detain us.[177] Hooker provides a fitting synopsis of his views on the exercise of the royal prerogatives:

> What power the *King* hath he hath it by law, the bounds and limits of it are known. The entire community giveth general order by law how all things

publically are to be done and the *King* as the head thereof the highest in authority over all causeth it according to the same law every particular to be framed
and ordered thereby. The whole body politic maketh laws which give power
unto the *King* and the King having bound himself to use according to law that
power, it so falleth out that the execution of the one is accomplished by the other
in most religious and peaceable sort.[178]

At this point we may summarize four critical themes in Hooker's political
philosophy, which were to exercise a profound impact on later political,
thought, and most especially the writing of John Locke.[179] First, Hooker acts
as mediator of the medieval natural law tradition, which was to continue to
have an important place in the early modern period. The fact that he mediated
this tradition within a Protestant culture is of particular note. Second, there is
Hooker's distinction of paternal and regal authority, the former being natural,
the latter artificial. The assertion of political authority being grounded in artifice rather then nature, and his specific repudiation of the equation of paternal and regal authority were to be of decisive importance in seventeenth-
century polemics as patriarchalism gained in importance and theoretical
development, and is of course central to Locke's project. Third, following
from Hooker's assertion that the origins of political authority lie in human artifice, there is the beginning of the conceptualization of an original pre-
political state. Thus we see the nascent origins of thinking about a state of nature and what conditions would apply therein. Hooker affirms an original,
pre-political state, and like Hooker sees the state as proceeding from artifice,
not nature. Fourth, there is Hooker's idea that original sovereignty is vested
in the whole people, and is then *delegated* by "conveyance" to the monarch.
The idea that sovereignty is not vested in the person of the king but in the
whole community was to supply a powerful argument to constitutionalists
who opposed royal absolutism. These themes will be more fully explored in
our next chapter.

NOTES

1. For an in-depth investigation of Hooker's specific political doctrine, there are
two articles, which perhaps most influenced my own exposition: W. D. J. Cargill
Thompson, "The Philosopher of the Politic Society"; A. Cromartie, "Theology and
Politics in Richard Hooker's thought." This text specifically dealt with the distinction
between Hooker's Aristotelian ethics and what he takes as a political theory focusing
on the notion of government only as ex post facto necessary to repress sin. The central point being that, unlike Aristotle, Hooker takes political society to be artificial and
a remedy against sin, not natural.

2. Cf. Cromartie, "Theology and Politics in Richard Hooker's Thought," p. 41

3. Augustine, *City of God*, 15.5.

4. *Ibid.*, 1.21.

5. S.T. I, Q. 94, art. 4.

6. Cf. C. Schmitt, *John Case and Aristotelianism in Renaissance England*. The information regarding alteration in an anti-scholastic direction at Oxford can be found, for example, on p. 63 where he writes, "the complete rejection of Scholastic theology in England during the middle years of the sixteenth century."

7. *Ibid.*, pp. 64–65.

8. See John Case, *Sphaera Civitatis*. (Francof: Sigifmundi, 1589), and John Case, "Speculum Moralium Quaestionem" in *Universam Ethicen Aristotelis*. (Oxford, Joseph Barnes, I Barnesti, 1585). The information on the status of Aristotelian and Scholastic studies in late Elizabethan England can be found in the cited parts of Schmitt's work.

9. Richard Tuck, *Philosophy and Government: 1572–1651*. (Cambridge: Cambridge University, 1993) pp. 147–148.

10. Peter Munz has indeed done an impressive study of directly parallel arguments in "Aquinas and the Laws" in his *The Place of Hooker in the History of Thought* (see, in particular, Appendix A).

11. Preface, 6: 7.3.

12. Preface, 6: 8.7.

13. An example may be found in Bodin's Republique in Book 10, "On the Marks of Sovereignty," published in *On Sovereignty*, Cambridge University Press (2004). Cf. Ernst H. Kantorowitz, *The King's Two Bodies: A Study in Medieval Political Theology*. (Princeton: Princeton University Press 1997).

14. For a survey of how different medieval concepts of natural law were employed during the period from the Renaissance to Hobbes, see Richard Tuck, *Natural Rights Theories: Their Origin and Development*. (Cambridge: Cambridge University, 1979). Tuck shows how the late medieval debate over whether ius (right) and domininium (property or mastery) were the same thing, blossomed into the first theories of rights (cf. "First Rights" pp. 5–31, and "The Renaissance" pp. 32–57. Tuck's account begins with fourteenth century figures like Jean Gerson, John Mair, and Alamain, and ends with John Selden and Thomas Hobbes.

15. The following quotations from Aquinas are generally taken from the collection edited by A.P. d'Entreves, *Aquinas: Selected Political Writings* (Oxford: Oxford University Press, 1978). The footnotes thus refer to the original texts from which they are derived.

16. S.T. I-II Q. 72, art. 4.

17. *De Regimine*, I, "Naturale Autem est Homine ut sit animal sociale et politicum . . ." Quotations taken from the *Omnia Opera* of Saint Thomas Aquinas on the University of Navarra website.

18. *Ibid*.

19. *Ibid*.

20. *Ibid*.

21. *Ibid*.

22. *Ibid.*

23. S.T. Q. 95, art. 9.

24. S.T. Q. 96, art. 4.

25. S.T. Q. 96, art 3.

26. S.T. Q. 92, art 1, AD 2 UM

27. As Walton renders the matter, " his [Hooker's] friendship was much sought for by Dr. Hadrian Saravia." Keble, Volume I, p. 74. Keep in mind however, the previously cited works by Novarr and Sisson which placed Walton's rendering of Hooker's life in its political and historical context.

28. First published in 1593, Hadrian Saravia, *De Imperandi Authoritate.* (London, deputies of Christopher Barker, 1593), the work was also reprinted in 1611 by Richard Field as part of a compendium. Cf. Saravia, Hadrian, *Diversi Tractatus Theologici.* (London: Richard Field, 1611).

See also J.P. Sommerville, "Richard Hooker, Hadrian Saravia, and the Advent of the Divine Right of Kings," in *History of Political Thought*, vol. 4 (1983), pp. 229–246. Because Sommerville relies on the 1611 version of Saravia's *De Imperandi Authoritate* it is this edition to which our page numbers will refer.

29. *Ibid.*, p. 240.

30. *Ibid.*, p. 241.

31. De Regimine Principium, I.

32. *Ibid.*, II.

33. *Ibid.*

34. In S.T. II-II, Q.42, art. 2, reply 3.

35. S.T. I-II ,Q. 90, Art. 3.

36. *De Regimine Principium*, IV.

37. "For it sometimes happens that men who are ruled by a monarch are slow to interest themselves in the common welfare; since they are of the opinion that whatever they do for the common good will in some way benefit themselves, but only serve to enrich whoever appears to control the public interest. But if there is no one person with power over the public interest, they go about the corporate task as though it were their own business and not merely profitable to another. So experience has shown that a single city, with an administration which is changed annually, can sometimes accomplish more than three or four cities under a monarchy." *De Regimine Principium*, IV.

38. *De Regimine Principium*, VI.

39. "With respect to the right ordering of power in a city or nation, two points are to be considered: the first is that all should in some respect participate in the government. It is this, in fact that ensures peace within the community as we are told in the *Politics* (II, Chaps 1 and 2), all people's prize and guard such a state of affairs. Among the various forms of government which the Philosopher enumerates in the third book of the *Politics* (Chap 5,6,7) the more important are the Kingdom in which one alone governs according to virtue; aristocracy, that is government by the best elements, in which a few hold office according to virtue. So the best ordering of power within a city or kingdom is obtained when there is one virtuous head who commands over all; and who has under him others who govern virtuously; and when furthermore all par-

ticipate in such government, both because all are eligible, and because all participate in the election of those who rule. This is the best form of constitution, which results from a judicious mixture of the Kingdom, in which there is one person at the head of it, of aristocracy in that many participate in the government according to virtue; and of democracy or popular rule, in that rulers may be elected from the people and the whole population has the right of electing its rulers" (S.T. I-II, q.105, art 1).

40. Thus Alan Cromartie writes in "Theology and Politics of Richard Hooker" that "examination of his[Hooker's] argument reveals a genuine tension between an Aristotelian ethical theory, and a picture of political arrangements as nothing but a means to cope with sin," p. 46.

41. Cromartie continues "This brings us to the central oddity of Hooker's political thought: the fact that though his ethics take an Aristotelian form, he did not accept the Aristotelian notion that man is naturally political. It is a basic principle for Hooker that 'we are not by ourselves sufficient to furnish ourselves with a competent store of things needful for such a life as our nature doth desire, a life fit for the dignity of man,' but the only natural form of government is 'the supreme power of fathers as 'lords and lawful kings in their own houses.' If human beings were untouched by sin, the state would not be a necessity" *Ibid.* p. 55

42. In another manner, Munz presents Hooker's thought as an inconsistent mixture of Thomistic ethics and philosophy, with the political theories of Marsilius of Padua.

43. The late printing of Book VIII could have been due to its highly circumscribed view of the role of the Crown, and as we shall see Royalist writers in the seventeenth century even shed doubt about its authenticity. While its authenticity is no longer in serious question among scholars, the reasons why it was not published during Hooker's lifetime remain speculative.

44. This is the title of Book VIII of Laws.

45. Thomas Stapleton was a leading English language Roman Catholic apologist of the sixteenth century. His main work, *Principiorum Fidei Doctrinalium Demonstratio Methodicum*, is quoted by Hooker several times, particularly in Book VIII (e.g. K.2.14, K.3.1.).

46. Marsilius of Padua perhaps began to be mentioned in connection with Hooker by A.P. d'Entreves, e.g. *The Medieval Contribution to Political Thought: Thomas Aquinas, Marsilius of Padua and Richard Hooker* (Humanities Press, 1959—originally 1939). The ostensible influence of Marsilius on Hooker with respect to notions the control of the Church by the Christian ruler, and the whole body-politic as the source of laws was mentioned at the 1935 proceedings of the British Academy (cf. Previte, C.W., "Marsilius of Padua" Proceedings of the British Academy, 1935). By the mid twentieth century the influence of Marsilius was accepted by scholars like Munz and Kearney (cf. Kearney, H.F. "Richard Hooker: A Reconstruction." *The Cambridge Journal*, Volume V, (Oct 1951–Sept.1952)), and questions were consequently raised regarding the philosophical coherence of his whole work, since the ethical as opposed to the political theory of Richard Hooker was held to be Thomistic. For more on that cf. Peter Munz both in his previously mentioned *The Place of Hooker in the History of Thought*, and in his article on Hooker for the Encyclopedia of Philosophy. Another brief reference is contained in A.S. McGrade´s commentary on Book VIII, which we cited earlier.

47. See, for example, Cary J. Nederman, *Community and Consent: The Secular Political Theory of Marsiglio of Padua's Defensor Pacis* (Lanham, MD: Rowman and Littlefield, 1995).

48. *Laws*, VII, K.9.11.1: "The power of the censures and keys of the church, and of ordaining and ordering ministers (in which two points especially this superiority is challenged), is not committed to any one pastor of the Church more than to another; but the same is committed as a thing to be carried equally in the guidance of the Church. Whereby it appeareth, that Scripture maketh all pastors not only in the ministry of the word but also in all ecclesiastical jurisdiction and authority, equal," from *Defensor Pacis*, Part II. The Latin text is found in the note in the Keble edition, Vol. III, p. 205.

49. *Ibid.*

50. *Ibid.*, K.11.2 ff.

51. Stephen Gardiner, *De Vera Obedientia.* trans. John Bale (in 1553), (Leeds: Scholar Press, 1966). Gardiner's *De Vera* was first published in 1535.

52. *Laws*, VIII.1.2.

53. *Ibid.*, 1.4.

54. *Ibid.*

55. *Ibid.*

56. See G. B. Elton, *England under the Tudors* (London: The Folio Society, 1997), p. 184.

57. Cf. McGrade, in Folger, p. 356, note.

58. *Ibid.*

59. Laws, VIII.1.2.

60. *Ibid.*, VIII.3.4.

61. *Ibid.*, VIII.3.2.

62. *Ibid.*, K VIII.1.2.

63. "With us therefore the name of a Church importeth only a Society of men first united into some public regiment and secondly distinguished from other societies by the exercise of Christian religion. With them on the other side the name of the Church in this present question importeth not only a multitude of men, so united and so distinguished, but also further the same divided necessarily and perpetually from the body of the commonwealth. So that even in such a politic Society as consisteth of none but Christians, yet the Church of Christ and the Commonwealth are two corporations independently each subsisting by itself" (Cf. *Ibid.* I.2).

64. Much of the remainder of the chapter is an exploration of the nature and extent of Royal supremacy over both the Church and the Commonwealth—an exploration of the question of how to determine "By what right, after what sort, in what measure, with that conveniency, and according to what example, Christian Kings may have it. In a word, their manner of holding dominion." "By what right" is indeed one of the most controverted questions of the age—how should political authority legitimate itself? Hooker grants to the King a certain pre-eminence over both civil and ecclesiastical affairs but he is concerned also to show the qualification and limits of Royal prerogatives in both civil and ecclesiastical affairs. In this respect, his argument seems to be developed consciously in response to the arguments of absolutist writers on Royal authority.

65. Frederick C Beiser. *The Sovereignty of Reason: The Defence of Rationality and the Early English Enlightenment*. (Princeton: Princeton University, 1996), 83

66. Bodin, *On Sovereignty*, 491, p. 56.

67. *Ibid.*, pp.358–359.

68. *Ibid.*, 361, p. 12.

69. Laws, VIII K.6.10.

70. Robert Eccleshall, "Richard Hooker and the Peculiarities of the English: The Reception of the 'Ecclesiastical Polity' in the Seventeenth and Eighteenth Centuries," in History of Political Thought II (1981) 63–117, here p.85. We shall turn to Eccleshall's article again in Part III.

71. We don't mean of course that representative institutions were unknown among continental kingdoms—the Cortes in Spain, and the Estates-General in France are two examples.

72. For a discussion of this issue see the excellent discussion in Lawrence Manley, *Convention 1500–1750* (Cambridge: Harvard University, 1980), particularly his chapter "Use becomes Nature:" pp. 90–106. Manley argues that the attack on English common law was centered on its reliance on custom—for how can the unity of law be harmonized with the variety of custom. For an example of this kind of polemic between partisans of Roman and Common Law, one may refer as an example to Thomas Starkey, *A Dialogue Between Cardinal Pole and Thomas Lipset*, ed. J.M. Cowper (London: Early English Texts Society, 1878).

73. Two of the most important advocates of the Roman law tradition in sixteenth century England were Alberico Gentilli whose most important work was his 1587 *De Iuris Interpretibus*, and Sir Thomas Smith of Cambridge, author of *De Republica Anglorum*. For information on the competition between common and civil lawyers in the English context see for example: Donald R. Kelley, "History, English Law, and the Renaissance:" *Past and Present*, Volume 65 (1974).

74. See George W. Keeton. *The Norman Conquest and the Common Law* (London: Benn / Barnes and Noble, 1966). As Keeton writes, "Further the lawyers as a learned profession, were fully responsive to prevailing habits of thought and their influence cannot be fully understood unless it is accepted that they had been educated in a system . . . in which the learning of the Christian philosophers, especially that of St. Thomas Aquinas was paramount." p. 216.

75. Henry Bracton, from the introduction of his *De Legibus* (numbers references removed); cf.the Harvard online edition(Latin text by George Woodbine, English translation by Samuel E. Thorne) In Latin the cited phrase is rendered: "Cum autem fere in omnibus regionibus utatur legibus et iure scripto, sola Anglia usa est in suis finibus iure non scripto et consuetudine. In ea quidem ex non scripto ius venit quod usus comprobavit. Sed non erit absurdum leges Anglicanas licet non scriptas leges appellare, cum legis vigorem habeat quidquid de consilio et consensu magnatum et rei publicæ communi sponsione, auctoritate regis sive principis præcedente, iuste fuerit definitum et approbatum."

76. *Laws*, VIII K.2.3, for information on Hooker's use of Bracton, see A.S. McGrade, "Constitutionalism Late Medieval and Modern-Lex facit Regem: Hooker's use of Bracton," from the *Acta Conventus Neo-Latini Bononiensis*. ed. R.J. Schoek, pp. 116–123.

77. Bracton, 33 d, in Latin: "Ipse autem rex non debet esse sub homine sed sub deo et sub lege, quia lex facit regem.Attribuat igitur rex legi, quod lex attribuit ei, videlicet dominationem et potestatem. Non est enim rex ubi dominatur voluntas et non lex."

78. *De Natura Legis Naturae*, I.16, see Cambridge Texts in the History of Thought Edition (1997), p. 128 (Appendix A).

79. Carlyle (In Volume VI, p.142) remarks that in fact the section of *De Regimine* used here by Fortescue (*De Regimine Principium* ii.8.19) is now thought to have been written by Ptolemy of Lucca.

80. From *De Laudibus*, IX, the Cambridge texts edition (1997) is an amended version of the Chrimes translation.

81. Cambridge edition (Appendix A), pp. 128–129

82. *Ibid.*, p. 232.

83. Christopher of St. Germain, *Doctor and Student*, fol.8ff.

84. By natural law constitutionalism, we refer primarily to such principles as that the civil law promulgated by the government must conform to the natural law.

85. See McGrade's commentary on Book VIII of Laws. McGrade develops the idea of three modes of qualification with respect to Hooker's view of Royal sovereignty.1) Qualification with respect to God, 2) Qualification with respect to the Law, and 3) Qualification with respect to the community.

86. *Laws*, C.3.1.

87. *Ibid.*, 4.5.

88. *Ibid.*

89. *Ibid.*, K.III.9.2, the quotation is from ST I-II, q. 91, art. 3.

90. *Ibid.*; interestingly, this passage is quoted by Locke (*Second Treatise*, 11.136) without any indication that it is Hooker's paraphrase of the words of St. Thomas (ST I-II, q.95, art. 3).

91. Laws, 3.1.

92. *Ibid.*, I.10.1.

93. All quotes from Saravia are taken from *De Imperandi Authoritate* (1611).

94. For an excellent overview see M.W.F. Stone, "The Nature and Significance of Law in Early Modern Scholasticism," in *A History of Philosophy of Law from the Ancient Greeks to the Scholastics*, ed. Fred Miller (Dordrecht: Kluwer, 2005), p. 15. See also the discussions of Thomistic Constiutionalism in Quentin Skinner, *The Foundations of Modern Political Thought* (Cambridge: Cambridge University Press, 1978). One of the most in depth contemporary references for the "second scholasticism" that was centered in the Spanish university of Salamanca is found in Belda Plans, Juan: *La Escuela de Salamanca y la renovacíon de la teología en el siglo XVI*. BAC maior, Madrid, 2000. For an excellent English language survey of sixteenth Century Spanish political thought, see Berenice Hamilton, *Sixteenth Century Spain: A Study of the Political Ideas of Vittoria, De Soto, Suarez and Molina* (Oxford: Clarendon, 1963). An important contemporary study is found in Brett, Anabel, *Liberty, Right and Nature*. (Cambridge: Cambridge University, 1997). Brett's study is valuable for showing how the subjective use of ius found in the Iberian scholastics, evolved from the late medieval debates about whether and how ius or "right" was or was not related to dominium which can mean the power to control, mastery, or ownership. While Aquinas

himself tended to favor the "objective" sense of ius, in writings of figures like Jean Gerson, John Mair, and Almain ius began to be thought of as a subjective power or faculty. The writings of the Spanish scholastics were profoundly influenced both by the "objective" tradition of Thomism, and the "Gersonian" understanding of ius and achieved a kind of synthesis. Cf. especially "Objective right and the Thomist tradition" pp.88–122 and "Subjective right and Thomism in Sixteenth-Century Spain," pp.123–164. For information on the theories of law among the Spanish scholastics see William Daniel's "The Purely Penal Law Theory in the Spanish Theologians from Vitoria to Suarez." Analecta Gregoriana, vol. 164, 1968.

95. Though in the case of the Catholic scholastics the concern about Caesarism in which Kings whose authority was merely earthly claimed power over the Church which received its authority from God was more prominent than in Hooker, who accepted a kind of Erastian model.

96. *Politics*, Book I, 1259b.

97. Lib 1, Cap.II p. 125 in *De Imperandi Authoritate*, cited in J.P. Sommerville, "Hadrian Saravia, and the Advent of the Divine Right of Kings," in *History of Political Thought* 4 (1983), p. 238.

98. *Ibid.*

99. Saravia argues that: "Falsum esse opinionem eorum qui credunt primos populos palentis incertis sedibus, more beastiarum, in antris et sylvis, sine lege et Rege vixisse." See *De Imperandi Authoritate*, Lib.2, Cap.XI, p.168, cited in J.P. Sommerville, p. 239.

100. *De Authoritate*, p. 167: "Seriam sacrae historiae qui considerabit attentius, primos hominum progenitores primos quoque fuisse Reges facile inveniet," cited in Sommerville, p. 238.

101. Saravia, *De Imperandi Authoritate*, Lib.II, Cap.XI, p.167.

102. *Ibid.*

103. *Ibid.*

104. *Ibid.*

105. *De Imperandi Authoritate*, p. 168, quoted in Sommerville, p. 239.

106. *Ibid.*, p. 167, quoted in Sommerville, p. 238.

107. *Tractatus de Legibus*, Book I, Caput II.3: 'Solum posset quispiam dicere, Adamum in principio creationis ex natura rei habuisse primatum, et conesequentur imperium in omnes homines.'

108. *Ibid.*

109. *Ibid.*, Book I, Caput III.3.5: "Unde Sicut illa communitas no coepit per creationem Adae, nec per solamvoluntatem eius, sed omnium qui in illa convenerunt, ita non possumus cum fundamento dicere Adamaum ex natura rei habuisse primatum politicum in illa communitate."

110. *Ibid.* "Verumtamen, ex vi solius creationis et originis naturalis solum colligi potest, habuisse Adamum potestatem oeconomicam, nonpoliticam." (boldface added)

111. *Politics*, Book I, 1252a.

112. This distinction was argued against by Bodin when he charged that Aristotle, 'without any probable cause . . . divided the Oecunomical government from the political, and the city from the family.' Cf. Schochet, "The Authoritarian Family and

Political Attitudes in seventeenth Century England," p. 32. Bodin, however, later argues that wives unlike slaves are members of the commonwealth because their subjection is not political (see *ibid.*, pp. 33–34). So if Bodin is to be considered a Patriarchalist, it is difficult to make his argument consistent on this point.

113. *Laws*, I.10.4 (Keble).

114. *Ibid.*

115. The reference occurs in Molina in his *De Iustitia et Iure Libri sex* (1689), where he refers to *rebus indito in statu natura integer.* While this state is pre-political (and post-lapsarian), the theological resonances of this concept in terms of the Catholic doctrine of grace may be more important to Molina than its political resonances.

116. *Laws*, I.10 (Keble, p. 139).

117. *Relectio on Civil Power*, 1.2.4 (see Cambridge p.7).

118. "Primum est, hominem esse animal sociale, et naturaliter recteque appetere communitate vivere," p. 161.

119. Suarez, *Tractatus*, Book I, Caput 3.1.

120. *Ibid.*, Caput 4:2, p. 169.

121. *Laws*, VIII, K. 2.5.

122. Suarez, *Tractatus*, Book I, Caput II, p.165.

123. *Ibid.*, Book I, Caput II,1.

124. De Soto, 102, quoted in Skinner, p.155.

125. Quoted in Skinner, p. 156.

126. "Ratio ex dictis est, quia haec potestas ex natura rei est immediate in communitate;ergo ut iuste incipiat esse in aliqua persona tamquam in supreme principe, necesse est ut consensus communitatis illi tribuatur." Suarez, *Tractatus*, Book I, Caput 4:2, p. 169 (italics added).

127. "Sed arbitrio ac beneplacito diursaru rerupublicarum instituti sint" (from *Tractatus* V, 1869).

128. Caput II, 1.

129. *Ibid.*

130. Cf. the previously quoted passage on p.162 of this work (i.e. Caput III. 3.5: "Unde Sicut illa communitas no coepit per creationem Adae, nec per solamvoluntatem eius, sed omnium qui in illa convenerunt, ita non possumus cum fundamento dicere Adamaum ex natura rei habuisse primatum politicum in illa communitate.")

131. *Laws*, I.10.4 (italics added).

132. Book II, Caput I, p. 162.

133. *Laws*, I.10.4.

134. *Ibid.*

135. *Ibid.*, I.10.5.

136. *Ibid.*, VIII.2.5.

137. *Ibid.*, VIII.2.5.

138. *Ibid.*

139. *Ibid.*, VIII.2.11.

140. *Ibid.*, I.10.7.

141. Hobbes, *Leviathan*, Part I, Chapt. XIII.8.

142. Lay investiture of bishops had been a common practice which enabled kings and emperors to retain leverage over the bishops in their jurisdiction symbolically expressed by the fact the emperor invested the bishops with the symbols of their authority. Gregory VIII, as part of his reforms, sought to free the Church from temporal control. In 1075, he forbade lay investiture, and after Henry IV's defiant attitude toward implementing this decree, Henry IV was excommunicated and his subjects absolved of their vow of obedience. Because the Pope was claiming the right to depose a sitting monarch, issues regarding the legitimate powers of pope and emperor soon became part of the disputation.

143. Quoted in Sabine, A History of Political Theory (Holt, Rinehart, and Winston press, 1961), p. 241—from Manegold's *Ad Gebehardum* 67: "Cum enim nullus se imperatorem ve regem creare possit, ad hoc unum aliquem super se populus exaltat, ut iusti ratione inperii se gubernet et regat, cuique sua distribuat, pios foveat, inpios perimat, omnibus videlicet iusticiam inpendat. At vero so quando pactum, quo eligitur, infringit, ad ea disturbanda et confundenda, que corrigere constitutus est, eruperit, iuste rationis consideratione populum subjectionis debito absolvit." Cf. also, Carlyle, *History of Medieval Political Thought* (1932), Vol.III, p. 164.

144. Giles of Rome, De Renuntiatione Papae (1555), Chap 16, p. 22: "Sed Quamvis sic requirit natura negotii, quod scientes melius pericula praeudire, aliis praeficiant[ur], ut sub eoru[m] multitudo saluetur[servetur], opportet tamen quod hoc compleat per consensum hominum. Et Sicut p[er] consensum hom[in]um p[rae]ficiturandcomplet[tur], et quis aliis praeficiant, sic per consensum homini[um]contrario modo factu[m]fieri pot[est], quod praefectus cedat, vel quod etian deponatur." (My orthographic modifications in brackets are based on the excerpt cited in Carlyle, Vol. V, p.117.) Parenthetically, another relevant medieval text on the subject of the pactum subjectionis is the *Tractatus de Potestate Regia et Papali* by John of Paris.

145. Cf. *Ibid.* (Carlyle), p. 116.

146. Hobbes, Thomas, *Leviathan*, ed. Richard Tuck. (Cambridge: Cambridge University Press, 1997), Chapter XVIII, p. 121.

147. While Hobbes and the Patriarchalists share an aversion for mixed or limited monarchy, it is interesting that Hobbes's contractualism in some respects is more opposed to the Patriarchalists then Hooker. For example, Hooker acknowledges the natural right of the father over his children, but denies that there is an analogy to be made about the non-consensual nature of government from the paternal example. Hobbes's contractualism is so thoroughgoing that for him even paternal authority is contractual. Thus he says, "[T]he right of Dominion by Generation is that, which the parent hath over his children and is called PATERNALL. And is not so derived from the Generation, as if therefore the parent had dominion over his child because he begat him; but from the childs consent, either expresse, or by other sufficient arguments declared." *Leviathan*, Chapter XX, p. 139.

148. Hobbes, *Leviathan*, Chap XVII, p. 120.

149. *Leviathan*, part I, chapter XIII, p. 90.

150. *Laws*, I. 10.1.

151. Hobbes, *Leviathan*, part II, chapt. XVII, p. 120. Noel Malcolm has some interesting comments on how Hobbes's quite original notion of the transferrence of

rights influenced other European thinkers such as Spinoza. Following this line of inquiry Malcolm suggests that in terms of understanding Spinoza's political ideas, it may be fruitful to examine the influence of Dutch "Hobbsians" like Johnan and Pieter de la Courts, rather than focusing primarily on Jewish religious influences.

152. Cf. Berenice Hamilton, p. 39.

153. *Ibid.*, p. 40.

154. *Ibid.*

155. *Laws*, VIII.2.7.

156. *Ibid.*, VIII.2.9–10 (italics added).

157. *Ibid.*, I.10.8.

158. *Ibid.*

159. *Ibid.*

160. *Ibid.*, VIII.2.11.

161. *Laws*, VIII. K. 2.5.

162. *Ibid.*, VIII.2.10.

163. *Ibid.*

164. *Ibid.*, VIII.2.8.

165. *Ibid.*

166. Thus Thompson writes in "The Philosopher of the Politic Society" that "Historically, the theory of social contract as it evolved in the late sixteenth and early seventeenth centuries was closely associated with the right of resistance and the doctrine of popular sovereignty. The majority of seventeenth century social contract theorists — whether they emphasized the idea of a contract of society or the older concept of a contract of government — were concerned to prove that political authority was ultimately derived from the people and that a ruler who broke the terms of the original contract might lawfully be resisted or deposed by his subjects. By contrast, Hooker was primarily interested in the idea of compact as a means of explaining how society and government came into existence, and it is hardly accidental that at no point in his argument does he draw the inference that because society originates in some kind of 'composition' or 'agreement' subjects are entitled to resist their rulers."

167. "It might be supposed that Hooker's argument at this point demonstrates his conservativism and his rejection of the resistance theories of the monarchomachs. This is unclear. Since contracts which did not infringe God's law could not be justly broken it was obvious that the people would be acting unjustly if they infringed the terms of the original contract with their king. It was not obvious, however, that they would be acting invalidly. A magistrate who condemns an innocent man is acting unjustly, but the condemnation remains valid until it is reversed by someone with authority superior to the magistrate's. Who in Hooker's theory, had authority superior to that of the whole commonwealth? Certainly the king did not have such authority, for Hooker took great pains to point out that his power was inferior to that of the people." J.P. Sommerville, "Richard Hooker, Hadrian Saravia, and the Advent of the Divine Right of Kings," *History of Political Thought*, IV (1983), p 234.

168. *Laws*, VIII.K.2.9–10.

169. *Ibid.*, I.10.5.

170. *Ibid.*, VIII,2.12.

171. *Ibid.*, VIII.K.2.13.

172. *Laws*, VIII.K.2.17 (italics added).

173. *Ibid.*

174. We have already seen this notion clearly enunciated in Bodin—viz. that the Crown is the source of law and not subject to the law. We have also seen it in Saravia, and it would be even further developed by seventeenth century Patriarchalists such as Filmer. The notion is closely related to the idea of law as command. To these writers it seemed evident that if law is the will of a superior toward an inferior it cannot be that the superior is bound to his own law, because it is nothing other then his will.

175. *Laws*, VIII.6.11.

176. *Ibid.*

177. After the discussion in chapter 5 of the meaning of the king's title as "head" of the Church and its inferiority to the headship of Christ, Hooker devotes chapter 5 to a discussion of the king's prerogative of calling ecclesiastical assemblies, arguing that this right belongs to the Roman Emperors in the ancient Church, and there is nothing repugnant to Scripture in it. In chapter 6 he discusses the Crown's authority to make laws but it is here he makes clear that the real source of such laws is the parliament of England together with the convocations of bishops, and the king only makes the law in the sense that his assent is required by the custom of the English constitution. In chapter 7 he argues for the right of the king to appoint bishops—parenthetically such lay investiture was a central issue in the middle ages. He argues for this prerogative on the grounds that the bishops are peers of the realm with seats in Parliament and just as the king creates titles of nobility, so does he have the right to invest bishops, however he calls on the king to exercise this right responsibly. In chapter 8 he discusses the right of the king to render judgment on ecclesiastical matters. His argument is based on the conviction that a finally binding authority is necessary to resolve cases of theological dispute. However he also warns kings that they are not specialists and so are not personally qualified to judge in matters of theology and that in the ordinary case theological judgments are to be rendered by the clergy. Hooker's general image is that the King acts only as executor of the law.

178. *Ibid.*, VIII.8.9. Parenthetically, chapter 9 of Book VIII concerns another special prerogative of the Crown namely his exemption from certain judicial penalties that might be imposed by ecclesiastical authority. Since these are of a somewhat technical nature, and do not concern our main themes we omit detailed discussion of them.

179. Cromartie also discusses most of these elements of Hooker's thought in specific reference to Locke.

Part II

Richard Hooker, John Locke, and The Great Debates of the Seventeenth Century

Chapter Four

The Tory Hooker and the Whig Hooker: Divergent Readings of the *Laws* in Stuart England

We will now move to consider the *legacy* of Richard Hooker in the development of modern constitutional thought. The main focus will be particularly his importance to political philosophy in seventeenth-century England. Certainly the most famous personage of English political philosophy to make extensive use of Richard Hooker's *Laws* in post-Restoration England was John Locke. A major part of our attention in Part II will therefore be devoted to understanding how Hooker's political philosophy informed Locke. It is not possible, however, to understand this question apart from the broader intellectual context of seventeenth-century England. To understand why Locke refers so frequently to Hooker's *Laws,* we must first understand the enormous position of veneration and authority that Hooker came to occupy by the later part of the seventeenth century. A proper introduction to our topic would therefore include a brief historical overview of the place of Hooker in Stuart and especially Restoration England.

This was a period of profound tumult for England, as Crown and Parliament clashed in a violent civil war. Much as Hooker had prophesied, rigorist Calvinism was transformed by choice and circumstance—and perhaps by the inexorable logic of its doctrine—from an ecclesiastical reform movement into a powerful and increasingly revolutionary faction. The Puritans by the first half of the seventeenth century had become a force ready, able, and willing to seize political power from the Crown in order to implement its reform project. The conflict therefore was as much about the struggle between Anglican conformists and Puritans, as about adjudicating the respective prerogatives of King and Parliament under the English constitution. After winning the support of Parliament, the famed military leader Oliver Cromwell led his "new model army" of Puritans to victory in the English civil war of 1642–1646. From this position of strength, Cromwell was able to overthrow the English monarchy, execute King Charles I, abolish the Anglican liturgy, and establish a Puritan protectorate from 1649–1660 that reorganized both the ecclesiastical and civil polity along Calvinist lines.

Needless to say, the breakdown of normal and orderly processes of government strained to their limit the traditional institutions that guarded the traditional order of English ecclesiastical and political government. This time of crisis was also the occasion of profound reflection on the origin and justification of political obligations. Both Royalists and Parliamentarians during and after the civil war developed theoretical arguments to support their positions on behalf of obedience or revolt against the Crown. The interest in exploring the foundations and origins of political obligation long survived the civil war and Cromwell's protectorate. The return of the monarchy in 1660 signaled the end of Puritan domination, but not of the need to justify either the political authority of the Crown, or the ecclesiastical polity of the Church of England. In spite of the mood of High Church Anglican triumphalism that followed the accession of Charles II, it remained necessary to produce a political and theological apologia for the conformist position on church government and liturgy. It was perhaps natural that Anglicans would canonize Richard Hooker, the most systematic defender of conformity, as the unofficial patron saint of Restoration England.

It is remarkable that throughout the seventeenth century, eminent men of opposing political allegiances employed Richard Hooker as a respected authority in ecclesiastical and political matters. Thus Robert Eccleshall is able to write: "In one sense it is misleading to suppose that the *Polity* belongs to a specific ideological tradition. It was used to justify parliamentary opposition to Charles I and James II, to uphold and condemn the Cromwellian regime, as well as to sustain more radical contractual arguments."[1] However, we ought not, on account of the many uses of Hooker, to presume that Hooker's thought was malleable to the point of incoherence. What is at play rather is that, in the *Laws of Ecclesiastical Polity*, Hooker strives to maintain a complex and delicate balance between various theological and political currents. In the partisanship of the seventeenth century, different factions were able to use—and often to misuse—different aspects of Hooker's system to their own advantage.

In terms of his ecclesiastical doctrine, Hooker is a strong defender of the existing government and ritual of the English church. Yet, as we have seen, Hooker has a political doctrine that argues against Patriarchalist and divine right theories of absolute monarchy. He stakes out clear positions on the consensual origins of government, the sovereignty of the community, the delegated power of the king, and the limitation of monarchical authority by divine law and civil law.

In the sixteenth-century context, the ecclesiological and political elements of Hooker's theory were relatively cohesive with each other. Crown and Parliament for the most part stood on the same side in upholding the Elizabethan settlement. In his ecclesiology, Hooker defends the broad competence of Parliament with the convocations of bishops over the rites and government of the Church (though restricted to "indifferent" matters not pertaining to salvation), while his political theory defends the broad competence of parliament (though restricted by divine law and the special prerogatives of the Crown) over the civil order. The Crown has a vital place as head of the body politic, but its powers were ultimately delegated by, and subordinate to, the body as a whole. It should be understood that Hooker's positions in this regard were rather conservative. Medieval political theory was generally averse to notions of absolutism, and Hooker's political doctrine, as we have seen, constituted for the most part a plausible interpretation and development of Thomistic political theory. In many particulars, his views shared much in common with other early modern developments of medieval political theory such as that of Suarez. It was the changing conditions of early modernity that gave rise to ascendance of centralized monarchies, and corresponding to this development, the effort to provide a theoretical defense of the new absolutism in notions of natural or divine right. In this context, figures such as Hooker (and Suarez) may be seen as traditionalists struggling against the modern trend toward more expansive state power, by appealing to an older, medieval tradition of a monarchy hedged in by custom and limited by divine, natural, and positive law. This idea was later to exercise a decisive influence on figures like Burke.

Hooker's work is characterized by a profound reverence for traditional English political and legal institutions. Hooker presents an image of harmony among the disparate elements within the English constitution. Parliament representing the community is related to the king, as the body to the head, each performing its proper function in relation to the whole. Yet, in the seventeenth century, the *modus vivendi* between crown and Parliament that existed in the Elizabethan era had broken down dramatically. Indeed, the whole period leading up to the civil war became more and more characterized by violent factionalism and partisanship between a party of "Cavalier" Royalists—mostly Anglicans—and a party of "Roundhead" Parliamentarians, largely Puritan. Parliament, in the period up to the civil war under increasing Puritan influence, sought not only to limit, but also even to overthrow Royal authority. Equally central to the Puritan agenda was to forcibly implement the Calvinist "purification" of the Anglican Church from those aspects in Church liturgy and government which derived from Roman Catholic provenance.

Richard Hooker was interesting to the Royalist party for a number of reasons. Hooker was the most sophisticated theologian which conformist Anglicanism had produced up to their time. Clearly he was also a passionate opponent of rigorist Calvinism, and a systematic defender of precisely those elements of Anglicanism that were attacked by their Puritan enemies. The controversial elements that the Puritans attacked and Hooker defended included the Episcopal government of the Church, many aspects of sacramental theology, the rejection of double predestination, and the retention of pre-Reformation liturgical reforms. Moreover, Hooker's temper was anti-revolutionary, having warned bitterly of the "seedsmen of rebellion" who preached revolt against established authority. Thus, Hooker was in many ways an ideal defender of the order that the Cavaliers sought to uphold.

Yet as we have seen, Hooker favored a crown limited by law, and referred to Parliament as that upon which "the very essence of all government within this Kingdom doth depend."[2] Royalists were anxious not only to preserve their power, but also to survive in the face of a violent rebellion fighting under the banner of parliamentary rule. It was thus natural that Royalists should emphasize the theological and ecclesiological aspects of Hooker's thought, more so than the political theory sketched out in Book VIII of the *Laws*. In political theory, the seventeenth century instead saw a wide variety of apologetics on behalf of a pure or unmixed monarchy. Some (like Sir Robert Filmer, who will be explored later) followed the lead of Saravia, in defending absolutism on Patriarchalist grounds, while others such as Hobbes deployed contractualism in defense of pure monarchy.

PURITANS, LAUDIANS, AND LATITUDINARIANS

Equally natural were those opponents of absolute monarchy before, during, and after the civil war, who saw fit to emphasize precisely those aspects of Hooker's political theory that sought to limit the prerogatives of the Crown. Thus, what emerges especially during the Restoration period is the construction of a "Tory" Hooker, and a "Whig" Hooker. Each side used for partisan advantage those aspects of Hooker's thought that cohered with their own ideas and purposes, while deliberately playing down those aspects that did not. The formation of these highly distinctive and partisan readings of Hooker has their early roots in the period of religious controversy leading up to the civil war. By the 1630s, at least three ecclesiastical factions had emerged: the Puritans, who hoped to implement a strict Calvinist reform of the Church; the Laudians, who insisted forcefully on conformity to the established liturgy and doctrine; and what we might describe as the Latitudinarian camp, who hoped a theological compromise could still be achieved, and civil war avoided. All three factions made some use of Hooker in support of one or another of their objectives. It was the ultimate failure of the Latitudinarian project that led to the polarization of English religion and politics into two contending factions.

Among the conformists of the early seventeenth century, the most prominent English religious leader in the period immediately preceding the civil war was William Laud, who became the Archbishop of Canterbury under Charles I in 1633. Possessed of strong "High Church" sensibilities, Laud was viewed as a crypto-Catholic by his Calvinist opponents. For his part, Laud was intolerant of Puritanism and was determined to put an end to the controversy over the government and ritual of the Church of England. Laud's chosen method was to enforce a stern ecclesiastical discipline that included extensive use of the Court of High Commission, the court that insured religious conformity through judicial penalties and to which was delegated the fullness of the Crown's ecclesiastical authority. Under Laud's direction, the High Commission proceeded to impose rigorous censorship against the printing of Puritan tracts under a law that required all books published in England to have the approval of an Archbishop. In some cases, authors of hostile pamphlets were cruelly punished, as in 1637 when the dramatist William Prynne, the doctor John Bastwick, and the clergyman Henry Burton, were publicly pilloried and their ears cut off.

Laud furthermore established his authority by the device of the Metropolitan Visitation, which gave to Laud a direct universal jurisdiction over every parish in England. Under this stewardship, the forms of worship were scrutinized to ensure their conformity with the official rubrics, and preachers suspected of Calvinist sympathies were silenced and/or removed. These measures aroused no little disquiet in the Puritan party; some of whom responded by seeking an exodus to the nascent English colonies in America, while others were motivated increasingly to consider open rebellion.

Although the *The Laws of Ecclesiastical Polity* was not as central to the theology of William Laud as to post-Restoration Anglicans, Hooker's hostility to Calvinist theology and defense of the duty of conformity against private judgment naturally commended itself to the aims of the Laudians. It is thus not surprising that Laud would refer to him as "that Worthy Author."[3] Surprisingly, a number of important supporters of the parliamentarian cause also looked upon Hooker with favor. One of the main Parliamentary leaders of the insurrection, Sir Henry Vane, was brought to trial for high treason following the Restoration. In his defense, Vane cited the *Laws* to make the argument that, under the natural law, sovereignty is vested in the community. Thus, in the case of the breakdown of normal political and legal procedures, Parliament was within its rights to assume power on behalf of the community.[4] Moreover, William Walwyn, one of the founding leaders of the Levellers,

named Hooker's *Ecclesiastical Polity* as part of his regular reading.[5] What attracted many of the anti-Royalists to Hooker were those aspects of his political theory that emphasized consent, the idea of the mixed monarchy where
royal authority is a delegated power from the community, and the idea of Parliament as the locus of law and government in the English Commonwealth.
Thus, Henry Parker—perhaps the single most significant political thinker on
the parliamentarian side—appealed to Hooker to promote his idea that sovereignty is vested in the community, and thus in a crisis, Parliament could reserve that sovereign authority to itself.[6] One of the most remarkable uses of
Hooker occurred after the Puritan victory in the civil war when John Hall, a
notable defender of Cromwell's protectorate, used the *Laws of Ecclesiastical
Polity* in support of precisely that Calvinist reformation of the English Church
that Hooker had labored to prevent.

> much more I might have alledged out of these authors I have pitched upon in
> justification of supream Magistrate's power in ordering the affairs of the
> Church: but these aleadged, being (as I conceive) plain and enough for satisfac-
> tion of any unprejudiced person, I have spared that labor: and also out of ease to
> the Reader, fortorn quotations of many famous men in our Church, concurring
> in the same judgement; and made most particular choice of *Mr. Hooker* and
> *Bishop Andrews.*[7]

Hall's argument was that, according to the *Laws,* Parliament under the secular power is competent to determine and even change the forms of government and worship of the Church of England. Hooker furthermore argued
(originally against the Calvinists!) that there was no right of private dissent
from the Ecclesiastical polity. Hall therefore argued that, since Parliament
was not in the hands of the Puritans and the monarchy abolished in favor of
Cromwell's protectorate, it was now the high church party that resisted the
Puritan reformation that was guilty of schism and sedition, and so they were
obliged on Hooker's logic to conform to the Calvinist order.[8]

Hooker's thought, however, had the most impact on a third party, which
was neither rigidly Laudian nor Puritan. Lord Falkland, secretary of state to
the King, gathered around him a circle of some of the most eminent figures
of seventeenth-century England at his home in Great Tew in Oxfordshire.
Many of these would later play central roles in the Restoration settlement.
Among those who gathered at Great Tew were: George Morely (Bishop of
Winchester); Edward Hydes (the first Earl of Clarendon) who, as Lord Chan-
cellor of Oxford, authored the Clarendon code to protect High Church An-
glicanism and was the author of a famous history of the English civil war;
Robert Sanderson, who would later serve as the Bishop of Lincoln during the
Restoration; John Selden, an important contractarian political philosopher;

and most likely Izaak Walton, who has already been mentioned as the author of a hagiographic biography of Richard Hooker.[9] The circle gathered at Great Tew held a variety of theological positions, but were all basically "Latitudinarian" in that they hoped to arrange a political and religious compromise between the Puritan and Laudian camps. They also shared a common reverence for Richard Hooker—indeed, Lord Falkland saw himself as Hooker's disciple.

In the period between late 1641 and 1642, the long simmering tensions between the Royalists and Puritans finally exploded. In November 1641, Parliament passed a petition of grievances against the King and Church, and on December 1, 1641, this *Great Remonstrance* of grievances was presented to King Charles I by a group of Parliament members led by John Pym. The remonstrance charged the bishops with being involved in "a malignant and pernicious design of subverting the fundamental laws and principles of government, upon which the religion and justice of this kingdom are firmly established."[10] It charged them with collaborating with Roman Catholics to subvert the Church and Kingdom and even with conspiring with foreign powers stating:

> The actors and promoters hereof have been . . . the Jesuited papists, who hate the laws . . . the Bishops, and the corrupt part of the clergy who cherish formality and superstition as . . . supports of their own ecclesiastical tyranny and usurpation.[11]

It demanded that the king restrict the Anglican bishops, and appoint a panel of Puritan-minded Protestants to oversee the reform of the Church. King Charles refused the petition on December 23, after which Pym called for a bill to give Parliament control of the army. In April 1642, Parliament issued nineteen propositions to the King, which under the circumstances amounted to an ultimatum. The propositions demanded, among other things, that power over major affairs be given to Parliament, that the education and marriages of the King's children be overseen by Parliament, and that the laws for repressing Roman Catholics be strictly enforced.

The circle at Great Tew played a profound role in crafting the King's response, entitled *His Majesty's Answer to the Nineteen Propositions of Both Houses of Parliament.* Many in the Great Tew Circle later became key figures during the Restoration who helped elevate Hooker to near sainthood. For this reason, it may be that the political conception portrayed in the reply owes much to Richard Hooker and his praise of the English constitution for providing for a mixed monarchy. We will recall Hooker's view that the form of government is determined originally by free consent of the community. In this regard, he praises the ancestors of the English constitution because it combines the advantages of a monarchy, while circumscribing the king's authority so as to prevent the degeneration of monarchy into tyranny. Thus, we have his statement that:

> I cannot but choose to commend highly their wisdom by whom the foundations of this Commonwealth have been laid, wherein though no manner person or cause be unsubject to the *King's* power, yet so is the power of the *King* over all and in all limited that unto all his proceedings the law itself is the rule.[12]

This preference for a mixed or limited monarchy is precisely what is sketched out in the *Answer*. Here the King praises the ancestors of the English constitution for creating a mixed constitution in which the potential pitfalls of the three "pure forms"—monarchy, aristocracy, or democracy—are to be avoided. Thus, he says that:

> Of the Government of this Kingdom . . . There being three kindes of Government amongst men, Absolute Monarchy, Aristocracy and Democracy, and all these having their particular conveniences and inconveniencies. The experience and wisdom of your Ancestors hath so moulded this out of a mixture of these, as to give to this Kingdom (as far as humane Prudence can provide) the conveniencies of all three, without the inconveniencies of any one, as long as the Balance hangs even between the three Estates, and they run jointly on in their proper Chanell . . . The ill of absolute Monarchy is Tyranny, the ill of Aristocracy is Faction and Division, the ills of Democracy are Tumults, Violence and Licentiousnesse.[13]

The potential for forms of government to degenerate is of course a staple of classical political philosophy, being discussed both in Plato's *Republic* and in Aristotle's *Politics*. What is interesting is the king's exposition of the tradition found in earlier writers like Fortescue and Hooker, that the English constitution found a way to wonderfully provide for the goods present in each of the three forms to be retained by its "mixed" constitution, which ably avoids the pitfalls of each form:

> The good of Monarchy is the uniting of a Nation under one Head to resist Invasion from abroad, and Insurrection at home: The good of Aristocracy is the Conjunction of Counsell in the ablest Persons of a State for the publike benefit: The good of Democracy is Liberty, and the Courage and Industry which Liberty begetts.[14]

However, he then argues that the Parliament was endeavoring to subvert the English constitution by usurping the prerogatives of the monarchy. We might recall Hooker's position on whether powers once granted by the body politic may be withdrawn:

May then a body politic withdraw in whole or in part that influence of dominion which passeth from it, if inconvenience doth grow thereby? It must be assumed that supreme governors will not in such case oppose themselves and be
stiff in detaining that, the use whereof is with public detriment. But surely without their consent I see not how the body should be able by any just means to help
itself, saving when Dominion doth escheat. Such things must be thought upon
beforehand, that power may be limited ere it be granted.[15]

Along similar lines, King Charles argues that Parliament already has sufficient power to check the monarchy from becoming absolute and arbitrary, and
now it is attempting to arrogate to itself even the legitimate authority given to
the King by the English system of laws:

Since therefore the Power Legally placed in both Houses is more sufficient to
prevent and restrain the power of Tyranny, and without the power which is now
asked from Us We shall not be able to discharge that Trust which is the end of
Monarchy, since this would be a totall Subversion of the Fundamentall Laws,
and that excellent Constitution of this Kingdom, which hath made this Nation so
many yeers both Famous and Happy to a great degree of Envie . . . We shall have
nothing left for Us.[16]

The final *Answer* of the Crown—*Nolumus Leges Angliae mutari*—was thus
not based on more modern theories of absolute or Patriarchal monarchy. It
was rather based on Hooker's conservative principle that powers once
granted by compact, law, and custom, and henceforth hallowed by long continuity ought not to be rescinded.

"THAT RICH AND INEXHAUSTIBLE ANTI-SECTARIAN PEN": HOOKER IN THE RESTORATION

Hooker's place in English ecclesiastical history reached its apogee with the
Restoration of the monarchy and correspondingly of traditionalist Anglicanism. Particularly, after the failure of the Savoy conference of 1661 to work out
a compromise between Presbyterian and Anglican positions, the Ecclesiastical policy of Charles II moved strongly in the direction of entrenching high
church Anglicanism. During this period, many figures that had been members
of Lord Falkland's Great Tew circle became intellectual leaders with a deter-
mining role in the direction of the religious and political life of the kingdom.

In 1645, the Puritans had banned the Anglican liturgy. In 1662, a new *Book
of Common Prayer* was issued, with a preface written by Bishop Sanderson
(a Great Tew veteran) that incorporated the central plank of Hooker's criticism of the Calvinists—that in addition to unchanging matters specified by

divine law in the Scriptures, there are *Adiaphora* or "things indifferent" to salvation, which are mutable and over which the authorities have legitimate jurisdiction. As Sanderson wrote:

> So on the other side, the particular Forms of Divine worship, and the Rites and Ceremonies appointed to be used therein, *being things in their own nature indifferent, and alterable*, and so acknowledged; it is but reasonable, that upon weighty and important considerations, according to the various exigency of times and occasions, such changes and alterations should be made therein, as to those that are in place of Authority should from time to time seem either necessary or expedient. Accordingly we find, that in the Reigns of several Princes of blessed memory since the Reformation, the Church, upon just and weighty considerations her thereunto moving, hath yielded to make such alterations in some particulars, as in their responsive times were thought convenient.[17]

Anglican conformity had no more able defender or capable theologian than Richard Hooker. We need not be surprised that in the Restoration ambience, no praise was too great if offered to the "Judicious Hooker." Hooker's place in the Restoration Church was more or less assured on the basis of: 1) his defense of the Church of England against Puritanism on a broad variety of fronts, but especially in regards to "things indifferent" and 2) his position on the need to defer to the corporate wisdom of the Church as opposed to the Puritan appeal to dissent based on private judgment. Hooker became the doctor of the Restoration, as seen in the many examples of lavish praise heaped upon his life and works. John Barbon[18] lauded him as "the profound and sweet-breath'd Mr. Hooker," and "That rich and *inexhaustible* anti-sectarian *Pen*."[19] Meric Casaubon[20] earnestly promoted the reading of Hooker's writings as among the most valuable of works:

> I would persuade men that have been buyers of books these 15, or 16 yeares, to burn one halfe at least, of those books they have bought . . . and then betake themselves to the reading of *Hooker*: not doubting, but by the time they had read him once, or twice over accurately they would thank me for my advice, but God much more, that put it into their hearts to follow it.[21]

Thomas Fuller wrote that the works of Richard Hooker were "prized by all, save such who out of ignorance cannot, or envy will not understand it."[22] Hooker's work was soon treated as an Anglican *Summa contra Gentiles* that had established the case for conformity beyond all refutation. John Gauden, in his own apology for the Church of England, *Ecclesiae Anglicanae Suspira*, wrote in 1659 that:

> Mr. Richard Hooker (one of the ablest *Pens* and best *Spirits* that ever England employed or enjoyed) abundantly examined every feature and dress of the

Church of England, asserting it by calm, clear and unanswerable demonstrations of reason and *Scripture*, to have been very far from having anything unchristian or uncomely.[23]

Gauden claims that Hooker had foretold the dreadful consequences that would follow were the Puritans ever to get power—a warning he feels was vindicated in the years of Cromwell's protectorate when the episcopacy of the Anglican Church was overthrown and the Anglican liturgy suppressed. Referring to the Puritans, he says that they were those:

> Whose wrathful menaces the *meekness* and *wisdome* of that good man [Hooker] forsaw, and in his Epistle foretold, would be very *fierce and cruel,* if once they got power answerable to their *prejudices* against the *Church of England*; which he fully proved to differ no more from the Primitive temper and prudence, then was either lawfull, convenient or necessary.

For writing an early account of the life of Hooker, Gauden was rewarded by the King, acceding to the Bishopric of Exeter.

Hooker was appreciated for his eloquent defense of the Anglican liturgy. Anthony Sparrow in his frequently reprinted gloss on the *Book of Common Prayer* refers to "the incomparable Hooker."[24] We also have George Masterson, in his 1661 work, *The Spiritual House in its Foundation, Materials, Officers and Discipline*, making the statement that Hooker had already refuted all attacks on the Book of Common Prayer. Along similar lines, Irenaus Freeman, addressing himself to Non-Conformists who attacked the Anglican liturgy, wrote that "All they write is no answer, till they undertake *Hooker's Ecclesiastical Polity* in the full body."[25] Claims about the nearly canonical nature of Hooker's opinions extended not merely to his views on liturgical issues, but also to his views regarding Church government. Edward Stillingfleet, in his work *Irenicum*, referred to the changeable character of the government of the Church as having been proved by Richard Hooker. "Those who please but to consult this the *third* book of learned and judicious Mr. *Hooker's Ecclesiastical Polity* may see the mutability of the form of Church Government largely asserted and fully proved."[26]

Hooker's role as the doctor of the Anglican Church was paralleled by his role as Saint. Thus, the Archbishop of Canterbury, Gilbert Sheldon, upon his accession, authorized the hagiographic account of Hooker's life by Izaak Walton.[27] Nonetheless despite Hooker's central place in the Restoration Church, it must be said that Hooker's specifically *political* doctrines were viewed with a certain diffidence by the Royalists of the Restoration. Hooker had argued for a mixed monarchy against theories of natural or divine right, and vested the source of sovereignty in the whole body politic rather than the person of the King. We have already seen how some of these ideas were used by figures like John Hall and Henry Vane to justify the rebellion. The question for the emerging Tory party of the Restoration then was how to "manage" the potentially dangerous interpretations of Hooker's political constitutionalism, while retaining what they found essential from his ecclesiology.

There were essentially three strategies for doing this. The first was to deny the veracity of the later books of the *Laws* in which his political theory is principally contained. This is precisely what, for example, Izaak Walton did in his *Life*. The theory that parts of the *Laws* were fraudulent was given additional credence when the Royalist historian Sir William Dugsdale claimed that Hooker's remark in Book VIII that the King was *major singulis, universis minor* was a later interpolation, and warned against the use of Gauden's biography since, unlike Walton, he regarded Book VIII as authentic.[28]

A second strategy was to place central emphasis on Hooker's polemic against private judgment in the Church. The idea being that by focusing on the duty of obedience and conformity to the civil power in religious matters, any subversive implications of Hooker's text could be ignored or mollified. For example, in a work by Samuel Parker in 1671 (*A Discourse of Ecclesiastical Polity*), Parker wrote against the absurdity of non-conformists quoting Hooker to their purpose:

> How long has his [Hooker's] incomparable book of *Ecclesiastical polity* bid shameful defiance to the whole [nonconformist] Party, and yet never found any so hardy as to venture upon an Encounter . . . the Book it self is as full and demonstrative a Confutation of their Cause, as the matters contained in it: i.e. 'tis Unanswerable.[29]

Another salient example can be found in John Nalson's work *The Countermine*.[30] Nalson characteristically praises Hooker effusively as "the Learned and Judicious Mr. Hooker"[31] when dealing with points of Church polity, yet mocks the idea of the subordination of the King to the community that was a central element of Hooker's political philosophy. Interestingly in Nalson's sarcastic screed, he uses Hooker's own formulation of the matter without naming Hooker:

> Have you never heard, that a King is *Major Singulis* but *Minor Universis*. A little better man then *Dick*, or *Tom* or *Will.*, if you take them by themselves in a frock with a cart-whip: but by your Majesties leave, good sir King, you are not so good a man as Mr. *Multitude*.[32]

Likewise, Clarendon, who strongly attacked Hobbes's contract-based theory of government for its individualist biases, commended Hooker in his *History of the Rebellion* for warning against the dangers of private judgment.[33] Eccleshall sees in Clarendon's use of Hooker an embryonic manifestation of the Burkean view of English society: a spiritual corporation developing organically from an ancestral constitution, as opposed to Hobbes's emphasis on the artificiality of society and the natural rights of the individual.

A third strategy to domesticate Hooker's political theory was to try and counter or reconcile it with political theories favoring a pure monarchy in which sovereignty is vested exclusively in the person of the King. Some Restoration theorists like Dudley Diggs adopted the contract-based argument of Hobbes in support of the King's authority. That is to say, the political obligation to obey the King is founded on the transference of rights to a sovereign, after which there is no longer any right of private dissent.[34] However, perhaps the most historically influential Tory tract of the time was Sir Robert Filmer's work, *Patriarcha*. Although Filmer died in 1653, his most famous work was not published until 1680. Filmer presents his views as broadly compatible with those of Hooker through several unctuous references to him. Yet, the whole tenor of the argument in *Patriarcha* is to promote precisely the Patriarchal theory of government that Hooker had sought to discredit. In essence, Filmer praises Hooker while proceeding to covertly but systematically assail his entire political doctrine by attacking those positions of Suarez and Bellarmine which were identical to Hooker's. Because of Filmer's importance to this discussion, we will provide separate treatment of the *Patriarcha* elsewhere (cf. chapter 11). Part of Filmer's importance is what occurred by way of reaction. The idiosyncratic use of Hooker by Filmer provided an occasion for the emergence of a distinct "Whig" interpretation of Hooker.

One of the first examples of this was in the work of Edward Gee, prior to the publication of the *Patriarcha*, but well after other Patriarchalist tracts of Filmer became well known. Gee's main work, *The Divine Right and Originall of the Civill Magistrate from God* (1658), uses Hooker to argue against Filmer's patriarchalism. While Filmer saw political structures on the model of the family, where there is a natural subjection to the rule of the father, Gee holds that, according to Hooker, "Power is originally in God, and from him passeth by means of the people's consent to the magistrate."[35] On this basis, Gee held that Hooker's theory would justify the deposition of rulers who usurped their authority.

Algernon Sidney, in his *Discourses Concerning Government*, made a similar argument claiming that Filmer had utterly distorted Hooker. Citing specific places where Hooker had specifically attacked the patriarchal theory of the origins of politics, Sidney's purpose was to highlight the dangers of unchecked or pure monarchy to degenerate into tyranny, and used Hooker for this purpose.[36] In 1690, William Atwood published his work, *The Fundamental*

Constitution of the English Government, again defending consensual government and attacking Filmer's use of Hooker as ludicrous:

> Many have cited the authority of the *Judicious Hooker* till it is thread-bare, to prove
> that it is impossible there should be a lawful Kingly Power which is not mediately,
> or immediately, from the Consent of the People where 'it's exercised.[37]

Likewise, James Tyrrell, in his *Bibliotheca Politica*, uses Hooker to defend
his consent theory and defense of mixed monarchy. We see therefore the development in England of a specific school of "Whig Hookerians" by the latter part of the seventeenth century. Originally, they had formed to combat the
Patriarchalist theory of government put forth by Sir Robert Filmer, who tried
to make Hooker compatible with a pure or absolute monarchy. It is within this
specific polemical context that we must understand the most historically important text to develop the Whig interpretation of Hooker—John Locke's *Two
Treatises of Government*.

THE RISE OF PATRIARCHALISM: SIR ROBERT FILMER
AND THE CHALLENGE TO THE CONSTITUTIONAL IDEA
IN STUART ENGLAND

Patriarchalism can be defined as the effort to understand political society as a
natural community, by means of symbols of another natural community—the
family. For Patriarchalists, each person is born a natural subject of political authority in precisely the same way as a child is born a natural subject of parental,
and specifically paternal authority. Patriarchalism thus envisioned a natural hierarchy, which was mirrored by the hierarchical relations of the social order it
defended. The defense of natural orders of privilege and hierarchy would soon
find itself attacked if not swept away by the reconceptualization of nature, and
the leveling social movements of modernity. And yet considered as an account
of the nature of political obligation, patriarchalism was an apology for a new and
characteristically *modern* form of political governance—royal absolutism. In the
political sense, the passage from the medieval to the early modern world was
marked by the ascent of the national monarchy. In theory, the politics of Latin
Christendom was based not on the nation-state, but on an ideal of a Christian
community, united under two swords—the temporal sword wielded by the Holy
Roman Emperor and the spiritual sword held by the Roman pontiff—both co-
operating to order human affairs to the glory of God and the salvation of souls.
In practice, the papacy and empire frequently had different conceptions of the respective prerogatives of the imperial and priestly power, and neither was able to
assert the kind of effective power that the theory maintained.

Moreover, we must recall that the political structure of medieval Europe was generally quite decentralized, with much of the military and political power being held by feudal lords, who in exchange for homage and vassalage to the king, enjoyed wide discretion in the governance of their fiefs. Thus the pragmatic organization of medieval political life, rested on a delicate balance of power between the kings, the feudal princes, and the Roman Catholic Church. So far from being an absolute ruler, the medieval king was often a relatively weak figure since he depended upon the feudal princes for military service, and so could not exert effective control over much of what theoretically was his realm. In addition to the practical limits to royal authority, medieval political theory had a marked aversion to absolutism, as we have seen in Aquinas's assertion that the unjust law is an act of violence that does not bind in conscience, that the ruler is subject to the directive (though not the coercive) power of the law, and that the deposition of a tyrant by the community can be lawful.

Between the late fifteenth and the seventeenth century however, monarchs in Spain, France, and England went quite far in centralizing power. They circumvented the feudal system, by creating professional national armies, and hiring civil servants to govern the realm. Systematically, the kings endeavored to assert their authority over the feudal princes, and curtailed the traditional prerogatives of the lords. Likewise the kings also asserted their authority over the Church—the high point being in England when King Henry proclaimed himself to be by law supreme in both ecclesiastical and civil affairs (though quite similar "Caesarist" tendencies were found for example with the case of Gallicanism in France).

Certainly by the seventeenth century, an entirely new situation had emerged in which the kings of nations like England and France ruled in a centralized manner unimaginable in earlier centuries. A regime that wishes to endure must rely not only on political power but also on moral suasion. Regimes that are seen as lacking in legitimacy, or engaged in usurpation, tend to be unstable in the best case. That being the case, it was necessary for supporters of royal absolutism to construct some mode of theoretical defense: an apologia, in other words, for the new prerogatives claimed for kings. A problem arose, however, because many of the available political theories (developed by early modern thinkers from medieval antecedents) were markedly hostile to the idea of absolutism. Early modern constitutionalism as developed by figures like Francisco Suarez and Richard Hooker, offered a broad and cogent account of political life and one that presupposed sharp limits to the legitimate exercise of political power. As noted in the introduction (cf. chapter 1), constitutionalism provided a theory of *law* in which the actions of rulers were seen as circumscribed by divine, natural, and positive law; a theory of *sovereignty* in which the lawful power to govern was seen as being vested first in the whole community rather then the prerogative of any particular individual; and a theory of the origins of *political obligation*, seeing the right of some to rule over others as rooted in an original act of consent.

Early modern constitutionalism also had the advantage that it could claim a highly traditional pedigree, and so could present itself as in basic continuity with a conception of a just political order sanctioned by habit and custom. Although there are important and new elements in early modern constitutionalism, it presented itself—quite plausibly—as a homogenous development from its medieval antecedents. Thus both Catholics like Suarez and Anglicans like Hooker drew upon a common heritage, particularly that of Thomism. Both of them accepted the Thomistic hierarchy of eternal, divine, natural, and positive law, and its corollary: that there is a moral order anterior to the human legislator to which the laws promulgated by human rulers like kings must conform. Suarez and Hooker put perhaps more emphasis on the community as the original locus of sovereignty than Aquinas; yet we find passages where St. Thomas presupposes that since the law is directed to the common good, law is only legitimate if promulgated by the community, or by one standing as representative of the community.[38]

Hooker and Suarez were arguably most original in their account of the origins of political obligation in consent; an idea nowhere explicitly found in Aquinas. Included in the conception is the notion of agreement or compact as the origin of political society, and thus there seems to be a much clearer notion of the distinction between (what we would call) the state and society in Hooker and Suarez. But since Aquinas himself provides no developed account of the origins of particular forms, Suarez and Hooker could argue from a Thomistic foundation that while society is natural, the particular political regime a community wishes to establish is a matter of convention. The idea of a *pactum subjectionis*, in which a community freely subjects itself to political rule, had at all events a respectable pedigree among not a few medieval thinkers.[39]

The formidable task confronting political theorists who wished to defend royal absolutism then was to answer the powerful case made by constitutionalism. This was necessarily to demand answering it in terms that would provide equally compelling accounts of: first, the question of *sovereignty* within a commonwealth, and; second the question regarding the origins and justification of the *political obligation*. In other words, from where derives the right of the ruler to rule, and the duty of his subjects to obey.

By the late sixteenth and seventeenth centuries, a *number* of defenses of absolute or "pure" monarchy were in play. We have already seen an early example of one kind of defense of absolutism in Bodin's *Les Six Livres de la Republique* (1576), which argues that it is the nature of sovereignty to be indivisible, and arguing within a Roman law tradition of *Princeps Legibus Solutus*. That is to say that as the sovereign *source* of law, he is absolved of any duty toward the law. Within the English context, the most famous defense of such absolutism is Hobbes's *Leviathan* of 1651, which we have already mentioned. One point, on which Strauss's analysis is insightful, is that Hobbes's theory seems to rest on a radical reconceptualization of the place of *nature*. Although constitutionalists like Hooker are prepared to allow that nature is insufficient to prescribe a particular polity, still there are modes of human community (like the family and society) which, for Hooker are natural; moreover, the law of reason can be discerned from nature, and this would bind man in man's natural condition even prior to political life. We have already seen that, for Hobbes, even the authority of parents within a household is a product of convention and consent rather then nature,[40] and that the "natural" condition of man is one in which there is no moral law to guide him.[41]

The natural condition therefore is one of equality, but also of equal misery since the state of nature is one of war given the lack of any protection against the natural selfishness and rapacity of other men. Nature therefore is unable even to supply the inclinations that lead to society—which is also a product of artifice. Only by transferring rights to a single will therefore is the minimal level of order necessary to secure human existence possible. Here absolutist conclusions are arrived at from thoroughly individualist and contractarian premises.

Although a Patriarchalist like Sir Robert Filmer would arrive at broadly similar conclusions to Hobbes about the need for an absolute and even arbitrary monarchy, the philosophical foundations on which it rested were diametrically opposed. Hobbes saw both society and the family as artificial constructions based originally on mechanisms of contract and consent. Filmer saw rule within the political, social, and the familial as resting on hierarchies within the order of nature, and denied that there was such a thing as a prepolitical condition.

THE NATURE AND HISTORY OF PATRIARCHALISM

In one of the most in-depth inquiries into the development of patriarchalism, *The Authoritarian Family and Political attitudes in 17th Century England*, Gordon Schochet notes that patriarchalism was in many ways a reaction to the new view of nature found in Hobbes and other thinkers. The "attack on nature" was a salient feature of early modern political thought:

> The conflict between nature and convention has been a part of a search for justifying standards that is among the salient features of political philosophy. The

appeal to nature is particularly congenial to political philosophy that looks to origins for justification because nature reveals the beginnings of civil society that are so important to such a theory. Prior to the reformation, naturalism was relatively unquestioned as a political standard . . . in Luther and especially Hobbes the attack on nature showed that it was incoherent, contradictory, anarchic, and dangerous . . . thus any order found among human beings had to be the result of imposition, that is, of convention. Order necessarily involves the will. It is in this context that Hobbes' view of the household as a conventional order becomes especially significant.[42]

Filmer's position was that the family was the *most* natural form of society, and the best way of understanding king's rule over a commonwealth was in terms of the father's rule over his household. Just as a child is born by nature subject to paternal authority, so is the member of a commonwealth born by nature subject to regal authority. If the natural state of man is not one of freedom, but one of subjection to political authority the whole logic of Hobbsian contractarianism with its corresponding notions of the state of nature as anarchy, the social contract, and the consensual and artificial origins of political society are overthrown. It is not surprising that Sir Robert Filmer (in spite of sharing Hobbes's preference for absolutism) launched a broad ranging attack on Hobbes in his *Observations Concerning the Originall of Government* (1652).

The idea of defending royal authority on the basis of nature rather then artifice was one that had broad appeal. Although in our own time, owing to the influence of contractarian political thought, Hobbes's *Leviathan* is thought of as a classic of political thought, in the seventeenth century the patriarchal account enjoyed wide favor as a way of defending the absolutist theory of government without adopting the quite radical implications of Hobbsian philosophy. As such, it was patriarchalist rather then contractarian defenses of absolutism which were dominant in the royalist world in this period, and indeed "Filmer's books became the backbone of the Tory ideology when they were republished in the 1680s."[43] It is not surprising then that the leading parliamentarian and later Whig theorists (like Locke) devoted so much time to refuting the patriarchalist thesis.

So what is patriarchalism? In essence, it is the view that associates the regal authority of the king (*regia potestas*) with the paternal authority of the father (*patria potestas*). Schochet distinguishes at least three forms of patriarchalism.[44] The first kind, *Ideological Patriarchalism*, sees an *analogy* between political and paternal authority and sees the father image as an appropriate one in describing the king, given the combination of authority with care and solicitude by which the just king governs his people. This type of patriarchalist symbolism is surely of venerable origin. Thus, we might recall Aquinas in his *De Regimine Principium* writing that: "The head of a household on the other hand, is not called king but father. Even so there is a certain similarity between the two cases, and kings are sometimes called the fathers of their people."[45] Aquinas's thesis that there was government in the condition of original justice was also important for Patriarchalists, since it suggested that the search for some pre-political "state of nature" was inherently illusory. Moreover, both Catholic and Protestant catechetical books down to our own time frequently place the duty to obey the political authorities under the heading of the commandment to "honor thy father and mother," thus seeing obedience to rulers in the analogy.

Second, *Anthropological Patriarchalism* is basically a *descriptive* account of the origins of government, without necessarily any value judgment as to the goodness or justice of patriarchal government. Aristotle provides an early version of this kind of patriarchalism. Thus, in the first book of the *Politics*, Aristotle describes the origins of politics as natural and rooted in the coming together of families ruled over by fathers:

> The family is the association established by nature for the supply of men's everyday wants, and the members of it are called by Charondas 'companions of the cupboard,' and by Epimenides the Cretan, 'companions of the manger.' But when several families are united, and the association aims at something more than the supply of daily needs, the first society to be formed is the village. And the most natural form of the village appears to be that of a colony from the family, composed of the children and grandchildren, who are said to be suckled 'with the same milk.' And this is the reason why Hellenic states were originally governed by kings; because the Hellenes were under royal rule before they came together, as the barbarians still are. Every family is ruled by the eldest, and therefore in the colonies of the family the kingly form of government prevailed because they were of the same blood. As Homer says: 'Each one gives law to his children and to his wives' . . . When several villages are united in a single complete community, large enough to be nearly or quite self-sufficing, the state comes into existence, originating in the bare needs of life, and continuing in existence for the sake of a good life. And therefore, if the earlier forms of society are natural, so is the state, for it is the end of them, and the nature of a thing is its end.[46]

Aristotle, moreover, describes government within the family in clearly Patriarchal terms, that is to say, conditioned by a natural hierarchy in which the wife and children are subject to the authority of the father. Thus, he says that "Again, the male is by nature superior, and the female inferior; and the one rules, and the other is ruled; this principle, of necessity, extends to all mankind."[47] The rule of the husband over his wife however differs from his paternal authority over his children, in that the subjection of the children to the father is more complete:

> Of household management we have seen that there are three parts—one is the rule of a master over slaves, which has been discussed already, another of a

father, and the third of a husband. A husband and father, we saw, rules over wife and children, both free, but the rule differs, the rule over his children being a royal, over his wife a constitutional rule. For although there may be exceptions to the order of nature, the male is by nature fitter for command than the female, just as the elder and full-grown is superior to the younger and more immature.[48]

Moreover, Aristotle's description of man's natural condition as political would support the major position that patriarchalists would want to uphold against contractualism—namely, that government is rooted in nature rather than convention ("Now, that man is more of a political animal than bees or any other gregarious animals is evident").[49] Yet, in a number of ways, Aristotle's position differs markedly from that of the English patriarchalists. Whereas the latter tended to *identify* the rule of kings with the rule of fathers, the tenor of Aristotle's theory of politics is to *distinguish* them. Thus, he says that:

> Some people think that the qualifications of a statesman, king, householder, and master are the same, and that they differ, not in kind, but only in the number of their subjects. For example, the ruler over a few is called a master; over more, the manager of a household; over a still larger number, a statesman or king, as if there were no difference between a great household and a small state. The distinction which is made between the king and the statesman is as follows: When the government is personal, the ruler is a king; when, according to the rules of the political science, the citizens rule and are ruled in turn, then he is called a statesman. *But all this is a mistake; for governments differ in kind*, as will be evident to any one who considers the matter according to the method which has hitherto guided us.[50]

The English patriarchalists wanted to say that the *regia postestas* was similar to the *pater potestas* in being monarchical. Yet this is precisely the opposite of Aristotle's point, which is that political rule is *unlike* paternal rule in that it is *not* monarchical. His conception of political rule is one where ideally there is a rule of law and not of men, and where the subjects of political rule are free men rather then children:

> The previous remarks are quite enough to show that the rule of a master is not a constitutional rule, and that all the different kinds of rule are not, as some affirm, the same with each other. For there is one rule exercised over subjects who are by nature free, another over subjects who are by nature slaves. The rule of a household is a monarchy, for every house is under one head: whereas constitutional rule is a government of freemen and equals.[51]

Aristotle's patriarchalism then is primarily a genetic account of how political society arose, not a claim that the authoritarian rule of the father is the ideal symbol for political governance. Significantly, the distinction in Aristotle between paternal rule over a household, and political rule over a society, is important for constitutionalists like Hooker and Suarez, who working within a broadly Aristotelian tradition make an emphatic distinction between domestic or "economical" authority of the father, and the consensually based authority of the king.

The final form of patriarchalism that Schochet discusses is *Moral Patriarchalism* and it is this form that is of the most interest to this discussion. Here, patriarchalism is more than a merely descriptive account of how governments came into being. We have rather a *prescriptive* account of sovereignty and the origins of political obligation. In other words, it is not merely that *de facto* the first kings were fathers, but that members of a commonwealth *ought* to view themselves as subject to kings in the same manner as children to their fathers. This type of patriarchalism sees the rule of kings as both natural and having a divine sanction. It is difficult to find examples of this form of patriarchalism before the sixteenth century.

In Elizabethan England, we have already seen that Hooker's contemporary, Hadrian Saravia, had a fully developed patriarchalist thesis in which all the elements of later versions of patriarchalism (like Filmer's) were already present. Saravia denies that there was ever a "state of nature" in which men were not subject to political authority—every man is born into a natural condition of political subjection, just as children are born into subjection to their parents. Saravia seems to inaugurate the tradition of annexing to patriarchalism a *scriptural politics*—something characteristic of the English Patriarchalist tradition. The objective of figures like Saravia and later Filmer here is to show both that *de facto* there never was a pre-political state of nature, and therefore that the state of being governed by kings was both natural and divinely sanctioned. Since the Bible was understood as both the Word of God and (especially in an age before modern Biblical criticism) a literal account of the historical record, the Scriptural politics of the patriarchalists had considerable power. For Saravia, Adam is presented in Scripture as both the father and king of the human race, and is given monarchical dominion. Thus, Saravia saw not merely an *analogy* between royal and paternal authority, rather the claim is that from the first the two modes of authority were *identical.* This paternal and monarchical authority descended from Adam by right of primogeniture to his descendents, and then at the time of Noah, the monarchical government of the world was divided among his three sons, indicating that the will of the father could also transfer paternal authority as he wished. This power in the period after the flood was given to the patriarchs who were both the fathers of their people, and their rulers. Only in the case of God's special election, or the express will of the holder of paternal authority was the

ordinary process of kingly and paternal rule descending from father to eldest
son by natural generation suspended.

Saravia is an important—if exceptional—example of a fully developed patriarchalism being put forth in an Elizabethan context. This type of position
was already significant enough for figures like Hooker to attempt to refute.
Yet it was not until King James I that the Patriarchalist position began to
emerge as a standard position. No king in European history was more forth-
right in putting forth the claims of royal absolutism; it thus is perhaps not surprising that while the author of *The True Law of Free Monarchies* (1598)[52]
reigned, patriarchalism found a hospitable environment to flourish. Shochet
points out that in his own tract, James's patriarchalism is more ideological
then moral. James employs paternal symbolism in stating that upon coronation, the King becomes father to his people, such that he is bound to care and
provide for them, as they like dutiful children are subject to his benevolent
rule.[53] Yet the relationship between paternal and regal authority in the *True
Law* is basically allegorical—no claim is made for example that the King receives authority by a literal inheritance from Adam's paternal rule. Yet under
the aegis of King James the equation of paternal and regal rule became far
more common. A 1615 treatise attributed to Richard Mocket entitled *God and
the King*[54] states that: "There is a stronger and higher bond of duety betweene
children and the Father of their countrie, then the fathers of private Families.
These procure the good only of a few, and not without the assistance and protection of the other, who are the common foster-fathers of thousands of families, of whole Nations and Kingdomes, that they may live under them an
honest and peacable life."[55] Mocket moreover invokes the common catechetical practice of placing duty to king under the precept to *honor thy father and
mother.*[56]

Schochet goes on to point out a number of cases in the early seventeenth
century in which the catechetical placing of the duty to one's rulers under the
heading of the commandment to honor one's parents were extended into legal usages. Thus, Edward Coke, the chief justice, stated:

> "within that Commandment of the Moral Law, *Honor Parte* . . . doubtless doth
> extend to him that is *pater patria.*" The *Convocation book of 1606* approved by
> the convocation of Bishops under the leadership of John Overall, was informed
> by a rather robust patriarchalist argument, in which Adam's authority as father
> of the human race is referred to as *"potestas Regias."*[57] This authority was
> passed down by natural generation to Adam's descendents, so that by the time
> of Noah: "Touching this patriarchal, or in effect regal government of Noah, there
> is more expressed in the Scriptures, then there was before the flood, of the
> power and authority of Adam, or of any of the chief fathers and rulers that were
> descended from him."[58]

Admittedly, Schochet may be somewhat overstating the case in his claim that the *Convocation Book* "provides the earliest example of the substitution of the patriarchal account of political origins for the anthropological underpinnings of populism." In support of this claim, Schochet refers to where John Overall writes that:

> If anyone shall affirm That men at the first, without all good education, or civility ran up and down in the woods and fields, as wild creatures, resting themselves in caves and dens acknowledging no superiority one over another . . . and that consequently all civil power, jurisdiction and authority was first derived from the people, and disordered multitude . . . he doth greatly err.[59]

Yet we have seen that almost identical language existed in Saravia who wrote over a decade earlier.[60] The essential point is nevertheless correct—Overall, like Saravia, was concerned to deny that there was any pre-political condition of man, and thus that the origins of political obligation were consensual. Although the *Convocation* was not published at the time due to the opposition of King James, its approbation by the convocation is evidence that patriarchalist thought was already a firmly entrenched line of thought among the English elite.

Schochet cites numerous other sources from the rule of King James that testify to the growing influence of the thesis that paternal and regal power are essentially one—thus, the Bishop of Winchester, George Carleton, wrote: "no man can conceive of any other gouernment of a family, then by one whom God and nature made *patrum familias* . . . and what is a King by nature, but the father of a great family? And what is the father of a familie by nature but a little king?"[61] Likewise, in Richard Field's 1606 text, *Of the Church*, there are passages that endeavor to uphold the thesis that Adam was a father, priest, and king. The debate on patriarchalism would become more important by the 1640s when England would move toward civil war, in a situation where the extent of the king's prerogatives was one of the most divisive issues.

From the beginning, the opposition to patriarchalism and advocacy of constitutionalism came from two sources—Roman Catholics and parliamentarians. Since Puritan anti-Catholicism often influenced the English Parliament in the seventeenth century, the conjunction of Roman Catholicism with parliamentarian populism in the polemical writings of the Patriarchalists may seem paradoxical, yet quite consistently Catholics are identified as a source of opposition to the theory of absolute monarchy. Thus, the most important Patriarchalist would write in *The Anarchy of a Limited or Mixed Monarchy* that:

> Since the growth of the new doctrine of the limitation and mixture of monarchy, it is most apparent that monarchy hath been crucified between two thieves, the

Pope and the people . . . indeed the only point of Popery is the alienating and withdrawing of subjects from their obedience to their prince, to raise sedition and rebellion.[62]

THE OPPONENTS OF PATRIARCHALISM

Sir Robert Filmer, as we shall see, would also direct many of the arguments of the *Patriarcha* specifically against Suarez and Cardinal Robert Bellarmine.[63] The same views are put forth by other Patriarchalists of the period. George Carleton would write, "some of the Pope's flatterers, as others also to open a wide gappe to rebellions, have written that the power of gouernment by the law of nature is in the multitude."[64] Somewhat later, John Spellman, a prominent royalist and patriarchalist, inveighed against the thesis that government has its origin in the consent of the community by saying that: "were we shie of *Jesuitism* as well as of *Popery* we would not with so little examination receive opinion which we know had their first hatchlings in the Schoole of the Jesuite."[65] Roman Catholic thinkers on the continent such as Suarez attacked the theses of English patriarchalism for a number of reasons. As scholastics, they continued the medieval tradition of suspicion toward absolutism and, as we have seen, Suarez explicitly attacks patriarchalism in favor of the notion the whole community originally held sovereignty, and that the origins of government were consensual. Moreover, since the persecuted Catholics in England were imperiled by claims of royal power in the form of the Act of Supremacy, they had little incentive to support the new claims made for the unlimited power of monarchy. Finally, the theory of the communitarian sovereignty and consensual origins of government served the purpose of contrasting the human and conventional origins of the secular authority with the divine origins of ecclesiastical authority vested in the Roman pontiff.

The second source of opposition to patriarchalism in the first half of the seventeenth century was of course among those who upheld the parliamentarian cause. For those who held that Parliament rather than the Crown was the locus of authority, the view that the community held sovereignty rather then the king was naturally more congenial to their ends. As we have already mentioned, among the most important of those political thinkers who supported the doctrine of parliamentary supremacy was Henry Parker. Parker explicitly rejected any attempt to identify regal and paternal authority. His reasoning is that unlike the father's relationship to the child, the relationship between the king and his subjects is reciprocal:

The father is more worthy then the son in nature, and the son is wholly a debtor to the father, and can by no merit transcend his dutie . . . yet the same holds not in the relation between King and subject for its more due in policie, and more strictly to be chalenged, that the King should make happy the people, then the People make glorious the King.[66]

Among Parker's opponents, two have already been mentioned: Sir John Spelman and Dudley Diggs, both of whom argued against the notion that the community or the people were the original source of government. Spelman employed the typical patriarchalist thesis that from the time of Adam's coronation in Eden, the plentitude of paternal and regal authority have descended from father to son by divine sanction rather than popular election:

> I shall observe that even in *Adam*, and after the patriarchs, *Noah, Abraham, Jacob* and others, the Common Fathers of mankind, Regall government was instituted by GOD himself without any election of the people; God created mankinde, *ex uno, ut esset inter homines non Democratia, sed Regnum.*[67]

Dudley Diggs's position waffled on the question of whether the father symbol was adequate to describe political rule.[68] Digg's primary polemical purpose was a practical one—the undermining of the legitimacy of the Puritan/Parliamentary rebellion. But in order to do this, he had to show that the theoretical notion that political rule was established through consent was implausible. In essence, this involved the idea that there was once a time in the history of mankind when there was no government.

Yet he found that idea that there once was a pre-political state of nature (on which the consenualist theory rested) as unintelligible, for in such a situation there would be no security for anyone's lives or possessions: "Yet we . . . cannot imagine that Anarchy was before a regulated government, and that God who had digested once *Chaos* into order, should now leave the most noble creatures in a worse confusion."[69] Two years after the publication of his *Observations*, Henry Parker addressed critics like Spelman and Diggs in his *Jus Populi.*[70] Parker defended his basic position that regal and paternal authorities were two distinct things. But now he also addressed some of the specific Scriptural claims of the Patriarchalists arguing, for example, that Adam had no political authority, otherwise he would have punished Cain himself, and that moreover there is no Scriptural evidence that Adam's political authority even if it existed has descended to his children.

Meanwhile, new and sundry pamphlet wars on patriarchalism erupted. Henry Ferne in *The Resolving of Conscience* (1642) argued that regal authority arose naturally and directly from paternal authority by divine right:

> When this Governing power was not a *populo efluxa* Governing power . . . but flowed from that providence at first, first through the veines of nature in a paternal or Fatherly rule, and by a pattern as a Kingly rule or Government, upon

the encrease of peoples and nations, for when the reins of Paternall Government could not reach them for their extent . . . it enlarged it selfe into a Kingly power.[71]

Charles Herle replied to him in an "answer"[72] that there is no evidence from Scripture that either Adam or his successors were universal monarchs.[73] In Scotland, the royalist ally of Charles I, John Maxwell, regarded a pure monarchy as the form of government which had existed in Paradise with Adam as father and king, and since this authority would pass to his descendents, all other modes of government were symptoms of the Fall—"It is not to be controverted, if Adam had never fallen, Aristocracie, or mixed government had never been existent or apparent in the world."[74] Against the argument that the kings of seventeenth century Europe could not trace their lineage directly to Adam, he argued that in that case kings were "surrogates" of natural fathers, and should be given the same plentitude of monarchical authority:

> The King elected to be Sovereragne to such a headlesse, discorded multitude as we suppose, is surrogated to the place of a common father to whole community over which he should beare rule . . . for my part a King designed in such a case, ought, should enjoy his Paternall right no less then *Malchisedeck*, or *Abraham*.[75]

In opposition to Maxwell's views, his fellow Scotsman Samuel Rutherford argued that even paternal rule is limited. Moreover, Rutherford reaffirmed the existence of a pre-political condition by arguing that in moving from nature to a condition of subjection to kingly rule the people gave up their power to harm other members of the community, but not their rights and legitimate liberty.

> men must have governours, either many or one supreme Ruler: and it is voluntary and dependeth on a positive institution of God whether the Government be one supreme Ruler as in a *Monarchie*; or in many as in an *Aristocracie*, . . . individual persons in creating a magistrate doth not properly surrender their right, which can be called a right, for they but surrender their power of doing violence to these of their fellows in the same communitie; for they shall not now have power to do injury without punishment.[76]

SIR ROBERT FILMER

It is in the context of this vibrant debate that we must understand the thought of Sir Robert Filmer, whose work is the apotheosis of English patriarchalism. The year 1648 was a fateful one for Europe. The Peace of Westphalia, while leaving unresolved the great confessional divide separating Roman

Catholic and Protestant Christianity, brought an end to the Thirty Years War that had ravaged the European continent. In England, King Charles I had already surrendered to Cromwell's Roundheads, but royalist resistance to Parliament continued and the nation remained deeply divided. It was in that year that Filmer published his first three works on politics on behalf of the royalist cause. In the *Free-holders Grand Inquest*, Filmer provides an extensive legal history of England as a response to the Parliamentarian arguments of William Prynne. The basic aim is to refute the claim that kings were always the source of law and authority in England, and to make the case that Parliament was only an advisory body, with no real legislative power or rights. Consequently, whatever rights Parliament had were by the grace and discretion of the King—"that Privilege of Parliament is the gift of the King."[77] Scarcely two months later, his *Anarchy of Limited Government* appeared in print. The work was a reply to Phillip Hunton's *Treatise on Monarchy* (1643), arguing that England was a strictly limited monarchy. His basic thesis is the defense of absolute and arbitrary monarchy and a rejection of the theory that there was a time when the community was not under such authority. As he states in the preface: "We flatter ourselves, if we hope ever to be governed without an arbitrary power . . . there never was, nor ever can be any people governed without a power of making laws, and every power of making laws must be arbitrary."[78]

The same year also saw the publication of Filmer's short tract, *The Necessity of Absolute powers of All Kings*. Filmer published two other significant political treatises four years later. *The Observations of the Originall of Government* was largely a polemic against the theory of the origins of government found in the *Leviathan* of Thomas Hobbes, where Filmer aptly notes that "I consent with him [Hobbes], about the rights of exercising government, but I cannot agree to his means of acquiring it. It may seem strange that I should praise his building, but mislike his foundation, but so it is."[79] Essentially, Filmer agrees with Hobbes on the necessarily absolute and arbitrary power of the monarch, but attacks the idea that there was once a state of nature which was anarchy without government, that the community and government were instituted by consent, and that the origins of sovereign authority were consequently based on contract and convention. Finally, in his *Observations upon Aristotle's Politiques Touching Forms of Government* (1652), the substance of Filmer's conclusions are given succinctly at the end of his treatise that provide an admirable summation of his whole political position:

1. That there is no form of government but monarchy only.
2. That there is no monarchy but paternal.
3. That there is no paternal monarchy but absolute and arbitrary.

4. That there is no such thing as an aristocracy or democracy.
5. That there is no such form of government as a tyranny.
6. That the people are not born free by nature.[80]

Filmer's most famous treatise, *Patriarcha*, was not published in his own lifetime, but was known to members of his circle who shared his political sympathies. However, in 1679, during the Exclusion controversy over whether Parliament had the right to exclude James, the Catholic brother of Charles II, the issues of the relative powers of king and Parliament resurfaced. Opponents of the Exclusion are the source of the revived interest in Filmer's thought during the Restoration, when *Patriarcha* was published for the first time. Since this treatise invokes Hooker specifically, and was the primary object of Locke's attack in the *Two Treatises* we will focus attention on the argument in this work without neglecting the other writings of Filmer where they shed light on the relevant issues.

Filmer's endeavor in the *Patriarcha* had both critical and constructive aims. His critical purpose is to undermine the constitutionalist theory of government; while his constructive purpose is to provide an alternative account based on the identification of paternal and regal authority. It might be best to discuss each of these in turn. As we have already seen in our discussion of Hooker and Suarez, a well-developed constitutional theory had already consisted of a number of claims such that there was an original pre-political condition of mankind which was one of liberty rather than subjection; that sovereignty was thus originally vested in the whole community rather than in a single man; that political authority has its origins in an act of consent by the community whereby it delegates its power to a king or other representative, that the powers of the king being delegated are limited, particularly by the positive law.

As we have seen, all four of these theses were notable aspects in the political philosophy of Richard Hooker. One might thus expect the *Laws of Ecclesiastical Polity* to be a primary object of attack in Filmer's treatise. Yet, Filmer instead focuses his polemic on Roman Catholic authors like Francisco Suarez and Cardinal Robert Bellarmine. Wherever Hooker is mentioned in the *Patriarcha*, Filmer seems in fact to take the rather hagiographic approach that became common during the Restoration. This is no doubt because Hooker's growing stature as the premier doctor and saint of the Anglican Church rendered him an unattractive target for a man of royalist and high church sympathies such as Filmer. His solution therefore is to attack the political philosophy, which an Anglican Thomist like Hooker *shared* with Catholic Thomists like Suarez and Bellarmine. Thus, he will cite only those passages in Hooker's laws which, taken in isolation from his whole argument, support the case Filmer is trying to build. Meanwhile, he will explicitly quote passages in Catholic authors like Suarez and Bellarmine that support constitutionalism, even though directly parallel passages can be found in the Laws.

NO ORIGINAL CONDITION OF LIBERTY

In the first chapter of the *Patriarcha*, Filmer takes aim at the tenet of original liberty taken to be the proposition that there existed a pre-political condition in which man was under no human government. He summarizes this view as follows: "Mankind is naturally endowed and born with freedom from all subjection, and at liberty to choose what form of government it please, and the power which any one hath over others was at first by human right bestowed according to the direction of the multitude."[81]

The origin of what Filmer sees as a pernicious tenet—that man is born free rather then under political subjection—is for Filmer the Jesuits and scholastics of the Catholic Church: "This tenet was first hatched in the schools, and hath been fostered by all succeeding papists for good divinity . . . never remembering that the desire for liberty was the cause of the fall of Adam."[82] Basing themselves upon the premise of the original freedom and sovereignty of the whole community, Filmer argues that those who reject royal supremacy, both Catholic and Calvinist, have used these doctrines to support a moral right to judge the king as unjust and resist his authority:

> Yet upon the grounds of this doctrine both Jesuits and some over zealous favourers of the Geneva discipline have built a perilous conclusion which is 'that the people or multitude have power to punish or deprive the prince if he transgress the laws of the kingdom' . . . this desperate assertion, whereby kings are made subject to the censures and deprivations of their subjects, follows (as the authors of it conceive) as a necessary consequence of that former position of the supposed natural equality and freedom of mankind, and liberty to choose any form of government it please.[83]

For the doctrine, the whole people rather than the person originally held sovereignty and consequently passed to a king or civil authority by way of the consent of the community. He points to Cardinal Bellarmine's remarks in *De Laicis*:

> 'Secular, or civil power,' saith he 'is instituted by men. It is in the people unless they bestow it on a prince. The power is immediately in the whole multitude as in the subject of it. For this power is by the divine law, but the divine law hath given it to no particular man. If the positive law be taken away, there is no

reason left why amongst the multitude (who are equal) one rather than another should bear rule over the rest. Power is given by the multitude to one man, or to more by the same law of nature, for the commonwealth of itself cannot exercise this power, therefore it is bound to bestow it upon some one man, or few. It depends upon the consent of the multitude to ordain for themselves a king, or consul, or other magistrate; and if there be lawful cause, the kingdom into an aristocracy or democracy.'[84]

NO SOVEREIGNTY IN THE COMMUNITY—AND A CRITIQUE OF REPRESENTATION

Filmer then launches a number of critiques of this idea that original sovereignty was vested in the multitude, first if God gave original power to the multitude, then it would follow that democracy would be the only lawful form of government; second Bellarmine in this passage is self-contradictory because he says that the people *must* delegate their power while at the same time states that democracy is a permissible form of government (in which the people *retain* their power); and third the idea that the multitude can judge which causes are lawful is a "pestilent and dangerous conclusion."[85]

Comparing Bellarmine's ideas to those of Hooker that we have examined, one finds little disagreement. The thesis that the community originally held sovereignty over itself before any specific form of government was erected was the clear teaching of Hooker: "It seemeth almost out of doubt and controversy that every independent multitude before any certain regiment established hath under God's supreme authority full dominion over itself."[86] Also similar to Bellarmine's position in *De Laicis* is Hooker's view that since there was no obvious relation of superiority and inferiority in the pre-political condition of human society, political authority requires the consent of those governed:

> There were no reason, that one should take upon him to be Lord or Judge over another; because although there be according to some very great and judicious men a kind of natural right in the wise, the noble and virtuous to govern them that are of servile disposition, nevertheless for manifestation of this right, and men's more peaceful contentment on both sides, the assent of them who are to be governed seemeth necessary.[87]

Given the virtual identity of their positions, it is remarkable then that Filmer has unreserved praise for the Hooker and stern condemnation for Bellarmine. Yet, Filmer nowhere explicitly acknowledges that the idea that sovereignty belonged to the community is the exact doctrine held by Hooker. The closest he comes is in a passage where he gives Hooker exalted praise, while perhaps making a veiled reference to their possible disagreement:

I must not detract from the worth of all those learned men who are of a contrary judgment concerning natural liberty. The profoundest scholar that ever was known hath not been able to search out every truth that is discoverable: *neither Aristotle in natural philosophy, nor Hooker in divinity.* They were but men, yet I reverence their judgments in most points, and confess myself beholden even in their errors in this. Something that I found amiss in their opinions guided me in the discovery of that truth which (I persuade myself) they missed.[88]

In other works, Filmer has a number of substantive arguments against consent and agreement of the community as the origin of political obligation, to which Schochet has directed our attention. Perhaps the most interesting is in the *Anarchy* written against Hunton. Here, Filmer asks how the community could even summon itself to meet and come to agreement without a government already preexisting:

For except by some mysterious instinct they should all meet at one time and place, what man or company of men less then the whole people hath power to appoint either time or place of elections, where all be alike free by nature? And without a lawful summons, it is most unjust to bind those that be absent. The whole people cannot summon itself. One man is sick, another is lame, a third is aged, and a fourth is under the age of discretion. All these at some time or other, or at some place or other, might be able to meet if they might choose their time and place, as men naturally free should.[89]

This argument is based on the fact that in the state of nature supposing it to be one of freedom and equality among men, some group would not be able to justly bind others to subjection. Thus Filmer argues that once it is postulated that by nature, men are born free rather than in subjection, nothing less than the unanimous consent of *all* human beings could justify subjection to government:

If they understand that the entire multitude or whole people have originally by nature power to choose a king, they must remember that by their principles and rules, by nature all mankind makes but one people, who they suppose to be born alike into an equal freedom from subjection—and where such freedom is, there all things must of necessity be common. From whence it follows that natural freedom being once granted, there cannot be any one man chosen a king without the universal consent of the people of the world at one instant, *nemine contradicente.*[90]

The reason for this requirement of unanimity is that, for Filmer, if we grant the premise of natural liberty, it will be an injustice to deprive any *individual* of his liberty, and subject him to authority without his *personal* consent:

As to the act of the *major* part of a multitude, it is true that by politic human constitutions it is oft ordained that the voices of the most shall overrule the rest. And such ordinances bind, because where men are assembled by human power, that power that doth assemble them can also limit and direct the manner of execution of that power . . . but in assemblies that take their authority from the law of nature it cannot be so. For what freedom is due to any man by the law of nature, no inferior power can alter, limit or diminish. No man nor a multitude can give away the natural right of another . . . it must follow that the acts of multitudes not entire are not binding to all but only to such as consent unto them.[91]

As to the claim that those who consented *represent* those not involved in the agreement, Filmer demands proof that those absent from deliberation *actually* and *personally* consent: "As to the point of Proxy, it cannot be showed or proved that all those that have been absent from popular elections did ever give their voices to some of their fellows. I ask but one example out of the history of the whole world."[92]

A related issue for Filmer is his critique of representative government—which is for him the notion that one person can consent in the place of another. Schochet elegantly summarizes Filmer's objections:

Filmer alleged that legislatures do not act as single representative bodies. The frequency and number of absences mean that the body truly representing all the people is rarely if ever assembled. Size is a further hindrance to the genuine operation of the representative principle. Because Republican bodies are so large and unwieldy, much important work is delegated to committees . . . third, Filmer charged that delegates do not represent the interests of their own areas or constituents on all issues but actually tend to vote as blocs and trade votes according to the design of their leaders . . . finally, Filmer said that electors are not prepared to choose the best qualified representatives because they do not know enough about politics.[93]

Since Filmer can find no plausible way in which the consent of the multitude can be the origin of government, he reaches the conclusion that strictly speaking the people neither choose their leaders, nor share in the sovereignty that belongs to kings. Parliament is at most an advisory body, meeting at the good grace of the King with no proper power of its own. If the people have no share in sovereignty even through representation, the idea that they may depose monarchs they deem unjust is the height of absurdity: "If it be unnatural for the people to choose their governors, or to govern and partake in the government, what can be thought of that damnable conclusion that the multitude may correct or depose their king if need be? Surely the unnaturalness and injustice of this position cannot sufficiently be expressed."[94]

THE IDENTITY OF *REGIA POTESTAS* AND *PATER POTESTAS*

For Filmer then, it is clear that the natural condition of man is not one of liberty, but rather one of subjection to authority. It is in this capacity that the image of paternal rule assumes its importance. Just as by nature the child is subject to the authority of the father, so by nature everyone is subject to the authority of the king:

> I see not then how the children of Adam, or of any man else, can be free from subjection to their parents. And this subjection of children is the only fountain of all regal authority, by the ordination of God himself. It follows that civil power not only in general is by divine institution, but even the assignment of it specifically to the eldest parent, which quite takes away that new and common distinction which refers only power universal as absolute to God, but power respective in regard of the special form of government to the choice of the people. Nor leaves it any place for such imaginary pactions between kings and their people as many dream of.[95]

Filmer does not simply employ the image of paternal authority to *symbolize* royal authority. Rather, his understanding of the relation between *regia potestas* and *pater potestas* approaches in fact complete identification of the two:

> If we compare the natural duties of a father with those of a king we find them to be all one, without any difference at all but only in the latitude or extent of them. As the father over one family, so the king as father over many families, extends his care to preserve, feed, clothe, instruct, and defend the whole commonwealth. His wars, his peace, his courts of justice and all his acts of sovereignty tend only to preserve and distribute to every subordinate and inferior father and to their children, their rights and privileges, so that all the duties of a king are summed up in an universal fatherly care of the people.[96]

Given Filmer's view on the unity of paternal and regal authority, it is not surprising that one of his main targets is Francisco Suarez. Filmer's issue with Suarez is not only that Suarez also accepts the idea that original sovereignty belonged to the community,[97] but also that Suarez explicitly distinguishes the *regia potestas* from the *pater potestas*. The issue took the form of whether Adam has only the paternal authority, or also royal power. The passage he quotes from Suarez is one we have already seen from the *Tractatus de Legibus* and is as follows:

> Adam had only economical power, but not political. He had power over his wife, and fatherly power over his sons, whilst they were not free . . . but political

power did not begin until families began to be gathered into one perfect community. Wherefore as the community did not begin with the creation of Adam, nor by his will alone, but of all them that did agree in this community, so we cannot say that Adam naturally had political primacy in this community. For that cannot be gathered from any natural principles, because by the force of the law of nature alone, it is not unto any progenitor to be also king of his posterity. And if this be not gathered out of the principles of nature 'God by a special gift of providence gave him this power.' For there is no revelation of this, nor testimony of Scripture.[98]

Filmer produces a number of arguments against Suarez. One of them involved the concept of nonage—that is, that the subjection to paternal authority is only for a limited time after which the children are emancipated. Suarez held that the authority of the father was limited in that, at a certain point, the children were emancipated. Parenthetically, Locke in the *Two Treatises* later took up this very argument. Filmer argues, however, that by the law of nature nonage does not exist, though the father may remit his authority freely. Filmer also finds the distinction between "economical" (domestic) authority and political authority untenable:

If Adam did or might exercise in his family the same jurisdiction which a king doth now in a commonweal, then the two kinds of power are not distinct though they may receive an accidental difference by the amplitude of the bounds of one beyond the other, yet since the like difference is also found in political states, it follows that economical and political power differ nowise then a little commonweal differ from a great one.[99]

Filmer earlier had referred to the catechetical tradition of placing obedience to rulers under the rubric of the commandment in the Decalogue to honor one's parents. He argues that if the duty to honor one's parents came from divine and natural law, and the duty to obey rulers only from positive law, then why is obedience to the king given primacy over the obedience to one's father:

To confirm this natural right of regal power we find in the Decalogue that the law which enjoins obedience to kings is delivered in the terms of 'honour thy father' (Exodus 12) as if all power were originally in the father. If obedience to parents be immediately due by natural law, and subjection to princes but by the mediation of a human ordinance, what reason is there that the law of nature should give place to the laws of men, as we see the power of the father gives place and is subordinate to the power of the magistrate.[100]

Against Suarez's position that since community did not begin with Adam, neither could political power, Filmer replies that the creation of communities followed his creation, and that as a father he determined what belonged to each of his children and what was common to them. Thus the paternal/regal care for the common good of subjects began with Adam. Against Suarez's position that the natural law does not make a father also a king of his children, Filmer cites Bellarmine against him.

What is odd is that in the discussion of paternal and regal authority, Hooker, who Filmer compares with Aristotle in authority, is not referenced. Filmer here continues the same tactic of critiquing figures that shared Hooker's views, while by omission and selective quotation making Hooker appear to agree with him. Thus, shortly after criticizing Suarez for making the distinction between regal and paternal authority, he quotes Hooker in Book VII against the argument that authority descends from the people to the king:

> So God must *eligere* [choose] and the people only do *constituere* [establish]. Mr. Hooker in his eight book of *Ecclesiastical polity* clearly expounds this distinction. His words are worth the citing: 'Heaps of Scripture' (saith he) are alleged concerning the solemn coronation or inauguration of Saul, David, Solomon and others, by nobles, ancients, and people of the commonwealth of Israel; as if the solemnities were a kind of deed, whereby the right of dominion is given. Which strange, untrue, and unnatural conceits set abroad by seedsmen of rebellion, only to animate unquiet spirits . . . for unless we will openly proclaim defiance unto all law, equity, and reason, we must (there is no remedy) acknowledge that in kingdoms hereditary birth giveth right unto supreme dominion.[101]

What Filmer does not note is that the views of Suarez are in fact virtually the same as Hooker's on these points. We have already seen how Hooker also carefully distinguished the *regia potestas* and the *pater potestas*:

> To fathers within their private families nature hath given a supreme power . . . . Howbeit over a grand multitude having no such dependency upon anyone . . . *impossible it is that any should have complete lawful power but by consent of men*, or immediate appointment of God; because not having the natural superiority of fathers their power must needs be either usurped, and then unlawful; or if lawful then granted or consented by them over whom they exercise the same.[102]

The passage Filmer quotes from Hooker refers to the illegitimacy of resisting a lawful sovereign *once the community has agreed to establish a hereditary monarchy.* It says nothing about the origins of this political obligation to accept a given king as sovereign. On the point of the original sovereignty of the community point, we have seen that Hooker's view is unambiguous and is essentially the same as that of Suarez:

> The lawful power of making laws to command whole political societies of men belongeth so properly unto the same entire societies, that For any Prince or

potentate of whatsoever kind to exercise the same of himself, and not either by express commission of God, or else by authority derived at the first from their consent upon those persons they impose laws, it is no better then tyranny.[103]

The question of the nature of Adam's paternal and regal authority was of fundamental importance for Hooker because "Filmer inextricably united his argument for the divine right of kings with patriarchal authority."[104] For Filmer, the authority of kings begins with the enthronement of Adam in paradise. Filmer's view is precisely that Adam's authority as father of the human race was also a royal authority, and that this very plenitude of authority passed on to his descendents. In order for Filmer to establish the right of kings to absolute and arbitrary power, he had to show that Adam's title to kingship was unimpeachable. Filmer argues that the title of Adam to regal authority exists not only by natural right of paternity, but also by divine right through God's grant of dominion over the world to Adam in Genesis. Thus, in his *Observations upon Aristotles Politiques*, Filmer states that:

> We must not neglect the Scriptures and search in philosophers for grounds of dominion and property, which are the main principles of government and justice. The first government in the world was monarchical, in the father of all flesh. Adam being commanded to multiply, and people the earth, and to subdue it, and having dominion given him over all creatures was thereby monarch of the whole world. None of his posterity had any right to possess anything but by his grant or permission, or by succession from him.[105]

The title of Adam to kingship by donation is likewise assumed in *Patriarcha*: "The lordship which Adam by creation had over the whole world, and by right descending from him the patriarchs did enjoy, was as large and ample as the absolutist dominion of any monarch which hath been seen since creation."[106]

Filmer sees the plentitude of Adam's regal power descending then to his successors. The tracing of the details regarding how Adam's regal authority descended through the genealogy of Biblical history, forms a central part of Filmer's argument. In this time in England, the Bible was generally viewed as a more or less literal and accurate historical account. Filmer's opponents like Locke neither dispute the accuracy of the Scriptural account nor the probative value of arguments from Scripture, but rather Filmer's particular interpretations.

To those who argued that there once was a time before government when people were not under the authority of kings, Filmer challenges them to find in the Scriptures where such an anarchical condition prevailed from the time of Adam onwards. This type of Biblical exegesis showing how regal power descended was of course not new—even in details Filmer's account resembled that of Saravia. Both, for example, trace the descent of royal power from Adam to the Flood, and then remark that the universal monarchy over the whole earth, ended after Noah chose to divide the world among his three sons, each having royal power over his own territories. Thus, Filmer comment that "The three sons of Noah had the whole world divided amongst them by their father,"[107] precisely echoes Saravia's comment that Noah was king of the whole world until he divided his rule among the three sons.[108]

After the flood, the rulers of the sundry peoples that emerged from the confusion of tongues after Babel were patriarchs of families like Abraham, Isaac, and Jacob. Filmer does not claim that the kings of his time owe their authority to a provable *natural* line of descent. Like Saravia, Filmer believes that kings are free to choose others than their eldest sons to bestow their authority, and furthermore that God by special election can transfer authority from one house to another:

> All such prime heads and fathers have power to consent in the uniting or conferring of their fatherly right of sovereign authority on whom they please. And he that is so elected claims not his power as a donative from the people, but as being substituted properly by God, from whom he receives his royal charter of an universal father.[109]

Since both God and kings themselves may transfer their authority to others then their firstborn sons, what is important is not so much the chain of natural descent, but the descent of *authority*:

> It may seem absurd to maintain that kings now are fathers of their people, since experience shows the contrary. It is true, all kings be not the natural parents of their subjects, yet they all either are or are reputed to be the next heirs to those progenitors who were at first the natural parents of the whole people, and in their right succeed to the exercise of supreme jurisdiction. And such heirs are not only lords of their own children, but also of their brethren, and all others that were subject to their fathers.[110]

Filmer's third and final chapter of the *Patriarcha* is devoted to proving that kings are not subject to human or positive law:

> Hitherto I have endeavored to show the natural institution of regal authority, and to free it from subjection to an arbitrary election of the people. It is necessary to enquire whether human laws have a superiority over princes, for those that maintain the acquisition of royal jurisdiction from the people do subject the exercise of it to human positive laws.[111]

Filmer's basic position is that the law is nothing other than the command or will of the king. Kings are therefore prior to laws as their source, and cannot be constrained by what is nothing but their own will "for as Kingly power is by the law of God, so it hath no inferior law to limit it . . . a proof unanswerable for the superiority of princes above laws is this, that they were kings long before there were any laws. For a long time the word of the king was the only law."[112]

Filmer defends this position on the basis of the special prerogative power of kings. Without such prerogative authority, the king cannot fulfill the task appointed to him by divine and natural law to exercise a paternal care for his subjects. Thus, he says: "That the prerogative of the King is to be above all laws, for the good only of them that are under the laws . . . howsoever some are afraid of the name of prerogative, yet they may assure themselves the case of subjects would be desperately miserable without it."[113]

Filmer naturally accepts the voluntarist position that the essential nature of law is that it is the command of a superior. Were the king himself bound by his own commands, he would cease on this account to possess true sovereignty:

> There can be no laws without a supreme power to command or make them . . . by the like reason in a monarchy the king must of necessity be above the laws. There can be no sovereign majesty in them that are under them. That which giveth the very being of a king is the power to give laws, without this power he is but an equivocal king.[114]

Regarding the argument that the common law of England was not derived from kings but from custom, and consequently is a limit to royal authority, Filmer answers that customs derive their authority only from the assent of kings:

> Customs at first became lawful only by some superior power which did either command or consent unto their beginning. And the first power which we find (as is confessed by all men) is the kingly power . . . from whence we must necessarily infer that the common law itself, or common customs of this land, were originally the laws and commands of kings unwritten.[115]

THE SUPREMACY OF THE CROWN OVER THE LAW

In defense of the notion of kings being above the law, Filmer refers to the Roman law principle of *Princeps Legibus solutus est*. We have already seen how the Roman law argument also formed an important part of Bodin's argument that kings are both the source of law and above the law. Filmer endeavors moreover to support his thesis of the "unlimited jurisdiction of kings" by marshalling a broad variety of examples from the Old and New Testament and the legal history of England. He even refers to the Thomistic distinction of *potestas directiva* and *potestas coactiva* in support of his claim, arguing that to be solely under the law's directive power is not being under the law at all:

> The familiar distinction of the schoolmen whereby they subject kings to the *directive* but not the *coactive* power of the law, is a confession that kings are not bound by the positive laws of any nation—since the compulsory power of the laws is that which properly makes laws to be laws . . . whereas the direction of the law is like advice and direction which the king's council gives the king, which no man can say is a law to the king.[116]

Remarkably, Filmer also quotes Richard Hooker in this chapter in support of his most "un-Hookerian" of conclusions. Thus, he argues that the King alone and not Parliament is the source of laws by using a quote from Hooker divorced from its context:

> A fourth point to be made is that in parliament all statutes or laws are properly made by the king alone at the rogation of the people, as his lare majesty of happy memory affirms in his *Trew Law of Free Monarchy* [by James I] and as Mr. Hooker teacheth us that 'Laws do not take their constraining force from the quality of such as devise them, but from the power that doth give them the strength of law.'[117]

We may be reminded that Hooker's position was precisely the reverse of Filmer's on the question of whether the King ought to be subject to human or positive law: "I mean not of the law not only of nature and of *God*, but every national or municipal law consonant thereunto. Happier that people whose law is their *King* in the greatest things, then that whose *King* is himself the law."[118] Or his position that "so is the power of the *King* over all and in all limited that unto all his proceedings the law itself is the rule."[119] We may also recall his position on whether it is the King alone who is the source of law: "The *Parliament* of England together with the *Convocation* annexed thereunto is that whereupon the very essence of all government within this Kingdom doth depend,"[120] or again "Touching the supremacy of power which our *Kings* have in this case of making laws it resteth principally in the strength of a negative voice."[121] It was in a certain sense a boon to his adversaries that Filmer chose to employ Hooker as an authority for his position, which in other ways had interesting criticisms of the consensual and contractual theory of government.

THE WHIG HOOKER: AN EXCURSUS
ON THE ANTI-FILMERIAN TRACTS

Before we move to a discussion of Hooker's influence on Locke in the next chapter it will be important to place Locke's work within its own proper historical context. The distorted use of Hooker by Filmer in the form of selective and misleading quotations in the *Patriarcha* allowed anti-patriarchalists and Whigs such as Edward Gee, Algernon Sidney, and James Tyrrell to appropriate Hooker, and thus argue against Filmer out of his own sources. Needless to say, the *Patriarcha*, upon its publication in 1680, unleashed a flurry of tracts responding to its claims. Among the tracts to adopt a Whig interpretation of Richard Hooker against Filmer was John Locke's *Two Treatises*. It would therefore be logical to briefly discuss this genre of Whig tracts, before moving to examine Locke's own use of Hooker in his most famous political work *The Two Treatises of Government*.

The appropriation of Richard Hooker by royalist writers set the stage for a great contention over the proper interpretation of the political doctrine found in his writings. The Restoration had essentially canonized Richard Hooker as the doctor and saint of Anglican conformism.[122] The reasons for this were primarily the fact there was no more systematic and theologically substantive apology for Anglican conformity than the *Laws of Ecclesiastical Polity* extant. The Cromwellian protectorate had swept away not merely the monarchy, but also the Anglican Church with its episcopal structure and its characteristic liturgical forms based on the Book of Common Prayer. However, upon the accession of Charles II, a mood of Anglican triumphalism prevailed, and the Book of Common Prayer was restored in a revised version in 1662. Under the Clarendon Code, nonconformity in relation to the Church of England retained at most a bare toleration to which many disadvantages were attached. Hooker's exhaustive polemic against Calvinist theology and discipline and his assertion of the rights of King and Parliament over "things indifferent" served the purposes of Restoration partisans well.

A problem existed, however, because Hooker's specifically political doctrine was notably hostile to Royal absolutism. Hooker asserted that there was no natural or divine right to rule, that the community was the original locus of sovereignty, that what authority the king possessed derived from an original act of consent by the community, that the king held his authority as a delegated power, and that as a subject of the community he was bound to obey not merely the divine and natural laws, but also the positive laws of the English realm. Royalists desirous of emphasizing the king's special and absolute prerogatives, and threatened directly by the doctrine of parliamentary supremacy, endeavored to maintain a kind of double position with respect to

Hooker. While exalting Hooker as nearly impeccable in theological matters, Royalist writers tended to turn to alternative and non-constitutionalist theories of government such as patriarchalism. The effort to maintain the hagiographic attitude to Hooker's theology, while rejecting his constitutionalism, resulted in strange readings of Hooker, such as that found in Filmer's *Patriarcha*. Here, Hooker is praised as an authority in divinity comparable to Aristotle in philosophy, while at the same time a Patriarchalist political theory is advanced which contradicts all the major tenets of Hooker's theory of political society. At various points in the *Patriarcha*, omission and selective quotation are used to make it appear as though Filmer's patriarchalism coheres with the politics of the *Laws*; yet, at the same time, figures whose political philosophy was actually close to that of Hooker like Francisco Suarez are relentlessly criticized.

EDWARD GEE

As patriarchalism ascended in importance as a defense of the Restoration polity, it was quite natural that opponents of royal absolutism in the second half of the seventeenth century would focus their energies on confuting Filmer as the preeminent Patriarchalist. A standard feature of the anti-Filmerian tracts was an appropriation of Hooker as a defender of the idea that the powers of the king derive from the community. One of the earliest examples of this kind of pamphlet and an ancestor of the later Whig tracts was the 1658 work, *Divine Right and original of the Civil Magistrate* by Edward Gee.[123] Because the *Patriarcha* was not published until 1680, this early Patriarchalist tract deals primarily with Filmer's *Anarchy of Mixed Government*. The cornerstone of Gee's argument is that Filmer wrongly equates paternal with regal authority. Gee does not deny that the father has legitimate authority, but merely denies that this paternal authority over a family and the authority of kings over a commonwealth are one and the same:

> The question is not . . . whether the father or the first-born have not some pre-eminency over their respective correlatives, to wit the Father over his children, the First-Born over his younger brethren, but whether the pre-eminency be the same as the Civill Magistracy: or whether the political power in a Commonwealth be not one thing, and that [paternal] superiority another, and those two be not really and essentially different.[124]

In other words even presuming that the child is a natural subject of the father, it does not follow that the citizen is a natural subject of the king because it has not been shown that *political* and *domestic* society are one and the same.

Indeed Gee writes that:

> Although it is granted that there is in the Father a power over his child, yet ever since the erection of the publique State, or commonwealth as a distinct society from that of a household . . . the paternal power hath been (and that duly and necessarily) taken to be another or a distinct authority from that of the Civil Magistrate, and inferior or subordinate to it.[125]

Gee sees as a point of weakness Filmer's admission that kings are not necessarily *natural* fathers of their people, and that the chain of natural inheritance of Adam's ostensibly regal authority has been broken. As we have seen, Filmer endeavored to answer this by asserting that where a usurpation of royal authority has been successfully maintained over time, this is a sign of God's providential transference of paternal and regal authority from one line to another. Gee regards Filmer's prescriptive account as equivalent to annulling the notion of a natural right to succession by fatherhood—for if usurpation can be sanctioned *ex post facto*, then how does natural paternity assert any title to royal authority? Gee writes:

> The saying that *Providence in dispossessing of a Crown him that is true heir (and so hath the right) and disposing it to the hands of an unjust invader, doth put fatherly authority in that invader, and adopt the subjects to an obligation to it*; is to deny the right both of paternity and of birth-right, and of the consent of the people, and of every other special way of conveying title to Government, and to make the right thereof consist only to follow, come by and consist in possession . . . and to what purpose then is all the plea for Fatherhood . . . ? What a void distinction is that of his when he distinguisheth of a natural and a usurped right? According to him [Filmer] there is no power, but Fatherhood, no Fatherhood but possession.[126]

Interestingly, Gee seems ready to accept what Schochet refers to as "Anthropological Patriarchalism" (i.e. that *de facto* government has its origins in paternal authority). Moreover, in response to Filmer's claim that the only legitimate consent would have to be universal, Gee replies that fathers of families have the authority to consent on behalf of their subjects.[127] What Gee argues is even supposing that the first kings happened to be fathers, this in no way implies that kings of his day can claim a moral right to royal authority by reason of paternity.[128] The *historical* question of how political societies formed is distinct from the *moral* question of how political authority becomes legitimate. This is a principle Gee also applies to the case of conquest. Conquest only confers the *right* to rule in the case that war which led to the conquest was a just war. Thus Gee writes:

Conquest is admitted to be . . . in government where it is the effect of a reall and just war. And so it makes no exception against any assertion. The Victory which is acknowledged justly to law claim to a Crown is the issue of such a war as supposeth the equity and necessity of the war to be on the victor's part.[129]

This relates to the fundamental distinction in Gee's thought—that between physical and moral power. Thus Gee writes:

Natural or *physical* power is the same which we call (more distinctly) *strength, might* and *vigor.* It consisteth in the ability to enforce or make impression upon another thing or to cause it to yield . . . *moral power* is that which call *property* or *dominion*; it consisteth in a right, title . . . to order or dispose or govern.

The influence of the medieval scholastics is here to be noted—as we immediately see the similarities between Gee's discussion of property, dominion, and right, and the issues of *dominium* and *ius* found in writers like Gerson and later in the Spanish scholastics. Gee in fact explicitly refers to the authority of Aquinas and Cajetan in that he equates moral power with the Thomistic *potestas directiva* and physical power with the *potestas coactiva*.[130] Interestingly, while Filmer denigrates the *potestas directiva* or the directive of moral power,[131] arguing that it is the constraining power that properly makes law to be law, Gee argues on the contrary that it is moral power which is primary.

The scepter goes before the sword is that which legitimates it: when it draweth its Sword the difference between its sword and anothers (that is armed only by natural strength) is that its edge is not merely backed by metal or in an arme of flesh and sinews, but with warrant and communion, and that signed by God.[132]

For this reason even if conquest or paternity were the *de facto* historical origins of governments it would not follow that paternity or conquest constitutes a *de jure* title to legitimate rule. Turning to the authority of Richard Hooker,[133] Gee argues that there is no natural political subjection of one man to another. Thus where political authority is asserted by force based on claims of conquest or paternity, there is no proper claim to power at all:

By Nature men are (in regard of Civill jurisdiction) all equal, no man a ruler or servant to another. So that the [effect of] natural power is . . . but to involve them that are under in an actual subordineis, that they couch down as a man doth to a lion being under his paw, or as a traveler doth to a highway robber that hath set his pistol to his breast, that is without either will owed to the prevailer, or obligation to go any further in subjection then self-preservation or the like considerations (irrespective to the invader) may suggest.[134]

So what conditions *do* create political obligation and render political authority legitimate? Gee essentially adopts Hooker's alternative account of the origins of political obligation. Essentially, his view is that sovereignty belongs originally to God and is then given to the people who delegate their authority to a magistrate. For Eccleshall, Gee is transforming Hooker's doctrine of consent from a doctrine about the *origins* of government to a more active theory in which royal authority requires communal assent.

In fact Gee reshaped Hooker's consensual theory into a doctrine of active consent in which legitimate magistracy proceeded from election or some similar procedure for registering communal approval. He even managed to extract support in the *Polity* for the rightful deposition of usurpers.[135]

RESISTANCE IN HOOKER: A QUESTION REVISITED

Eccleshall here raises two issues: one is concerned with whether Hooker's doctrine of consent is a merely passive one, and the second concerns Hooker's attitude to resistance. In regard to the first, certainly Eccleshall is correct that, for Hooker, the legitimacy of a king's rule is not contingent on election for "in Kingdoms hereditary birth giveth right unto supreme dominion."[136] The reason for this is that in a monarchy like England at least, Hooker believed that there was some form of original compact whereby the community decided to have succession to the throne proceed by natural heredity. Consequently, to challenge the right of a natural heir to rule in a hereditary monarchy would be to act against the terms of the original compact. Evidence for this is certainly to be found in the "passive" consent by which institutions attain prescriptive authority through "silent allowance":

> Touching Kings which were instituted by agreement and composition made with them over whom they reign and how far their power may lawfully extend, the articles of compact between them must show, not only the articles of compact at the first beginning which for the most part are worn clean out of knowledge . . . but whatsoever hath been after in free and voluntary manner condescended whether by express consent, whereof positive laws are witnesses, or lese by silent allowance famously notified through custom reaching beyond the memory of man.[137]

However, it is also clear that for Hooker the act of communal consent by which a king rules is not simply a question of *origin* of his authority, but something that continues to condition his rule: "Original influence of power from the body to the King is cause of the King's dependency in power upon the body. By dependency we mean subordination and subjection."[138] At least in a regency like England, Hooker's principle that "Laws they are not which public approbation hath not made so"[139] is given concrete expression in institutions like Parliament. We must therefore state that while the passive or prescriptive consent has a primary role for Hooker, it would be going too far to say that he rejects the present and active role of the community.

The question of Hooker's attitude toward resistance has already been discussed previously. Certainly, we can agree that Hooker used the "notion of consent to disclose the prescriptive authority of constitutional arrangements"[140] rather than elaborating the conditions under which resistance was justified. Any theory of resistance to constituted authority was contrary to the express purpose of the laws, which was to demonstrate the competence of the Crown and Parliament to govern the civil and ecclesiastical polity of England. As Eccleshall aptly notes, "far from wishing to justify the deposition of arbitrary rulers, his intention was to suggest that the English had been peculiarly adept in using the opportunity afforded to them to construct a sound polity. For, having institutionalized co-operation in their constitutional procedures, they had insured the congruity of their public regulations with precepts of eternal justice."[141]

And yet if the community rather then the king is sovereign, there is the question that Hooker does not directly touch upon—namely, what happens when the king becomes a tyrant and refuses to accept the "subjection" and "subordination" to divine, natural, and human law that Hooker regards as his obligation? If the authority of kings is a power delegated by the community rather than a natural or divine right, may not then the community refuse obedience to a tyrant that refuses to be constrained by law? And may they depose him? Certainly St. Thomas Aquinas, on whom Hooker relied for much of his doctrine, recognized cases in which laws that contravene the order of justice should be disobeyed and even cases in which the deposition of a tyrant by an act of the community is not seditious. Nevertheless, it would perhaps be anachronistic to put an answer in Hooker's mouth to a question with which he did not feel confronted.

Yet, the efforts of "Whig Hookerians" like Sidney, Tyrrell, and Locke were precisely aimed at transposing the political philosophy of Hooker into a time, context, and political purpose that differed from Hooker's own. They sought, in other words, to deploy the premises involved in Hooker's theories of sovereignty, consent, and compact to a new goal. Whereas Hooker's own doctrine of consent and communal sovereignty was meant to buttress the competence of established English institutions, the Whigs sought to draw up a theory of resistance to (what they saw as) the arbitrary and illegitimate use of power by kings. In turning to Hooker, they were able to appeal to a respected tradition of constitutionalism and limited government; a tradition older in fact than the Patriarchalist theory that justified absolute and arbitrary government based on natural prerogative authority.

ALGERNON SIDNEY

The flashpoint for the emergence of an articulated Whig position was indubitably the Exclusion controversy between 1679 and 1681.[142] One of the main Parliamentary advocates of Exclusion was the Earl of Shaftesbury, who in 1667 became John Locke's patron and close associate. Because the issue of Exclusion once again pitted the Crown against Parliament, the issues soon raised philosophical questions regarding whether authority was prerogative or consensual in its origins. Tory opponents of Exclusion published new editions of Filmer's writings including the *Patriarcha* for the first time in 1680. A Tory leader, Edmund Bohun, published a more accurate text of the *Patriarcha* in 1685 from a manuscript provided by the Archbishop of Canterbury, William Sancroft.[143] A number of Whig authors undertook detailed responses to Filmer's *Patriarcha*. Algernon Sidney's *Discourses Concerning Government* was written between 1680 and 1683, but not published until 1698. Here, Sidney takes issue with Filmer's fundamental contention that the natural state of man is one of subjection to authority rather than liberty. Sidney argues that to depend on the absolute and arbitrary will of a single man is slavery: "As liberty solely consists in an independency upon the will of another, and by the name of slave we understand a man, who can neither dispose of his person nor goods, but enjoys all at the will of his master; there is no such thing in nature as a slave."[144]

Sidney calls upon Hooker as a defender of the natural liberty of man. Indeed, Sidney mocks Filmer's veiled critique of Hooker in the first chapter of the *Patriarcha* saying that:

> I cannot but commend his modesty and care *not to detract from the worth of learned men*; but it seems they were all subject to error, except himself [Filmer], who is rendered infallible through pride, ignorance, and impudence. But if Hooker and Aristotle were wrong in their fundamentals concerning natural liberty, how could they be in the right when they built upon it? Or if they did mistake, how can they deserve to be cited? or rather, why is such care taken to pervert their sense? It seems our author is by their errors brought to the knowledge of the truth. *Men have heard of a dwarf standing upon the shoulders of a giant, who saw farther than the giant*; but now that the dwarf standing on the ground sees that which the giant did overlook, we must learn from him.

Sidney makes many arguments against the patriarchalist thesis, arguing that the Patriarchs of the Bible were not kings, the power of a father belongs only to him, God left man free to determine his political forms so monarchy is neither natural nor divinely mandated, and the lawful power to govern derives from the whole people. In 1683, Sidney was implicated in the Rye House Plot to overthrow King Charles, and after his execution the same year he became a martyr for the Whig cause.

JAMES TYRRELL: *PATRIARCHA NON MONARCHA*

Another anti-Filmerian tract that directly influenced Locke was that written by his close friend James Tyrrell—*Patriarcha non Monarcha* (1681). Tyrrell's basic thesis is that the authority of fathers and kings are fundamentally distinct:

> I will not deny that the Heads of separate families, being out of Commonwealths have many things analogous to them, though they are not Commonwealths themselves: and the reason why I do not allow them to be so is, because the ends of a family and the ends of a Commonwealth are divers: and so many parts of a Monarchical Empire are not to be found in families.[145]

In establishing the distinction between regal and paternal authority, Tyrrell relies in part on the *Laws of Ecclesiastical Polity* and it is perhaps in Tyrrell's writings that Hooker first becomes for Whigs "the Judicious Hooker." Thus Tyrrell writes:

> the Government of such Heads or Fathers of families was only an *Oeconomical* and not a *Civill power* . . . I think I may safely affirm that *Kingly*, or *Monarchical power* cannot be proved to be of divine institution by this Argument: and I have a greater man than Sir. R. F. viz. the Judicious Mr.Hooker on my side, who makes a plain distinction between such a Head or Master of a family and the king.[146]

Tyrrell denies moreover Filmer's fundamental thesis that the authority of fathers is absolute and arbitrary. "The Author [Filmer] . . . affirms that a childe, a slave, and servant, were all one without any difference. I see no divine charter in scripture of any such absolute, despotick power granted to Adam or any other Father."[147] The authority of fathers over children like all just and legitimate authority exists for the good of the subject, in this case for the good of the children themselves.[148] Taking up a theme that would later be echoed by Locke, Tyrrell argues that the authority of fathers is temporary, arising from the as yet imperfect rational judgment of the minor.

> In the first period [of a child's life], all the actions of Children are under the absolute dominion of their parents: for since they have not the use of Reason, nor are able to judge what is good and bad for themselves . . . yet this [parental] power is still to be directed to the Good and Preservation of the child.[149]

While in the "third period" when the child has both the discretion of reason and is no longer in his parent's household he is emancipated:

> In the third Period they [the children] are in all their actions free, and at their own dispose; yet still under obligations of Gratitude, Piety, and Observance toward their parents as their greatest benefactors.[150]

This principle of *nonage*,[151] that time in which a child lacks the discretion of reason, was a crucial one for the anti-patriarchalist polemic of the late seventeenth century. The idea being that human beings are and ought to be free insofar as they are rational. Those who lack the discretion of reason whether through minority or other conditions (such as lunacy) lack the requisites for the exercise of freedom and hence must be under the custodianship of others for their own good.

Tyrrell spends a great deal of time attacking Filmer's Biblical account of a chain of paternal authority that can be traced starting with Adam and continuing down to the kings of the seventeenth century. This type of Biblical exegesis was part of the anti-Filmerian polemic, and was also the main theme of Locke's *First Treatise*. But Tyrrell also holds that Filmer confuses origins with moral right. Even assuming that the first to exercise political authority were fathers, it does not follow that the rule a man exercises as father is one and the same as that which he exercises as a political leader, nor that paternal authority *remains* the basis of political authority for all future time. Thus, even supposing that Adam was a king:

> God's bare approbation, lays no Obligation for all mankind to practice it now, any more then it is a good Argument to say that it is not onely lawful, but necessary for men to marry their sisters, because God approved of that way of propagation at first.[152]

Like Edward Gee, Tyrrell also contends that Filmer's equation of regal with paternal power cannot be rendered coherent with his view that those who are not actual fathers can hold the *authority* of fathers. Filmer we will recall believed that fathers could transfer their authority as they pleased, and that even usurped authority can become legitimate through prescriptions since prolonged possession of power is a sign of providential favor. Thus for example Noah transferred his authority not to his eldest son, but to all three equally. But, Tyrrell says that for Noah paternal power could be divided into many sons at his will: "Why might they not do so *in infinitum*? And then there could never be any common Prince or Monarch set over them all, but by force and Conquest, or else by Election, either of which destroys the notion of the natural Right of Eldership."[153]

Tyrrell and Locke were both working on their texts against *Patriarcha* around the same time and were in close communication, though it is unclear (in spite of their very similar lines of argument) whether they were directly collaborating.[154] It is also interesting to note that Tyrrell, like Locke, would also turn to Richard Hooker—if less extensively—to establish the doctrine of consent as the basis of government.[155]

OTHER WHIG TRACTS

The period following the revolution of 1688 brought forth a flurry of lesser known Whig tracts defending the deposition of King James II, and many of these make use of Hooker's *Laws*. Thomas Harrison's *Political Aphorisms or the Maxims of Government Displayed* is one noteworthy example.[156] Harrison begins with Hooker's idea that "It is evident that no Rule or Form of Government be prescribed by the Law of God and Nature for then they would be both immutable."[157] Since then no political form is mandated by natural law, it follows that political subjection itself is not natural, so that in the pre-political condition all are equal:

> By the State of Nature we are all equal, there being no Superiority or Subordination to one above another: there can be nothing more rational then that Creatures of the same species and rank promiscuously born to all the same advantages of Nature and the use of the same Faculties all be equal one amongst another, without God by any manifest declaration of his Will had set one above another.[158]

This being the case, sovereignty is originally vested in the whole community and political authority is only legitimate when it is established through the consent of the community:

> All Politick Societies began from a voluntary Union and mutual agreement of Men, freely acting in the choice of their Governours, and Forms of Government. All Kings receive their Royal Dignity from the Community by which they are made the Superior Minister and Ruler of the People.[159]

Harrison then proceeds to justify his theory by turning to the authority of Richard Hooker, citing the First Book of the Laws.[160] Hooker makes an appearance in several other Whig tracts of the period. In Timothy Wilson's *The Vanity and Falsity of the History of Passive Obedience Detected* (1690), Wilson is taking issue with the doctrine of passive obedience to government which was associated with some of the Protestant reformers like Luther. Wilson turns to Hooker to establish the principle of limited government:

> Wherefore I shall only observe what the Author confesseth of the meek, wise, and ever reknowned *Hooker* in this (I Queen Elizabeth's) reign, Mr.Hooker published his Judicious Books of *Ecclesiastical* Polity, from the first of which it must be confessed, it is observed that he lays the Foundation of Government in Agreement he herein following the Schools too strictly . . . but be it as it will, we are sure Aristotle, the Schoolmen and *Mr. Hooker* are all ours in the Controversie. And if Mr. Hooker's Eight Book be Authentick[161] . . . I desire no better Authority.[162]

Thus it is clear that by the end of the seventeenth century, Hooker was regularly invoked by Whig writers to attack the patriarchalist theory of government, to establish the sovereignty of the community, and to argue for the origins of government in consent and agreement, in some cases even basing their resistance theories on these premises. As one contemporary writer put it:

> Many have cited the Authority of the *Judicious Hooker* till it is thread-bare to prove, that it is impossible that there should be a lawful Kingly power which is not mediately, or immediately, from the Consent of the People where 'tis exercised.[163]

It is no strange thing then that the most famous Whig writer would turn to the "Judicious Hooker" as his most cited authority in political philosophy. In October of 1689 John Locke's *Two Treatises of Government* was published.

NOTES

1. Robert Eccleshall, "Richard Hooker and the Peculiarities of the English," p. 64; this thoroughly researched article is the source of many of the references used in this section.

2. *Laws*, VIII.6.11.

3. The quote is from *A relation of the conference between William Lavvd, then, lrd. Bishop of St. Davids; now, lord arch-bishop of Canterbvry: and Mr. Fisher the Jesuite, by the command of King James* (1639). It dates originally to the 1620s before Laud ascended to the See of Canterbury. Given that Laud was frequently considered sym-

pathetic to Roman Catholicism, it is significant that this is an apologetic work designed to meet Catholic objections to Anglicanism (cf. http://www.prbm.com/interest/17c-k-la.shtml). For the quote and information on Laud and Hooker see Eccleshall, "Richard Hooker and the Peculiarities of the English," pp. 72–73.

4. *Ibid.*, p. 75.

5. *Ibid.*, p. 72; for information on Walwyn, note the text cited by Eccleshall: *Walwyn's just defence*, in *The Leveller Tracts 1647–1653.* eds. W. Haller and G. Davies (Gloucester, Mass., Peter Smith, 1964).

6. Cf. Eccleshall, "Richard Hooker and the Peculiarities of the English," p. 75.

7. John Hall, *The True Cavalier.* (London: Tho. Newscomb, 1656), p. 87.

8. *Ibid.*, pp. 88–89.

9. For information on the Great Tew circle, see *ibid.*, pp. 71–74.

10. http://www.thevickerage.worldonline.co.uk/ecivil/grand_remonstrance.htm

11. *Ibid.*

12. *Laws*, VIII.2.13.

13. http://www.thevickerage.worldonline.co.uk/ecivil/nineteen_propositions.htm

14. *Ibid.*

15. *Laws*, VIII.2.10.

16. Found online at http://www.thevickerage.worldonline.co.uk/ecivil/nineteen_propositions.htm

17. http://www.eskimo.com/~lhowell/bcp1662/intro/preface.html (italics added). This website has been sold, but an online copy of the 1662 prayer book remains intact.

18. John Barbon, *Liturgie a Most Divine Service.* (Oxford: AandL Lichtfield, 1663), p. 13

19. This is quoted also in Eccleshall, "Richard Hooker and the Peculiarities of the English," p. 68. Parenthetically Barbon also references Meric Casaubon's favor of Hooker.

20. Meric Casaubon was the son of the famous classical scholar Isaac Casaubon, the great classical scholar of Huguenot heritage who sought refuge in England in the late sixteenth century, at Archbishop Bancroft's invitation. Meric was also a notable classical scholar in his own right, penning works on Marcus Aurelius as well as on issues of Christian doctrine. See *Oxford Dictionary of National Biography.*

21. Meric Causabon, *A Vindication of the Lord's Prayer.* (London: Thomas Johnson, 1660), p. 82. An interesting aspect of this work is Casaubon's mention of Grotius's interest in having Hooker translated into Latin (p. 81), and the inclusion of the Latin letter from Grotius in which he mentions his interest in Hooker (cf. p. 81, and the non-paginated end of the work).

22. *Ibid.*, pp. 68–69, quoting *The History of the Worthies of England,* p. 69.

23. *Ibid.*, p. 70.

24. *Ibid.*, p. 67, Sparrow's text is a *Rationale upon the Book of Common Prayer of the Church of England* (1655?).

25. *Ibid.*, quoting Freeman's *The Reasonableness of the Divine Service: or Non-Conformity to Common-Prayer, proved not conformable to Common Reason* (1661).

26. Edward Stillingfleet. *Irenicum* (London: Henry Mortlock and John Simmes, 1662), p. 394. Cited by Eccleshall, p. 67.

27. Eccleshall, pp. 70–71.

28. *Ibid.*, p. 93.

29. *Ibid.*, p. 94.

30. John Nalson, *The Countermine*. (London: Jonathan Edwin, 1678).

31. Nalson, p. 6.

32. Nalson, p. 175.

33. Cf. Eccleshall, *ibid.*, 91.

34. *Ibid.*, p. 87.

35. *Ibid.*, p. 90, quoting *The Divine Right*, p. 138–139.

36. *Ibid.*, p. 95.

37. *Ibid.*, p. 99, quoting *The Fundamental Constitution of the English Government*, p. 4.

38. Cf. Aquinas, S.T. I-II, q.90, art. 3 .

39. For example, confer with the works of Manegold of Lautenbach, Giles of Rome, and John of Paris.

40. Cf. the previously quoted passage in chapter VII where he says of paternal authority that it "is not so derived from the generation, as if therefore the parent had dominion over his child because he begat him; but from the child's consent, either express, or by sufficient arguments declared" (As noted this is from *Leviathan*, chap. 20).

41. "To this war of every man against every man, this also is consequent; that nothing can be unjust. The notions of right and wrong, justice and injustice have no place. Where there is no common power there is no law: and where no law, no injustice" (*ibid.* 13.13).

42. *Ibid.*, introduction, xvii and xviii.

43. *Ibid.*, p. 120.

44. *Ibid.*, pp. 11–16.

45. Aquinas, *De Regimine Principium*, 1.

46. Aristotle, *Politics* I, II (trans. Jowett).

47. *Ibid.*, I,V.

48. *Ibid.*, I,XII.

49. *Ibid.*, I,II.

50. *Ibid.*, Book I,I (italics added).

51. *Ibid.*, I, VII.

52. James, *The True Law of Free Monarchy*. (Edinburgh, Robert Waldegrave, 1598), p. 5. "By the Law of Nature the King becomes a natural father to his lieges at his Coronation. And as a Father of his fatherly duety is bounde to care for the nourishing, education and vertuous gouernment of his children: euen is the King bounde to care for all his subjects."

53. Schochet, *The Authoritarian Family and Political Attitudes in 17th Century England*, p. 89.

54. Richard Mocket. *God and the King*. (London: John Beale, 1615), p. 3.

55. *Ibid.* p. 3, quoted with modernized spelling in Schochet, 89.

56. Mocket, p. 4.

57. *Ibid.*, p. 92.

58. Quoted in Schochet, *Ibid.*, p. 93.

59. *Ibid.*, pp. 92–93.

60. See J.P. Sommerville, "Hadrian Saravia, and the Advent of the Divine Right of Kings," p. 239 (quoting Saravia's *De Imperandi Authoritate*, 168, already quoted in chapter VII: "falsum esse opinionem eorum qui credunt primos populos palentis incertis sedibus, more beastiarum, in antris et sylvis, sine lege et Rege vixisse").

61. George Carleton. *Iurisdiction Regall, Episcopall, and Papall*(London, John Norton, 1610), p. 12.

Found cited in Schochet, *The Authoritarian Family and Political Attitudes in 17th Century England*, p. 95.

62. Sir Robert Filmer, *Patriarcha and Other Writings*, ed. Johann P. Sommerville (Cambridge: Cambridge University Press, 1991), pp. 132–133.

63. Robert Bellarmine (1542–1621) was one of the most central intellectual figures of the sixteenth and early seventeenth centuries and is a canonized saint of the Roman Catholic Church. Born in Tuscany, Bellarmine later became the first Jesuit to teach at the Catholic University of Louvain. Called to Rome in 1576, Bellarmine became a Papal Theologian and later in 1599, he became a Cardinal. The author of a large number of works on theology and philosophy, including his text *De Laicis*, Bellarmine argued that governments are established by consent. It was this theory that made Bellarmine, together with his fellow Jesuit Suarez, the target of Filmer's polemics. Bellarmine is also well known for his prominent role in the Galileo controversy.

64. Carleton, George, *Iurisdiction Regall, Episcopall, and Papall.* (London, John Norton, 1610), p. 12.

65. Spelman, Sir John, *Certain Consideration upon the Duties both of Prince and People* (Oxford: Leonard Lichfield, 1642), p. 2.

66. Schochet, p. 100, quoting from *Observations upon some of his late majesties answers and expresses*.(London, 1642), p. 18–19, quoted also by Schochet, p. 100.

67. *Ibid.*, pp. 100–101, quoting from Spelman's *A View of a printed Book.*

68. *Ibid.*, p. 102.

69. Dudley Diggs, *An Answer to a Printed Book.* (London: Leonard Lichfield, 1642), p. 4, quoted in Schochet, p. 10.

70. Henry Parker, *Jus Populi.* (London: Robert Bostock, 1644).

71. Ferne, Henry. *Conscience Satisfied.* (Oxford or London: Leonard Lichfield, 1643), p. 8, found quoted in Schochet, pp. 107–108.

72. Charles Herle, *An Answer to Doctor Ferne's reply* (London: Tho Brudenell, 1643); this was actually part of a short pamphlet war between Herle and Fern.

73. Schochet., p. 108–109.

74. *Ibid.*, p. 111, quoting from *Sacro Sancta Regum majestas or, the Sacred and Royal prerogative of Christian Kings.* (London: Tho. Dring, 1689).

75. *Ibid.*

76. Samuel Rutherford, *Lex, Rex: The Law and the Prince.* (London: John Field, 1644), p. 44.

77. Filmer, *Patriarcha and Other Writings*, p. 120.

78. *Ibid.*, p. 132.

79. *Ibid.*, pp. 184–185.

80. *Ibid.*, p. 281.

81. *Ibid.*, p. 2.

82. *Ibid.*

83. *Ibid.*, p. 3.

84. *Ibid.*, p. 5, quoting *De Laicis*, Book 3, Chapter 4.

85. *Ibid.*, p. 6.

86. *Laws*. VIII. K.2.5.

87. *Laws*, I.10.4.

88. Filmer, *Patriarcha and Other Writings*, 4 (italics added).

89. *Ibid.*, pp. 141–142.

90. *Ibid.*, p. 140.

91. *Ibid.*, pp. 20–21.

92. *Ibid.*, p. 21.

93. Schochet, *The Authoritarian Family and Political Attitudes in 17th Century England*, p. 131.

94. Filmer, *Patriarcha and Other Writings*, p. 32.

95. *Ibid.*, p. 7.

96. *Ibid.*, p. 12.

97. Dicendum ergo est hanc potestatem ex sola rei natura in nullo singulari homine existere sed in hominum collectione (Previously quoted in Part II from the *Tractatus De Legibus*, Book I, Caput 3:1).

98. Filmer, *Patriarcha and Other Writings*, p. 15, quoting *Tractatus De Legibus*, Book I, Caput 3:2.

99. *Ibid.*, p. 18.

100. *Ibid.*, pp. 11–12.

101. *Ibid.*, p. 22, quoting *Laws,* VIII.2.1.

102. *Laws*, I.10.4.

103. *Ibid.*, I,10.7.

104. Schochet, *The Authoritarian Family and Political Attitudes in 17th Century England*, 139.

105. Filmer, *Patriarcha and Other Writings*, p. 236.

106. *Ibid.*, p. 7.

107. *Ibid.*

108. *Ibid.*, p. 171.

109. *Ibid.*, p. 11.

110. *Ibid.*, p. 10.

111. *Ibid.*, p. 35.

112. *Ibid.*

113. *Ibid.*, p. 44.

114. *Ibid.*

115. *Ibid.*, p. 45.

116. *Ibid.*, p. 40.

117. *Ibid.*, p. 57.
118. *Ibid.*, p. 207.
119. *Laws*, VIII.2.13.
120. *Ibid.*, VIII.6.11.
121. *Ibid.*
122. Cf. Eccleshall, "Hooker and the Peculiarities of the English."
123. Edward Gee, *The Divine Right and Originall of the Civill magistrate from God.* (London: George Eversden, 1658); all references to Gee will be refering to this work.
124. Gee, ch. V, p. 144.
125. *Ibid.*, p. 145.
126. *Schochet*, pp. 172–173.
127. *Ibid.*, p. 173.
128. *Ibid.*, p. 172.
129. Gee, ch.V, p. 160.
130. Gee, ch. I, p. 20.
131. We had the earlier quoted statement of Filmer's "the compulsory power of the laws is that which properly makes laws to be laws . . . whereas the direction of the law is like advice and direction which the king's council gives the king, which no man can say is a law to the king."
132. Gee, chap 1, p. 21.
133. Cf. Gee's reference to Hooker's *Laws* on p. 22.
134. Gee, chap. 1, p. 22.
135. Eccleshall, "Hooker and the Peculiarities of the English," p. 90.
136. *Laws*, VIII.2.8 (Keble edition); Gee in fact cites Hooker on precisely this point, arguing from the legitimacy of hereditary monarchy (where its origins are consensual), cf. Gee, ch. VII, p.225, and ch. 8, p. 265.
137. *Ibid.*, VIII.2.11, (Keble edition).
138. *Ibid.*, VIII.2.9–10 (Keble edition).
139. *Ibid.*, I.10.8.
140. Eccleshall, "Hooker and the Peculiarities of the English," p. 115.
141. *Ibid.*, p. 85.
142. During the "Cavalier Parliament" of 1661–1679, King Charles II enjoyed a certain grace period, in which the conflict over the respective prerogatives of the Crown and Parliament abated. It might have seemed in the early Restoration as if the wounds opened by the civil war had healed. By the 1670s, cracks in the apparently harmonious arrangement began to break down. An important factor was the anti-Catholic sentiment that gripped many English Protestants, and the accompanying suspicion regarding the religious sympathies of the Stuarts. In 1670, Charles broke from the Protestant triple alliance with Holland and Sweden, and instead came to terms with the French King Louis XIV in the treaty of Dover. In a secret and possibly opportunistic passage in the treaty Charles agreed to convert to Catholicism and promote the Catholic cause among his subjects. The foreign policy of England then shifted to a Pro-French policy with England joining France in a war against Holland in 1672. The same year, Charles published a *Declaration of Indulgence* that ended most penalties

for non-conformists, and religious tests for office. While the *Indulgence* might be seen today as one of the most tolerant acts of the seventeenth century, in its own time the fact that the act ended most legal penalties for the practice of Catholicism (along with other faiths) and allowed Catholics to hold office increased suspicions that the King was in league with the forces of Roman Catholicism. In 1673, Parliament reacted by passing the Test Act that compelled office holders to take an oath upholding the Anglican Act of Supremacy and rejecting Catholic doctrines such as transubstantiation. In 1678, anti-Catholic sentiment in England reached the level of national hysteria when two Anglican clergyman, Titus Oates and Israel Tongue, made wild claims that there was a "Popish plot" led by the Jesuits to murder the king, burn down the city of London, butcher England's Protestant population, and install James the Catholic brother of Charles on the throne of England. As a result of the alleged Popish Plot, dozens were executed. In this atmosphere, the following year Parliament introduced the first bill to exclude James from the succession. Between 1679 and 1691, a total of three exclusion parliaments met. The last one met at Oxford in 1681 and was dissolved by the King's order.

143. Schochet, "The Authoritarian Family and Political Attitudes in 17th Century England," p. 193.

144. Algernon Sidney, *Discourses Concerning Government* (1698), p. 5 .

145. See Tyrrell, James. *Patriarcha Non Monarcha.* (London, Richard Janeway, 1681),p.35. All quotations refer to this work except where explicitly indicated. Cited also in Schochet, "The Authoritarian Family and Political Attitudes in 17th Century England," p. 199.

146. James Tyrrell *Bibliotheca Politica: An Enquiry into the Ancient Constitution of the English Government* (London: Richard Baldwin, 1694), p. 129; the work is framed as a series of dialogues between a Tory Filmerian, Mr.Meanwell, and a Whig gentlemen Mr. Freeman. Tyrrell in the person of Mr. Freeman quotes in this passage from Hooker's *Laws* Book I.10.

147. Tyrrell, p. 10.

148. "But God hath not delivered one man into the power of another merely to be tyrannized over at his pleasure; but that the person who hath this Authority may use it to the good of those he governs . . . in his [the father's] children he is chiefly to design their good advantage" (cf. Tyrrell, p. 17).

149. Tyrrell, p. 19.

150. Tyrrell, p. 20.

151. Tyrrell, p. 75, " [T]he Author [Filmer] is here mistaken, and that there really is in nature an Age of Nonage . . . in which the Child be indeed free, yet(by reason of his want of strength and discretion to judge what is necessary for his own preservation) is obligated to submit himself to his parents judgement in all things concerning that end."

152. Tyrrell, p. 94.

153. Schochet, p. 196, quoting Tyrrell, p. 35.

154. See Laslett's introduction to John Locke, *Two Treatises of Government* (Cambridge: Cambridge University Press, 1999), p. 60.

155. Eccleshall, "Richard Hooker and the Peculiarities of the English: The Reception of the 'Ecclesiastical Polity' in the Seventeenth and Eighteenth Centuries," p. 99, quoting Tyrrell, *Bibliotheca Politica* 4, p. 99.

156. Thomas Harrison, *Political Aphorisms or the Maxims of Government Displayed.* (London: printed for Thomas Harrison, 1690). In fact, this tract is only signed "T.H." and could thus be considered anonymous, but it is catalogued in "Early English Books Online" with Harrison as the author.

157. Harrison, p. 1.

158. Harrison, p. 2.

159. Harrison, p. 4.

160. See Harrison's citations of Hooker on p. 5 and p. 12.

161. We here recall the efforts by Tories to cast doubt on the authenticity of Book VIII.

162. Wilson, Timothy. *The Vanity and Falsity of the History of Passive Obedience Detected.* (London: George Croom, 1690), p. 8.

163. William Atwood, *The Fundamental Constitution of the English Government.* (London, J.D., 1690), p. 4.

about Ʒi Theriac Androm ut[er]
every night

M[r]s mary Percivall had a 3[an] ague
last winter was cured with Cortex
Peru. About the later end of may
or m[i] June (about what time many of
those agues returned ag[n]) she w[as]
very much out of order ag[n] every other
day & could not eat her meat Coo[k]
very ill & was sick & though it were
not a perfect ague was plainly an
aguish distemper

℞ Theriac Androm ut Ʒi
Ent veneris g[r] vi. m·f· bolus
cui[us] qualibet nocte horâ somni
she tooke this about a week
et convaluit

_____

The works of Mr Richard
Hooker fol London 76 p 553
Scores the wittyest of the schoole
Divines Hooker 553 p 93

74

That wch doth assigne to each thing
the kinde, that wch doth moderate
the force & power, that wch doth
appoint the forme & measure the
same we terme Law Hooker 553
p 70 §2.

I am not ignorant yt by law Eternall
the learned for the most part doe understand
ye order not wch god hath eternally purposed
himself in all his workes to observe: but
rather yt wch with himself he hath
set downe as expedient to be kept
by all his creatures according to the
severall conditions where with he hath
endued them. They who thus are accustomed to
speake apply the name of Law unto
that only rule of working wch superior
authority imposeth whereas we somewhat
more inlarging the sense thereof
terme any kinde of rule or canon
whereby actions are framed a law. Now
that law wch as it laid up in the bosome
of god they call Eternall receiveth

according to the different kinde of things
wᶜʰ are subiect unto it different &
sundry kindes of nature that part
of it wᶜʰ ordereth naturall agents
wee call vsually **naturs law**. That
wᶜʰ angells doe clearly behold & wᵗʰout
any ~~error~~ swerveing observe is
a Law **Celestiall**. The law of reason
yᵗ wᶜʰ bindeth creatures reasonable in
this world & wᶜʰ wᵗʰ by reason they most
plainly perceive themselves bound.
That wᶜʰ bindeth them & is not knowen
but by speciall revelation from god
Divine law. Humane law yᵗ wᶜʰ
out of thᵗ law either of reason or of
god men probably gathering to be
expedient they made it a law
The **first Eternall law** is yᵗ wᶜʰ god
himself hath eternally purposed to keepe
& doth himself worke according to
The **second eternall law** Is that law
wᶜʰ he hath imposed upon his creatures

The "Judicious Hooker": *The Laws of Ecclesiastical Polity* in the Political Writing of John Locke

So accustomed have we become to thinking of John Locke as "the Father of Liberalism" that we forget that the early Locke was in many respects a staunchly conservative figure. In his first political writings, Locke greeted the Restoration of King Charles II in jubilant terms: "All the freedom I can wish for my country or myself is to enjoy the protection of those laws which the prudence and providence of our ancestors established and the happy return of his Majesty hath restored."[1] It was here at the very beginning of the Restoration that Locke first began to turn to Hooker as an authority in questions of ecclesiastical and political philosophy. The restoration of the Crown meant also the restoration of the Church of England, and the efforts of the King to enforce his authority over the ritual and government of the Church opened the same kinds of questions that Hooker himself had dealt with. Though now in a disadvantageous political position on account of the Cavalier Parliament, certain Presbyterians and other non-conformists continued to view the Anglican Church as un-Biblical and riddled with "Popish remnants," and contested the authority of the Crown over Church ritual and government. In 1660, Edward Bagshaw wrote a text entitled *The Great Question Concerning Things Indifferent,*[2] which argued that "things indifferent" (i.e. questions of ritual and ceremony) ought to be left to private judgment and should not be adjudicated by the civil magistrate. The Bagshaw/Locke debate is thus surprisingly similar in content to the debate between Hooker and Whitgift on one side, and Thomas Cartwright and the Admonitioners on the other. The main difference is that while Cartwright denied the existence of things indifferent and wanted to purge the Church of England from such practices, Bagshaw's position is defensive. He wants to preserve the liberty of conscience of those who did not want to be constrained in "things indifferent."[3] Against those who argue from

Biblical examples of Hebrew Kings adjudicating religious issues, Bagshaw acknowledges that the Jews in the Old Covenant were bound to observe uniform rites and rituals,[4] but argues that Christian liberty consists precisely in freedom from being bound in such indifferent matters of rite and ceremony. Bagshaw thus takes up once again the Calvinist theme of solicitude for indifferent matters as a cause of scruples and dissension, and a form of bondage that fetters Christian liberty:

> And it seems altogether needless, that the *Jewish Ceremonies,* should as to their Necessity at least, expire and be abrogated, if others might succeed in their roome, and be as strictly commanded, as ever the former were. For this returns us to our *Bondage* again, which is so much the more intolerable, in that our religion is [titled] the *Perfect Law of Liberty* which *Liberty* I understand not wherein it consists, if in things *Necessarie,* we are already commanded by God and in things *Indifferent* we may still be tied up to *Humaine Ordinances*, and *Outside Rites* at the pleasure of our *Christian Magistrates*.[5]

Bagshaw next takes issue with another argument for civil authority's intervention in the *adiaphora* that he attributes to Richard Hooker among others. Since the civil authority has no power over "things necessary," if it also had no power in "things indifferent" it would seem to follow that the civil authority would be abridged of any role in religious life at all.

> That things necessary to the worship of God, be already determined by God, and over them the *Magistrate* has no power; if likewise he should have no Power in *Indifferent Things* that it would follow, that in things appertaining to religion, the *Christian Magistrate* hath no power at all—which they think to be very absurd—so the Reverend and very learned Mr. Hooker and Dr. Sanderson.[6]

Bagshaw launches two rebuttal arguments, first that the "imposing power" of the civil authority has no warrant in Scripture,[7] and secondly that the existence of things indifferent in the Christian dispensation so far from being an argument in favor of civil authority's role in such matters, is an argument against them, since what is of its nature indifferent, should not be made necessary.[8] Bagshaw thus sets himself against a Constantinian Christianity in which the civil authority governs religious matters by coercive penal laws. Indeed he names Constantine as the author of an "Antichristian Tyranny."[9] By abstaining from the use of constraint in things indifferent for Bagshaw, the prince both honors God, and ensures the felicity of the commonwealth.

> Where the *Magistrate* most consults God's honour and his own duty, it being strict to himself, he leaves all others in their *Outward Ceremonies*, to their Inward Convictions. Which *Liberty* is so far from weakening, that it is indeed the

security of a Throne: since besides gaining the Peoples Love . . . it doth in an especial manner entitle him to Gods Protection since in not pretended to be wiser then God, he gives Religion the free and *Undisturbed Passage* which our Savior seems by his life and death to have opened for it.[10]

The publication of this text mobilized Locke to respond with his *Two Tracts on Government* defending the right of the Crown over the *adiaphora*.[11] In the Second Tract in particular, Locke proposes to address the question: "Can the Civil magistrate specify indifferent things to be included within the order of divine worship and impose them on the people?"[12]

As we have seen, the question of whether the civil authority has to right to legislate in "things indifferent" was a central question for Hooker as well. In addressing this question, the one who would later author the *Essay on Toleration* complains against those who are always:

Bitterly crying out that the liberty of the Gospel, the fundamental entitlement of all Christians, is being tyrannically denied them, and the rights of their consciences trampled upon. This view leads to contempt for the magistrate and disrespect for the laws, whether secular or spiritual, for they believe people can do what they like, so long as they defend liberty of religion and liberty of conscience two slogans which people are extraordinarily quick to rally around. Indeed the burning zeal of those who discover the rashness and ignorance of the multitude by appealing to conscience often ignites a fire capable of devastating everything.

Vindicating the authority of the English Crown and Parliament over "things indifferent" was a central purpose of the *Laws*, as has already been shown. In defending the same position, Locke's emphasis was that the religious passions unleashed by the Puritan attack on the civil and ecclesiastical polity of England had led to a destructive period of chaos and warfare, and now the only thing rational and sober minds ought to do is recognize the need for Ecclesiastical order through obedience to established authority:

Now God has restored peace to our land . . . we must hope that nobody will now be so pig headed and obstinate as to try once again to destabilize society, or to question the magistrate's authority to legislate on indifferent things. Now that civil strife has died away and religious enthusiasm is on the wane, more sober minds will recognize that civil obedience, even in the indifferent aspects of divine worship, is not one of the least important of civil obligations, and that our only hope lies in punctilious obedience.[13]

Locke asserts the right of the magistrate to command as necessary in order to maintain public peace and, in terms almost echoing Bodin, writes that the power to make law by his commands is precisely the mark of a sovereign. For him the King:

> Has the overall authority to make and repeal laws. *It is this which gives the magistrate that supreme right of command* which alone enables him to command others, and direct societies affairs to the public good, according to his understanding of, and by any means he sees fit, and which enables him to order and dispose the people so as to keep them in peace and concord.[14]

It is formulating his theory of law in relation to "things indifferent" that Locke first turns to Richard Hooker:

> If we are to have an adequate understanding of indifferent matters we must give some account of law. The judicious Hooker describes it as follows (bk.1, ch.2): 'That which doth assign the force and power, that which doth appoint the form and measure of working, that we term a law.'[15]

From Hooker's definition, Locke proceeds to discuss the hierarchy of laws in relation to the question of "things indifferent." Thus, he first discusses divine law, which is further divided into the familiar scholastic divisions of natural and divine positive law according to whether it is knowable by reason or through revelation:

> The divine law is that which has been given to men by God. It is a rule and pattern of living to them. According as it becomes known by the light of natural reason, implanted in men, or is declared by supernatural revelation it is further divided into natural law and positive divine law . . . I call both of them 'moral' as well as 'divine.' For the divine law is the great measure of justice and rectitude, and the eternal foundation of all moral good and evil.[16]

The concept of the divine law as well as the moral law allows Locke to elucidate the notion of "indifferent matters." An action, which is not commended as a good by divine law or prohibited by it as an evil, is "indifferent," deriving its goodness or malice from the circumstances. Thus, he says: "Whatever, therefore, this [divine] law either orders or forbids is always of necessity, either good or bad; all other things which do not fall within the decrees of this law are left subject to men's free choice and are by their nature indifferent."[17] Locke, in the *Second Tract*, next turns his attention to the human law that he defines as:

> that which is enacted by someone who holds authority over others and has the right to make laws for them. Rather any instruction given by a superior to an inferior over whom he excercises legitimate authority, for instance the command of a parent to a child, or of a master to a servant, can be termed a human law and

requires obedience. However since the public decrees of a community, issued by a magistrate, are especially important . . . it is these in particular that we mean to refer to by the term human law.[18]

According to Locke, it is precisely those "things indifferent" on which the divine or moral law is silent that are the proper sphere of the human law. Were the ruler merely to decree laws already part of the moral law, he would not be promulgating any specifically new form of law:

> The proper subject-matter of this law is those indifferent matters which have not been included within a higher—that is to say, the divine—law, and are thus not yet layed down and determined. It is true that the magistrate may forbid theft, or insist on chastity, but in doing so he is merely recapitulating the divine law: he is not enacting new law so much as disseminating the existing law and requiring obedience to it. Chastity and respect for private property remain necessary even if he does not legislate for them, and the obligation on the consciences of the faithful remains in any case.[19]

Since the divine or moral law cannot cover every conceivable case concerning the particular circumstances of a commonwealth, God leaves such "things indifferent" to the discretion of the civil authority:

> God has left many indifferent things which are not included within his laws to the care of his deputy, the magistrate. It is right that government, should concern itself with indifferent things, for the magistrate can order or forbid them as the circumstances require, and by wisely regulating them he can successfully pursue the welfare of his people.[20]

Since indifferent questions are specific subjects of the human or positive law, Locke argues that the authority of the civil magistrate extends to *all* indifferent matters. He holds that it is vain to make a distinction between "secular" indifferent matters and the indifferent forms and rituals of the Church of England:

> All things which are indifferent are so for the same reason; and in both secular and spiritual indifferent matters, the logic is the same, and indeed the very same objects are in question, seen only from two different points of view. There is no more difference between them then between the jacket I wear on a weekday, and the very same jacket when I wear it to church. It follows that the magistrate must embrace both categories of indifferent things, unless God has somewhere that the magistrate's authority should be restricted within narrower limits.[21]

Locke then turns briefly to the great question of seventeenth century English thought between Patriarchalists and consensualists about the origins of political obligation and whether the natural condition of man were one of liberty or subjection:

> There are some who claim that men are born to servitude; others that they are born to freedom. The latter affirm that all men are equal according to the law of nature; the former stress that fathers have authority over their children, and that this is the origin of political authority.[22]

It was a question which Locke would later address definitively in his *Two Treatises*. At this stage, his point is that if *either* of these is correct, the civil authority still has jurisdiction in indifferent matters. Taking first the case of patriarchalism:

> If he occupies the throne by divine institution and by reason of birthright and natural superiority, it follows that he is the sole ruler both of the earth and its inhabitants, without any contract or limitation, and that he can do whatever is not prohibited by God, to whom alone he is subject . . . nor can anyone deny that all indifferent actions, no matter what category they belong to, are under his command, for to his discretion are delivered the liberty, possessions, and life of each of his subjects.[23]

However, says Locke, even if one accepts the premise of natural liberty and the consensual origins of government one and the same conclusion would follow:

> On the other hand if men have a right to equal liberty by virtue of the fact that there is no difference between them at birth and they are entitled to equal rights, it is nevertheless clear that men could establish no social life, no law, no institution or commonwealth . . . unless each man had given up their native liberty . . . and transferred his rights to another, whether that other be an individual ruler or an assembly, depending on the form of state they wish to establish. It is indispensable that this instituted authority should hold supreme power, for no commonwealth has ever existed, or ever could exist without human laws, and laws can bind only if they are imposed by supreme authority . . . the consequence of this is that whatever any individual was entitled to do he can now be commanded to do by the magistrate, for he embodies the authority and natural right of each individual by virtue of their mutual contract. Consequently all indifferent things, whether sacred or secular, are subject to his legislative authority and the right of command.[24]

Locke's concern in the *Second Tract* is thus not to determine whether the Patriarchalist or consensualist account of political authority is correct, but rather to show that whatever the origins of political obligation, the scope of civil authority over indifferent matters is unaffected:

I do not intend to defend any one of these approaches, nor is it relevant to our present controversy to establish which one of them is true. For in all events, this is true: God intends there to be ordered society and government amongst men, or in other words he wants commonwealths to exist. In every commonwealth there must be a supreme authority, for without such an authority a common-wealth cannot exist. The supreme authority is in every state of the same type, for it is always the legislative which is supreme. As we have shown above the subject-matter of all legislative authority is all indifferent things.[25]

The staunchly royalist and authoritarian sympathies of the early Locke are shown by his attitude to resistance, which certainly went well beyond anything that had existed, for example, among medieval scholastics. At this period of time, Locke did not believe there were *any* circumstances in which active resistance to civil authority was justified: "The subject is bound to obey any decree of the magistrate whatsoever, whether it is just, or unjust. There can be no possible justification for a private citizen resisting the decrees of the magistrate by force of arms, although if the subject-matter of the decree is unlawful then the magistrate sins in commanding it."[26]

Events during the early years of the Restoration went very much in the direction that Locke at this stage of his life would have approved. Between 1661 and 1665, the Cavalier Parliament enacted the four laws making up the Clarendon code that excluded non-conformists from public office and placed restrictions on their ability to legally meet, worship, and disseminate their doctrines. By 1667, however, Locke wrote his *Essay on Toleration* calling for end to civil penalties for Protestant (though not Roman Catholic) non-conformists. Clearly, Locke had undergone a considerable evolution in his religious and political ideas. Many attribute the change of perspective to his increasing association with the Earl of Shaftesbury.[27] Shaftesbury would later become one of the most important Whig leaders during the Exclusion controversy (1679-1681), and it is in this context that we must understand the *Two Treatises of Government*,[28] which is the next time Locke makes explicit use of Hooker's *Laws* in a political treatise, though for a rather different purpose.[29]

HOOKER IN LOCKE'S TWO TREATISES

To discuss the debt of Locke's *Two Treatises* to Hooker's *Laws* is virtually to seek an overview of Locke's entire argument. Locke purchased three different editions of the *Laws* for his private library.[30] His primary source—the 1666 edition—was purchased in 1681 while he was writing the *Two Treatises* and he wrote extensive notes about it in his journal.[31] Locke's 1681 personal journal[32]—included in the Lovelace collection donated to Oxford—provides a lot of evidence of Locke's personal fascination with Hooker's writings. On June 13, Locke records that he purchased a copy of the '66 edition of Hooker's *Laws* and for the next few weeks Locke took down extensive notes based on citations from the *Laws*. On June 17, Locke includes a note about Hooker's comment on Scotus as the "wittiest of the school-divines". The following day Locke wrote several pages on Hooker's doctrine of law, citing his Hooker definition of law as what assigns to each thing its force and power. Locke also wrote on the hierarchy of eternal, celestial, divine, and human law, and on Hooker's distinction between first and second law eternal. On June 27, Locke took notes on Hooker's doctrine of the will, mentioning that the will necessarily is directed toward the good, and choosing is willing one thing before another. On June 28, Locke noted Hooker's interest in Law as a directive rule, and distinguished how this directive rule applied in the case of voluntary and involuntary agents. Since many of these ideas were never actually incorporated into Locke's published works, one wonders whether Locke was more influenced by Hooker's natural law theory that most imagine. Another important reference in Locke's unpublished manuscripts is found under the heading "Ecclesia" in a 1682 manuscript. Here Locke focuses on Hooker's distinction between the Church as a supernatural society based on revealed law, and that aspect of the life of the Church whose origins are "the same as other societies viz an inclination unto sociable life and a consent to the bond of association." Oddly, Locke concludes from this that "noe body can impose any ceremonys unless positively and clearly by revelation enjoyned . . . for if his conscience condemns any part of unrevealed worship he cannot by any sanction of men be obliged to it."[33] This manuscript is a kind of dictionary of terms Locke wrote for himself, and he gives Hooker central place in the heading "ecclesia." Hooker did indeed argue that the Church is not exclusively a supernatural society, but also contains elements of a "natural society" based on consent and sociability. But his purpose here was not to promulgate a modern doctrine of religious freedom, of the type that Locke would later favor. It was rather to endeavor to demonstrate that Crown and Parliament are morally competent to govern the Church in so far as its legislation concerns "things indifferent" about which revelation is silent.

Hooker is used by Locke to support his major premises in three basic areas: 1) Locke's argument regarding regal and paternal authority; 2) Locke's concept of the state of nature; and 3) Locke's conception of consent and agreement as the origin of political obligation. We shall discuss each of these in turn.

First, however, we might ask the question of why Locke turned so extensively to Hooker? In part, of course, it was because Locke was deeply fascinated and influenced by the arguments found in the *Laws*. We have noted that in Locke's earlier *Two Tracts*, Locke pleaded agnosticism on the great question of whether the origins of government were Patriarchal or consensual. Yet, by the time of the *Two Treatises*, Locke had clearly adopted as his own Hooker's views on the existence of a pre-political condition of man and on consent and agreement as the origins of political obligation. Nonetheless, it is also clear that for Locke turning to Hooker's authority also served a polemical purpose. This factor was due to the eminence and authority that Hooker enjoyed among nearly all factions of English political opinion during the post-Restoration era. As we have seen, the Tory position eagerly assimilated Hooker's theology as virtually the measure of orthodox Anglicanism, even while sidelining his constitutionalist political theses in favor of Filmer's patriarchalism. To depose Filmerian patriarchalism from its position of dominance, it was thus quite logical for Locke to turn to Hooker. As a revered theologian of impeccable conservative credentials, Hooker was under no suspicion of the radicalism associated with the Puritan revolution. Moreover, though clearly in the scholastic mold, Hooker had none of the disadvantages associated in the English Protestant mind with those medieval or early modern Catholic scholastics who also held anti-Patriarchalist theses.[34] Locke, like Gee, Tyrrell, and Sidney, could thus turn to Hooker as a way of refuting the Tories from the very authority that they venerated. This is precisely what Locke suggests is his reason for turning to Hooker in the *Second Treatise*: "I thought *Hooker* alone might be enough to satisfy those men, who relying on him for their ecclesiastical polity, are by a strange fate carried to deny those principles upon which he builds it."[35]

LOCKE'S USE OF HOOKER ON THE DISTINCTION OF PATERNAL AND REGAL POWER

The *Two Treatises* belong to the same family of Whig and anti-Filmerian tracts as Algernon Sidney's *Discourses* and James Tyrrell's *Patriarcha non Monarcha*. Locke's argument naturally shares with these treatises many elements of form and content. The contemporary obsession with comparing Locke to Hobbes rather then Filmer has perhaps blinded many scholars to the importance of Locke's *First Treatise* as the edifice upon which his whole argument rests. Only if patriarchalism is false can we make sense of the major tenets of Locke's political philosophy, such as the natural liberty of man, the consensual rather then natural origins of government, and the right of resistance. Locke's first step therefore is a critical one—to demonstrate the distinction between paternal and regal authority.[36] Locke holds that Filmer's entire argument against man's natural liberty hinges upon his identification of paternal with regal authority. Filmer's basic thesis is the fact that a child is born not into freedom but into a condition of subjection, and that this natural subjection of children to parents is identical with political subjection. Thus, Locke says that:

> SIR *Robert Filmer*'s great position is, that *men are not naturally free.* This is the foundation on which his absolute monarchy stands, and from which it erects itself to an height, that its power is above every power, *caput inter nubila,* so high above all earthly and human things, that thought can scarce reach it; that promises and oaths, which tye the infinite Deity, cannot confine it. But if this foundation fails, all his fabric falls with it, and governments must be left again to the old way of being made by contrivance, and the consent of men . . . making use of their reason to unite together into society. To prove this grand position of his, he tells us: *Men are born in subjection to their parents,* and therefore cannot be free. And this authority of parents, he calls *royal authority. Fatherly authority, right of fatherhood.*[37]

Against this view, Locke will strive to prove the opposite position that:

> But these two *powers, political* and *paternal,* are so perfectly distinct and separate; are built upon so different foundations, and given to so different ends, that every subject that is a father, has as much a paternal power over his children, as the prince has over his: and every prince, that has parents, owes them as much filial duty and obedience, as the meanest of his subjects do to theirs; and can therefore contain not any part or degree of that kind of dominion, which a prince or magistrate has over his subject.[38]

As we have seen, this was far from an original position—Locke was merely *reaffirming* the respected and traditional position that distinguished that *Regia Potestas* from the *Pater Potestas*. The distinction was already made by Aristotle,[39] and was a common assertion among the Catholic scholastics on the continent.[40] We have already seen that it received particular emphasis in Richard Hooker's *Laws*:

> To fathers within their private families nature hath given a supreme power . . . . Howbeit over a grand multitude having no such dependency upon anyone . . . impossible it is that any should have complete lawful power but by consent of men, or immediate appointment of God; because not having the natural superiority of fathers their power must needs be either usurped, and then unlawful; or if lawful then granted or consented by them over whom they exercise the same.[41]

It was Filmer's view that paternal and regal authority are identical which represented a more novel and radical position though it had certain important antecedents, like Saravia's *De Authoritate Imperandi*. Yet, as our survey has indicated, patriarchalism became a dominant position in political philosophy in the seventeenth century. By Locke's time it had become an establishment doctrine favored by partisans of the Stuart restoration. Locke, in the beginning of his *First Treatise* decries the consequences of this Patriarchalist thesis:

> In this last age a generation of men has sprung up amongst us, that would flatter princes with an opinion, that they have a divine right to absolute power, let the laws by which they are constituted, and are to govern, and the conditions under which they enter upon their authority, be what they will, and their engagements to observe them never so well ratified by solemn oaths and promises. To make way for this doctrine, they have denied mankind a right to natural freedom; whereby they have not only, as much as in them lies, exposed all subjects to the utmost misery of tyranny and oppression, but have also unsettled the titles, and shaken the thrones of princes: (for they too, by these mens system, except only one, are all born slaves, and by divine right are subjects to *Adam*'s right heir); as if they had designed to make war upon all government, and subvert the very foundations of human society, to serve their present turn.[42]

Locke holds that all of the elaborate arguments Filmer uses can be reduced to a simpler one:

> His system lies in a little compass, it is no more but this,
> *That all government is absolute monarchy.*
> *And the ground he builds on, is this,*
> *That no man is born free.*[43]

In other words, since monarchy is held by Filmer to be both absolute and *natural*, it follows that all mankind is born not free, but in a condition of absolute subjection to the will of another. Filmer's argument had essentially three planks—first that God had enthroned Adam in Eden as the sovereign ruler over the earth, and thus Adam enjoyed the prerogatives of a king by special divine right; second that the paternal and regal authority is one and the same. Thus Adam had a paternal right of dominion over his descendents, as their king as well as their father, and third that Kings rule by the *natural* right of paternity, though for Filmer this is also confirmed by a precept of the divine law—*Honor thy father and mother*—by the fact that a discernible line of inheritance links the authority exercised by Adam to the authority of kings in all later ages.

Locke sets about in his *First Treatise* endeavoring to systematically undermine each of these tenets. The first of Filmer's tenets that God bestowed upon Adam a proprietary right over the earth Locke terms "Donation" and he deals with this claim by means of fairly elaborate biblical exegesis.[44] However, it is Filmer's argument for Adam's title by *paternal right* that is perhaps of the most direct interest to us. The identity of paternal with regal authority was of course the core of the Patriarchalist position. It is clear evidence that the *Second Treatise* was also a reply to Filmer's patriarchalism, that he devotes a full chapter to the issue of paternal authority, as if the long arguments in the *First Treatise* were not yet sufficient. The authority of Hooker's *Laws* has an important place in the course of Locke's counterargument. Filmer makes four basic contentions regarding paternal authority, that the authority to govern is given divine sanction in the commandment of the Decalogue to honor one's father;[45] that the authority of fathers is an absolute and unlimited authority extending even over the lives and goods of their children;[46] that the authority of kings is one and the same as paternal authority;[47] that consequently kings have an absolute and unlimited right to rule.[48]

Locke addresses each of these contentions in turn. Regarding the commandment in the Decalogue to honor one's father, Locke notes frequently that the whole commandment is, "honor thy father *and mother*." Had the intention of the verse commandment been to bestow absolute political authority there would have been as much of an argument to equate *maternal* with regal authority, as to identify paternal with regal authority. Thus, in the *Second Treatise*, Locke writes:

> Had but this one thing been well considered, without looking any deeper into the matter, it might perhaps have kept men from running into those gross mistakes . . . if this supposed absolute power over children had been called *parental*; and thereby have discovered, that it belonged to the *mother* too: for it will but very ill serve the turn of those men, who contend so much for the absolute power and authority of the *fatherhood,* as they call it, that the mother should have any share in it; and it would have but ill supported the *monarchy* they contend for, when by the very name it appeared, that that fundamental authority, from whence they would derive their government of a single person only, was not placed in one, but two persons jointly.[49]

Locke had made the same point in the *First Treatise*:

> The scripture joins *mother* too in that homage, which is due from children; and had there been any text, where the honour or obedience of children had been directed to the *father* alone, it is not likely that our author, who pretends to build all upon scripture, would have omitted it: nay, the scripture makes the authority of *father and mother,* in respect of those they have begot, so equal, that in some places it neglects even the priority of order, which is thought due to the father, and the *mother* is put first, as *Lev.* xix. 3. from which so constantly joining father and mother together, as is found quite through the scripture, we may con-

clude that the honour they have a title to from their children, is one common right belonging so equally to them both, that neither can claim it wholly, neither can be excluded.[50]

Locke will want to argue that the authority of parents over their children is neither absolute and arbitrary nor essentially political. This leads him to inquire as to the nature and limits of parental authority and why children are subject to it. His answer is founded on the intimate relationship he sees between rationality and freedom:

> The *freedom* then of man, and liberty of acting according to his own will, is *grounded on* his having *reason,* which is able to instruct him in that law he is to govern himself by, and make him know how far he is left to the freedom of his own will. To turn him loose to an unrestrained liberty, before he has reason to guide him, is not the allowing him the privilege of his nature to be free; but to thrust him out amongst brutes, and abandon him to a state as wretched, and as much beneath that of a man, as their's. This is that which puts the *authority* into the *parent's* hands to govern the *minority* of their children. God hath made it their business to employ this care on their off-spring, and hath placed in them suitable inclinations of tenderness and concern to temper this power, to apply it, as his wisdom designed it, to the children's good, as long as they should need to be under it.[51]

Man, for Locke, is under an obligation to obey the natural law that he discovers by means of his own reason. Locke here defines natural law in a rather scholastic/teleological manner as a rule by which a free and rational agent is directed to his due end: "for *law,* in its true notion, *is* not so much the limitation as *the direction of a free and intelligent agent* to his proper interest."[52] Since the natural law is discerned by means of man's reason, it follows that an agent is not responsible to the law except in so as he or she is rational and able to freely direct his or her actions. However, children are not born into the world having the full advertence of reason and, consequently, they are unable to freely direct their actions in a responsible manner:

> The law, that was to govern *Adam,* was the same that was to govern all his posterity, the *law of reason.* But his offspring having another way of entrance into the world, different from him, by a natural birth, that produced them ignorant and without the use of *reason,* they were not presently *under that law;* for no body can be under a law, which is not promulgated to him; and this law being promulgated or made known by *reason* only, he that is not come to the use of his *reason,* cannot be said to be *under this law;* and *Adam's* children, being not presently as soon as born *under this law of reason,* were not presently *free.*[53]

On this account, parents have only a *custodial* authority over their children until such time as they are free and responsible agents able to guide their own actions. This concept of *non-age*—the time of childhood or minority before human beings are left in the power of their own counsel is a crucial one for Locke. It means that parental authority is thus limited both in time (until the child attains majority) and extent (it must be exercised in accordance with its end of providing care and education). Once the child is recognized as a free and rational agent, he becomes a free man or woman:

> The *power*, then, *that parents have* over their children, arises from that duty which is incumbent on them, to take care of their off-spring, during the imperfect state of childhood. To inform the mind, and govern the actions of their yet ignorant non-age, till reason shall take its place, and ease them of that trouble, is what the children want, and the parents are bound to: for God having given man an understanding to direct his actions, has allowed him a freedom of will, and liberty of acting, as properly belonging thereunto, within the bounds of that law he is under. But whilst he is in an estate, wherein he has not *understanding* of his own to direct his *will,* he is not to have any *will* of his own to follow: he that *understands* for him, must *will* for him too; he must prescribe to his will, and regulate his actions; but when he comes to the estate that made his *father a freeman*, the *son is a freeman* too.[54]

On this point of the connection between reason and freedom, Locke turns to Hooker, who argues in the *Laws* that there are three classes of persons who being unable to guide their actions by right reason to the goods proper to human nature must be subject to the custodial authority of others. For such persons have neither the capacity to know the law that they ought to obey nor the freedom to act in accordance with it. The three categories are madmen, innocents (probably those who are born with a defective intelligence), and children.[55] Of these three categories, madmen and innocents are generally never able to be freemen, since they are deprived of the use of right reason. However, children are released into the power of their own counsel as soon as they attain the use of reason sufficiently to understand and keep the law. Here again Locke turns to Hooker:

> If any body should ask me, when my son is *of age to be free*? I shall answer, just when his monarch is of age to govern. *But at what time,* says the judicious *Hooker,* Eccl. Pol. l. i. sect. 6. *a man may be said to have attained so far forth the use of reason, as sufficeth to make him capable of those laws whereby he is then bound to guide his actions: this is a great deal more easy for sense to discern, than for any one by skill and learning to determine.*[56]

The subjection of children to parental authority is then, according to Locke, due to a special and temporary circumstance, viz. the fact that when born into the world the child does not yet have the full use of reason. If the duty to *honor* one's parents never ceases, parental authority itself is temporary and far from a supreme and unlimited power. It must be exercised prudently for the good to which it is directed, namely, the care and well being of the children.[57] Since the authority of fathers (and parents) is founded on the particular circumstance that children cannot yet direct their actions freely through right reason, it follows that there is no analogy between the rule that parents exercise over their own children, and the rule that public authority exercises. This is because the subjects of civil authority, unlike the subjects of parental authority are free adults able to govern themselves. There is, for Locke, no natural prerogative (like paternal right) of some free and rational persons to rule over others, and thus the authority of civil government is only legitimate if the free persons consent to be governed for their own good and that of the community. Locke concedes that what Schochet would term "anthropological" patriarchalism is a possibility — namely, that the first kings were *historically* fathers of families.[58]

However, Locke argues that even in that case, insofar as the rule of fathers was *political*, it would have to be derived from at least the tacit consent of the subjects, and not from any inherent right in some to rule:

> But that this was not by any *paternal right,* but only by the consent of his children, is evident from hence, that no body doubts, but if a stranger, whom chance or business had brought to his family, had there killed any of his children, or committed any other fact, he might condemn and put him to death, or otherwise have punished him, as well as any of his children; which it was impossible he should do by virtue of any paternal authority over one who was not his child, but by virtue of that executive power of the law of nature, which, as a man, he had a right to: and he alone could punish him in his family, where the respect of his children had laid by the exercise of such a power, to give way to the dignity and authority they were willing should remain in him, above the rest of his family.[59]

To summarize, Locke contends that while the first kings happened to have also been fathers, this was not as a result of natural or divine right. There is in fact no particular form of government that is ordained by nature. Government therefore derives its legitimacy from consent and agreement. For all of these ideas, Locke quotes Hooker for support. This passage from *Laws* is the one Locke uses to defend these contentions. In it we find Hooker's tenet that government arose from consent rather than natural prerogative and that the natural law does not mandate any special mode of governance:

> It is no improbable opinion therefore, which the archphilosopher was of, that the chief person in every houshold was always, as it were, a king: so when numbers of housholds joined themselves in civil societies together, kings were the first

kind of governors amongst them, which is also, as it seemeth, the reason why the name of fathers continued still in them, who, of fathers, were made rulers; as also the ancient custom of governors to do as *Melchizedec,* and being kings, to exercise the office of priests, which fathers did at the first, grew perhaps by the same occasion. Howbeit, this is not the only kind of regiment that has been received in the world. The inconveniences of one kind have caused sundry others to be devised; so that in a word, all public regiment, of what kind soever, seemeth evidently to have risen from the deliberate advice, consultation and composition between men, judging it convenient and behoveful; there being no impossibility in nature considered by itself, but that man might have lived without: any public regiment, *Hooker's Eccl. P. lib.* i. *sect.* 10.[60]

We thus see that Locke *follows* Hooker's position that government is the product of artifice rather than nature. It is from this idea that Locke develops his notion of the "state of nature," and this is the next aspect of Hooker's influence on Locke's thought which is worthy of examination.

LOCKE'S USE OF HOOKER ON THE STATE OF NATURE

Hooker held that government is not as primordial as human history itself, but arose through agreement and consent at some definite point. It is worth recalling in this regard the notion of the pre-political condition of man as charted by Richard Hooker (as well as other early modern scholastics like Suarez) so as we may determine to what degree Locke's "state of nature" is continuous or discontinuous with it. In essence, for Hooker, four things characterized the condition of man before any political "regiment." First the pre-political condition of man was *social.* Hooker concurs with the Thomistic/Aristotelian tradition that sees human beings as naturally social, and so even before a form of government is established, human beings would live in community. In short, the pre-political state was not *pre-social.* Second, even before "politic society," every human being would be subject to the *law of nature* or reason as well as divine law. The pre-political condition was not a state of amorality or complete anarchy, but one in which human beings are able to discern and responsible to obey the moral law. In short, the pre-political state was not *pre-moral.* Third, the pre-political state was a state of *equality.* Since there is no obvious prerogative of some to rule over others, all persons with the faculties of reason and free will would be in a basically equal station with every other person. And finally, the pre-political state was one of *liberty* not in the sense that persons were from the moral law, but in the sense that in the absence of political rulership each person was free to guide their actions according to their own counsel subject only to God.

Hooker together with figures like Suarez and Vitoria can be said to constitute a tradition of early modern scholasticism that drew upon similar medieval sources like St. Thomas Aquinas and developed their ideas about society and politics along basically similar lines. Thus Hooker's conception of the pre-political condition of man has remarkable similarities with that of Roman Catholic scholastics of the sixteenth century and early seventeenth century. Thus, Quentin Skinner writes concerning the Thomistic revival in sixteenth-century Spain (e.g. Suarez, Molina, Vitoria): "The Thomists may be said to emphasize three aspects of the natural condition of mankind: it would involve a natural community; it would be governed by the law of nature; and it would be based on acknowledging the natural freedom, equality, and independence of all its members."[61]

By elucidating the conditions that Hooker and other early modern scholastics stipulated regarding the pre-political condition, it is possible to discern which thinkers are more or less continuous with this tradition and which thinkers depart from it. Thus, for example, Hobbes, while accepting the late scholastic idea of a pre-political condition, departs radically from it in his notions of what it would involve. For Hobbes, the first condition would not hold since, in the *Leviathan*, there is no *natural* community. Society itself is the product of artifice and contract. In the state of nature, human beings would be solitary individuals in a state of war with one another. Moreover, the second condition would not hold either since, for Hobbes, there is no law or morality in the state of nature. Law is a product of the social contract that creates the lawgiver, and where there is no law, neither are there any moral obligations: "To this war of every man against every man, this also is consequent; that nothing can be unjust. The notions of right and wrong, justice and injustice have no place. Where there is no common power there is no law: and where no law, no injustice."[62]

Locke's conception of the state of nature is, however, quite different from that of Hobbes. We turn then to the question of whether or not the substance of Locke's idea of the pre-political state is continuous or not with the tradition represented by Hooker. Locke, in fact, explicitly uses the authority of Hooker as support for his idea of the state of nature:

> To those that say, there were never any men in the state of nature, I will not only oppose the authority of the judicious *Hooker, Eccl. Pol. lib.* i. *sect.* 10. where he says, *The laws which have been hitherto mentioned,* i. e. the laws of nature, *do bind men absolutely, even as they are men, although they have never any settled fellowship, never any solemn agreement amongst themselves what to do, or not to do: but forasmuch as we are not by ourselves sufficient to furnish ourselves with competent store of things, needful for such a life as our nature doth desire, a life fit for the dignity of man; therefore to supply those defects and imperfections*

which are in us, as living single and solely by ourselves, we are naturally in-
duced to seek communion and fellowship with others: this was the cause of
men's uniting themselves at first in politic societies. But I moreover affirm, that
all men are naturally in that state, and remain so, till by their own consents they
make themselves members of some politic society; and I doubt not in the sequel
of this discourse, to make it very clear.[63]

The four conditions that Hooker stipulated regarding the pre-political condition—sociality, subjection to natural law, equality, and liberty—provide a
good template for us to examine to what degree Locke's notion of the state of
nature coheres with Hooker. We may deal with these issues in turn, turning
first to the question of whether man is naturally social. Hooker is clearly in
the same tradition as Aristotle, Aquinas, and Suarez in affirming that man is
naturally social.

But forasmuch as we are not by ourselves sufficient to furnish ourselves with
competent store of things needful of such a life as our nature doth desire, a life
fit for the dignity of man; therefore to supply those defects and imperfections
which are in us living single and solely by ourselves, we are naturally induced
to seek communion and fellowship with others.[64]

Did Locke believe that society is a result of artificial contract like Hobbes, or
did he hold like Hooker that man was a social animal with a natural inclination to live in community? He appears to provide a rather direct answer in the
Second Treatise:

GOD having made man such a creature, that in his own judgment, it was not
good for him to be alone, put him under strong obligations of necessity, convenience, and inclination to drive him into *society,* as well as fitted him with understanding and language to continue and enjoy it.[65]

Locke in this passage even tacitly appeals to the characteristic Aristotelian argument for man's natural sociality—the natural human capacity for language.
For both Hooker and Locke then that nature is sufficient to account for society. However, for neither thinker can any particular form of government be
described as natural. Locke thus inherits Hooker's distinction between society and the particular forms and procedures of the "politic society."

The next question to examine is the issue of whether in the state of nature
human beings would be subject to natural law. Locke's natural law doctrine
has proven to be among the most contentious in Locke scholarship. It impacts
upon our study because while we have tried to make an argument for certain
broad continuities between Hooker and Locke other scholars have made the
case for a basic discontinuity between Locke and Hooker which they locate

on the point of natural law. The most radical of these forms of interpretation is that of Leo Strauss and the Straussian school which reads Locke in continuity with Hobbes rather than Hooker. If Strauss is correct in reading Locke as a Hobbesian, then the whole thesis we have developed regarding the importance of Hooker to Locke would be mostly meaningless. Hobbes held that society itself is artificial, that the pre-political condition of man was also pre-moral, and the public authority is a transferred rather then delegated power — all positions directly opposed to those of Hooker. But this reading has little support in the text. Hobbes, as we have seen, holds that morality and justice can exist only once political society is established. For Hooker (in the very passage Locke quoted), it is evident that even before human beings come together to form political societies they are subject to the natural law:

> We see then how nature itself teacheth laws and statutes to live by. The laws which have hitherto been mentioned do bind men absolutely even as they are men, although they have never any settled fellowship, never any solemn agreement among themselves what to do, or not to do.[66]

Here again Locke explicitly concurs with Hooker on the point that the state of nature is not Hobbes's lawless anarchy, but rather a condition in which human beings would still be responsible to keep the precepts of the natural law ordained by God:

> But though this be *a state of liberty,* yet *it is not a state of licence:* though man in that state have an uncontroulable liberty to dispose of his person or possessions, yet he has not liberty to destroy himself, or so much as any creature in his possession, but where some nobler use than its bare preservation calls for it. *The state of nature has a law of nature to govern it*, which obliges every one: and reason, which is that law, teaches all mankind, who will but consult it.[67]

The misreading of Locke in terms of Hobbes — or for that matter in terms of the later developments in liberalism — has been an obstruction to understanding Locke's political theory on its own terms. We have provided in Appendix 1 a more extensive examination of Strauss's reading of Locke and an explanation of why it must be firmly rejected. Suffice it to say at this point that the Straussian reading of Locke is an example of the imposition of an a historical approach to texts which imposes an intellectual framework worked out in advance *a priori*, on a text, and for this reason it has been rejected by the consensus of contemporary intellectual historians. Locke's natural law theory was (as modern scholars have come to recognize) a development from late medieval doctrines. The debate among historians and Locke scholars has moved to another plane — was Locke's natural law theory an *intellectualist* doctrine and thus in a homogeneous development from the natural law teachings of Thomas Aquinas and Richard Hooker, or was it a *voluntarist* doctrine descended from William of Ockham and the nominalists. The main lines of this debate are explained in Appendix 2. As we have seen, it is clear from Locke's personal notes that he was deeply engaged with Hooker's doctrine of eternal and natural law, and he gives no hint of any sharp disagreement with it. This provides perhaps some indication that Locke saw his own theory of natural law as in basic continuity with Hooker's intellectualism. But the debate between the voluntarist and intellectualist readings of Locke's natural law theory is not of the most practical importance for our thesis. Even if we accept that Locke was a voluntarist, it is not with relation to natural law theory where one finds most of the references to Hooker in Locke. Rather, Locke refers most to Hooker principally in the context of formulating his critiques of prerogative government, his idea of the state of nature, his notions of consent and compact as the origins of civil society, and the idea of government as a delegated power. Whether or not Locke's natural law theory was voluntarist or intellectualist, it would still be important to evaluate how and why Locke uses Hooker in building up the main points in his theory of political society.

The third issue to deal with is the issue of freedom and equality in the state of nature. Hooker, as we have seen, argued against any idea of a natural prerogative of some to rule over others in virtue, for example, of paternal right. Although he sees some merit in the Aristotelian view that the good and the wise ought to rule over the servile, he sees no way that this right could be manifested without the consent of those who are to be ruled. It would seem then that before human beings consented to form political societies, they were free from subjection to the rule of others and equal in station:

> There were no reason, that one should take upon him to be Lord or Judge over another; because although there be according to some very great and judicious men a kind of natural right in the wise, the noble and virtuous to govern them that are of servile disposition, nevertheless for manifestation of this right, and men's more peaceful contentment on both sides, the assent of them who are to be governed seemeth necessary.[68]

Locke also holds that since barring a special divine appointment there is is no natural right of some to rule others, the state of nature is:

> A *state* also *of equality,* wherein all the power and jurisdiction is reciprocal, no one having more than another; there being nothing more evident, than that creatures of the same species and rank, promiscuously born to all the same advantages of nature, and the use of the same faculties, should also be equal one

amongst another without subordination or subjection, unless the lord and master of them all should, by any manifest declaration of his will, set one above another, and confer on him, by an evident and clear appointment, an undoubted right to dominion and sovereignty.[69]

Here again is another place where Locke relies explicitly on the authority of Richard Hooker's *Laws*:

This *equality* of men by nature, the judicious *Hooker* looks upon as so evident in itself, and beyond all question, that he makes it the foundation of that obligation to mutual love amongst men, on which he builds the duties they owe one another, and from whence he derives the great maxims *of justice* and *charity*. His words are, *The like natural inducement hath brought men to know that it is no less their duty, to love others than themselves; for seeing those things which are equal, must needs all have one measure; if I cannot but wish to receive good, even as much at every man's hands, as any man can wish unto his own soul, how should I look to have any part of my desire herein satisfied, unless myself be careful to satisfy the like desire, which is undoubtedly in other men, being of one and the same nature? To have any thing offered them repugnant to this desire, must needs in all respects grieve them as much as me; so that if I do harm, I must look to suffer, there being no reason that others should shew greater measure of love to me, than they have by me shewed unto them: my desire therefore to be loved of my equals in nature, as much as possible may be, imposeth upon me a natural duty of bearing to them-ward fully the like affection; from which relation of equality between ourselves and them that are as ourselves, what several rules and canons natural reason hath drawn, for direction of life, no man is ignorant.* Eccl. Pol. Lib. 1.[70]

Locke, like Hooker, is also clear that his concept of equality in no way opposes the idea that there may be a hierarchical order of precedence based on natural gifts or the attainments of virtue. The relevant issue is political dominion—there is no *natural* right of some to subject others to their authority, and thus, in respect of dominion, all are equal:

Though I have said above, *Chap.* II. *That all men by nature are equal,* I cannot be supposed to understand all sorts of *equality: age* or *virtue* may give men a just precedency: *excellency of parts* and *merit* may place others above the common level: *birth* may subject some, and *alliance* or *benefits* others, to pay an observance to those to whom nature, gratitude, or other respects, may have made it due: and yet all this consists with the *equality,* which all men are in, in respect of jurisdiction or dominion one over another; which was the *equality* I there spoke of, as proper to the business in hand, being that *equal right,* that every man hath, *to his natural freedom,* without being subjected to the will or authority of any other man.[71]

A final issue to consider in regard to the state of nature is that of freedom. Some figures have argued that the issue of freedom in the state of nature is one that separates Hooker from Locke. Thus, Russell Kirk writes that "it remains true that Locke's emphasis upon primitive freedom endangers that spiritual continuity which we call human society."[72] There is certainly a marked difference in *emphasis* between Hooker and Locke on this question. Hooker stresses that human action is placed within a teleological structure of divine, natural, and human law, and the "compact" he speaks of is one, as we have seen, that binds each generation to the agreements made by their ancestors. Thus, Hooker's doctrines militate against an individualistic notion of freedom and against a mechanical view that society can be changed at any moment by the free consent of its members. And yet if we examine the *substance* of Locke's notion of freedom, it is unclear that it differs radically from Hooker's. We have noted that Locke clearly does not have in mind a *moral* freedom from divine or natural law, but rather a *political* freedom from subjection to the rule of others: "But though this be *a state of liberty,* yet *it is not a state of licence* . . . The *state of nature* has a law of nature to govern it, which obliges every one: and reason, which is that law, teaches all mankind, who will but consult it."[73]

The freedom of which Locke is speaking thus follows as a natural inference from the very fact that the state of nature is *pre-political*. No free and rational agent was subject to the dominion of any other before by common consent political authority was established. This is precisely the view of Hooker. Locke's position then is not saying much more then a scholastic like Suarez did when he said that "man is born free."[74] Both Locke and Suarez are referring to the fact that in the pre-political condition, no one has dominion over another or is subject to human authority. Locke makes the issue of natural freedom a quite central notion of his doctrine of the state of nature, and yet it is clear that this freedom is only in regards to subjection to political dominion. Locke, like Hooker, insists that in the state of nature, man remains a subject of divine and natural law:

> To understand political power right, and derive it from its original, we must consider, what state all men are naturally in, and that is, a *state of perfect freedom* to order their actions, and dispose of their possessions and persons, as they think fit, *within the bounds of the law of nature*, without asking leave, or depending upon the will of any other man.[75]

LOCKE'S USE OF HOOKER
ON SOVEREIGNTY AND COMPACT

Another important nexus between Hooker and Locke lies in their conception of sovereignty. One of the great debates of sixteenth and seventeenth century political philosophy concerned the question, where is the locus of sovereignty? For Filmer or Bodin, the power of making and enacting laws derived from the *person* of the sovereign. Locke is explicit that sovereign power is always vested in the *whole community*:

> [T]he *community* perpetually *retains a supreme power* of saving themselves from the attempts and designs of any body, even of their legislators, whenever they shall be so foolish, or so wicked, as to lay and carry on designs against the liberties and properties of the subject . . . And thus the *community* may be said in this respect to be *always the supreme power*.[76]

Here again Locke turns to Hooker as an authority to establish that the locus of sovereignty lies with the body-politic as a whole and not with any particular person: "The lawful power of making laws to command whole politic societies of men, belonging so properly unto the same intire societies."[77] We may recall that Hooker based his defense on the original sovereignty of the community on his understanding of the pre-political condition. Since before government, there is neither natural subjection nor any natural prerogative of rulership, sovereignty must be vested in the whole community: "It seemeth almost out of doubt and controversy that every independent multitude *before any certain regiment established* hath under God's supreme authority full dominion over itself."[78] Hence, for Hooker, the sovereignty of the community *precedes* the governing power of any settled political society. The question of sovereignty is closely connected to those of *consent* and the compact to form a political society. The issue of consent is of central importance for Locke's political philosophy. As John Yolton notes, "consent is the central device controlling the move from the state of nature into the civil society, consent to allow a formal governmental framework to assume the rights and powers of every man in the state of nature for the sake of security and possessions."[79] For Locke, consent is the very origin of political obligation. Since in the state of nature no one has any divine or natural right to subject others to their authority, political subjection can only be legitimate if it is voluntary: "MEN being, as has been said, by nature, all free, equal, and independent, no one can be put out of this estate, and subjected to the political power of another, *without his own consent*."

Locke quotes several passages from the *Laws* to bolster his views on consent. Thus, in a footnote in the *Second Treatise*, he quotes from Book I, 10, of the *Laws* where Hooker says that "Laws therefore human, of what kind so ever, are available by consent." Earlier in a note, he quotes Hooker to the effect that:

> Finally, they knew that no man might in reason take upon him to determine his own right, and according to his own determination proceed in maintenance

thereof, in as much as every man is towards himself, and them whom he greatly affects, partial; and therefore that strifes and troubles would be endless, *except they gave their common consent*, all to be ordered by some, whom they should agree upon, *without which consent there would be no reason that one man should take upon him to be lord or judge over another*, Hooker's *Eccl. Pol. l. i. sect.* 10.[80]

Given that the state of nature is one of equality and freedom, the question naturally arises of *why* persons would *voluntarily* subject themselves to the authority of others. As Locke puts the matter:

IF man in the state of nature be so free, as has been said; if he be absolute lord of his own person and possessions, equal to the greatest, and subject to no body, why will he part with his freedom? Why will he give up this empire, and subject himself to the dominion and controul of any other power?[81]

The basic answer Locke provides is the "inconveniences" of the pre-political condition. Since each person in the state of nature is the judge of his own cause, there is no common power to adjudicate in disputes and to defend the members of the community from injustice. Thus, Locke notes that:

[F]or where-ever any two men are, who have no standing rule, and common judge to appeal to on earth, for the determination of controversies of right betwixt them, there they are still *in the state of nature*, and under all the inconveniencies of it.[82]

Locke has a note on this passage, supporting his view on the inconveniences of the state of nature with a quote from Hooker's *Laws*:

To take away all such mutual grievances, injuries and wrongs, *i. e.* such as attend men in the state of nature, there was no way but only by growing into composition and agreement amongst themselves, by ordaining some kind of government public, and by yielding themselves subject thereunto, that unto whom they granted authority to rule and govern, by them the peace, tranquillity and happy estate of the rest might be procured. Men always knew that where force and injury was offered, they might be defenders of themselves; they knew that however men may seek their own commodity, yet if this were done with injury unto others, it was not to be suffered, but by all men, and all good means to be withstood... Hooker's *Eccl. Pol. l. i. sect.* 10.[83]

In regard to the issue of the "inconveniences" of the state of nature, it is certainly the case that Locke places much more importance on the issue of *property* than Hooker. This is important because the issue of property is closely related to the inviolable private sphere. The public/private distinction plays little role in Hooker's political philosophy. Thus, a statement like "The great and *chief end,* therefore, of men's uniting into common-wealths, and putting themselves under government, *is the preservation of their property*"[84] is nowhere found in the *Laws.* It must therefore be said that Locke's elaborate and important theory of property and his emphasis on individual property rights owes little to the influence of Hooker. But when we turn to what Locke sees as the lacks or "wants" of the state of nature—the absence of established settled law, of disinterested judges to arbitrate disputes, and the absence of a common power to execute judgments, there seems to be fairly broad agreement on many points between Hooker (in the above quoted passage) and Locke in regard to the substance of *why* pre-political society gave way to political society.[85] There is also close agreement on *how* political society came into being—namely, through an agreement or *compact* whereby the community consents to be governed in order to avert the aforementioned inconveniences of the state of nature. Thus, Locke writes that:

> The only way whereby any one divests himself of his natural liberty, and puts on the *bonds of civil society,* is by agreeing with other men to join and unite into a community, for their comfortable, safe, and peaceable living one amongst another, in a secure enjoyment of their properties, and a greater security against any, that are not of it. This any number of men may do, because it injures not the freedom of the rest; they are left as they were in the liberty of the state of nature. When any number of men has so *consented to make one community or government,* they are thereby presently incorporated, and make *one body politic,* wherein the *majority* have a right to act and conclude the rest.[86]

Hooker refers to the agreement to form a political society as consisting of "articles of compact," while Locke speaks of it as an "original compact." By this agreement, each member of the community consents to give up some of his original liberty and to submit to political authority:

> And thus every man, by consenting with others to make one body politic under one government, puts himself under an obligation, to every one of that society, to submit to the determination of the *majority,* and to be concluded by it; or else this *original compact,* whereby he with others incorporates into *one society,* would signify nothing, and be no compact, if he be left free, and under no other ties than he was in before in the state of nature.[87]

Locke had earlier quoted Hooker on the question of the compact whereby political society is created through the consent of the community:

> To take away all such mutual grievances, injuries and wrongs, *i. e.* such as attend men in the state of nature, there was no way but only by growing into

composition and agreement amongst themselves, by ordaining some kind of government public, and by yielding themselves subject thereunto, that unto whom they granted authority to rule and govern, by them the peace, tranquillity and happy estate of the rest might be procured.[88]

Further support of this position from the *Laws* is given later:

Two foundations there are which bear up public societies; the one a natural inclination, whereby all men desire sociable life and fellowship; *the other an order, expresly or secretly agreed upon, touching the manner of their union in living together:* the latter is that which we call the law of a common-weal, the very soul of a politic body, the parts whereof are by law animated, held together, and set on work in such actions as the common good requireth.[89]

This last passage is significant because in it Hooker gives his clearest case for a distinction between *society* (brought together by natural inclination) and *political society* (constituted through the artifice of "composition and agreement"). This is relevant to the question of whether the "original compact" Locke refers to is a *pactum societatis* whereby society itself is constituted by a contract or a *pactum subjectionis* in which an already existing natural community binds itself to obey a political authority. So the question becomes whether, for Locke, society is the product of nature or artificial contract. There are times when Locke indeed speaks as if the compact itself forms the society. Thus, we have seen him say that by the original compact "he with others incorporates into *one society*."[90] Yet earlier he had said God "put him [human beings] under strong obligations of necessity, convenience, and inclination to drive him into *society*"; while here he quotes Hooker with approbation regarding his Aristotelian idea that society is a product of "a natural inclination, whereby all men desire sociable life and fellowship."[91]

Given that the context in which he speaks about the compact as incorporating men into society was "the bonds of *Civil* Society" and that he refers to the formation of society as an "obligation of necessity, convenience and inclination," there is a strong case to be made that Locke holds communities themselves to be natural.[92] If this is the case then, for Locke, compact is merely a *pactum subjectionis* not different in kind from that spoken of by medieval and early modern scholastics. The conception of society that Locke is here developing is not as radically individualistic as is sometimes supposed. Certainly individual rights of liberty, property, and self-preservation have an important place in the *Two Treatises*. Yet, Locke makes clear that it is not the self-preservation of the *individuals* within society that has first primacy, but the preservation of society itself. Thus, the common good takes precedence over the individual good:

THE great end of men's entering into society, being the enjoyment of their properties in peace and safety, and the great instrument and means of that being the
laws established in that society; the *first and fundamental positive law* of all
common-wealths *is the establishing of the legislative* power; as the *first and fundamental natural law,* which is to govern even the legislative itself, *is the
preservation of the society,* and (*as far as will consist with the public good*) of
every person in it.[93]

Once the members of the community enter into political society, they are obligated to obey to civil authority:

for the *end of civil society,* being to avoid, and remedy those inconveniencies of
the state of nature, which necessarily follow from every man's being judge in
his own case, by setting up a known authority, to which every one of that society may appeal upon any injury received, or controversy that may arise, *and
which every one of the society ought to obey.*[94]

Locke in a note here cites Hooker in defense that since the public authority
ought to be obeyed except where its enactments conflict with divine or natural law:

The public power of all society is above every soul contained in the same society; and the principal use of that power is, to give laws unto all that are under it,
which laws in such cases we must obey, unless there be reason shewed which
may necessarily inforce, that the law of reason, or of God, doth enjoin the contrary, *Hook. Eccl. Pol. l. i. sect. 16.*

LOCKE'S USE OF HOOKER ON THE LIMITS OF
GOVERNMENT IN POLITICAL SOCIETY

However, Locke is also clear that political authority once established is subject to determinate limits. These limits include: 1) the need to respect *natural
law*; 2) the need for public authority to respect *positive law*; and 3) the limitation in terms of its *end* for which public authority was established. We may
deal with each of these in turn.

In the first place, there remains an order of natural law which binds man
even in the state of nature, which remains operative in the state of political
society: "The obligations of the law of nature cease not in society, but only in
many cases are drawn closer, and have by human laws known penalties annexed to them, to inforce their observation. Thus the law of nature stands as
an eternal rule to all men, *legislators* as well as others."[95] Thus, the enactments

of the public authority are bound to respect a moral order, which is antecedent
to and transcends its own scope of legitimate action:

> The *legislative,* or supreme authority, cannot assume to its self a power to rule
> by extemporary arbitrary decrees, but *is bound to dispense justice,* and decide
> the rights of the subject *by promulgated standing laws, and known authorized
> judges:* for the law of nature being unwritten, and so no where to be found but
> in the minds of men, they who through passion or interest shall miscite, or mis-
> apply it, cannot so easily be convinced of their mistake where there is no estab-
> lished judge.[96]

Locke again cites Hooker on the need for the civil law to conform to the
moral law:

> Human laws are measures in respect of men whose actions they must direct,
> howbeit such measures they are as have also their higher rules to be measured
> by, which rules are two, the law of God, and the law of nature; so that laws hu-
> man must be made according to the general laws of nature, and without contra-
> diction to any positive law of scripture, otherwise they are ill made. *Hooker's
> Eccl. Pol. l.* iii. *sect.* 9.

Interestingly, this passage that Locke cites in Hooker's *Laws* is an explicit
paraphrase from St. Thomas Aquinas in the *Summa Theologiae* I,II, q.95.[97]
Locke thus simultaneously reveals both the chain that links his own formulation to the medieval scholastics (through Hooker's mediation) and, at the
same time, the fact that Locke fails to cite Aquinas by name indicates perhaps
a certain reticence in the Whig theorist to recognize Roman Catholic influences.

The second limitation that Locke places on government pertains to positive
law. Locke argues that governments as much as individuals are prone to
abuses. In order then to prevent the public authority from abusing the power
that the community placed in it, it is necessary to have rules to keep government within its delegated and assigned powers:

> yet, when ambition and luxury in future ages would retain and increase the
> power, without doing the business for which it was given; and aided by flattery,
> taught princes to have distinct and separate interests from their people, men
> found it necessary to examine more carefully *the original* and rights *of govern-
> ment;* and to find out ways to *restrain the exorbitances,* and *prevent the abuses*
> of that power, which they having intrusted in another's hands only for their own
> good, they found was made use of to hurt them.[98]

Locke, in this same passage, cites Hooker on why the rule of law was found
to be preferable to the rule by the will of a man:

At first, when some certain kind of regiment was once approved, it may be nothing was then farther thought upon for the manner of governing, but all permitted unto their wisdom and discretion which were to rule, till by experience they found this for all parts very inconvenient, so as the thing which they had devised for a remedy, did indeed but increase the sore which it should have cured. *They saw, that to live by one man's will, became the cause of all men's misery. This constrained them to come unto laws* wherein all men might see their duty before hand, and know the penalties of transgressing them. *Hooker's Eccl. Pol. l. i. sect.* 10.[99]

The third mode of limitation pertains to the end for which government was established. For Locke government is established for the public or common good, and its activities are necessarily ordered to this end. Were a government therefore to be acting contrary to the common good, it would be behaving without legitimacy. As Locke puts it:

Their [Governmental power], in the utmost bounds of it, is *limited to the public good* of the society. It is a power, that hath no other end but preservation, and therefore can never have a right to destroy, enslave, or designedly to impoverish the subjects.[100]

Here Locke quotes Hooker on the common good as the end of human law:

[T]he latter is that which we call the law of a common-weal, the very soul of a politic body, the parts whereof are by law animated, held together, and set on work in such actions *as the common good requireth.* Laws politic, ordained for external order and regiment amongst men, are never framed as they should be, unless presuming the will of man to be inwardly obstinate, rebellious, and averse from all obedience to the sacred laws of his nature; in a word, unless presuming man to be, in regard of his depraved mind, little better than a wild beast, they do accordingly provide, notwithstanding, so to frame his outward actions, *that they be no hindrance unto the common good, for which societies are instituted.* Unless they do this, they are not perfect. *Hooker's Eccl. Pol. l. i. sect.* 10.[101]

Closely related to this idea is Locke's notion of government as a delegated power. Unlike Hobbes who viewed the social contract as transferred to a sovereign, for Locke, sovereignty is retained by the community and merely delegated to the public authority as a trust:

Political power is that power, which every man having in the state of nature, has given up into the hands of the society, and therein to the governors, whom the society hath set over itself, with this express or tacit trust, that it shall be employed for their good, and the preservation of their property.[102]

The question then arises of what to do when a political authority abuses its trust and uses its power to harm the common good or do violence against the members of the community? It is on the basis of his notion of government as a delegated power that Locke constructs his argument for the legitimacy of *resistance*. In his discussion of the nature of tyranny, he says that:

> *Tyranny is the exercise of power beyond right,* which no body can have a right to. And this is making use of the power any one has in his hands, not for the good of those who are under it, but for his own private separate advantage. When the governor, however intitled, makes not the law, but his will, the rule; and his commands and actions are not directed to the preservation of the properties of his people, but the satisfaction of his own ambition, revenge, covetousness, or any other irregular passion.[103]

In addressing the question of whether it is lawful to resist a lawless tyranny, Locke is quite clear:

> Whosoever uses *force without right,* as every one does in society, who does it without law, puts himself into a *state of war* with those against whom he so uses it; and in that state all former ties are cancelled, all other rights cease, and every one has a right to defend himself, and *to resist the aggressor.*[104]

To the argument that allowing for resistance to tyrants will lead to anarchy and chaos, Locke argues that only in the case of a manifestly immoral use of force by the tyrant in which he endeavors to unjustly despoil the people of their lives, liberty, and property is resistance justified. In other cases, to resist lawful authority is execrable:

> May the *commands* then *of a prince be opposed?* may he be resisted as often as any one shall find himself aggrieved, and but imagine he has not right done him? This will unhinge and overturn all polities, and, instead of government and order, leave nothing but anarchy and confusion . . . To this I answer, that *force* is to be *opposed* to nothing, but to unjust and unlawful *force;* whoever makes any opposition in any other case, draws on himself a just condemnation both from God and man; and so no such danger or confusion will follow, as is often suggested.[105]

Locke's essential argument is that the community as a whole remains the ultimate locus of sovereignty even in political society. Since government only holds its authority as a trust from the community, in the extreme case that the government acts despotically for the private good of the ruler or uses its power to violate the law of nature by abusing the lives, liberty, and property of the people and when furthermore it leaves the community with no means of redress, then the community may reserve again to itself the authority which it had delegated:

> *[T]he legislative can never revert to the people* whilst that government lasts; because having provided a legislative with power to continue for ever, they have given up their political power to the legislative, and cannot resume it. But if they have set limits to the duration of their legislative, and made this supreme power in any person, or assembly, only temporary; or else, when by the miscarriages of those in authority, it is forfeited; upon the forfeiture, or at the determination of the time set, *it reverts to the society,* and the people have a right to act as supreme, and continue the legislative in themselves; or erect a new form, or under the old form place it in new hands, as they think good.[106]

ASSESSING LOCKE'S DEBT TO HOOKER

Having surveyed Locke's use of the *Laws*, we are now in a good position to summarize the relationship between the political philosophy of Richard Hooker and that of John Locke. Certainly we can concur with those critics who note that the *intentions* of Hooker and Locke in formulating their respective forms of constitutionalism were entirely different.[107] Hooker's purpose was essentially traditional– perceiving a Puritan attack on the foundations of civil and ecclesiastical life, he wishes to demonstrate the sound foundations of the English constitution by showing that its characteristic institutions of Crown, Parliament, and common law are grounded in consent, tradition, and natural law. Given his objective of defending the Elizabethan settlement from subversion we waste our time seeking to find any defense, even hypothetical for rebellion. Hooker was by temper a deeply conservative thinker, admiring of tradition and continuity, reverent of established authority, and eager to defend against the nascent Puritanism of his time the existing institutions of the Crown, Parliament, and the Church by law established. Nowhere in the political writings of Hooker does he ever elaborate a doctrine of resistance similar to Locke's.[108] Although it is anachronistic to speculate, had Hooker been a contemporary of Locke's he might possibly have regarded him as one of those "seedsmen of rebellion" whose *Two Treatises* were apt to "animate unquiet spirits." Hooker, like Bracton and Fortescue before him and like Burke after him, was endeavoring to defend the wisdom and prudence of England's ancestors for devising a system which guaranteed the consonance of England's laws with divine and natural law and with the consent of the commonwealth. What this traditional theory never adequately addressed was this question—what is to be done if the King endeavors to subvert the constitutional arrangements and usurp for himself more power then the law allows? Hooker never, in fact, considers the case of the tyrant who acts to subvert the laws and acts against divine, natural, or human law in persecuting his subjects. Such a consideration would naturally fall outside the scope and purpose of the *Laws* that were primarily a defense of the English ecclesiastical polity. Yet given Hooker's premises, it is difficult to see how resistance can be altogether ruled out in the case of a tyrant.[109]

And what of John Locke—called the "father of liberalism" and luminary of the Enlightenment? Certainly in one respect Locke is a progenitor of liberalism in a way Hooker was not. In works like his *Letter on Toleration* he defends the concept of an individual right to religious liberty that was not part of Hooker's world view. Locke moreover rejects the Erastian conception of the ecclesiastical polity that animated Hooker's vision of the Elizabethan settlement as a unity of church and state. For Locke, church and state so far from being intimately united have separate provinces, the one over temporal, the other over spiritual welfare. And yet, on the basis of our study, Locke inevitably appears as a more traditional and in some respects less original figure. Locke seeks to explicitly justify a theory of resistance on the basis of the ready to hand principles provided by traditional thinkers like Hooker. It is no slight to say that many of Locke's fundamental political ideas—the notion of a pre-political community, his concepts of sovereignty, the consensual origins of government, and compact—had been developed in early modern scholasticism by various figures including Hooker (as well as other important late scholastic figures like Francisco Suarez). Locke's natural law theory was, as we have seen and as modern scholars have come to recognize, a development from late medieval doctrines. Even Locke's notion of resistance was not as radical as it might seem. Theories of resistance had existed in medieval thought and an authority like St. Thomas Aquinas did not have the reticence about discussing the licit nature of rebellion against tyrants. By linking himself with this older tradition Locke is endeavoring to depict himself as the true conservative, and the patriarchalists as dangerous innovators.[110] For example, Locke defines one of the attributes of a tyrant that he "makes not the law, but his will, the rule; and his commands and actions are not directed to the preservation of the properties of his people, but the satisfaction of his own ambition, revenge, covetousness, or any other irregular passion."[111]

On the basis of the tyrant's pursuing his own rather than the common good, he concludes that:

> it is the tyrant who is guilty of rebellion, rather than the community who resists him. In both the fore-mentioned cases, when either the legislative is changed, or the legislators act contrary to the end for which they were constituted; those who are guilty are *guilty of rebellion:* for if any one by force takes away the established legislative of any society, and the laws by them made, pursuant to their

trust, he thereby takes away the umpirage, which every one had consented to, for a peaceable decision of all their controversies, and a bar to the state of war amongst them.[112]

These formulations are strikingly similar to what we find in Aquinas:

> A tyrannical government is not just because it is directed not to the common good, but to the private good of the ruler, as the philosopher states. Consequently there is no sedition in disturbing a government of this kind . . . *indeed it is the tyrant rather that is guilty of sedition*, since he encourages discord and sedition among his subjects.[113]

Locke explicitly acknowledges his profound debt to Hooker for many of the key ideas in the *Two Treatises*. Locke drew upon many of Hooker's premises regarding the distinction of paternal and regal authority, the sovereignty of the community and the origin of political obligation in consent and compact, but reached conclusions regarding the right of resistance that Hooker himself did not reach. Thus, Locke transposed some of the fundamental ideas of Hooker's political philosophy into the service of his own quite different political purpose—namely, the ultimately successful Whig cause in late seventeenth-century England. In an era of growing literacy, Locke helped to popularize many of the ideas in Hooker's *Laws* in ways that would have a most profound impact on political thought and practice in Europe and North America. Though ideas regarding the king as the sovereign source of the law and above the law would occasionally resurface in English history, we can say that in the broad sweep of history, Locke's *Two Treatises* fatally undermined intellectual support for the Patriarchalist theory of government and provided a constitutionalist vision that would echo through the centuries. And to no small degree in this achievement Locke relied on the arguments and principles supplied by his most venerated authority—"the judicious" Richard Hooker.

NOTES

1. See John Locke, "Preface to the First Tract on Government" (1661), in John Locke, *Political Writings*, ed. David Wootton (Harmondsworth: Penguin / Mentor, 1993).

2. Edward Bagshaw. *The Great Question Concerning Things Indifferent* (London, 1660)—all references to Bagshaw are to this tract unless otherwise indicated.

3. Part of the difference is also of course the historical moment in which they were writing. Cartwright was writing during the nascent period of Puritanism, while Bagshaw was writing at the dawn of the Restoration when Puritanism was already a spent force in the English politics, and now had to struggle to survive in the midst of Anglican triumphalism.

4. "Yet I will grant that the piety of the *Jewish* is, and ought to be exemplary to the *Christian Magistrates*—but withal I shall deny the *Influence* since the Jewish *Princes* when they Reformed *Religion*, they followed a *Divine Law*, which did command it from them, and which in the minutest circumstances, had provided for *uniformity of Worship*: from which rigor and restraint all Christians are absolved," Bagshaw, p. 14.

5. Bagshaw, pp. 3–4.

6. *Ibid*, p. 14.

7. *Ibid.*

8. "It is so far from being an argument for *Impositions*, to urge that the thing being Imposed is *Indifferent*; that there cannot be stronger argument against them: since it is requisite for *Christian Practice* that *Things Indifferent* should be kept *Indifferent* as *Things Necessary* be held *Necessary*," *Ibid*. p.15.

9. *Ibid.*, p.15.

10. *Ibid.*, p.16.

11. The *Two Tracts* remained unpublished until 1967.

12. Locke, *Political Writings*, 152.

13. *Ibid.*, p. 153.

14. *Ibid.*, p. 154 (italics added).

15. *Ibid.*, p. 160.

16. *Ibid.*, p. 161.

17. *Ibid.*

18. *Ibid.*

19. *Ibid.*

20. *Ibid.*

21. *Ibid.*, p. 167.

22. *Ibid.*, p. 168.

23. *Ibid.*

24. *Ibid.*, p. 169.

25. *Ibid.*

26. *Ibid.*, p. 159.

27. Cf. David Wootton's introduction in *ibid.*, 36–49; and Peter Laslett's introduction to John Locke, *Two Treatises of Government*, pp. 26–37.

28. Two of the advances of recent Locke scholarship have been first to dispel the belief that the *Two Treatises* were written against Hobbes and, secondly, that they represented a defense of the revolution of 1688. The consensus of modern Locke experts is that Locke was already working on the *Two Treatises* in the period between 1679 and 1683 (Ashcraft, Laslett, and Marshall differ somewhat) and were related rather to the exclusion crisis in which his patron, the Earl of Shaftesbury, was personally involved. See Wootton's introduction in Locke, *Political Writings*, 50–55 and Laslett's introduction in Locke, *Two Treatises of Government*, pp. 45–66.

29. Locke's interest in Hooker while beginning with his early unpublished essays would last his entire life. In one of his last essays "Some Thoughts Concerning Reading and Study for a Gentleman"(1703), Locke distinguishes in politics between "two parts very different the one from the other, the one containing the original of societies

and the rise and extent of political power, the other, the art of governing men in society." In regard to the first or theoretical aspect of politics Locke places among the list of worthy books for a gentleman to study "the first book of *Mr. Hooker's Ecclesiastical Polity*—cf. James Axtell (ed.). *The Educational Writings of John Locke.* (Cambridge: Cambridge University, 1968), p. 400.

30. Cf. John Harrison and Peter Laslett, *The Library of John Locke*, 2nd ed., (Oxford: Clarendon, 1971), 157 (entries 1490, 1491, and 1492). The three printings of the *Laws* are the 1676 edition, the 1666 edition, and the 1632 edition.

31. Cf. Laslett's introduction in Locke, *Two Treatises of Government*, pp. 56–57. In this famous scholarly introduction to Locke's *Two Treatises,* Laslett uses these facts to help fix the date of Locke's first work on the *Second Treatise*: "We may take a further particular example in confirmation [of the *Second Treatises*'s date of composition] , a work of much more importance to his [Locke's] political philosophy than Knox-Hooker's *Ecclesiastical Polity*. He had read Hooker before, though perhaps not far into that tall folio. But it was not until 1681 that he bought in London 'Hooker Ecclesiasticall Politie fol. London 66.' He read the book during the rest of the month, making lengthy extracts from it into his journal. Now there are sixteen passages from Hooker quoted in the *Second Treatise* . . . when the quotations in his diary are set alongside those in the *Second Treatise* they are seen to alternate never overlapping. The conclusion must be that in June 1681, Locke was working on the *Second Treatise* incorporating lengthy extracts from Hooker into it, and at the same time copying other passages of philosophical interest." It should be noted on this point that Laslett's opinion on the date and order of when Locke began composing *Two Treatises* is contested." For an opinion opposed to Laslett's see Ashcraft, Richard. *Locke's Two Treatises of Government.* (London: Unwin Hyman, 1989): pp. 286–295 (Appendix).

32. Locke's personal journal is part of an Oxford collection of his unpublished writings – cf. John Locke Bodleian(Oxford) MSS f 5(1681). See illustration 4 at the beginning of the chapter.

33. Nuovo, Victor. *John Locke: Writings on Religion.* (New York: Oxford University, 2002) citing Bod MS Locke d.10, Lemmata Ethica, pp. 43–44.

34. Whigs like Locke in their assertions of natural liberty and the distinction of paternity from kingship were in fact reviving an earlier conception of politics that came to full fruition in a late form of Thomistic scholasticism to which both Hooker and the School of Salamanca can be considered to belong. However, given the general anti-Catholicism of this period in English history, and the efforts of Tories to depict the doctrines of natural liberty and consensual government as subversive ideas hatched by Jesuits, "papists," and schoolmen, it is not surprising that Locke turns to a respected Anglican scholastic like Hooker, while keeping more or less silent about any connection between his ideas and the continental Roman Catholic scholastics.

35. John Locke, *Second Treatise of Government*, §239.

36. As we have seen, this was far from an original position—Locke was in a sense *reaffirming* a respected and traditional position held by late scholastics like Richard Hooker (and for that matter Francisco Suarez and St. Robert Bellarmine). Filmer's more novel thesis that saw paternal and regal authority as identical had certain important antecedents like that of Saravia's *De Authoritate Imperandi*, but as our survey

indicated, patriarchalism only became a dominant position in political philosophy in the seventeenth century.

37. John Locke, *First Treatise of Government*, §6, cf. the 1764 edition of the *Two Treatises of Government*, ed. Thomas Hollis. (London: A. Millar et al., 1764): http://oll.libertyfund.org/Texts/Locke0154/ TwoTreatises/0057_Bk.html#hd_lf057. head.007. (Locke's page numbers from Filmer deleted.)

38. Locke, *Second Treatise on Government*, §71

39. Aristotle, *Politics*, Book I, 1252a

40. It has already been noted that the distinction between regal and paternal authority was strongly asserted by Suarez who explicitly distinguished Adam's domestic authority from political power: *Verumtamen, ex vi solius creationis et originis naturalis solum colligi potest, habuisse Adamum potestatem oeconomicam, nonpoliticam.* (See his *Tractatus de Legibus*, Book I, Caput 3.5, and Locke's defense of the natural condition of man as being one of liberty has its analogue in Suarez's position that *ex natura rei omnes homines nascuntur liberi.*) Similar quotations can be found in relation to other Roman Catholic scholastics including other members of the Spanish school and St. Robert Bellarmine.

41. *Laws*, I.10.4.

42. Locke, *First Treatise on Government*, §3 (Introduction).

43. *Ibid.*, §2.

44. In his endeavor of refuting that Adam possessed such a prerogative by divine right, Locke does not reject Filmer's method of "*conferring these proofs and reasons, drawn from the authority of the scripture.*" Instead, he endeavors through biblical exegesis to demonstrate that Scripture does not provide the foundation for Adam's title by donation that Filmer claims it does. We shall not discuss the exegetical details of the *First Treatise* in an in-depth way, but the argument from donation plays a large enough role in Locke's *First Treatise* to merit some attention; it is, moreover, a good example of the kind of approach Locke adopts in the *First Treatise*. Filmer relied for the claim of Adam's rule by divine right on Genesis 1:28, where God gives to Adam a mandate: "Be fruitful and multiply and fill the earth and subdue it: and have dominion over the fish of the sea and over the birds of the air *and over every living thing that moves upon the earth*" (From *Oxford Annotated Bible, Revised Standard Version*, italics added). The question dividing Locke and Filmer on this question of donation was whether the phrase, "every living thing that moves on the earth," was meant to include his own human descendents. For Filmer, it is clear that God was bestowing upon Adam personally a special proprietary prerogative of rulership that would extend over the whole earth. Locke provides the relevant citations: "Our author tells us in the words of Mr. *Selden*, that *Adam by donation from God*, Gen. i. 28. *was made the general lord of all things, not without such a private dominion to himself, as without his grant did exclude his children. This determination of Mr.* Selden, says our author, *is consonant to the history of the* Bible, *and natural reason*, Observations, 210. And in his Pref. to his Observations on *Aristotle*, he says thus, *The first government in the world was monarchical in the father of all flesh*, Adam *being commanded to multiply and people the earth, and to subdue it, and having dominion given him over all creatures, was thereby the monarch of the whole world: none of his posterity had*

any right to possess any thing, but by his grant or permission, or by succession from him: The earth, saith the Psalmist, *hath he given to the children of men, which shew the title comes from fatherhood*" (Locke, *First Treatise*, §21). Locke responds that Filmer's error is due largely to his apparent ignorance of Hebrew, noting that the Hebrew term *Hayah Romeset* translated in the English Bible as "living thing" is in fact a synonym for "terrestrial animal." This can be seen also from the immediate Biblical context. In Genesis 1:24, the same term is used before the creation of man: "Let the earth bring forth living *creatures* according to their kinds." Thus, Locke notes: "That this donation, i. Gen. 28. gave Adam no power over men, will appear if we consider the words of it: for since all positive grants convey no more than the express words they are made in will carry, let us see which of them here will comprehend mankind, or Adam's posterity; and those, I imagine, if any, must be these, every living thing that moveth: the words in Hebrew are, *Haya Romeset* i. e. *Bestiam Reptantem*, of which words the scripture itself is the best interpreter: God having created the fishes and fowls the 5th day, the beginning of the 6th, he creates the irrational inhabitants of the dry land, which, v. 24. are described in these words, let the earth bring forth the living creature after his kind; cattle and creeping things, and beasts of the earth, after his kind, and, v. 2. and God made the beasts of the earth after his kind, and cattle after their kind, and every thing that creepeth on the earth after his kind: here, in the creation of the brute inhabitants of the earth, he first speaks of them all under one general name, of living creatures, and then afterwards divides them into three ranks." (*ibid.*, §25, Hebrew not transliterated in the original). Moreover, if *Haya Romeset* (i.e. "living thing") were meant in the Bible to include human beings, then on Filmer's logic Adam and those who inherit his regal prerogatives would have the right to cannibalism as well since the identical term is found in Genesis 9:2, "Every living thing that moves shall be food for you." Thus, Locke says: "And if God made all mankind slaves to *Adam* and his heirs by giving *Adam* dominion over *every living thing that moveth on the earth,* ch. i. 28. as our author would have it, methinks Sir *Robert* should have carried his monarchical power one step higher, and satisfied the world, that princes might eat their subjects too, since God gave as full power to *Noah* and his heirs, *ch.* ix. 2. to eat *every living thing that moveth,* as he did to *Adam* to have dominion over them, the *Hebrew* words in both places being the same" (*ibid.*, §27). Locke instead interprets the dominion verse in Genesis 1:28 in line with that of Genesis 1:26 where God says, "Let us make man in our image, after our likeness and let them have dominion over the fish of the sea, and over the birds of the air, and over the cattle, and over every creeping thing that creeps upon the earth." This dominion is not a *private* dominion over earthly creatures but a *general* dominion of mankind as a whole (both males and females) over the irrational creatures." "Whatever God gave by the words of this grant, i. *Gen.* 28. it was not to *Adam* in particular, exclusive of all other men: whatever *dominion* he had thereby, it was not a *private dominion,* but a dominion in common with the rest of mankind. That this donation was not made in particular to *Adam,* appears evidently from the words of the text, it being made to more than one; for it was spoken in the plural number, God blessed *them,* and said unto *them,* Have dominion" (*ibid.*, §29). Thus, Locke holds that: "1. That by this grant, i. *Gen.* 28. God gave no immediate power to *Adam* over men, over his children, over those of his own species; and so he was not made ruler, or *monarch*, by this charter. 2. That by this grant God gave him not *private dominion* over the inferior creatures, but right in common with all mankind; so neither was he *monarch*, upon the account of the property here given him" (*ibid.*, §24).

45. Filmer writes that "to confirm this natural right of regal power, we find in the decalogue the law which enjoins obedience to kings is delivered in the terms of 'honour thy father' [Exodus 20:12] as if all power were originally in the father" (*Patriarcha* 1.10). Locke quotes from Filmer "that this command, *Honour thy father*, gives the right to govern, and makes the form of government monarchical." Cf. John Locke, *First Treatise*, §66.

46. "The Father of a family governs by no law other then his own will, not by the will of his sons or servants. There is no nation that allows children any action for being unjustly governed" (Filmer, *Patriarcha* 3.1).

47. "If we compare the duties of a father with those of a king, we find them to be all one,without any difference but only in the latitude and extent of them" (Filmer, *Patriarcha* 1.10).

48. At the end of his *Observations on Aristotles Politiques*, Filmer concludes that "there is no monarchy, but paternal" and "There is no paternal monarchy but absolute, or arbitrary."

49. Locke, *Second Treatise*, §53.

50. Locke, *First Treatise*, §61.

51. Locke, *Second Treatise*, §63.

52. *Ibid.*, §57.

53. *Ibid.*

54. *Ibid.*

55. See Locke *Second Treatise* §60: "But if, through defects that may happen out of the ordinary course of nature, any one comes not to such a degree of reason, wherein he might be supposed capable of knowing the law, and so living within the rules of it, he is *never capable of being a free man*, he is never let loose to the disposure of his own will (because he knows no bounds to it, has not understanding, its proper guide) but is continued under the tuition and government of others, all the time his own understanding is uncapable of that charge. And so *lunatics* and *ideots* are never set free from the government of their parents; *children, who are not as yet come unto those years whereat they may have; and innocents which are excluded by a natural defect from ever having;* thirdly, *madmen, which for the present cannot possibly have the use of right reason to guide themselves, have for their guide, the reason that guideth other men which are tutors over them, to seek and procure their good for them, says* Hooker, Eccl. Pol. *lib.* i. *sect.* 7. All which seems no more than that duty, which God and nature has laid on man, as well as other creatures, to preserve their offspring, till they can be able to shift for themselves, and will scarce amount to an instance or proof of *parents* regal authority.

It is interesting to note the remarkable similarity between Hooker's discussion and the categories of persons prospectively unable to govern themselves in Francisco Vitoria's discussion regarding Spain's claim to hold the Indians in tutelage. Cf. M. W. F. Stone, "The Nature and Significance of Law in Early Modern Scholasticsm."

56. Locke, *Second Treatise*, §61.

57. "The first part then of *paternal power,* or rather duty, which is *education,* belongs so to the father, that it terminates at a certain season; when the business of education is over, it ceases of itself, and is also alienable before . . . But all the *duty of honour,* the other part, remains never the less entire to them; nothing can cancel that: it is so inseparable from them both, that the father's authority cannot dispossess the mother of this right, nor can any man discharge his son from *honouring* her that bore him. But both these are very far from a power to make laws, and inforcing them with penalties, that may reach estate, liberty, limbs and life. The power of commanding ends with nonage; and though, after that, *honour* and respect, support and defence, and whatsoever gratitude can oblige a man to, for the highest benefits he is naturally capable of, be always due from a son to his parents; yet all this puts no scepter into the father's hand, no sovereign power of commanding. He has no dominion over his son's property, or actions; nor any right, that his will should prescribe to his son's in all things; however it may become his son in many things, not very inconvenient to him and his family, to pay a deference to it." *Ibid.,* §69.

58. "To conclude then, tho' the *father's power* of commanding extends no farther than the minority of his children, and to a degree only fit for the discipline and government of that age; and tho' that *honour* and *respect,* and all that which the *Latins* called *piety,* which they indispensibly owe to their parents all their life-time, and in all estates, with all that support and defence is due to them, gives the father no power of governing, *i. e.* making laws and enacting penalties on his children . . . yet it is obvious to conceive how easy it was, in the first ages of the world, and in places still, where the thinness of people gives families leave to separate into unpossessed quarters, and they have room to remove or plant themselves in yet vacant habitations, for the *father of the family* to become the prince of* it; he had been a ruler from the beginning of the infancy of his children: and since without some government it would be hard for them to live together, it was likeliest it should, by the express or tacit consent of the children when they were grown up, be in the father." *Ibid.,* §74.

59. *Ibid.,* §74.

60. Quoted in *ibid.*

61. Quentin Skinner, *The Foundations of Modern Political Thought,* 2, p. 158.

62. Hobbes, *Leviathan,* I.13.13.

63. Locke, *Second Treatise,* §15.

64. *Laws,* I.10 (Keble, 139).

65. Locke, *Second Treatise,* §77ff.

66. *Laws,* I,10.1.

67. Locke, *Second Treatise,* §6.

68. *Laws,* I.10.4.

69. Locke, *Second Treatise,* §4.

70. *Ibid.,* §5.

71. *Ibid.,* §54.

72. See Russell Kirk, *The Roots of the American Order.*

73. Locke, *Second Treatise,* §6.

74. See Suarez, *Tractatus de Legibus*, I: *ex natura rei omnes* homines nascuntur liberi, *et ideo nullus habet iurisdictioonem politicum in alium, sicut nec dominium* (emphasis added).

75. Locke, *Second Treatise*, §4 (1st emphasis in the original; 2nd emphasis added).

76. *Ibid.*, §149.

77. *Ibid.*, §134 (note), quoting *Laws*, I.10.

78. *Laws*, VIII. K.2.5.

79. John Yolton, "Locke on the Law of Nature," in *Critical Assessments* II, 29.

80. For the earlier passage, see Locke, *Second Treatise*, §134; for this passage, see §91 (emphasis added).

81. *Ibid.*, §123.

82. *Ibid.*, §91.

83. *Ibid* (note).

84. *Ibid.*, §124.

85. *Ibid.*, §124–126.

86. *Ibid.*, §95.

87. *Ibid.*, §97.

88. *Ibid.*, §91, quoting *Laws* 1.10 (previously quoted in this work).

89. *Ibid.*, §135, quoting *Laws* 1.10 (emphasis added).

90. *Ibid.*, §97.

91. *Ibid.*, §77.

92. *Ibid.*, §95 (emphasis added).

93. *Ibid.*, §134 (emphasis added).

94. *Ibid.*, §90 (emphasis added).

95. *Ibid.*, §135.

96. *Ibid.*, §136.

97. Cf. Peter Laslett's note in John Locke, *Two Treatises on Government*, p. 358.

98. Locke, *Second Treatise*, §111.

99. *Ibid.* (emphasis added).

100. *Ibid.*, §135.

101. *Ibid.* (emphasis added).

102. *Ibid.*, §171.

103. *Ibid.*, §199.

104. *Ibid.*, §232.

105. *Ibid.*, §202–203.

106. *Ibid.*, §243.

107. "Hooker sought to refine the patriotic doctrine of the English constitution which ran from Bracton . . . through Fortescue and Reformation writers. Long ago the English had sensibly agreed to establish a limited monarchy 'for their own most behoof and security' in which the king was *major singulis, universis minor* and where consequently, arbitrary power was excluded by the rule of law (VIII.ii.7; VIII.ii.13). The result was that the monarch could make statutes only with the approval of the body politic assembled in parliament (VIII.vi.11). The ancestral bequeathal of procedures for mobilizing communal agreement provided the assurance that nothing was

done in English public life to infringe the divine moral order. Eccleshall, "Hooker and the Peculiarities of the English," p. 86.

108. Consequently, Eccleshall rightly concludes that (contrary to Locke): "Far from wishing to justify the deposition of arbitrary rulers, his intention was to suggest that the English had been peculiarly adept in using the opportunity afforded to them to construct a sound polity. For, having institutionalized co-operation in their constitutional procedures they had ensured the congruity of their public regulations with precepts of eternal justice." *Ibid.*

109. We have seen that Sommerville argument that: "It might be supposed that Hooker's argument at this point demonstrates his conservativism and his rejection of the resistance theories of the monarchomachs. This is unclear . . . .Who in Hooker's theory, had authority superior to that of the whole commonwealth? Certainly the king did not have such authority, for Hooker took great pains to point out that his power was inferior to that of the people." Cf. J.P. Sommerville, "Hadrian Saravia, and the Advent of the Divine Right of Kings," p. 234.

110. This fact is mentioned by John Marshall who writes that "Locke, was also attempting to argue, of course, that it was only in 'this Latter age' that the legitimacy of resistance was completely denied and political authority had become *jure divino*. By using Richard Hooker, whose works supported *jure divino* episcopacy but only *jure humano* monarchy, and was thus a basis for 'their arguments' on church government, Locke was indicating that the elevation of monarchy as *jure divino* was particularly novel . . . .this was all part of Locke's attempt to show that his defence of resistance was restorationist." Marshall, John. John Locke: *Resistance, Religion, and Responsibility*. Cambridge: Cambridge University Press, 1994, cf. note on p.114.

111. Locke, *Second Treatise*, §199.

112. *Ibid.*, §227.

113. Aquinas, S.T. II-II, q.42, art. 2, Reply 3 (italics added).

Chapter Six

Conclusion

Part of what I hope is achieved by this work is a more complex understanding of the relationship between the medieval tradition of political thought and the modern political philosophy represented by thinkers like John Locke. We have seen how Richard Hooker's political philosophy outlined in the *Laws of Ecclesiastical Polity* drew heavily upon scholastics such as St. Thomas Aquinas, even while serving as a central authority for John Locke in his *Two Treatises*. A sixteenth-century figure like Hooker can be seen as a kind of "missing link," a mediator between the medieval and the modern worlds, of a type that has been neglected by contemporary scholars for too long. This neglect has contributed to significant errors of historical understanding. The evidence I have adduced strongly suggests that particular standard historical narratives of how and why constitutionalism emerged need to be reconsidered in light of historical evidence. A prevalent "textbook" account sees European culture and society as hopelessly mired in autocratic government and clerical obscurantism throughout the medieval and early modern period, until Enlightenment figures such as Locke, Rousseau, Voltaire, Diderot, and Montesquieu at last challenged the *status quo* by laying the foundations of the ideas of popular sovereignty and constitutional government. In this narrative, the *coup de grace* to the old order was delivered by the "age of revolutions" that based themselves on these enlightened figures. After the English Revolution of 1688, the American Revolution of 1776, and the French Revolution of 1789, the great principles of popular sovereignty, rule of law, and constitutional government at long last were secure and established for posterity.

   This present study, however, reveals the gross simplification of this historical narrative. Medieval scholastic thought was notably hostile to notions of absolutism. We have seen, for example, how St. Thomas Aquinas (like many other figures of the age) regarded the unjust law as an act of violence by the ruling authority rather than a true law. Martin Luther King, in his *Letter from a Birmingham Jail*, famously referred to this constitutionalist element of the doctrine in Aquinas in defense of resistance to laws mandating segregation in the American South. Aquinas moreover regarded the tyrant (rather than those who resist him) as guilty of sedition, and he favored a "mixed" mode of government in which monarchy would be limited so that it could not easily degenerate into tyranny. Absolutist theories of government became more prevalent only in the early modern period when centralized monarchy began to emerge. Against this trend, early modern scholastics, including Francisco Suarez and Richard Hooker, drew upon the resources of medieval scholasticism to develop a broader constitutionalist theory. This theory includes such concepts as the consensual origins of government, sovereignty as originally vested in the community, and government as a delegated power that must be ordered to the common good. Early modern absolutists (such as the Patriarchalists in England) subsequently attacked constitutionalism, but Whig theorists such as John Locke defended it (albeit for their own partisan political purposes). Many of the main themes of Locke's *Two Treatises*—the state of nature, consent as the origin of government, the sovereignty of the community, and so forth—were already part of a traditional account of the origins and legitimation of government. It is for that reason that Locke is able to turn so frequently to a traditional authority such as Hooker for the vindication of his claims. Locke was appealing to this established tradition as a reply to the patriarchalist theory of government.

Judged in this broader context, it is possible to view the "ascent of constitutionalism" not as emerging from a radical effort to overthrow the traditional order of thought and society, but as an effort to *preserve* elements of this order from the novel claims made on behalf of modern state power in the person of the king. It should be noted, however, that this account is problematic not merely for the modernist enlightenment myth, but also for anti-modernist projects like that of Leo Strauss. Straussianism's conceptual framework draws on an overly rigid distinction between premoderns and moderns that overlooks important lines of continuity and development. Too much of our understanding of intellectual history remains trapped in a simple duality between medieval and modern political thought. For a writer like Strauss, modernity signifies a shift from the classic "natural law" discourse that emphasizes a natural order prior to human volition to a "natural rights" discourse that emphasizes the nonexistence of any theological or natural order prior to the claims of the subject.

On his binary categorization between "natural law" premodern thinkers and "natural rights" moderns, Locke becomes for Strauss a quintessential "modern" following the lead of Hobbes in rejecting the existence of a binding order of natural law. As he puts it: "Locke deviated considerably from the traditional natural law teaching, and followed the lead given by Hobbes."[1] However, looking at more recent and more historically attentive studies like those of Annabel Brett and Brian Tierney, it is clear that Strauss's twofold distinction is rather simplistic: the concept of rights long predates the period ordinarily understood as *modern*, being found in the canonist tradition of the High Middle Ages, among the Franciscan school of the fourteenth century and the School of Salamanca in the sixteenth century. And yet, this schema remains hugely influential. I hope that more attention will be given to the political thought of early modern scholastic figures like Hooker as both significant in its own right and as mediating between the medieval and modern outlooks.

THE RELEVANCE OF HOOKER TO CONTEMPORARY DEBATES IN POLITICAL PHILOSOPHY

This work has been an effort to contribute to intellectual history, but it is up to the reader to judge how successful this project has been in realizing its objectives. In these concluding remarks, we should also examine how Richard Hooker and the issues discussed in this work may be of continued relevance to the problems of political philosophy. This would include not merely *historical* relevance, in that Hooker was one of the figures who helped to shape modern constitutional thought. In fact, it should also consist of *philosophical* relevance in that Hooker's understanding of the nature of the political may assist us in illuminating broader and more general issues that remain of concern in our own time. It would of course be an absurd anachronism to transpose Hooker into our own era and ask what solutions he would recommend to the great political questions of our contemporary age. Political conditions have altered radically enough since the sixteenth century, and thus, many of the concrete questions that loomed so large in Hooker's time and that he addressed are of diminished import today. For example, Hooker's *erastianism*, in regard to the ecclesiastical polity, is inextricably tied to a conception of church and commonwealth that *de facto* no longer pertains to any contemporary Western society.

Yet, any great political philosopher is not merely addressing matters that belong to the realm of historical contingency. Political philosophy also strives to address *perennial questions* and thus to find universal goods that are not circumscribed by a particular time and place. For example, Aristotle's position that human beings are by nature social and political animals may be correct or incorrect, but the question it addresses is a universal, and his answer is meant to make a statement regarding human societies *as such* and not about any society in particular. In what follows, I will suggest certain broad ideas in Hooker that might be helpful in contributing to contemporary debates in political philosophy.

THE HIERARCHY AND PLURALITY OF LAW

As we have seen, Hooker played an important role in relation to the natural law tradition. On the one hand, he received the medieval, and specifically Thomistic, concept of law and, on the other hand, he mediated this tradition in early modern English political philosophy. The notion of a *hierarchy* and *plurality* of orders in law—the eternal law, the divine positive law, the natural law, and the human positive or civil law—is central to the medieval concept of law as understood by Aquinas and received by Hooker. Each order of law must be governed by the norm of the order of law above it. Thus, since there is a moral law knowable by reason antecedent to the human act of legislation, a law must conform to the natural moral law and may not justly contravene it for it to be legitimate. As Hooker put the matter, "Laws Humane must be made according to the general Laws of Nature and without contradiction to any positive Law of Scripture."[2]

Perhaps one of the consequences of secularism has been the tendency to reduce law to a *single* order of law—that of the human or positive law. Such *legal positivism* involves the notion that the (civil) law does not depend on any principles external to it for its validity; what it requires for validity is merely adherence to a set of defined norms and procedures—for example, that the law is enacted through democratic processes according to the rules of a written constitution. It would seem that legal positivism depends on procedural conformity (rather than content) for legitimacy. Thus, legal positivism rejects the notion that the civil or juridical order must conform to a moral order that transcends it.

The tendency of contemporary Western societies to adopt legal positivism is perhaps linked to the widespread acceptance of *relativism*, which is grounded in a general skepticism that there is something like a universal "moral truth" that can be known. From this view, moral concepts are relative to cultures and even individuals. Indeed, cultural elites often believe that relativism is the most secure foundation for pluralistic and democratic values, since differing perspectives can coexist without seeking to impose their truths on others when everyone accepts that there is no truth to which society ought to conform. Yet, the experience of totalitarianism in both its Communist and National Socialist forms in the twentieth century has led in some circles to a renewed appreciation of the need for some form of natural law to undergird positive law. When the Nuremberg trials convened, a problem immediately arose: the mass extermination of millions of human beings, of which the Nazi leaders were accused, was in fact legal according to the positive laws of Germany and its duly constituted legal authority. Indeed, in his last published book, *Memory and Identity*, Pope John Paul II noted that:

> It was a regularly elected parliament that consented to Hitler's rise to power in Germany in the 1930s. And the same *Reichstag* by delegating full powers to Hitler (*Ermachtigungsgesetz*) paved the way for his policy of invading Europe, for the establishment of the concentration camps, and for the implementation of the so called 'final solution' to the Jewish question, that is to say the eliminations of millions of the sons and daughters of Israel.[3]

He concludes that the traditional teaching that human law must conform to moral law has perennial value, given that the positive law can sanction any crime:

> Suffice it to recall these events, so close to us in time, in order to see clearly that the law established by man has definitive limits, which it must not overstep. *There are limits determined by the law of nature*, through which God himself safeguards man's fundamental good.[4]

We must then consider whether in fact relativism and positivism provide the best foundation for the values of modern constitutional democracies, or whether they in fact tend to undermine them. The natural law tradition as enunciated by figures like St. Thomas Aquinas and Richard Hooker provides an *independent standard* by which the actions of a state can be judged. But, taken to their logical extremes, legal positivism and relativism leave human beings with no conceptual defense against the claims of a state to absolute power. If there is no law or principle higher than the state to which its enactments must conform, then there are no grounds by which state action can be condemned.

For Hooker, of course, the challenge was not the efforts of legal positivists to reduce all law to the single order of human law, but the effort of Calvinists to reduce all law to the single order of *divine* or *revealed* law. Thus, we have Whitgift's complaint that if the Puritans triumph,

> All the laws of this land, that be contrary to these judicial laws of Moses, must be abrogated: the prince must be abridged of that prerogative which she hath in pardoning such as by the law be condemned to die . . . to be short, all things must be transformed: lawyers must cast away their huge volumes and multitude of cases, and content themselves with the books of Moses: we of the clergy would be the best judges; and they must require the law at our hands.[5]

As we have seen, the Puritan tendency to replace all other law with Biblical law arose from their basically pessimistic conception of nature. Human nature, they thought, was so radically depraved that reason was no longer competent either to discern the ends of nature (the foundation of natural law) or to frame wise ordinances for its governance (human law). Consequently, in such a fallen state, the only reliable guide was Scripture, and so, the Puritans advocated a politics of divine law. Though there remains a skepticism regarding the natural law tradition and a desire to create a "political theology" based on scriptural resources in some Protestant circles, the rigid advocacy of *theonomy* in the civil sphere, for the most part, is no longer a central feature of any mainstream Christian theology.[6] It must be argued, however, that this monistic[7] tendency to abolish the order of human law and reduce all law to a single order of divine law remains relevant in our times, particularly within the Islamic world.

ISLAMISM AND THE POLITICS OF DIVINE LAW

The essential effort of the modern *Islamiyya* movement has been to replace the civil law systems (largely introduced after the fall of the Ottoman empire in World War I) with Islam's own tradition of divine positive law (*Sharia*). This is precisely what animates the religious revolutionaries of the Middle East, namely, the desire to overthrow the "apostate" regimes of the region and replace them with regimes prepared to implement their politics of divine law. For these Islamists (a term we use to describe those who wish to implement *Sharia* as the law of the land, as opposed to the mere practice of Islam as a faith), the law of God embodied in the texts of the *Quran* and the Hadiths is understood as a single, all embracing order of divine law, which essentially constitutes a rule for all of human life. All of man's activities, public and private, social and individual, are to submit to the divine law and its mandates. The *Shariah*, therefore, regulates not merely such matters as personal morality and prayer, but criminal law, issues of property and inheritance, the correct form of government, matters of war and peace, economic policies, the position of religious minorities, and so forth. Behind this idea is the theological concept of the sovereignty of God. As Bernard Lewis writes:

> There is another interpretation of the term 'theocracy,' in its original and literal meaning, that is, 'the rule of God.' In the juristic conception of the Muslim state, God alone is the supreme sovereign, the ultimate, indeed the sole source of authority. In this conception only God makes law; only God confers, or at least legitimizes, authority.[8]

Thus, the ideal polity for Islamists is one in which God rules human society *directly* through his divine law. Syed Qutb, perhaps the leading intellectual theorist of Islamist ideology, contrasts the "rule of God" advocated by Islam and the law of the *Quran* with the "rule of man" characterized by laws framed by human legislators:

> When in a society, the sovereignty belongs to God alone, expressed in its obedience to the Divine Law, only then is every person in that society free from servitude to others . . . in a society in which some people are lords who legislate and some others are slaves who obey them, there is no freedom in the real sense.[9]

This robust Islamist conviction regarding the earthly kingship of God is precisely why historically, democracy has made such little headway in the Middle East, and why the present effort to transpose Western democracy into the Middle East is a difficult task. For the Islamist, the divine law is the *only* law by which man should be governed; consequently, the effort to supplant the law of God with a democratic system of laws contracted by human beings is tantamount to rejecting the sovereignty of God. As Qutb puts it, Islam is a

> declaration that sovereignty belongs to God alone and that he is the Lord of all the worlds. It means a challenge to all kinds and all forms of systems that are based on the concept of the sovereignty of man; in other words where man has usurped the Divine attribute. Any system in which the final decisions are referred to human beings and in which the sources of all authority are human, deifies human beings by designating others than God as lords over men. This declaration means that the usurped authority of God be returned to Him and the usurpers thrown out . . . in short to proclaim the sovereignty of God means to eliminate all human kingship and to announce the rule of the Sustainer of the universe over the entire earth.[10] (Milestones, p. 4)

It is this notion that establishes the basis for the doctrine of *Jihad* or "striving" by military and nonmilitary means to establish divine sovereignty:

> The establishing of the dominion of God on earth, the taking away of sovereignty from the usurper to revert it to God, and the bringing about of the enforcement of the Divine Law (Shari'ah) and the abolition of man made laws cannot be achieved only through preaching . . . anyone who understands the particular character of this religion will also understand the place of Jihad bis saif (striving through fighting) which is to clear the way for striving through preaching in the application of the Islamic movement. He will understand that Islam is not a 'defensive movement' in the narrow sense which is today technically called a 'defensive war.'[11]

Indeed, for Islamists, not only democracy, but any form of civil law, would seem to contradict this vision. Traditional Islam divides the world between *Dar al Islam*, which submits to the kingship of God and is governed by his law, and *Dar al Kufr*, that unbelieving part of mankind, which rejects the kingship of God. The tension that this conception creates with Western models is admirably described in Paul Berman's book *Terror and Liberalism*; there, he discusses the work of Syed Qutb—perhaps the foremost intellectual behind the twentieth century Islamic revival. For Syed Qutb, the West is in the grip of a "hideous schizophrenia" in which religious and secular human activities are distinguished and compartmentalized. As Qutb puts it, for the West and its imitators:

> God's existence is not denied, but His domain is restricted to the heavens and his rule on earth is suspended. Neither the Shari'ah nor the values prescribed by God and ordained by Him as eternal and invariable find any place in this scheme of life . . . thus such a society denies or plainly suspends God's sovereignty on earth, while God plainly says 'It is he who is Sovereign in the heavens and Sovereign in the earth.'[12]

While, in the course of Western history, the proper relations between church and state have been debated, discussed, and even fought over, the legitimate existence of two separate orders (and thus the legitimate existence of a secular sphere) rarely has been questioned within the normative Christian discourse prior to the Reformation. Even in the medieval period when the relationship between church and state was most intimate, the functions of the priestly power (*sacerdotium*) and the royal power (*regnum*) were identifiably distinct. The position of Roman Catholicism recognized a hierarchy of laws (as opposed to a single order of law) in which there was a clear space reserved for the order of human law promulgated by the civil legislator. The normative expression of this view can be found in the text of St. Thomas Aquinas:

> There is a three-fold order to be found in man. The first is that which derives from the rule of reason: insofar as all our actions and experiences should be commensurate with the guidance of reason. The second arises from comparison with the rule of divine law, which should be our guide in all things. And if man were a solitary animal, this double order would suffice: but because man is naturally a social and political animal, as is proved in I. *Politics,* chap 2; it is necessary that there should be a third order, regulating the conduct of man to his fellows with whom he has to live.[13]

This Thomistic concept of a *plurality* of orders in law—divine, natural, and human—was taken up in the English-speaking world by Richard Hooker. This notion leaves ample room for legitimate human autonomy without in any way negating the notion of divine sovereignty. As Hooker put the matter, "it seemeth almost out of doubt and controversy that every independent multitude before any certain regiment established *hath under God's supreme authority full dominion over itself.*"[14] In contrast to the notion of direct and unmediated divine sovereignty, as promoted by the Puritans, Hooker emphasized the idea of a *mediated* sovereignty in which the sovereignty is ultimately vested in God, but expressed *through* the community. Hooker thus leaves ample space for legitimate human freedom and judgment in devising rules that best serve the common good of the community. The community is obligated to frame laws that *conform* to the general precepts of divine and natural law, but nonetheless: "God creating mankind did naturally endow it with full power to guide itself in what kind of societies soever it should choose to live."[15]

We thus see that the traditional conception of natural law promoted by Hooker avoids the problems associated either with a legal positivism that reduces all law to human law (and thus tends to provide the state with few moral constraints), or a theocratic conception that reduces all law to divine law. It will be interesting to observe whether some form of indigenous natural law theory will emerge to harmonize human law with classical Islam's emphasis on the direct and undivided sovereignty of God as the Islamic world struggles to carve a legitimate space for consensually-based human or positive law.

STATE AND SOCIETY

We have seen that one of Hooker's most important contributions is his distinction between society and the political society. The Aristotelian tradition asserted that "politics" and what we today would call "the state" both arose from the order of nature. Hooker operates within an Aristotelian perspective in so far as he sees human beings as having a social nature, but more so than Aristotle, he emphasizes that the character of particular *political* institutions arises from conscious human agreement:

> Two foundations there are which bear up public societies, the one a natural inclination, *the other an order expressly or secretly agreed upon, touching the manner of their union together. The latter is that which we call the law of a commonweal, the very soul of a politic body,* the parts whereof are by law animated, and set on work as the common good requireth.[16]

Hooker's explicit distinction between state and society opens up a space for a consensual theory of government. Were particular political *forms* natural, the Patriarchalist position that the natural state of human beings is one of subjection to political authority would then have some validity; if however, the society or the community *precedes* political rule, there are valid reasons to see state authority as inherently limited to the powers assigned to it by the community.

In the modern epoch, the state's tendency to equate itself with society has led to dramatic abuses of political power reaching their apotheosis in totalitarian systems in which the state aims to bring all spheres of culture and society under its domain. A just social doctrine will accept the principle of subsidiarity in which there are a variety of institutions within society; and, the public authority should limit itself to performing only those functions that cannot be effectively performed by other institutions. Fr. Richard John Neuhaus ably describes the connection between the state/society distinction, subsidiarity, and the principles of limited or constitutional government:

> Democratic government is limited government. It is limited in the claims it makes and in the power it seeks to exercise. Democratic government understands itself to be accountable to values and to truth which transcend any regime or party. . . . *limited government means that a clear distinction is made between the state and the society.* Other institutions—notably the family, the Church, educational, economic and cultural enterprises—are at least equally important actors in the society. They do not exist or act by sufferance of the state. Rather, these spheres have their own peculiar sovereignty which must be respected by the state . . . Most importantly democratic government does not seek to control or restrict the sphere of religion in which people affirm, exercise and share their ultimate beliefs about the world and their place in it.[17]

SOVEREIGNTY AND CONSENT

Closely connected to Hooker's distinction between society and government are his notions of sovereignty and consent. If, as he holds, divine or natural law ordains no particular form of government, it follows that the subjection of some to the rule of others does not arise from a special divine or natural prerogative. Therefore, original sovereignty is vested not in a particular person, but in the whole body of the people who "hath under God's supreme authority full dominion over itself."[18] The people's obligation to the ruler therefore has its origin in the *consent* of the community to be governed. Ultimately then, "laws they are not which public approbation hath not made so."[19] That is to say, each community is free and entitled to compose arrangements for their governance within the due limits imposed by the natural law, and civil laws derive their authority from the consent of the governed. These principles in Hooker's thought came to influence Locke and other thinkers and became part of the great constitutional tradition that has so influenced our world. Though much of the twenty-first century's population continues to labor under autocratic dictators who make no pretense to base their rule on the consent of their people, the principles of constitutional self-government remain the dominant understanding in the Western world (and much beyond it) of what makes government *legitimate*. Governments whose authority is merely based on force and the arbitrary will of the leader are widely viewed as "no better then mere tyranny."[20]

The principle of sovereignty has also become an essential component of international law. Given that each national community is understood to be self-governing, international law generally condemns attempts by one government to interfere in the internal affairs of another nation. The principle of sovereignty, of course, also has due limits, and discussions are increasing, for example, on humanitarian interventions through which foreign states intervene in order to end a tyrannical government's gross mistreatment of its own citizens. Though the notion of humanitarian interventions has gained currency in contemporary times, early modern scholars did not neglect it. For them, the principle of sovereignty did not do away with the precept of charity that requires that one not stand by the shedding of an innocent neighbor's blood. In a case where a people are unable to defend themselves against a murderous tyrannical regime, other nations may intervene to deliver a people from tyranny and appoint new authorities who will rule with greater justice. Luis de Molina recognizes this exception when he writes that:

> It is quite proper to end by force the atrocities and cruel behavior due to wickedly unjust laws, if necessary by declaration of war and using all the rights of war, even to deposing wicked rulers, and if necessary appointing others. It does not matter if the barbarians and their subjects are in favour of such customs and sacrifices and do not want outsiders to attack them, for everybody has the right to save a man who is being unjustly killed, even if the victim does not want to be saved, as in the generally agreed case of a man trying to hang himself, or to commit suicide in some other way.[21]

Nonetheless, the principles of sovereignty and consent that figures like Hooker developed have become an essential template for judging regimes. Constitutional government recognizes that for civil law to be legitimate, it must somehow derive from the consent of those who are subject to them, even if only tacitly or by means of representatives. It is a mark of constitutionalism's broad appeal that the principles of sovereignty and consent are broadly accepted today, even if they remain contested both by autocratic rulers, and in some cases, more subtly by international institutions.

PRESCRIPTION AND CONTINUITY

In a certain sense, Hooker was the father not only of Locke but also of Burke.[22] For Hooker, the "social compact" exists not only between the ruler and the ruled, but also between the living and the dead:

> Wherefore as any man's past deed is good as long as he himself continueth: so the act of a public society of men done five hundred years since standeth as theirs, who presently are of the same societies, because corporations are immortal: we were alive in our predecessors and they in their successors do live still.[23]

For Hooker, the consensual agreements that create the "politic society" are bequeathed to each new generation. Each generation is thus entrusted to keep faith with their ancestors by maintaining the continuity of the fundamental institutions of the commonwealth. Prescription—a tacit assent of a community to its inherited traditions—becomes one of the primary manners through which consent is expressed:

> The articles of compact between them must show, not only the articles of compact at the first beginning which for the most part are worn clean out of knowledge . . . but whatsoever hath been after in free and voluntary manner condescended whether by express consent, whereof positive laws are witnesses, *or lese by silent allowance famously notified through custom reaching beyond the memory of man.*[24]

One of Hooker's major problems with the Puritans was that their scriptural politics presumed to transcend the two most hallowed inheritances of the English constitutional system: the common law and the parliament. After the destructive seventeenth century, which resulted in the rending of English traditional institutions during a period of civil war and the Cromwellian protectorate (ultimately, the Crown, Parliament, and established Church were overthrown), the English adopted a much more temperate and evolutionary approach to social change. With this approach, reforms were gradual and did not tamper with fundamental institutions. To this day, the medieval institutions of Crown, the lords spiritual, the lords temporal, and the commons, remain part of the English system. This English tradition treats society on the whole as a spiritual corporation or organism where growth and change is gradual and roots are preserved, as opposed to being a mechanism that can be taken apart and reassembled at will.

This approach is sharply contrasted against the *revolutionary* attitude that has inspired other nations. By "revolutionary," I do not mean resistance to a particular tyrant with the aim of restoring the *status quo ante* but instead the kind of ferment that desires to replace one political, economic, and cultural order with an entirely new one. We may think, for example, of the French Revolution of 1789, the Russian Revolution of 1917, the Chinese Revolution of 1949, and the Iranian Revolution of 1979. The destructive potential of the revolutionary ethos is seen in all these cases in spite of their different ideological commitments (Jacobinism, Bolshevism, Maoism, and revolutionary Islam, respectively).

Tradition is the memory of a community, and just as a human being without memory has lost his or her identity, so a community that strives to eliminate its past seems to lose its bearings. Thus, all of these revolutions follow a familiar pattern—attacks on the ruling elites, a descent into chaos and civil war, foreign intervention, the effort to implement the revolutionary agenda, and the emergence of a centralized state apparatus to employ terror against real or perceived enemies of the revolution. It generally takes decades, if not centuries, to heal the tissues of a society damaged by this kind of revolution— if indeed complete healing ever occurs at all.

HOOKER, LOCKE, AND AMERICA

Is the American form of constitutionalism rooted in precisely this kind of revolutionary radicalism? Or, on the other hand, can it be understood as congruent with the natural law tradition represented by Hooker? Given Locke's central importance in the American founding, the answer to this question hinges in no small degree on how we read Locke. Leo Strauss bases his understanding of Locke on a rather binary categorization between "natural law" premoderns and "natural rights" moderns. Locke is thus cast as a quintessential "modern," following the lead of Hobbes in rejecting the existence of a binding order of natural law, or as he puts it: "Locke deviated considerably from the traditional natural law teaching, and followed the lead given by Hobbes."[25] It was left to one of Leo Strauss's most important followers, Alan Bloom, to draw out the implications. The moral relativism, secularism, and radical libertarianism he associates with the 1960s were not the subversion of the American order, but the working out of conceptual implications present already at the founding. Yet, on the basis of this reading, Bloom endeavors to identify Locke with Rousseau and, thus, the American with the French Revolution: "What was acted out in the American and French Revolutions, had been thought out beforehand in the writings of Locke and Rousseau." This is because Bloom follows Strauss in interpreting Locke, and thus the American founders, as cautious and modified Hobbesians, meaning that rights, rather than duties, are primary. Likewise, the state of nature is premoral, and thus morality, rights, and duties come into being only with the contract that creates civil society. For Bloom, the pioneers of modernity—Locke, Hobbes, and Rousseau—see a world where:

> God neither looks after him nor punishes him. Nature's indifference to justice is a terrible bereavement to man. He must care for himself without the hope that good men have always had: that there is a price to be paid for crime, that the wicked will suffer. But it is also a great liberation, from God's tutelage.[26]

It must be said at the outset that the search for a "monolithic" political philosophy embraced by "the founders" as such is largely illusory. Certain key figures in the American founding like Thomas Paine were indeed deeply influenced by the radicalism of the French *philosophes*. Yet, if we look at other figures like Alexander Hamilton, Bloom's representation of the founders appears as precisely the inverse of the truth. Alexander Hamilton, in his letter *A Farmer Refuted*, associates Hobbes with the notion of a state of nature in which men are not subject to any moral law:

> There is so strong a similitude between your political principles and those maintained by Mr. Hobbs [*sic*], that, in judging from them, a person might very easily *mistake* you for a disciple of his. His opinion was, exactly, coincident with yours, relative to man in a state of nature. He held, as you do, that he was, then, perfectly free from all restraint of *law* and *government*. Moral obligation, according to him, is derived from the introduction of civil society; and there is no virtue, but what is purely artificial, the mere contrivance of politicians, for the maintenance of social intercourse. But the reason he run into this absurd and impious doctrine, was, that he disbelieved the existence of an intelligent superintending principle, who is the governor, and will be the final judge of the universe.[27]

Hamilton counterpoises this view of the state of nature to that of Locke stating that he:

> would recommend to your perusal, Grotius, Puffendorf, Locke, Montesquieu, and Burlemaqui. I might mention other excellent writers on this subject; but if you attend, diligently, to these, you will not require any others.[28]

And what is the view of the state of nature that Hamilton commends? He asserts that even prior to civil society, human beings were subject to the natural moral law and its divine sanctions:

> Good and wise men, in all ages, have embraced a very dissimilar theory. They have supposed that the deity, from the relations we stand in, to himself and to

each other, has constituted an eternal and immutable law, which is, indispensably, obligatory upon all mankind, prior to any human institution whatever. This is what is called the law of nature, "which, being coeval with mankind, and dictated by God himself, is, of course, superior in obligation to any other. It is binding over all the globe, in all countries, and at all times. No human laws are of any validity, if contrary to this; and such of them as are valid, derive all their authority, mediately, or immediately, from this original.[29]

In direct contrast to the view of Strauss and Bloom that the founders privileged rights above duties, Hamilton explicitly grounds rights in a natural law that is primary:

Upon this law, depend the natural rights of mankind, the supreme being gave existence to man, together with the means of preserving and beatifying that existence. He endowed him with rational faculties, by the help of which, to discern and pursue such things, as were consistent with his duty and interest, and invested him with an inviolable right to personal liberty, and personal safety. Hence, in a state of nature, no man had any *moral* power to deprive another of his life, limbs, property or liberty; nor the least authority to command, or exact obedience from him; except that which arose from the ties of consanguinity.[30]

James Wilson of Pennsylvania, a signer of the 1776 Declaration of Independence and active participant in the 1787 Constitutional convention, provides another important discussion of Locke and Hooker on the nature of law in the eighteenth-century Wilson's 1790 work "Of the General Theory of Law and Obligation"[31] defends the classical natural law tradition. Wilson holds a high opinion of Locke, but he also is convinced that the irreligious figures of the eighteenth century made use of his works and perverted his intentions:

I am equally far from believing that Mr. Locke was a friend to infidelity. But yet it is unquestionable, that the writings of Mr. Locke have facilitated the progress, and have given strength to the effects of scepticism[sic]. The high reputation, which he deservedly acquired for his enlightened attachment to the mild and tolerating doctrines of christianity [sic], secured to him the esteem and confidence of those, who were its friends. The same high and deserved reputation inspired others of very different views and characters, with a design to avail themselves of its splendour, and, by that means, to diffuse a fascinating kind of lustre over their own tenets of a dark and sable hue. The consequence has been, that the writings of Mr. Locke, one of the most able, most sincere, and most amiable assertors of christianity and true philosophy, have been perverted to purposes, which he would have deprecated and prevented, had he discovered or foreseen them.[32]

It is perhaps for this reason that Wilson turns to Hooker as his primary authority on the question of law and its nature. Using Hooker's authority, he remarks that divine wisdom is the ultimate foundation of law:

> Order, proportion, and fitness pervade the universe. Around us, we see; within us, we feel; above us, we admire a rule, from which a deviation cannot, or should not, or will not be made . . . . Let humble reverence attend us as we proceed. The great and incomprehensible Author, and Preserver, and Ruler of all things—he himself works not without an eternal decree. Such—and so universal is law. "Her seat," to use the sublime language of the excellent Hooker,* "is the bosom of God; her voice, the harmony of the world; all things in heaven and earth do her homage; the very least as feeling her care, and the greatest as not exempted from her power. Angels and men, creatures of every condition, though each in different sort and manner, yet all with uniform consent, admiring her as the mother of their peace and joy.[33]

Wilson, moreover, divides the divine law in the manner of Hooker into the following: *eternal law* governing the divine decrees; *celestial law* governing angels; the *law of nature* governing inanimate beings; and the *law governing man*, which is in turn divided into the *natural law* discerned by reason and the *revealed law* found in Scripture.[34]

Wilson is sympathetic to an understanding of law that is related to an end or *telos*. This is to say that law is a rule that governs the actions of a being so that it may attain its end, or perfection. Inanimate beings are guided to their end by necessity or instinct, but human beings are guided to their end by reason and will. Again, Wilson refers to the authority of Hooker:

> When we speak of a rule with regard to human conduct, we imply two things. 1. That we are susceptible of direction. 2. That, in our conduct, we propose an end. The brute creation act not from design. They eat, they drink, they retreat from the inclemencies of the weather, without considering what their actions will ultimately produce. But we have faculties, which enable us to trace the connexion between actions and their effects; and our actions are nothing else but the steps which we take, or the means which we employ, to carry into execution the effects which we intend . . . Hooker, I think, conveys a fuller and stronger conception of law, when he tells us, that "it assigns unto each thing the kind, that it moderates the force and power, that it appoints the form and measure of working." Not the direction merely, but the kind also, the energy, and the proportion of actions is suggested in this description.[35]

Wilson's emphasis, then, is on the positive function of law in assisting the attainment of an end, rather than on a merely negative understanding of law as a command to do or refrain from doing:

Some are of opinion, that law should be defined "a rule of acting or not acting"; because actions may be forbidden as well as commanded. But the same excellent writer, whom I have just now cited, gives a very proper answer to this opinion, and shows the addition to be unnecessary, by finely pursuing the metaphor, which we have already mentioned. "We must not suppose that there needeth one rule to know the good, and another to know the evil by. For he that knoweth what is straight, doth even thereby discern what is crooked. Goodness in actions is like unto straightness; wherefore that which is well done, we might term right."[36]

Wilson argues energetically for an "intellectualist" concept of law as a rational order of human acts to ends, rather than a "voluntarist" account of law as grounded solely in the command of a superior. In the sphere of human law, Wilson attributes this theory of superiority as a necessary feature of law to Puffendorf:

By comparing what is said in the Commentaries on this subject, with what is mentioned concerning it in the system of morality, jurisprudence, and politicks written by Baron Puffendorff, we shall be satisfied that, from the sentiments and opinions delivered in the last mentioned performance, those in the first mentioned one have been taken and adopted. "A law," says Puffendorff, "is the command of a superiour." . . . "A law," says Sir William Blackstone, "always supposes some superiour, who is to make it."[37]

According to Wilson, if a superior preeminence is a *necessary* part of the definition of law, what is the source of the preeminence of the persons who promulgate *human* law? If not by agreement of their subjects, this superiority must have been found in some special prerogative. Thus, Wilson sees a connection between the voluntarist theory of law, and the notions of the divine and natural right of kings that Locke spent so much time trying to refute:

When I entered upon the disquisition of the doctrine of a superiour as necessary to the very definition of law; I said, that, if I was not mistaken, this notion of superiority contained the germ of the divine right of princes to rule, and of the corresponding obligation on the people implicitly to obey. It may now be seen whether or not I have been mistaken; and, if I have not been mistaken, it appears, how important it is, carefully and patiently to examine a first principle; to trace it, with attention, to its highest origin; and to pursue it, with perseverance, to its most remote consequences. I have observed this conduct with regard to the principle in question. The result, I think, has been, that, as to human laws, the notion of a superiour is a notion unnecessary, unfounded, and dangerous; a notion inconsistent with the genuine system of human authority.[38]

Wilson regards it as inherently untenable to think that there is some natural prerogative that renders certain men the superiors of others and thus enables them to impose laws without their consent:

> Had it been the intention of Providence, that some men should govern the rest, without their consent, we should have seen as indisputable marks distinguishing these superiours from those placed under them, as those which distinguish men from the brutes . . . These pretensions to superiority, when viewed from the proper point of sight, appear, indeed, absurd and ridiculous. But these pretensions, absurd and ridiculous as they are, when rounded and gilded by flattery, and swallowed by pride, have become, in the breasts of princes, a deadly poison to their own virtues, and to the happiness of their unfortunate subjects.[39]

Since, then, there are no manifest signs in nature that give some the right to rule, Wilson views consent as the origin of political obligation—again citing the "judicious Hooker":

> If this superiour cannot rest a title on any inherent qualities; the qualities, which constitute his title, if any title he has, must be such as are derivative. If derivative; they must be derived either from a source that is human or from a source that is divine. 'Over a whole grand multitude,' says the judicious Hooker, 'consisting of any families, impossible it is, that any should have complete lawful power, but by consent of men, or by immediate appointment of God.'[40]

Wilson, of course, acknowledges that the divine and natural law bind human beings absolutely, since God is man's superior and not in virtue of some agreement by God's subjects to obey. However, in the case of human law, Wilson uses Hooker to argue that the ultimate source of the legitimacy is consent:

> One reason, why he urges their expressions to be inaccurate, is, that "neither the divine positive laws, nor the laws of nature had their rise from the agreement of men." All this is, at once admitted; but the present disquisition relates only to laws that are human . . . I am now unsolicitous to repel the accusation: it seems, it was conceived to arise from a reference, by the ancients, to their democratical governments. Let them be called covenants, or agreements, or bargains, or stipulations, or any thing similar to any of those, still I am satisfied: for still every thing mentioned, and every thing similar to every thing mentioned, imports consent. Here history and law combine their evidence in support of consent. Let us listen to the judicious and excellent Hooker: what he says always conveys instruction. 'The lawful power of making laws to command whole politick societies of men, belongeth so properly unto the same entire societies, that for any prince or potentate of what kind soever upon earth, to exercise the same of himself, and not either by express commission immediately and personally received

from God, or else by authority derived, at the first, from their consent, upon whose persons they impose laws, it is no better than mere tyranny. Laws they are not, therefore, which publick approbation hath not made so.' 'Laws human, of what kind soever, are available by consent.'[41]

To treat the influence of Hooker on early American religious and political thought in great detail would fall outside the scope of this work. However, the foregoing should be sufficient to indicate that Hooker exercised an influence on some of the American founders both directly (as with James Wilson) and indirectly (through Locke's Whig interpretation of Hooker). The influence was felt particularly in terms of his conception of natural law, his notion of sovereignty, and his concept of consensual government.

It should also be clear that the Straussian reading of Locke and the American founding—as radically divorced from the natural law tradition, as emphasizing rights to the virtual exclusion of duties, and as radically secularist in inspiration—is largely incorrect. Though representing a variety of religious perspectives from deism to Christianity, many the American founders emphasized the reality of transcendent moral law anterior to government that no temporal ruler could legitimately trespass. The founding documents of the United States undeniably combined certain ideas of the eighteenth-century Enlightenment—relatively recent values, such as freedom of speech, freedom of the press, and freedom of religion. But, they understood these in continuity with ideas drawn from the much older and broader tradition of European constitutionalism, which I have described in this work.

The great modern achievement of constitutionalism as we have received it from Locke drew upon certain central tenets that have their origins in antiquity and the Middle Ages. However, they were more clearly articulated by the thought of the early modern scholastics of the sixteenth century, such as Richard Hooker. These tenets include the following: the existence of a law above human government by which it may be judged; the dependence of a government's legitimacy on consent; and the belonging of sovereignty to a community as a whole, as opposed to the person of the ruler. The future stability and security of our political culture and civilization may well depend upon the degree to which we are able to maintain an understanding of the truth and value of these ideas and a conviction regarding the worthiness of defending them.

NOTES

1. Leo Strauss, *Natural Right and History*, p. 221.
2. *Laws*, I.3.9.

3. John Paul II, *Memory and Identity: Conversations at the Dawn of a Millennium* (London: Weidenfeld and Nicolson, 2005), p. 151.

4. Ibid., pp. 151–152 (emphasis added).

5. Cited in McGinn, *Admonition Controversy,* p. 120.

6. Exceptions are the advocates of *Christian reconstructionism* or *Dominion theology* who are a fringe group primarily within American Protestantism and associated with R. J. Rushdoony. Basing themselves on Calvinist theology, they advocate the replacement of civil law with the judicial law of the Old Testament and see the existence of non-biblical law as infringing upon the "Crown rights of Jesus Christ."

7. The famous John Courtney Murray SJ investigated the concept of monistic approaches to the civil in a number of works. In his context the main concern was to interpret the Catholic critique of liberalism represented by the Leonine encyclicals as an effort to uphold "Gelasian Dualism" against the efforts of liberal states like postrevolutionary France to deny that the state has any obligations to a moral law beyond itself. Part of this was also an effort to distinguish the American and European forms of liberalism, the former being more defensible from his perspective. For one example of his analysis, see John Courtney Murray. *Leo XIII and Pius XII: Government and the Order of Religion.* Edited by Leon Cooper SJ, (Louisville, KY: Westminster/ John Knox Press, 1993), it is available online: http://woodstock.georgetown.edu/ library/Murray/rel-liberty/rl-chap1a.htm (accessed December 30, 2007). It is clear, however, that "monism" can occur not just when *only* civil or positive law is recognized, but also where only divine law is recognized and the legitimacy of the order of civil law is questioned, as in certain forms of theocracy.

8. Bernard Lewis. *The Political Language of Islam.* University of Chicago, 1988.

9. Syed Qutb. *Milestone.*(Berlin and New York: Globusz Publishing,), chapter 7. Cf. http://www.globusz.com/ebooks/Milestone/00000010.htm (accessed 1/27/08).

10. *Ibid,* chapter 4. Cf. http://www.globusz.com/ebooks/Milestone/00000010.htm (accessed 1/27/08).

11. *Idem.*

12. *Idem.*

13. Aquinas, S.T. I-II, q.72, art. 4.

14. *Laws.* VIII.K.2.5.

15. *Idem.*

16. *Ibid.,* I.10.1 (emphasis added).

17. http://www.acton.org/publicat/occasionalpapers/sintax.html—quoting Richard John Neuhaus, "New Hymns for the Republic," in *On Freedom,* ed. John Howard (Greenwich, Conn: Devin-Adair Publishers, 1984, emphasis added).

18. *Laws*, VIII.K.2.5.

19. *Ibid.* I.10.8.

20. *Ibid.* I.10.7.

21. Luis de Molina, *De Justitia et Jure*, Volume I, treatise ii, disputation 106, par 5 (1597).

22. In *The Portable Conservative Mind* (Harmondsworth: Penguin Books, 1982), Russell Kirk writes that "'The wisdom of our ancestors' is one of the most important

phrases in the writings of Burke; presumably Burke derived it from Richard Hooker" (p. xvi).

23. *Laws*, I.10.8.

24. *Ibid.*, VIII.2.11 (Keble edition, emphasis added).

25. Leo Strauss, *Natural Right and History*, p. 221.

26. *Ibid.*, p. 163.

27. Cf. Alexander Hamilton, *The Farmer Refuted* (available online: http://www .founding.com/library/lbody.cfm?id=148andparent=56). My attention was drawn to this work by an article by Thomas G West, "Allan Bloom and America" (available online: http://www.claremont.org/writings/890101west.html).

28. Alexander Hamilton, *The Farmer Refuted* (1775) (available online: http:// www.founding.com/library/lbody.cfm?id=148andparent=56.

29. *Ibid.*

30. *Ibid.*

31. Originally I used the online version at http://www.founding.com/library/ (accessed 2005). But this text can be found in Kermit Hall and Mark David Hall(eds.) *The Collected Works of James Wilson.* (Indianapolis: The Liberty Fund, 2007), Vol I. References refer to page numbers in this text.

32. *Ibid.* p. 472–473.

33. *Ibid.* p. 464.

34. Wilson writes,

The laws of God may be divided into the following species: I. That law, the book of which we are neither able nor worthy to open. Of this law, the author and observer is God. He is a law to himself, as well as to all created things. This law we may name the "law eternal." II. That law, which is made for angels and the spirits of the just made perfect. This may be called the "law celestial." This law, and the glorious state for which it is adapted, we see, at present, but darkly and as through a glass: but hereafter we shall see even as we are seen; and shall know even as we are known. From the wisdom and the goodness of the adorable Author and Preserver of the universe, we are justified in concluding, that the celestial and perfect state is governed, as all other things are, by his established laws. What those laws are, it is not yet given us to know; but on one truth we may rely with sure and certain confidence — those laws are wise and good. For another truth we have infallible authority—those laws are strictly obeyed: "In heaven his will is done." III. That law, by which the irrational and inanimate parts of the creation are governed. The great Creator of all things has established general and fixed rules, according to which all the phenomena of the material universe are produced and regulated. These rules are usually denominated laws of nature. The science, which has those laws for its object, is distinguished by the name of natural philosophy. It is sometimes called, the philosophy of body. Of this science, there are numerous branches. IV. That law, which God has made for man in his present state; that law, which is communicated to us by reason and conscience, the divine monitors within us, and by the sacred oracles, the divine monitors without us. This law has undergone several subdivisions, and has been known by distinct appellations, according to the different ways in which it has been promulgated, and the different objects which it respects. As promulgated by reason and the moral sense, it has been called natural; as promulgated by the holy scriptures, it has been called revealed law. (*Ibid.* p.497-498).

35. *Ibid*. p. 468.
36. *Ibid*. p. 469.
37. *Ibid*. p. 473-474.
38. *Ibid*. p. 494.
39. *Ibid*. p. 477-478.
40. *Ibid*. p. 483.
41. *Ibid*. p. 495-496.

Straussianism and its Discontents

It is in part due to Straussianism that the rather facile assumptions of complete continuity between Hooker and Locke—and thus the simplistic reading of Hooker as an early proponent of a Whig political doctrine—have by now been generally replaced. The particular contribution of Leo Strauss to the question of Locke's relationship to Hooker was to expose some of the ambiguities within Locke's text, and to raise the question of whether his claim to be continuing rather then innovating upon the "classic" or traditional concept of natural law can be taken at face value.

An unfortunate side effect has been to contribute to the trend toward a general neglect of research into the place of Hooker within the debates of seventeenth-century political philosophy. Since Strauss constructs Locke as a "modern," it follows that the extensive references to Hooker in his major texts are seen as merely part of a structure of subterfuge through which Locke is concealing his true aims and intentions. If this reading is correct, a close historical scrutiny of the place of Hooker in the late seventeenth century is of little intrinsic value in understanding Locke's political argument. Because Straussianism is a prominent influence in American scholarship, and on this account has a role in obstructing an understanding of the relevance of Locke's use of Hooker. We would do well to investigate some of the key themes that inform Strauss's hermeneutics.

The Straussian project can be understood on one level as an effort to defend the idea of an eternal standard of moral and political truth, against what has occurred in modernity, specifically "the attack on natural right in the name of history."[1] Whereas ancient political philosophy viewed it as possible for rational men through philosophical inquiry to attain knowledge of immutable goods, modern historicism has argued that, on the contrary, "history shows us that all principles of justice are mutable."[2] The problem of history then is at the root of modern relativism. If truth in the moral and political sphere is radically contingent upon the historical conditions under which it is promulgated or apprehended, then the very notion of an unchanging and therefore supra-historical truth is brought into sharp question. Yet the notion that human reason is competent to discern moral standards by reflection upon the unchanging and universal ends and verities of nature, is precisely what for Strauss is at the core of what he terms *classic natural right*. This is the doctrine first promulgated by "the Ancients" (e.g. Socrates, Plato, and Aristotle) that more or less holds until the onset of modernity. Strauss places a special emphasis on the radicalism of the modern break from classic natural right. Neil G. Robertson has written that:

> For Strauss, the history of political thought in the West is broken in two: the thought of the ancients, and that of the moderns . . . As an anti-historicist, Strauss does not characterize this break as a result of historical causes; but rather he sees it as a result of a re-conception of moral and political thought, a fundamental restructuring of how we conceive moral and political life.[3]

What characterizes this break for Strauss is the reconceptualization of the concept of *nature*. This took place when the Aristotelian teleological model, in which there are intrinsic ends within nature independent of the human subject, was replaced with the ascent of modern science by a mechanistic model, in which nature has no intrinsic purposes and purpose is something imposed by the human subject. Thus, Robertson continues:

> At the centre of our moral and political self-understanding, for Strauss, is the notion of "nature," i.e., what is given prior to human willing. From his earliest writings, the division between modern and ancient was characterized by a distinction concerning what is meant by "nature." In "Comments on *Der Begriff des Politischen*" Strauss points to two fundamental concepts of nature: "whether as an order seen as a model or whether as disorder which is to be removed." In *The Political Philosophy of Hobbes*, Strauss writes: *"Traditional natural law is primarily and mainly an objective "rule and measure," a binding order prior to, and independent of, the human will, while modern natural law is, or tends to be, primarily and mainly a series of "rights," of subjective claims, originating in the human will."*

This manner of presenting the matter leaves the "ancients" and the "moderns" in a condition of radical opposition, with little room for synthesis, or for explicating lines of historical development from one to the other. Where a thinker appears to have certain elements characteristic of the "ancients" and others of the "moderns," ultimately they must stand to the one side or the other of the chasm, and the discrepancies are either a consequence of inconsistency or a consequence of mechanisms of concealment by which "moderns" aim to make their positions seem continuous with their antecedents. Thus, Robertson writes:

> The ancients in one way or another conceived of nature as a restraining order within which human beings lived out lives of lesser or greater virtue; the moderns saw nature as an alien other to be overcome through human activity. The distinction between the ancients and the moderns lies in determining which is the central grounding principle for moral and political life—nature's order, or humanity's will. The simplicity of this opposition is what gives such force to Strauss's account of the history of political thought. Implicit in it is the assumption that any position that argues for a synthesis of these two sides is inherently contradictory. The originators of modernity, the early modern thinkers, appear to argue for such a synthesis, and so for Strauss, either they were contradictory or their apparent contradictions hid a deeply consistent radical humanism. The argument of this paper is that Strauss's conception of the nature of moral and political thought in general renders impossible an appreciation of early modern political thought in its own terms: Strauss allows modernity to be understood only in its revolutionary form. In this sense, he has closed the early modern mind.

This picture has no doubt been particularly serviceable for various sides of *parti pris* discourse. Thus, for some American conservatives, Strauss is valuable because he confirms the view that the nihilism and subjectivism they associate with modernity is simply the playing out of the implications of the liberal theory of rights associated with Locke.[4] On the other hand, this schema equally plays into the more widespread prejudice that notions like consent, limited government, and the language of rights were purely products of the Enlightenment and owe little if anything to premodern classical and Christian thought. Thus, in spite of the strength of many of Strauss's claims, we may however ask whether his basic hermeneutical model is the best possible one for advancing understanding of the relevant intellectual history. One can sympathize with Strauss's well-known critique of historicism that he saw as one more manifestation of modernity's nihilism and relativism. To historicize the truth-value of ideas that manifest themselves in history is to render them context-dependent, and thus relative. Certainly, the truth-value or validity of a philosophical argument, for example, can and should be considered as independent from the time and place in which it was promulgated. Philosophical accounts of truth manifest themselves within history, but their logical validity and truth value is not in the ordinary case contingent on the historical context in which they were first promulgated. A metaphysical theory like Aristotle's notion of hylomorphic composition may be true or false, and the arguments for it may be valid or invalid, but the answers to these questions are not dependent on the fact that Aristotle was born in Thrace in the fourth century B.C. Nonetheless, knowledge of Greek intellectual history is essential if we wish to reconstruct how Aristotle's theories arose, and even to understand what is the nature and meaning of his arguments. Many misconceptions are possible if we do not know what the extant questions of the time were, which schools of philosophy figures like Aristotle were seeking to address, and how the terms and language that Aristotle employed were used.

In relation to the question of Locke, Strauss is engaged in a project that is not merely logical and philosophical but historical. He is aiming to show how the idea of "modern natural right" arose. Strauss thus involves himself in a set of hypotheses about how the thought of Locke is related to earlier notions of natural law and natural right. Such a question cannot be answered according to the *a priori* methods of logic—we must carefully reconstruct the world in which Locke lived, and recover the questions of the time which his political philosophy was seeking to answer. Even as Strauss correctly points to the dangers of relativism posed by historicism, so we must also point out the danger in an *ahistoricism* that proceeds by imposing an *a priori* structure on the history of ideas. To see the "ancient" and the "modern" as pure forms into which the major figures in the history of the ideas can be elegantly categorized, superimposes a template which can obscure the rich complexities of historical development. Once one adopts such a paradigm one is tempted to look at all the evidence that conforms to the model, and explain away whatever does not. Thus, if a "modern" employs language characteristic of "classic natural right," he is dissimulating his purposes to seem respectable; while if there are references to characteristic ideas of "modern natural right" in an "ancient," it must be a relatively unimportant idea in the context of his thought that can be ignored. Strauss takes it as a given for example that the "ancients" work within a framework of *natural law*, while the concept of *natural rights* is the characteristic "modern" idea that comes into importance only with Hobbes. Between the concept of natural law and that of natural rights, there is an almost unbridgeable chasm. For Strauss then, the use of natural rights language is almost by necessity a rejection of traditional natural law theories and the teleological concept of nature which undergirded it.

NATURAL RIGHTS, NATURAL LAW, AND HISTORY

The problem with this view regarding how the idea of natural rights arose with Hobbes—as a modernist rejection of classical and Christian natural law—is that it fails to accord with the actual historical process by which the idea of natural rights developed. Medieval political thought for Strauss has no proper identity of its own, being considered a theological variant of Aristotelian or "classic natural right" with little or no originality of its own. Yet, the weight of recent scholarship has shown that the theory of natural rights has its roots not in Hobbes and the "moderns" but instead deep in the traditions of the medieval canonists and scholastics.[5] Thus, natural rights theory arose not in reaction to the natural law discourse, but in great part directly from it. In his pioneering study, *The Idea of Natural Rights*, Brian Tierney remarks that:

> There exists a considerable school of thought maintaining that Hobbes—not Ockham, not Gerson, not Grotius—was the true originator of a modern theory of natural rights and that he expounded his theory with rigorous logic in his political writings . . . to me it seems that Hobbes' work is best seen as an aberration of natural rights thinking that flowed from the medieval jurists through Ockham, Gerson, and Grotius.[6]

Part of the difficulty in tracing the origin of the idea of natural rights is that the Latin terms *ius* and *iura* are somewhat ambiguous, since they can be used to refer either to what we would call an "objective" order of law, or they can refer to a "subjective" moral claim or right to something. Tierney meticulously surveys the usage of the concept of *ius* in a wide variety of canonists (e.g. Gratian, Huguccio, Rufinus, Simon of Bignano, Odo of Dover, Sicardus) and concludes that the subjective sense of *ius* was firmly established no later then the twelfth century:

> In reading the language of the twelfth century canonists, or Gerson's later adaptations of it, one is often reminded of the Stoic doctrine of the natural law in man. But a decisive shift in meaning and emphasis occurred in the twelfth century. For some of the Stoics and Cicero there was a force in man through which he could discern *the ius naturale,* the objective natural law that pervaded the universe; but for the canonists *ius naturale* itself could be defined as a subjective force or faculty of power inherent in human persons . . . although such definitions do not in themselves express a doctrine of natural rights, once the term *ius naturale* was defined in the subjective sense the argument could easily move in either direction, to specify natural laws that had to be obeyed, or natural rights that could licitly be exercised; and canonistic argument soon did move in both directions.[7]

By the thirteenth and fourteenth centuries scholastic philosophers incorporated more usage of the language of natural rights. The objective and subjective senses of right are poignantly illustrated in a passage of the thirteenth century figure Godfrey of Fontaine: "By the law of nature *(iure naturae)* each one has a certain right *(ius)* in the exterior goods of the world, which right cannot licitly be renounced."[8]

Tierney explicitly takes issue with Strauss's contention regarding the antinomy of natural rights and natural law: "Despite the assertion of Villey (and similar assertion by Leo Strauss in America) it is just not true that 'the notion of subjective right is logically incompatible with classical natural right.'"[9] Evidence for the falsehood of Strauss's position can be shown by reference to figures in the Franciscan school, for whom the language of subjective rights became particularly important as issues property were matters of frequent debate. Turning to Peter Olivi's specific uses of concepts like "right of property" and "right of royal power," Tierney notes that, "Olivi did not regard subjective rights as somehow contrary to his overarching structure of natural law or natural right, but as implicit in it. Rights of rulership and of property were a part of the divine scheme of things."[10]

By the fourteenth century, fully developed theories of *particular* natural rights belonging to the subject had emerged. Thus Jean Gerson speaks of right as "an immediate faculty or power pertaining to anyone according to the dictate of right reason,"[11] and goes on to enumerate specific rights such as the "*jus nutriendi corpus*"[12]—the natural right to nourish one's body, of which a person might not be justly deprived. The *locus classicus* in regard to fourteenth century discussions of natural rights would of course be William of Ockham in whom the doctrine of rights forms a central part of ethical theory due to his personal involvement in disputes on evangelical property and the respective rights of the papal and imperial authority. Thus, Ockham in his *Opus Nonaginta Dierum* explicitly distinguishes different kinds of rights in the context of somewhat technical debates with Pope John XXII. Concerning whether the use of goods by the Franciscans was a right, Ockham makes a distinction between natural rights and positive rights, which exist in virtue of some permission by civil and ecclesiastical authority. Thus, Ockham writes that, "Every right of using [*ius utendi*] is either a natural right [*ius naturale*] or a positive right [*ius positivum*] . . . [Nicholas] did not take right of using for a natural right. Therefore he took right of using for a positive right."[13] In Ockham's development of the doctrine of the right to property, Ockham concludes that, "The Right of private property is thus a natural right, willed by God, and as such is inviolable, in the sense that no one can be despoiled of this right by an earthly power."[14]

On the other hand, one of the principal figures of the thirteenth century, St. Thomas Aquinas, rarely if ever employs the concept of *ius* in the subjective sense. Some debate has occurred among scholars over whether there is any notion of rights in St. Thomas Aquinas, and perhaps more importantly whether the doctrine of natural rights is compatible with Thomism. In this regard, it is relevant to once again refer to the so-called School of Salamanca. In the sixteenth century, there was a profound revival of scholasticism in Spain led by Dominicans and Jesuits who were profoundly indebted to Thomas. In their works, there are explicit examples of both the objective and subjective uses of the concept of *ius naturale*. The notion of natural rights was quite important at this time, for example, because of the debates regarding the rights of the Indians. The way in which members of the school of Salamanca used the subjective concept of natural rights suggests at the very least that they viewed the language of rights as completely commensurable with and derivative from the Thomistic doctrine of natural law. Thus, Vitoria would remark that: "Thomas says that all things are common in extreme necessity. So if they are common, I have a right to them."[15] In his *De Indis*, Vitoria moreover enumerates certain particular rights including both the rights of the Indians, and certain rights which if violated by the Indians might constitute a legitimate *casus belli*. These include the *ius peregrinandi*, or right to travel and trade, and the *ius praedicandi* or right to preach the Gospel.[16]

Since Aquinas does not often employ the language of rights in the subjective context, the question among scholars is whether the language of rights represents a homogenous development from Thomism, or whether it was something incorporated through interaction with the Franciscan nominalists. Quentin Skinner, for example, locates the shift to the language of subjective rights in Spanish scholasticism in the influence of Ockhamism through the mediation of figures like John Mair:

> The willingness to endorse the more radical outlook originally associated with the exponents of the *Via Moderna* can be observed in relation to the theory of political society which the Thomists began to evolve in the latter part of the sixteenth century. One notable innovation was that they took over the 'subjective' view of rights which had originated with Ockham and his followers, and had been restated by Alamain and Mair at the start of the sixteenth century."[17]

For Skinner, the Spanish scholastics completed the incorporation of the basically Ockhamist notion of subjective rights onto the structure of the Thomistic natural law theory. By the time we come to Suarex's discussion in the *Law and God the Lawgiver*, we find a complete endorsement of the "subjective view" which Mair in particular had developed a century earlier.[18]

Tierney, however, turns to the language of the *Decretals* and its commentators. Tierney shows that the seminal importance of Ockham in any discussion of the topic must be recognized, the concept of natural rights as such does not *originate* with Ockham, nor is it exclusive to the Nominalist school. His work takes note of the existence of subjective uses of *ius* in canonists who preceded Ockham by nearly two centuries. Neither was it the Ockamists alone who took the subjective concept of natural rights, for example, writers like Jean Gerson, Henry of Ghent, and Godfrey of Fontaine can hardly be called followers of the *Via Moderna*.

Given the openness of a figure like Suarez to a variety of sources in addition to Aquinas, it is not absurd to suggest that the use of natural rights language in the *Escuela de Salamanca* owes something to the Ockhamist inheritance. But neither can one dogmatically assume that this natural rights language is simply incommensurable with Thomistic ethical theory, and not a plausible development from it. As Tierney notes:

> Although Thomas himself did not choose to develop a doctrine of subjective rights, there was nothing in his work that necessarily excluded such a concept. One can now add that the principles of Thomist philosophy and the idea of subjective rights were not only theoretically compossible: they actually coexisted. . . the combination of professed Thomism with an acceptance of rights language derived ultimately from medieval jurisprudence was characteristic of the greatest thinkers of the Spanish 'second scholasticism' whose work provides the principal link between medieval and modern rights theories.[19]

To fully engage the debate over where precisely in the medieval tradition the notion of natural rights begins, and over how much weight to give to the specifically Ockhamist theory of rights, would fall outside of the scope of this present disquisition. Our purpose was to consider Strauss's contentions that: 1) the idea of subjective rights emerged as a modernist rejection of traditional natural law and 2) that the key figure in regard to enunciating the theory of natural rights was Hobbes. It is clear that these positions of Strauss will not stand criticism under the sheer weight of historical evidence. The tendency of Strauss to rigidly separate the "ancients" and the "moderns" leads in the direction of seeing the "moderns" as *sui generis*, and so carries the danger of ignoring the important ways in which early modern figures were deeply informed by an existing intellectual inheritance. The difficulties of a rigid adherence to Straussian hermeneutics become clear when we look at how Straussian hermeneutics functions in relation to the specific texts that are most relevant to our discussion.

STRAUSS ON LOCKE'S SIGNIFICANCE

In perhaps his best-known text, *Natural Right and History*, Strauss places a special emphasis on John Locke. If the whole structure of his thought presumes a sharp dichotomy between the "classic" or "ancient" concept of natural right and "modern natural right," then Strauss makes clear that in the transition to "modern natural right" John Locke is the most central figure. Yet the fact that much of Locke's terminology is dependent upon more traditional formulations constitutes an apparent obstacle to the schema into which he wishes to place him. Thus, he writes that, "The most famous and most influential of all modern natural right teachers was John Locke. But Locke makes it particularly difficult to recognize how modern he is, or how much he deviates from the natural right tradition."[20]

Strauss recognizes that Locke relies extensively on the work of Hooker for his argument on the origin and nature of political obligation. However, for Strauss, Hooker's importance is purely exoteric, and of little import for the substance of Locke's argument. Hooker simply represents the kind of respected and tradition-minded authority through which Locke can conceal the very radical and "modern" quality of his teaching. Thus, Strauss writes:

> His [Locke's] authority seems to be Richard Hooker, the great Anglican divine, distinguished by elevation of sentiment and sobriety; 'the judicious Hooker' as Locke, following others, likes to call him. Now Hooker's conception of natural right is the Thomistic conception, and the Thomistic conception, in its turn, goes back to the Church Fathers, who, in their turn, were pupils of the Stoics, of the pupils of pupils of Socrates. We are then apparently confronted with an unbroken tradition of perfect respectability that stretches from Socrates to Locke.[21]

Thus, by linking himself to Hooker, Locke is able to endow his political theory of obligation with a "respectable pedigree."[22] However, Locke's ruse is exposed once we begin to examine the substance of the doctrines as opposed to nominal resemblance.

> The moment we take the trouble to confront Locke's teaching as a whole with Hooker's teaching as a whole, we become aware that, in spite of a certain agreement between Locke and Hooker, Locke's conception of natural right is fundamentally different from Hooker's.[23]

The core of this difference is the altered conception of nature that occurred between the sixteenth and seventeenth centuries, in which the Aristotelian concept of nature as guided by final causality and immanent teleology was replaced by a scientific conception of nature as an inert mechanism without intrinsic purpose except that imposed on it by man: "The period between Hooker and Locke had witnessed the emergence of modern natural science, the non-teleological natural science, and therewith the destruction of the basis of traditional natural right."[24]

In order to clarify what is meant by "modern natural right" and how it differs from "classic natural right," Strauss realizes that he must turn to a thinker less "esoteric" in his exposition than Locke. For Strauss, Thomas Hobbes is the emblematic "modern" because he exhibits its principles in a rather raw and undisguised manner. Although Locke rarely mentions Hobbes, and then only in a derogatory manner, for Strauss it is Hobbes rather than Hooker who is Locke's true authority. His method involves three stages: 1) illustrating the doctrine of Hobbes; 2) turning to the text of Locke, exposing how Locke's arguments are inconsistently judged according to their plain sense; and 3) showing how sense can be made of Locke's arguments only if we presume them to be broadly Hobbesian.

THE QUINTESSENTIAL MODERN: THOMAS HOBBES

For Strauss, the specific character of "modern natural right" is derived from Hobbes. It is in the *Leviathan* for him that the modern critique of classic natural right is most clearly illustrated. Strauss understands the traditional theory as embracing a number of assumptions such as: the idea that nobility and justice is a distinct question from what is pleasant or unpleasant; the question of right as independent from human convention and contrivance; and that man is by nature a social being and thus there is a naturally best form of political organization.[25] All of these assumptions Hobbes aims to stand on their head.

Strauss sees that Hobbes's creativity lies in accepting the hedonistic theories of certain ancient Greek schools of philosophy, but using them as the edifice for a new form of political philosophy.

> He [Hobbes] traces the failure of the idealistic tradition to one fundamental mistake: traditional political philosophy assumed that man is by nature a political or social animal. By rejecting this assumption, Hobbes joins the Epicurean tradition. He accepts the view that man is by nature or originally an a-political or even an a-social animal, as well as its premise that the good is fundamentally identical with the pleasant. But he uses that a-political view for a political purpose . . . he thus becomes the creator of political hedonism, a doctrine which has revolutionized human life everywhere on a scale never yet approached by any other teaching.

Hobbes accomplishes this, for Strauss, by reconceptualizing the natural law tradition. The traditional natural law theory presumed that nature had a teleological structure in which every being had its own proper end. Natural law was thus the rule of reason by which every being is guided to its own proper perfection and end. Since man forms part of this natural order, and since man also has his proper end, natural law is therefore a rule of action, whereby human acts are ordered to man's final end and whereby he achieves his final end. For Hobbes, however, this entire teleological conception of the cosmos is abandoned. The important ends are those which human desires and impulses impose on the world:

> To return to Hobbes, his notion of philosophy or of science has its root in the conviction that a teleological cosmology is impossible and in the feeling that a mechanistic cosmology fails to satisfy the requirements of intelligibility . . . all intelligibility or all meaning has its ultimate end in human needs. The end or the most compelling end posited by human desire, is the highest principle, the organizing principle. But if the human good becomes the highest good, political science or social science becomes the most important kind of knowledge.[26]

Hobbes therefore develops his notion of "natural law" in a manner utterly distinct from that of the classical natural law tradition. This tradition sought to discern the end of man, that universal good the attainment of which would bring the natural potencies and inclinations of human nature to their perfection and fulfillment. Natural law in this reading constitutes a rational rule by which human actions can be ordered to their proper end. For the "moderns," on the contrary, there is no inherent or universal end, which is intelligible to reason reflecting on human nature. Thus, the science of politics must be built up in an "empirical" way by studying the forces which actually shape and motivate human action. Consequently, Strauss sees Hobbes following in the footsteps of Machiavelli in that, for both, "The complete basis of natural law must be sought, not in the end of man, but in his beginnings, in the *prima naturae*, or rather in the *Primum Naturae*."[27]

Only by taking men as they actually are can one hope to construct a stable political order. And what stands out in studying how actual human beings behave? For Hobbes, it is not rationality, but self-regarding passions, and at the deepest level the urge for self-preservation: "Death takes the place of *Telos*. Or, to preserve the ambiguity of Hobbes's thought, let us say that the fear of violent death expresses most forcefully the most powerful and most fundamental of all natural desires, the initial desire, the desire for self-preservation."[28]

By making a passion or urge within the human subject the starting point of a theory of law, justice, and the origins of political obligation, Hobbes accomplishes for Strauss the essential "Copernican turn" in political thinking. That is to say, the modern transition from the primacy of duties, to the primacy of rights is given form at the point when Hobbes makes the naked self-will to live the basis on which he constructs the entire edifice of his political philosophy.

> The pre-modern natural law doctrines taught the duties of man; if they paid any attention at all to his rights, they conceived them as essentially derivative from

his duties. As has frequently been observed, in the course of the seventeenth and eighteenth centuries a much greater emphasis was put on rights then ever had been done before. One may speak of a shift of emphasis from natural duties to natural rights . . . The fundamental change from an orientation by natural duties, to an orientation by natural rights finds its clearest and most telling expression in the teaching of Hobbes, who squarely made an unconditional natural right [i.e. the right to self-preservation] the basis of all natural duties, the duties being therefore only conditional. He is the classic and the founder of the specifically modern natural law doctrine.[29]

The particular political implications Hobbes drew from his anthropology were authoritarian. The only manner of safeguarding the right of self-preservation against the aggressive and egotistical drives of others was to transfer all authority to a sovereign. Nonetheless, for Strauss, Hobbes becomes ironically one of the most important progenitors of modern liberalism: "If we may call liberalism that political doctrine which regards as the fundamental political fact the rights, as distinguished from the duties, of man and which identifies the function of the state with the protection or the safeguarding of these rights, we must say the founder of liberalism was Hobbes."[30]

For Strauss, perhaps the most central and revolutionary aspect of Hobbes's development of "modern natural right" is how it reconceived the relationship between man, nature, and society. As we have seen, in the Aristotelian tradition (here broadly conceived to include men such as St. Thomas Aquinas and Richard Hooker), man is by nature a social animal. This is evidenced, for example, by the fact of language and speech and the fact that man needs others for his necessities. In order to attain his end, man therefore requires society.

For Hobbes, in contrast, the natural condition of man is egotistical, violent, and anarchic. The primordial reality then is the individual and his drive for survival. Nature becomes in Strauss's language, not a principle of association but of *dis*association. In such a view, society itself is not natural, but the product of deliberate artifice—since in order to avert the state of war it is necessary to come to agreement and contract. Strauss considers this assertion to be a necessary condition for liberalism, in the sense that as long as the society has primacy over the individual, no doctrine of rights could flourish:

The tradition which Hobbes opposed had assumed that man cannot reach the perfection of his nature except in and through civil society and, therefore, that civil society is prior to the individual. It was this assumption that led to the view that the primary moral fact is duty and not rights. One could not assert the primacy of natural rights without asserting that the individual is in every respect prior to civil society: all rights of civil society or of the sovereign belonged to the individual. The individual as such—and not merely as Aristotle had contended, the man who surpasses humanity—had to be conceived of as essentially complete independently of civil society. This conception is implied in the contention that there is a state of nature which antedates political society.[31]

THE STRAUSSIAN READING OF JOHN LOCKE

To observe how, in the Straussian model, Hobbes's ideas contributed to liberalism, one must turn to his treatment of the figure who has been dubbed "the father of liberalism," that is John Locke. The essence of Strauss's treatment of Locke is his notion that to interpret his texts correctly one must distinguish their esoteric from the exoteric significance. Concretely, this reading suggests that Locke wishes to dissimulate his true position by appearing to render his understanding of natural law coherent with the classical tradition. Among the elements of this "classic natural right" is the idea that the law of nature and the duties it imposes are anterior to human society, and that this law is intelligible to all rational creatures, which is eternal and universally binding on all mankind. Thus, Strauss says:

> At first glance, Locke seems to reject altogether Hobbes' notion of natural law, and to follow the traditional teaching. He certainly speaks of natural rights as if they were derivative from the law of nature, and he accordingly speaks of the law of nature as if it were a law in the strict sense of the term. The law of nature imposes perfect duties on man as man, regardless of whether he lives in the state of nature or in civil society.

Strauss maintains however that a close reading of the text establishes that Locke's *actual* doctrine of natural law is inconsistent with "classic natural law" and is also basically continuous with the doctrine of Hobbes. This "esoteric" natural is disclosed when one takes account of the tensions between what Locke takes to be the conditions of a genuinely binding natural law and what he takes to be actually established about the natural law. In the second chapter of his *Essay on Human Understanding*, Locke tries to reject both the extreme positions that either knowledge of the first principles of morality is innate and so in no need of demonstration, or that there is no possible knowledge of natural law. Thus, he writes that: "And I think they equally forsake the truth who, running into contrary extremes, either affirm an innate law, or deny that there is a law knowable by the light of nature, i.e. without the help of positive revelation."[32] Locke famously held that a rationally demonstrable science of ethics was possible, whose conclusions had as much certitude and necessity as mathematics, writing that: "Wherein I doubt not but from self-evident propositions, by necessary consequences, as incontestable as those in mathematics, the measures of right and wrong might be made out to any one that will apply himself with the same indifference and attention to the one, as he does to the other of these sciences."

However, according to Strauss, Locke never elaborates such a science of ethics in detail ("Locke never made a serious effort to elaborate that code.").[33] Instead, Locke endeavors to establish the natural law on a voluntarist foundation. According to Strauss, for Locke, "The law of nature is a declaration of the will of God. It is 'the voice of God' in man . . . it is the law of God not only in fact. It must be known to be the law of God, in order to be law. Without such knowledge man cannot act morally. For 'the true ground of morality . . . can only be the will and law of a God'."[34] While, for Locke, both the revealed law and the natural law emanate from and derive their binding force from the will of God, they differ in that the law of nature binds man insofar as he is human, while the "law of the Gospel" implies certain positive precepts particular to the Christian dispensation.[35] "As men, we have God for our King and are under the law of reason, as Christians we are under Jesus the messiah for our king, and are under the law revealed by him in the gospel. And every Christian both as a deist and a Christian, be obliged to study both the law of nature, and the revealed law."[36]

The problems in the consistency of Locke's explanation arise from the tension between what Locke holds to be the necessary conditions for an authentic law, and what Locke thinks can actually be known by reason about the law of nature. One of the basic conditions for an authentic law in Locke's view is that the law must have a sanction. Since the law of nature is not a civil law, its sanction cannot be the penalty, which is the just recompense, which comes with the transgression of the positive law. Thus, the sanctions of the law of nature must be in another life. But Locke holds that natural reason cannot demonstrate the existence of another life, but only faith. Thus, Strauss carries Locke's positions to their logical conclusion: "Only through revelation do we know of sanctions for the law of nature, or of 'the only true touchstone of human rectitude.' Natural reason is therefore unable to know the law of nature as a law. This would mean there does not exist a law of nature in the strict sense."[37]

According to Strauss, Locke's recourse is to say that natural reason is able to demonstrate the veracity of the Gospels, and thus of the truth of Divine sanction in the afterlife. As Strauss puts it:

> Natural reason is able to demonstrate that the New Testament is the perfect document of revelation. And since the New Testament teaches that the souls of the just shall live forever, natural reason is able to demonstrate the true ground of morality, and therewith to establish the dignity of the law of nature as a true law.[38]

But if the law of nature requires revelation to acquire its status as a true law, then strictly speaking it is not a fully natural law, in that reason unaided by revelation would not be able to discern it in its fullness. God's revelation in the Scripture is basically required for the natural law to have binding force. The logic of Locke's position would therefore lead him to precisely the kind of Scriptural politics against which he argues. If the entire law of nature is available in Scripture, and is only a true law in virtue of Scripture then:

> The complete and perfectly clear natural law teaching in concerning government in particular would consist of properly arranged quotations from Scripture and especially from the New Testament. Accordingly, one expects that Locke would have written a 'politique tiree des propres paroles de l' Ecriture Sainte.' But in fact he wrote the *Two Treatises of Government*. What he did stands in striking contrast to what he said.

This apparent discrepancy between "what he did" and "what he said" is the opening for Strauss to insinuate his hidden meaning hypothesis. Strauss believes that Locke understands the contradiction between his view of natural law and revealed law or between both and his political theses, but he feels they must be dissimulated. This comes forth particularly in Strauss's view of "noble caution":

> Caution is a kind of noble fear . . . there may be extremely relevant facts, which if stressed will inflame popular passion, and thus prevent the wise handling of these very facts. He would avoid mention of everything which would 'displace the veil beneath which' the respectable part of society 'dissembles its divisions.' Whereas the cautious theoretician would scorn the appeal to prejudices, the cautious man of affairs would try to enlist all respectable prejudices in the service of a good cause. Acting in this spirit, the statesmen of 1689 which Locke defended in his *Two Treatises* 'cared little whether their major agreed with their conclusion, if their major secured 200 votes, and their minor 200 more.'[39]

Strauss, in his analysis of the texts, endeavors to show how, if taken exoterically, Locke's natural law theory would lead to various contradictions. For example, in spite of his claim that the law of nature is confirmed and harmonious with revealed law, a close reading indicates that Locke views them as opposing each other. There are, for example, contradictions between the *First Treatise*, which focuses on refutations (largely from Scripture) of Sir Robert Filmer's *Patriarcha*, and the *Second Treatise on Government* where natural law plays a larger role. For example:

> The tension between Locke's natural law theory and the New Testament is perhaps best illustrated by his teaching about marriage and related topics. In his

First Treatise he characterizes adultery, incest, and sodomy as sins. He indicates that they are sins independently of the fact that they 'cross the main intention of nature.' One is therefore forced to wonder whether they're being sins is not chiefly due to 'positive revelation.' Later on he raises the question 'what in nature is the difference betwixt a concubine and a wife?' He does not answer the question, but the context strongly suggests that natural law is silent about the difference.[40]

Strauss shows a similar, apparent, textual contradiction concerning the biblical command to honor one's parents by noting that, "he gives the biblical commands an unbiblical meaning by disregarding the biblical distinctions between lawful and unlawful unions of men and women."[41]

But if there were a contradiction between the natural law and the scriptural law, then the edifice of Locke's moral system would seem to come apart. In order to be a true law, the law of nature must be known to have come from God. But if the law of nature and scriptural law do not cohere with each other, then "we thus arrive at the conclusion that Locke cannot have recognized any law of nature in the proper sense of the term." Yet "this conclusion stands in shocking contrast to what is generally thought to be his doctrine and especially the doctrine of the *Second Treatise*."[42]

One might adopt the position that Locke was not able to discern the antinomies within his own political philosophy and thus was only unconsciously contradicting himself. In fact not a few scholars have argued that Locke is a less then fully consistent thinker. Thus, Strauss refers to the fact that "the accepted interpretation of Locke leads to the consequence that 'Locke is full of logical flaws and inconsistencies.'"[43] In defense of his esoteric interpretation, Strauss declares that the inconsistencies are "so obvious that they cannot have escaped the notice of a man of his rank and sobriety."[44] He views the "inconsistency" in Locke, therefore, to be a device, which allows him to dissemble his true doctrine so as to make it oblivious to the *hoi polloi*. Thus, Strauss attributes the apparent inconsistencies to "a kind of caution which is, to say the least, compatible with so involving one's sense that one cannot easily be understood and with going with the herd in one's outward professions."[45]

LOCKE AS A DISCIPLE OF HOBBES

The true doctrine or esoteric political philosophy of Locke, for Strauss, is built upon the "Copernican revolution" of Hobbes. Even when Locke arrives at somewhat different specific conclusions than Hobbes, the foundations of his philosophy are the same. Thus, Strauss remarks that:

It is on the basis of Hobbes' view of the law of nature, that Locke opposes Hobbes' conclusions. He tries to show that Hobbes' principle—the right of self-preservation—far from favoring absolute government requires limited government. Freedom, 'freedom from arbitrary, absolute power' is the 'fence' to self-preservation.[46]

Likewise, even if Locke imposes more restrictions on the civil power then Hobbes does, he has a similar basic conception of both the state and society as constituted by a contract:

> In spite of the limitations which Locke demands, the commonwealth remains for him, as it was for Hobbes, the 'mighty leviathan' in entering civil society . . . Just as Hobbes did, so Locke admits only one contract: the contract of union which every individual makes with every other individual of the same multitude is identical with the contract of subjection.[47]

Strauss sees Locke as following Hobbes' lead in terms of making the drive to self-preservation, rather then natural teleology, the starting point of his politico-ethical theory. Thus, for example, Locke deduces additional rights like the right to property from the more primordial right to exist: "The Natural right to property is a corollary of the more primordial right of self-preservation; it is not derivative from compact, from any action of society. If everyone has the natural right to preserve himself, he necessarily has the right to everything that is necessary to his self-preservation."[48]

The distinguishing attribute of this modern doctrine is thus seen in a certain shift from the view that natural duties are primary, and rights deduced from these, to the view that rights are primary and duties deduced from these. The shift is corollary with the change from a teleological conception of nature in which the purposes inscribed in the natural order can be discerned, to viewing nature as a blind and inert mechanism that must be domesticated by human activity. Strauss sees both these trends at work particularly in Locke's doctrine of property that emphasizes both men's *right* to property, and the work of human labor in transforming the natural order. Thus, he says that:

> Locke's teaching on property, and therewith his whole political philosophy, are revolutionary not only with regard to the biblical tradition, but with regard to the philosophical tradition as well. Through the shift of emphasis from natural duties to natural rights, the individual, the ego has become the center of the moral world, since man—as distinguished from man's end—has become that center or origin . . . . according to Locke, man and not nature, the work of man, and not the gift of nature is the origin of almost everything valuable.[49]

Locke furthermore follows Hobbes on this reading in emancipating the human individual not only from both nature *and* society. Nature is something inert, and human society itself is not something natural, but also the product of human artifice and contrivance. Thus, he says:

> Man is effectively emancipated from the bonds of nature, and therewith the individual is emancipated from those social bonds which antedate all consent and contract . . . the world in which human creativity reigns supreme is replaced by the rule of convention. From now on nature furnishes only the worthless materials as in themselves; the forms are supplied by man, by man's free creation.[50]

On Strauss's reading then, Hooker has no *intrinsic* importance within Locke's doctrine. Locke's frequent references to Hooker are meant rather to conceal Locke's radicalism by making his positions seem coherent with a figure who is both reverenced by his audience and an archetypal representative of "classic natural right." Thus, for example, Strauss writes that:

> Acting in the same spirit [of dissimulation], Locke in his defense of revolutionary settlement, appealed as frequently as he could to the authority of Hooker— one of the least revolutionary men who ever lived. He took every advantage of his partial agreement with Hooker. And he avoided the inconveniences which might have been caused by his partial disagreement with Hooker, by being practically silent about it.[51]

As we have seen, for Strauss, Locke is essentially a Hobbesian. Yet his political "caution" leads him to refer to Hobbes as that "justly decried name" while presenting himself as a disciple of Hooker. The mechanism of this deceptive process is evident for Strauss in the *Second Treatise*: "Already a summary comparison of its [Locke's] teaching with the teachings of Hooker and of Hobbes would show that Locke deviated from the traditional natural law teaching and followed the lead given by Hobbes."[52] Even on the *unique* occasion where Locke gives voice to a personal disagreement with Hooker, Strauss holds that he distorts Hooker's meaning so as to make it appear coherent with his own. Thus:

> There is indeed only one passage where Locke explicitly notes that he deviates from Hooker. But the passage draws our attention to a radical deviation. After having quoted Hooker, Locke says: but I moreover affirm that all men are naturally in [the state of nature]. He thus suggests, that, according to Hooker, some men were in fact or accidentally in the state of nature. Actually Hooker had not said anything about the state of nature: the whole doctrine of the state of nature is based on a break with Hooker's principles, i.e. with the principles of the natural law doctrine.[53]

In fact, Strauss's confidence about this point is excessive. Clearly the term "state of nature" is not the language of Hooker; yet, as we have seen, Hooker clearly believes there is a pre-political condition of society, since political authority requires the assent of the community. This state or condition is "natural" in the sense that it precedes the artificial construction of determinate structures of political governance. Hooker sees this view as perfectly compatible with the notion that in this natural, pre-political condition, human communities would still be subject to "traditional natural law." If one wanted to make the case for an essential discontinuity between Locke and Hooker, one could not do so on the basis of differing language used to describe the pre-political condition. One would have to demonstrate that the substance of their doctrines regarding the pre-political condition was incommensurable.

If Strauss's interpretation of Locke as a Hobbesian is correct, then Hooker is of little intrinsic interest for an understanding of Locke's texts. Hobbes' particular views (as specified by Strauss)—the state of nature as pre-social and pre-moral, society itself as an artificial product of contract, and the priority of natural rights (in this case of self-preservation) over natural law—are profoundly discontinuous with the Anglican Thomism of the *Laws*. Hooker's constant presence in the *Two Treatises* for Strauss is merely there to throw the undiscerning reader off track. The ascription of Hobbesian views to Locke is by no means new. Locke refers to an accusation against him by Jonathan Edwards, "that the doctrine proposed in the 'reasonableness of Christianity' was borrowed, as he says from Hobbes' Leviathan?" to which he replies "This, whether it be the doctrine of the Leviathan, I know not. This appears to me out of the New Testament, from whence (as I told him in the preface) I took to be the doctrine of our Savior and his Apostles."[54] Locke thus clearly disassociates himself from Hobbes, and even refers to him as that "justly decried name." Since Locke acknowledges no debt to Hobbes, how is one to assess Strauss's contention that Locke is in spite of his protestations an esoteric Hobbesian? One might say that given the fact that Locke nowhere refers to Hobbes in support of his natural law theory, the Straussian contention should only be given weight, if upon a careful reading of the texts, the substance of Locke's argument is so similar to that of Hobbes' as to permit no other plausible or consistent explanation.

NOTES

1. Cf. Leo Strauss, *Natural Right and History* (Chicago: University of Chicago Press, 2001), p. 9.

2. *Ibid.*

3. Cf. Neil Robertson, "The Closing of the Early Modern Mind: Leo Strauss and Early Modern Political Thought" (from http://www.mun.ca/animus/1998vol3/robert3 .htm).

4. This type of view is associated with Allan Bloom, *The Closing of the American Mind*.

5. Cf. Brian Tierney, *The Idea of Natural Rights: Studies on Natural Rights, Natural Law and Church Law 1150–1625* (Atlanta: Scholar's Press, 1997); and Annabel S. Brett, *Liberty, Right and Nature: Individual Rights in Later Scholastic Thought.* (Cambridge: Cambridge University Press, 1997).

6. Tierney, *The Idea of Natural Rights*, p. 340.

7. *Ibid.*, p. 65.

8. *Ibid.*, p. 75, quoting Godfrey's *Summa Theologia* 2.2 ae 66.7.

9. *Ibid.*, p. 33.

10. *Ibid.*, p. 39.

11. *Ibid.*, p. 210, quoting *Oeuvres*, 3:141.

12. *Ibid.*, p. 75, quoting *Oeuvres* 3:156.

13. *Ibid.*, p. 121, quoting *Opus Nonaginta Dierum*, p. 556.

14. Frederick Copleston, *A History of Philosophy, vol II: Medieval Philosophy from Augustine to Scotus.* New York: Image / Doubleday, 1993 (reprint), 112.

15. Tierney, *The Idea of Natural Rights*, p. 75, quoting *Commentaria*, 3:340.

16. Cf. M.W.F. Stone, "The Nature and Significance of Law in Early Modern Scholasticism," in *A History of Philosophy of Law from the Ancient Greeks to the Scholastics*, ed. Fred Miller (Dordrecht: Kluwer, 2005), p. 15.

17. Quentin Skinner, *The Foundations of Modern Political Thought* (Cambridge: Cambridge University Press, 1978), 2, p. 176.

18. *Ibid.*

19. Tierney, *The Idea of Natural Rights*, p. 108.

20. *Ibid.*, p. 165.

21. *Ibid.*

22. Cf. Haugaard in *Laws*.

23. Tierney, *The Idea of Natural Rights*, p. 165.

24. *Ibid.*, p. 166.

25. *Ibid.*, p. 167.

26. *Ibid.*, p. 177.

27. *Ibid.*, p. 180.

28. *Ibid.*, p. 181.

29. *Ibid.*, p. 182.

30. *Ibid.*, pp. 181–182.

31. *Ibid.*, p. 183.

32. John Locke, *An Essay concerning Human Understanding*, ed. Peter H. Nidditch (Oxford: Oxford University Press, 1975), Book I, chapter II, section 13.

33. Strauss, *Natural Right and History*, p. 202.

34. *Ibid.*, pp. 202–203.

35. *Ibid.*

36. Strauss, *Natural Right and History*, p. 202, quoting Locke's *Treatise on the Reasonableness of Christianity* (Works VI, 229).

37. *Ibid.*, p. 204.

38. *Ibid.*

39. *Ibid.*, p. 206.
40. *Ibid.*, p. 217.
41. *Ibid.*, p. 218.
42. *Ibid.*, p. 220.
43. Strauss's reference is to J.W. Gough, *John Locke's Political Philosophy.*
44. Strauss, *Natural Right and History*, p. 220.
45. *Ibid.*
46. *Ibid.*, p. 231.
47. *Ibid.*, pp. 231–232.
48. *Ibid.*, p. 235.
49. *Ibid.*, p. 248.
50. *Ibid.*, pp. 248–249.
51. *Ibid.*, p. 207.
52. *Ibid.*, p. 221.
53. *Ibid.*, p. 221–222.
54. John Locke, *The Reasonableness of Christianity as Delivered in the Scriptures* (1997), pp. 420–421.

The Question of Intellectualism and Voluntarism in Locke's Natural Law Theory

In fact, while the issue of Locke's natural law theory remains contentious, major Locke scholars have reached a fairly broad consensus that Strauss's reading of Locke's natural law theory as Hobbesian is fundamentally flawed. Francis Oakley notes, "While it is rare for major interpretations to be superceded in any definitive fashion, Strauss's viewpoint on this particular issue [Locke's natural law] has been . . . effectively sidelined,"[1] and he refers to Strauss's essay "Locke's Doctrine of Natural law" as "a veritable *tour de force* of learned obfuscation."[2] John Yolton, in his essay "Locke on the Law of Nature,"[3] undertakes a detailed refutation of Strauss's ascription of the Hobbesian views on natural law, state of nature, and civil society to Locke:

> The doctrine is clearly Hobbes' but Strauss credits it to Locke. That this reading of Locke is almost wholly erroneous should be obvious to any reader of Locke. Were it not for the seriousness of the charges, and the method of supporting them, the importance which Strauss's name commands, and the illumination of Locke's doctrine which the unraveling of some of Strauss's more glaring mistakes produces, it would be a waste of time to undertake an exposure of such a misrepresentation.[4]

Yolton mentions four assertions of Strauss regarding Locke's doctrine of natural law—that it is different from and opposed to scriptural law, that it is based on an innate right to happiness, that it is sanctioned by a hedonistic theory of pleasure and pain, and that the state of nature is one of conflict without any moral law. Yolton goes on to show using textual evidence that while all four views were part of the Hobbesian model, Locke explicitly rejected three of the four, with only the hedonistic theory having any foundation in Locke's writings. With the general rejection of Strauss's contentions the debate is no longer centrally about whether Strauss should be 'read out of the classical and Christian natural law tradition'" as Strauss wants to do, or "securely reinstated within it."⁵ Instead, modern scholarship has shown:

> It was simply improper to speak of any single 'classical and Christian' or even 'medieval' notion of natural law which could then be contrasted with a 'modern' notion of natural law. On the contrary, in the later Middle Ages and persisting on into the sixteenth and seventeenth centuries there had been two major traditions of natural law thinking. One of them was grounded on one or other form of essentialism (or realism, to use the medieval term). The other was grounded in the type of theological voluntarism characteristic of William of Ockham (d.1349) and of his fourteenth- and fifteenth-century successors.⁶

Thus, the argument has shifted from whether Locke was a Hobbesian or stood in continuity with the natural law tradition, to what *kind* of natural law tradition informed Locke's theory. We have already seen the issue of intellectualist and voluntarist natural law come up in relation to Hooker and other Protestant scholastics. In the case of Hooker, it is quite evident that he stood in the realist/intellectualist tradition. With Locke, however, the case is far less clear. In order to assess the matter, we should have a clear understanding of how these terms are being used. Otto von Gierke provided an elegant definition of the distinction between the intellectualist/realist and voluntarist/nominalist understandings of natural law, which though stating the matter in too unqualified a way, provides a clear basis for the discussion:

> The older view which is especially that of the Realists explained the *Lex Naturalis* as an intellectual act independent of Will—as a mere *Lex indiciativa*, in which God was not a lawgiver but a teacher working by means of reason—in short as the dictate of Reason as to what is right, grounded in the Being of God by him . . . the opposite opinion proceeding from pure nominalism, saw in the Law of Nature a mere Divine command, which was right and binding merely because God was the law giver.⁷

If then the natural law proceeds from divine reason, then a given act may be good or evil in virtue of its own intrinsic nature. Since goodness belongs to the very nature of the divine essence, God could not will that an intrinsically evil act be good. If however the natural law proceeds solely from divine will, then there is nothing intrinsic to any given act to make it good or evil—it derives its moral character solely from the divine command. The debate on Locke's natural law theory has been much deepened by the relatively recent emergence of eight previously unpublished Latin essays in the Lovelace collection, which were purchased by Oxford, edited by Wolfgang van Leyden, and published in 1954 under the title *Essays on the Law of Nature*. These essays are the only place where Locke presents his views on natural law in any broad detail. Yet, while this discovery has provided a wealth of new material, it has not definitively settled the debate on the status of natural law in Locke, because different passages suggest different things, and the text itself raises difficult questions of interpretation.

Thus, certain passages would seem to support a voluntarist reading:

> Hence, the law of nature can be described as being a *decree of the divine will* discernible by the light of nature and indicating what is not in conformity with rational nature, and for this reason commanding or prohibiting. *It appears to me less correctly termed by some people the dictate of reason*, since reason does not so much establish and pronounce the law of nature as search for it and discover it as a law enacted by a superior power and implanted in our hearts . . . hence it is pretty clear that all the requisites of a law are found in natural law. *For, in the first place, it is a decree of a superior will.*[8]

On the other hand, there are other passages that support an intellectualist reading:

> *In fact this law does not depend on an unstable and changeable will, but on the eternal order of things.* For it seems to me that certain essential features of things are immutable, and that certain duties arise out of necessity and cannot be other then they are. And this is not because nature or God (as I should say more correctly) could not have created man differently. Rather the cause is that, since man has been made such as he is, equipped with reason, and his other faculties . . . there necessarily result from his inborn constitution some definite duties for him, which cannot be other then they are . . . *For according to His infinite and eternal wisdom,* He has made man such *that these duties of his necessarily follow from his very nature* . . . the natural law stands or falls together with the nature of man as it is at present.[9]

In essence, modern scholarship, after surveying these new essays on the question, is divided into three broad camps: 1) those who read Locke's natural law theory in continuity with the intellectualist/realist tradition of Thomas Aquinas (and Richard Hooker); 2) those who see Locke as standing in continuity with the voluntarist/nominalist tradition of Ockham; and 3) those who regard Locke's views as a mixture of the two, either because Locke's position is inconsistent, that is, he changed his views, or because there is some way in which voluntarist and intellectualist components of Locke's theory can be reconciled.[10] Because the literature on this topic is by now vast and involves a large number of scholars with subtle differences in interpretation, a complete survey of the relevant literature is outside the scope of the present work. Perhaps then, the best way to make clear the lines of this debate is to outline the clearest and most representative examples of the respective arguments for the intellectualist and voluntarist readings of Locke's natural law.

LOCKE AS AN INTELLECTUALIST: RAGHUVER SINGH

Perhaps the classic presentation of the case for Locke as an intellectualist was that made by Raghuver Singh in his 1961 essay, "John Locke and the Theory of Natural Law." Singh notes that there has been a failure to properly understand Locke because of the tendency of historians to group thinkers into fixed categories:

> Locke has suffered at the hands of historians of ideas who first classify individual thinkers according to fixed and almost exclusive categories of thought like rationalism-empiricism, idealism-realism, individualism . . . just as in the history of philosophy he is often uncritically linked with empiricist successors like Berkeley and Hume, similarly in political theory he is often bracketed with Thomas Hobbes . . . the description of Locke as a typical empiricist corresponds to the description of his ethical and political theory as utilitarian, hedonistic, and individualistic.[11]

Singh targets Strauss's interpretation in particular as engaged in "violent and sometimes most learned and elaborate distortions,"[12] and sets out to show that "Locke is not a Hobbist in the usual sense of the term, and that his version of natural law is a continuation of the classical natural-law philosophy and not a deviation from it as Hobbes' certainly is."[13] Singh first deals with the argument that Locke's position on natural law is inconsistent with his philosophical position, specifically his rejection of innate ideas in the *Essay Concerning Human Understanding*. The argument seems to be that the natural law theory presupposes some doctrine of innate ideas. But Singh points out that in the *Essay* itself, Locke distinguishes between *innateness* and *naturalness*—the natural law for Locke is natural because it is knowable by man's natural faculties, not because it is innate. Thus Locke writes:

> I would not be mistaken, if because I deny an innate law I thought there were none but positive laws. There is a great deal of difference between an innate law, and a law of nature; between something imprinted on our minds in their very original, and something that we, being ignorant of may attain to the knowledge of, by the use and due of application of our natural faculties. And I think they equally forsake the truth who, running into contrary extremes, affirm either an innate law, or deny that there is a law knowable by the light of nature i.e. without the help of positive revelation.[14]

Singh furthermore denies that Locke is a radical empiricist or sensationalist, who reduces knowledge to particular sense impressions. If this was the case, then for Singh there could be no genuine natural law in Locke because "natural law can only have a place in some sort of realist-rationalist meta-physics."[15] In Singh's understanding of Locke's epistemology:

> All knowledge, according to him, is based on experience, that is on ideas of sensation and reflection. But ideas alone do not constitute knowledge, which consists in their relation to one another. Where this relation is perceived to be absolutely certain and necessary there we have knowledge in the highest sense . . . thus universality and strict intellectual necessity are the hallmarks of knowledge as Locke conceived it.[16]

Singh endeavors to show that Locke's putative "nominalism" has been wildly misunderstood. Thus, he refers to those passages in Book III of the *Essay on Human Understanding* in which Locke distinguishes *real* from *nominal* essences, and concludes that for Locke real essences mean the nature of things and that "one such 'nature' is intrinsically incapable of separation from another. In so far as this is the case, there arise class-concepts of which the definitions are inherent in the nature of things, not arbitrary and contingent."[17] On the basis of this, universal and necessary judgments are possible, which would not be the case if all knowledge were of singulars. Locke extends the notion of universal and necessary knowledge into the moral sphere. Hence, Locke famously affirms that a demonstrable science of ethics is possible for reason to achieve: "I cannot but thinke morality as well as mathematiques capable of demonstration if we would employ their understanding to think more about it."[18] Singh holds that it is in this context that his natural law theory must be understood. Thus, Locke refers to the natural law in rather traditional terms as practical principles of action which accord with right reason.[19] Locke uses three arguments in the *Essays on the Law of Nature* to demonstrate the existence of a universal and necessary natural law. Singh notes that Locke follows Hooker's definition of law as 'that which prescribes to everything the form and manner and measure of its working.' Locke then follows Aristotle in noting that 'the specific function of man is the active exercise of mind's faculties in accordance with rational principles.'[20] Therefore, in order to fulfill the function proper to his nature man must live in accord with right reason. The second argument he provides is the testimony of conscience, which all men possess. The third is from the order of the world in which all things obey a law proper to their particular nature.[21]

Singh cites a number of passages that indicate that the binding force of the moral law is such that even God cannot alter it. Thus, in the *Second Treatise*, Locke notes "No power can exempt them [princes] from the obligation of that eternal law. They are so great and so strong, in the case of promises that, omnipotence itself can be tied by them. Grants, promises and oaths are bonds that hold the Almighty."[22] Further passages that are much in line with an intellectualist reading can be found in his *Essay Concerning Human Understanding*. If Locke were a voluntarist we would expect him to hold that God's will was *definitive* of the good, not bound by the good. Yet Locke remarks that: "And if it were fit for such poor finite creatures as we are to pronounce what infinite wisdom and goodness could do, I think we might say, that God himself cannot choose what is not good; the freedom of the Almighty hinders not his being determined by what is best."[23]

In the same essay, he refers to the "eternal and unalterable nature of right and wrong." Singh also quotes from the above-cited paragraph in the *Essays on the Law of Nature* that the law of nature is immutable, arising from the very nature of man, and not dependent on a changing will. It is on the basis of this textual evidence that Singh pronounces that:

> Thus we see that extracts may be cited from almost all the major writings of Locke to prove that his conception of natural law is continuous with the classical Stoic and Christian tradition represented by Cicero and St. Thomas and coming down to Richard Hooker. It rests on a belief in the eminent dignity of human Reason proceeding from and in conformity with the cosmic and Divine Reason, in the existence of an 'eternal, rational and divinely ordained system of Order, embracing both morality and law.'[24]

In addressing those passages in the *Essays* where Locke speaks of the law taking its foundation from God's will, Locke makes a distinction between the formal *cause* of moral obligation, which is the will of a sovereign God, and the means by which it is discerned, which is reason. Citing Gierke, Singh sees this position as "similar to St. Thomas and his followers."[25]

Singh then turns to Locke's position that divine sanction, in the form of reward and punishment is necessary for something to be law in the true sense. As we recall, Strauss used this position of Locke's to argue that since we cannot know of divine rewards and punishments by natural reason, and since this is required in order to have a law in the true sense, Locke could not have had any genuine notion of natural law. Singh however argues that, for Locke, the sanctions attached to the law provide the motives for obedience, but not its objectivity. Thus, he quotes Locke to the effect that God has "by an inseparable connection joined virtue and happiness" in the form of sanctions, yet there is an "eternal and unalterable nature of right and wrong." It is in apprehension of this moral law through *right reason*, not dread of divine sanction that constitutes the origin of moral duty. Thus, in the *Essays on the Law of Nature*, Locke says that:

Indeed all obligation binds conscience and lays a bond on the mind itself, so that not fear of punishment, but a rational apprehension of what is right, puts us under an obligation, and conscience passes judgment on morals, and if we are guilty of a crime declares that we deserve punishment.[26]

It is in this connection of sanction as a motive rather then the source of moral life, that Singh discusses the "hedonism" of Locke. If we recall, Strauss interpreted Locke in an opposite manner, viz, as one who rejected the classical natural law tradition in favor of a Hobbesian reading of natural law. Singh argues, on the contrary, that for Locke, pain and pleasure are not the *foundation* of moral virtue or natural law, but merely the motivation for observing the precepts of the moral law. Thus, for Singh, Locke is not a radical ethical hedonist, but merely a psychological hedonist, not so different from thinkers in the Eudemonistic tradition for whom happiness and virtue are closely related. As Singh puts it, "Though he defines good and evil in terms of pleasure and pain, they are to him only *consequences* of a morally right action; they never constitute its *essence*. A moral law is eternal and it is obligatory independently of its pleasurable consequences."[27]

Turning to Locke's social and political theory, there are two related claims that Strauss makes regarding Locke to place him in the Hobbesian camp. The first is that Strauss sees both Locke and Hobbes as putting forward an *individualist* theory quite foreign to the natural law tradition, which consistently agreed with Aristotle on the social nature of man, and privileged the common good over the private good. The second following from it is that "modern natural right," represented for Strauss by both Hobbes and Locke, made subjective *rights* the starting point, from which moral duties are merely derivative. Singh responds that while for Locke there is a natural right to self-preservation, this need not be interpreted as giving *primacy* to the individual over the community. Thus, passages in the *Second Treatise* suggest that the self-preservation of *society* is what is primary for Locke: "The *First and fundamental natural Law*, which is to govern even the legislative itself, *is thepreservation of the society*, and (as far as will consist with the public good) of every person in it."[28] Thus, while Locke holds there is an individual right to self-preservation, this right is strictly subordinate to the right of the community to preserve itself, and in cases of conflict, Locke would hold with the natural law tradition, that the private good of the individual must yield to the common good of the community. Singh further refers to a letter in which Locke explicitly says that "the fundamental law of nature being the preservation of mankind . . . the injury and mischief done to society are much more culpable then those done to private men."[29]

Regarding the point about whether Locke derives human rights to life and liberty from the law of nature or the reverse, Locke's position was stated fairly clearly in the *Second Treatise*:

> The *freedom* then of man, and liberty of acting according to his own will, is *grounded on* his having *reason*, which is able to instruct him in that law he is to govern himself by, and make him know how far he is left to the freedom of his own will. To turn him loose to unrestrained liberty, before he has reason to guide him, is not allowing him the privilege of his nature to be free; but to thrust him out amongst brutes, and abandon him to a state as wretched, and as much beneath that of a man, as their's.[30]

While Hobbes at points defined liberty in negative terms as the silence of the law—and thus set law and liberty at odds—Locke at points describes the law in a basically teleological framework. Thus, the law is that which directs man to his proper end, and so far being an enemy of freedom, liberates man to attain this end:

> For law, in its true notion, is not so much limitation as the direction of a free and intelligent agent to his proper interest, and prescribes no further then is for the general good of those under the law . . . the end of the law is not to abolish or restrain, but to preserve and enlarge freedom; for in all the states of created beings, where there is no law there is no freedom.[31]

In contrast to the intellectualist Locke depicted by Singh, perhaps the clearest and most eloquent case for the voluntarist interpretation of Locke was that put forth by Francis Oakley.

LOCKE AS A VOLUNTARIST: FRANCIS OAKLEY

In his 1997 article, "Locke, Natural Law and God-again," Oakley begins by aptly noting that: "Of the many *questiones disputatae* rolling the fast-moving waters of Locke scholarship, few have evinced a more persistent capacity to stimulate disagreement then the matter of his natural law teaching—its status, significance, coherence, consistency."[32] After surveying the history of twentieth-century Locke scholarship from Lamprecht to the present, Oakley notes that there is as yet no scholarly consensus on Locke's natural law theory, in spite of much ink spilled on the subject, and the twentieth-century publication of Locke's *Essays on the Law of Nature*. Oakley is convinced that modern scholars of the late medieval background to Locke's natural law theory base much of the confusion on this topic on an inadequate understanding. The position that Oakley will defend is that: "Locke's own natural law theory

. . . could be most accurately understood as a pretty faithful continuation of the late-medieval voluntarist tradition."[33] Naturally enough, Oakley gives primary weight to the passages from the *Essays* where Locke states that natural law is obligatory because of "the decree of a superior will, wherein the formal cause of a law appears to consist"[34] and Locke's statement that: "Neither is reason so much the maker of the law as its interpreter, unless violating the dignity of the supreme legislator, we wish to make reason responsible for that received law which it merely investigates."[35]

Oakley acknowledges that advocates like Singh of the intellectualist interpretation of Locke can produce texts that indicate that the natural law is a "Law of reason," that this "law does not depend on an unstable and dangerous will, but on the eternal order of things"; or that "Omnipotency itself can be tied" by its immutable precepts. Thus he says that, "such texts would appear to insert some sort of rationalistic qualification into what otherwise has to be acknowledged as the controlling voluntarism of Locke's natural law thinking."[36] However, Oakley goes on to argue that this conclusion is premature until the intellectual context of Locke's ideas is more fully understood:

> The fleeting and fragmentary nature of the statements [supportive of intellectualism] involved, as well as Locke's manifest uneasiness with any probing discussion of the divine nature, suggest the wisdom of refraining from conceding the point until the texts in question have been appraised more fully.[37]

This appraisal must take into account not only the immediate context of Locke's own milieu, but also "the advances evident both in recent Locke scholarship and in our knowledge and understanding of the nominalist thinkers of the fourteenth and fifteenth centuries" from which, Oakley holds Locke's natural law theory takes it start. Oakley's confidence is that once the nominalist/voluntarist tradition in late scholasticism is understood, the apparent inconsistencies in Locke's position can be made coherent.

Oakley traces the nominalist movement as essentially a revolt against the effort to integrate the natural theology of Hellenistic metaphysics with the God of Biblical revelation. Oakley then takes us on a brief tour of the long history of ideas that preceded this revolt. Oakley sees the "God of the philosophers" as acquiring definite shape with Neoplatonism that assimilated the Platonic demiurge, with Aristotle's unmoved mover, and came to see the "exemplar ideas" of Plato, as subsisting within a divine mind. Thus, by the late antiquity a clear notion had emerged within Greek thought that there is a "transcendent God, at once the Highest Good, to which all things aspire, the First Cause to which all things owe their being, the Supreme Reason from which all things derive their order and intelligibility."[38] Though the effort to reconcile the heritage of Greece with the heritage of Israel, can be traced as

far back as Philo Judaeus, Oakley sees in St. Augustine the "further confla-
tion of the Neo-Platonic God—the God of the philosophers, as it were, in its
final and most developed version—with the biblical God of Abraham, Isaac,
and Jacob, the personal God of power and might who not only transcends the
universe but created it out of nothing."[39] Thus, there is the Augustinian tradition of exemplarism that, in a sense, reconciled the Biblical doctrine of creation with the Greek metaphysics of essences. Oakley remarks that for Augustine—"by agreeing with Philo, the Neo-Platonists, and many of his
Christian predecessors that the creative act was indeed an intelligent one
guided by Ideas of the Platonic mould but ideas located now in the divine
mind, he responded to the Greek concern to vindicate philosophically the order and intelligibility of the universe."[40] The process of assimilating Hellenistic natural theology into Christianity for Oakley, reaches its culmination
in the Christian Aristotelianism of St. Thomas Aquinas. Oakley holds that
Aquinas by arguing for the legitimacy of analogical predication of concepts
derived from human knowledge of created things was "vindicating the order,
rationality, and intelligibility of the universe"—a central goal of Greek philosophy. This element of Aquinas's synthesis is particularly evident in the primacy, which Aquinas seems to give to the divine wisdom or reason, culminating in his notion of the eternal law:

> Assuming the primacy of reason over will not only in man but in God, he
> [Aquinas] regarded what in later parlance would be called the (moral) natural
> law, and the (physical) laws of nature in comparatively 'Greek' fashion as both
> of them the external manifestations of an indwelling and immanent reason. Thus
> he spoke of an 'eternal law' that orders to their appropriate ends all created be-
> ings, irrational no less then rational . . . it was the advantage of this way of look-
> ing at things that it enabled one to regard the whole of being, the realm of na-
> ture no less then that of man as in its own fashion subject to the norms of the
> same eternal law.[41]

This is, of course, the very doctrine that Hooker inherited from Aquinas,
the rooting of all law in the eternal law. However, Oakley remarks that the
synthesis between Greek philosophy and biblical revelation is inherently unstable—"in the historic encounter between the Greek philosophical tradition
and religious views of biblical provenance, the great stumbling block has
been (and necessarily remained) the difficulty of reconciling the personal
and transcendent biblical God of power and might . . . with the characteristically Greek intuition of the divine as limited . . . and of the universe as necessary and universal."[42] The Thomistic position might seem to limit God's
omnipotence, by compelling him to create in accord with universal essences,

and to act in accord with reason. This later is an issue particularly with respect to the idea of an eternal law by which God acts—as Oakley remarks, "The subjection to law could arguably be taken to extend to God himself, thus threatening his freedom and omnipotence. For the eternal law is no more then one aspect of the divine reason itself, and in God reason is prior to will."[43] Although Thomism in later centuries received official favor from ecclesiastical authority, in the late thirteenth and early fourteenth century matters looked quite different. In 1277, a number of Aquinas's propositions were condemned at Paris and a search was soon under way for new philosophical approaches which would challenge "the priority accorded [by Thomism] to the divine intellect over the divine will and the confidence in the capacity of analogical reasoning to cast a conceptual net really capable of encompassing in a meaningful commonality of discourse the natures of both God and man."[44]

If the Greek metaphysics of essences seemed to many to impose a limitation of God's power, a need arose to find a philosophical system, which would safeguard God's omnipotence and freedom. In particular this new philosophy would tend to emphasize God's inscrutable *will* as the source of both creation and the moral law itself. As Oakley writes,

> the tendency was now to make the divine omnipotence the fundamental principle, to accord to the divine will the primacy in God's workings *ad extra* [i.e. in relation to the created order] and to understand the order of the created order (both the moral order governing human behavior and the natural order governing the behavior of irrational beings) no longer as a participation in a divine reason that is in some measure transparent to the human intellect, but rather as the deliverance of an inscrutable divine will.[45]

These philosophers are those that Oakley is referring to as the "voluntarists." He places particular emphasis on two thinkers in relation to Locke's natural law theory, namely, William of Ockham (d.1349) and Pierre D'Ailly (d. 1420).

Voluntaristic ethics is conventionally thought of as the view that what makes an act good or evil is whether or not it is commanded by God. There is therefore nothing *intrinsic* to the species of a given action that makes it good or evil. An intellectualistic approach, on the other hand, would see the good or evil of a given action as something intrinsic to the nature of the action. Thus, the moral law is basically universal, unchangeable, and knowable by reason. Since Locke speaks of the law of nature as immutable and knowable to natural reason, scholars like Singh are able to argue that Locke was an intellectualist. Oakley, however, points out that this way of conceptualizing the matter vastly oversimplifies the position of the fourteenth and fifteenth

century voluntarists. Indeed, by this criterion Ockham and D'Ailly are themselves intellectualists. As Oakley puts it:

> All one would have to do, would be to adopt an interpretive stance akin to that
> used by Singh in his approach to Locke . . . thus according to d'Ailly, morally
> correct action is nothing other then action in conformity with 'the dictates of
> reason,' and 'the light of natural reason' and, according to Ockham . . . no act
> 'perfectly virtuous unless it is elicited in conformity to right reason' . . . to fol-
> low the dictate of right reason is nothing other then to obey the natural law,
> which he describes as 'aboslute,' immutable, and admitting of no dispensation.[46]

What such an interpretation would miss is the central distinctions these
thinkers made between the ordained power (*potencia ordinata*) and absolute
power (*potencia absoluta*). According to what God has actually ordained in
the order of the universe as it is, there are universal moral principles discoverable by reason. However, God is not bound in any way by the particular
moral and physical order he has ordained and He is perfectly free to will any
other possible order into being:

> God's absolute power, by virtue of which he can anything that does not involve
> a formal contradiction, is a potentially active power whereby he can contravene
> . . . the laws—moral, natural, and salvational—which he has by his ordained
> power in fact established.[47]

The voluntarist vision of Ockham and d'Ailly was appealing to certain
English Protestants of the seventeenth century, because it appeared to correspond to a biblically based *covenantal* understanding of God's relationship to
man. God being the all-powerful sovereign of the creation is not limited by
anything. Yet God is able to freely bind Himself by promises and covenants
in His relations to man. Thus, in the Scriptures, God enters into a series of
covenants with Abraham, with the people of Israel, and with the Church, and
He is depicted as ever faithful. Voluntarism seemed therefore to a strain of
English Protestantism as providing an understanding that accorded with the
"God of Abraham, Isaac, and Jacob" and conceded less to the "God of the
philosophers."

> Its impact was such as to underline the contingency of the entire order while at
> the same time affirming its *de facto* contingency. That impact was two fold pre-
> cidely because it inserted, side by side with the Old Testament vision of Yahweh
> as a God of power and might, another fundamentally biblical theme—that of
> God's covenant and promise . . . While God cannot be said to be bound by the
> canons of any merely human reason or justice, he is certainly capable by his own
> free decision of binding himself to follow a certain pattern in dealing with his
> creation.[48]

This covenantal understanding based on voluntarism was widely popularized in the seventeenth century with works such as William Ames's *The Marrow of Sacred Divinity*.[49] Oakley also holds that this is the context in which we must understand Locke's apparently contradictory assertions in the *Essays on the Law of Nature* that, on the one hand, God's will is the source of the binding power of the law of nature and, on the other hand, that the natural law can be discerned by right reason from human nature. Thus, Locke's position "is equally in harmony with Ockham's earlier insistence that while it is the divine will that is the source of obligatory moral precepts, nonetheless, in the divinely-ordained moral economy presently prevailing, our right reason dictates to us what it is that we must do if we are to act virtuously."[50]

What has made Locke's position so difficult to understand for Oakley is the ignorance of so many scholars of the importance of late scholastic philosophy to a proper understanding of Locke. Once the distinctions of voluntarists like Ockham and d'Ailly are well understood, apparently intellectualist passages in Locke's work can be properly understood. Oakley draws our attention to the fact that voluntaristic qualifications of Locke's natural law doctrine in texts that might seem to a reader unfamiliar with the nuances of the late medieval tradition rather intellectualist. This point can be perhaps best understood by Oakley's careful use of italicization in a passage often cited by proponents of the "intellectualist" interpretation:

> 'Human beings cannot alter this law' but also '*because God would not wish to do so*.' For since, according to His infinite and eternal wisdom, He has made man such that these duties of his follow necessarily from his very nature. He *surely would not alter* what has been made and create a new race of men, who would have another law and moral rule, seeing that natural law stands and falls together with the nature of man *as it is at present*.

So basically, God does not alter the moral law, not because it is intrinsically unalterable, but because God has bound Himself by a promise. Oakley concludes that:

> So far as his natural law thinking is concerned, the Locke who emerges is unquestionably, and unqualifiedly a voluntarist. But he is a voluntarist of the late-medieval stamp whose emphasis on the divine omnipotence is so modulated as to accommodate a firm commitment to the existence of an order—seemingly intellectualistic in nature but actually grounded in the divine will, choice, promise.[51]

Thus having surveyed the case for intellectualism and voluntarism in Locke's natural law, how are we to assess the evidence? Certainly the voluntarist case is far from completely proven. Even Oakley will admit that sentences like 'God himself cannot choose what is not good' or 'the freedom of the Almighty hinders not his being determined by what is best'[52] cannot be so easily explained on voluntarist grounds. In order to bring the debate to a definitive resolution, it would be necessary to adduce more than is so far in evidence regarding the voluntarist sources of Locke's theory. It is not clear, for example, that Locke himself anywhere explicitly references a distinction between *potestate ordinata* and *potestate absoluta*; nor are there abundant citations of late scholastic voluntarists in the *Essays on the Law of Nature*. On the other hand, Locke cites St. Thomas Aquinas favorably in the work.[53] Still Oakley's resolution is arguably the more elegant one. Through the distinction between God's ordained and absolute power, it seems possible to interpret Locke's "intellectualistic" passages in terms of an underlying voluntarism. On the other hand, Singh's account does not allow us to easily read passages that support voluntarism in terms of an underlying intellectualism.

What does this debate mean for our primary discussion of assessing Hooker's influence on Locke? Since Hooker's natural law theory stands unquestionably in the realist-intellectualist tradition of St. Thomas Aquinas, the matter has a certain importance. If Oakley is correct, then clearly there is a significant discontinuity between Hooker and Locke on the issue of natural law. Though both thinkers would be deriving their respective positions from scholastic discussions of the topic, they would stand in continuity with different medieval schools of natural law thinking. However, whether Locke's natural law is continuous with Aquinas and Hooker, or Ockham and d'Ailly, both Singh and Oakley are willing to introduce qualifications into their positions that significantly narrow the ground between them. Thus, Singh is willing to concede that, "for Locke the will of God is the formal cause of obligation without which an action is without moral foundation."[54] For his part, as we have seen, Oakley is ready to recognize that the natural law for Locke is universal, immutable, and discernible by man's natural reason. Thus, neither side represents Locke as an example of either "pure" intellectualism or "pure" voluntarism—if such a position ever existed. The differences then come down to issues of natural theology such as whether God could have created a moral order different from the one He has actually ordained; or whether the natural moral law proceeds primarily from the wisdom of God, or rather from His will.

NOTES

1. Francis Oakley, "Locke, Natural Law and God-again," *History of Political Thought* 18 (1997), p. 625.

2. John Yolton, "Locke on the Law of Nature," in *John Locke: Critical Assessments*, ed. Richard Aschraft (New York: Routldege), p. 78.

3. *Ibid.*, p. 16ff.

4. *Ibid.*, p. 21.

5. Oakley, "Locke, Natural Law and God-again," p. 628.

6. *Ibid.*

7. Otto von Gierke, *Political Theories of the Middle Age*, trans. Frederic William Maitland (Cambridge: Cambridge University Press, 1900; reprint, Bristol: Thoemmes Press, 1996), p. 173 (page references are to reprint edition).

8. John Locke, *Essays on the Law of Nature*, ed. W. von Leyden (Oxford: Clarendon Press, 1958; reprint, 1988) I (page references are to reprint edition; italics added); in Locke's original: "*Haec igitur Lex naturae ita describi potest quod sit ordinatio voluntatis divinae lumine naturae cognosibilis, quid cum natura tationali conveniens ve disconveniens sit indicans eoque ipso jubens aut prohibens. Minus recte enim mihi videtur a nonullis dici dictatum rationis, ratio enim legem hance naturae non tam condit dictatque quam a superiore potestate sancitam et pectoribus nostris . . . Ex his facile patet in ea omnia reperir quae ad legem requiruntur. Name primo declaratio est superioris voluntatis.*"

9. *Ibid.*, pp. 199–201; in Locke's original: "*Non enim fluxa et mutabili voluntate pendet haec lex, sed Aeterna rerum ordine; mihi enim videntur quidam immutabiles esse rerum status et quaedam official ex necessitate orta, quae aliter esse non possunt, non quod natura vel(ut rectius dicam) Deus non potuit fecisse hominem, sed cum ita factus sit, rationis et aliissuis facultatibus intructus, as hanc vitae conditionem natus, sequuntur necessario ex nativa ipsius constitione aliqua certa officia, quae aliter esse non possunt . . . ex infinita et aeterna sua sapientia ita fecit hominum ut haec illius officia ex ipsa hominis natura necessartio sequerentur . . . quandoquidem cum humana natura, quae jam est, lex naturae stat simul caditque.*"

10. Von Leyden for example argues that Locke's voluntarist statements are somewhat provisional. Locke indeed defines law as the declaration of a superior will, but (according to Von Leyden) Locke finds this voluntarist definition inadequate to completely secure the morally binding character of the natural law. Thus Von Leyden writes "Locke advances . . . the 'voluntarist theory' (or rather definition) that law or men's duties are the expression of a superior will." Yet "the 'voluntarist' theory carries with it an implication which Locke obviously found dissatisfying, for together with the concept of will it introduces an arbitrary element into morality." Thus Von Leyden suggests that to avert the seemingly arbitrary character of a natural law theory based purely on divine commands, Locke introduces a second edifice on which the morally binding character of the natural law could be based, viz. the foundation of moral probity in reason and human nature. As Von Leyden puts it "In order to make his theory more perfect, Locke attempts to derive moral obligation in some other way. He does this as part of his endeavor to arrive at a purely rational foundation of ethics. For him human reason not only indicates or teaches what man's duties are, but at the same time makes his duties binding; it is thus a self-depending source of obligation. He maintains that natural law is coeval with the human race and that all men are subject to it since it is 'so firmly rooted in the soil of human nature.' W.Von Leyden.

"John Locke and Natural Law" in John Locke, *Critical Assesments*. (New York: Rout-ledge, 1991), vol. II, p. 11. Interestingly, Ian Harris takes an almost diametrically op-posed view, arguing that in fact it is Locke's emphasis on God as the legislator of the moral law that is meant to buttress weaknesses in a purely rationalist account of nat-ural law. Thus Harris writes that "Whilst Locke by no means neglected reason he wished to align it conceptually not to man's desire, but to God's will. Consent was not enough to establish a law. At the beginning of the first essay he contrasted a concep-tion of the natural law intelligible 'only' by the light of nature, and 'one which is the decree of the will of God.' He added that it seemed incorrect to speak of the law as dictated by reason, since reason only discovered what a superior had prescribed." Cf. Ian Harris, *The Mind of John Locke*. Cambridge: Cambridge University Press, 1994, 98.

11. Raghuveer Singh, "John Locke and the Theory of Natural Law," *Political Stud-ies* 9 (1961), pp. 105–106.

12. *Ibid.*, p. 105.

13. *Ibid.*, p. 106.

14. *Ibid.*, p. 106–107, quoting Book I of Locke's *Essay*.

15. *Ibid.*, p. 108.

16. *Ibid.*, p. 109.

17. *Ibid.*, p. 111.

18. *Ibid.*, p. 109.

19. *Ibid.*, p. 110; in Locke's original: *Sed Quaedam practica principia e quibus emanant omnium virtutem fonts et quicquid necessarium sit ad mores bene efforman-dos; quod ex his principiis recte deducitur id jure dicitur rectae rationi conforme.*

20. *Ibid.*, p. 111.

21. *Ibid.*

22. John Locke, *Second Treatise of Government*, §195 (hereafter shortened to *Sec-ond Treatise*).

23. John Locke, *An Essay concerning Human Understanding*, Book II, chapter 21, section 50.

24. Singh, "John Locke and the Theory of Natural Law," p. 112.

25. Whether St. Thomas Aquinas himself saw the will of God as the formal cause of obligation is a highly disputable point. Though for St. Thomas, God is certainly the promulgator of the natural law, the position identified with Thomist realism by Gierke and Singh might be more closely associated with his "followers" if by that we mean Suarez and others in the School of Salamanca. Thus, Oakley remarks that Gierke was "improperly ascribing thereby to the earlier Thomists the distinctly Suarezian teach-ing that the binding force of the natural law, though not its content, was to be ascribed to legislation by the divine will" (*ibid.*, p. 629).

26. Locke, *Essays on the Law of Nature*, 185: *Omnis enim obligatio conscientiam alligat et animo ipsi vinculum injicit (f. 86) adeo ut non poenae metus sed recti ratio nos obligat, et conscientia de moribus fert sententiam et admisso crimine nos merito poenae obnoxious esse judicat.*

27. Singh, "John Locke and the Theory of Natural Law," p. 114.

28. Locke, *Second Treatise of Government*, §134.

29. Singh, "John Locke and the Theory of Natural Law," 119, quoting Lord King's letters of Locke, ii.95.

30. Locke, *Second Treatise of Government*, §63.

31. Singh, "John Locke and the Theory of Natural Law," p. 116.

32. Oakley, "Locke, Natural Law and God-again," p. 624.

33. *Ibid.*, p. 628.

34. *Ibid.*, p. 631, quoting *Essays on the Law of Nature*, pp. 186–187.

35. *Ibid.*

36. *Ibid.*, p. 633.

37. *Ibid.*

38. *Ibid.*

39. *Ibid.*, p. 634.

40. *Ibid.*

41. *Ibid.*, p. 635.

42. *Ibid.*, p. 634.

43. *Ibid.*

44. *Ibid.*

45. *Ibid.*, pp. 635–636.

46. *Ibid.*, pp. 637–638.

47. *Ibid.*, p. 639.

48. *Ibid.*, p. 640.

49. *Ibid.*, p. 639; Ames's remarkable work *The Marrow of Sacred Divinity.* (London: Henry Overton and Edward Griffin, 1642, provides a strongly voluntaristic perspective on such points as predestination, divine command as the source of moral obligation, the attack on Molina's theory of middle knowledge, and the primacy of the will in ethics. If there were strong evidence that Locke's natural law theory was directly influenced by this work, Oakley's case would be immeasurably stronger. However, while Locke did have one book of Ames in his library—*Declaration of Ye Witnesses of God*, London, 1656—this work concerned conversion experience, not philosophical theology. In the absence of evidence that Locke made use of the *Marrow*, Oakley's suggestion that Locke's view on natural law may have been mediated through the influence of Ames must be considered speculative.

50. *Ibid.*, p. 645.

51. *Ibid.*, p. 649.

52. *Ibid.*, p. 651, quoting *Essays on the Law of Nature*, p. 21, p. 49.

53. In Book I of the *Essays on the Law of Nature*, Locke cites Aquinas to the effect that all things are subject to the eternal law: *Id Omne quod in rebus creatis fit, material est legis aeternae inquit Aquinas* (116). Van Leyden notes that this is not an exact quote of S.T. I-II, q.93, art. 4, but rather a paraphrase based on Hooker's formulation of Aquinas's thoughts in *Laws*, I.2.1 Locke goes on to note his concurrence with this position: "this being so, it does not seem that man alone is independent of laws while everything else is bound. On the contrary a manner of acting is prescribed to him that is suitable to his nature; for it does not seem to fit in with the wisdom of the Creator to form an animal . . . to endow it above all others with mind, intellect, reason . . . and yet not assign to it any work, or again to make man alone susceptible

of law precisely in order that he may submit to none" (cf. *Essays on the Law of Nature*, translation on p. 117).

54. Singh, "John Locke and the Theory of Natural Law," p. 113; Singh's error seems to be that he sees this view as continuous with Aquinas based on Gierke's misreading. The differences between the Thomist and Suarezian versions of "intellectualism" seem inadequately explored here.

Bibliography

BOOKS (INCLUDING ANTHOLOGIES AND BOOKS ONLINE)

Allen, J. W. *A History of Political Thought in the Sixteenth Century*. London: Methuen, 1951.

Ames, William. *The Marrow of Sacred Divinity*. London: Henry Overton and Edward Griffin, 1642.

———. *Declaration of Ye Witnesses of God*. London: 1656.

Aristotle. *Politics*. Translated by William Ellis. Buffalo, N.Y.: Prometheus, 1986.

———. *Politics*. Translated by Benjamin Jowett (online) classics.mit.edu/Aristotle/politics.html

Aquinas, St. Thomas. *Summa Theologica*. Five Volumes. Translated by Dominican Fathers. Christian Classics. New York: Benziger Bros., 1948.

———. *Selected Political Writings*. Translated by A.P. Entreves. Oxford: Blackwell, 1978.

Atwood, William. *The Fundamental Constitution of the English Government*. London: J. D., 1690.

Augustine. *Against Julian*. Translated by Matthew Schumacher. New York: Fathers of the Church, 1957.

———. *The Confessions. The City of God. On Christian Doctrine*. In Great Books of the Western World. Chicago: Enyclopaedia Britannica, 1990 (reprint).

———. *Four Anti-Pelagian Writings*. Translated by John A Mouran and William Collinge. Washington D.C.: Catholic University of America Press, 1986.

Ashcraft, Richard, ed. John Locke: *Critical Assesments*. New York: Routledge, 1991.

Ashcraft, Richard. *Locke's Two Treatises of Government*. London: Unwin Hyman, 1989.

Bancroft, Richard. *A Survey of the Pretended Holy Discipline*. Amsterdam: Theatrum Orbis Terravm, 1972.

Barbon, John. *Liturgie a Most Divine Service*. Oxford: A and L Lichfield, 1663.

Beiser, Frederick. *The Sovereignty of Reason: The Defence of Rationality in the Early English Enlightenment.* Princeton, N. J.: Princeton University Press, 1996.

Bellarmine, Robert Cardinal. *De Laicis.* Translated by Kathleen E. Murphy. Westport, Conn.: Hyperion, 1979.

Belda Plans, Juan. *La Escuela de Salamanca y la renovacíon de la teología en el siglo XVI.* Madrid: BAC maior, 2000.

Bloom, Allan. *The Closing of the American Mind: How Higher Education has Failed Democracy and Impoverished the Souls of Today's Students.* New York: Simon and Schuster, 1987.

Blum, Carol. *Rousseau and the Republic of Virtue: The Language of Politics in the French Revolution.* Ithaca, N.Y.: Cornell University Press, 1986.

Bodin, Jean. *On Sovereignty.* Edited and translated by Julian H. Franklin. Cambridge:Cambridge University Press, 1992.

The Booke of Common Prayer, and Administration of the Sacraments. And Other Rites and Ceremonies of the Church of England. London, 1549, 1552, 1559, 1662.
    justus.anglican.org/resources/bcp/1552/BCP_1552.htm
    virginia.edu.anglican.org/logue/bcpframe.htm
    justus.anglican.org/resources/bcp/1559/BCP_1559.htm
    www.eskimo.com/~lhowell/bcp1662/

Bracton, Henry. *De Legibus et Consuetudinibus Angliae.* Translated by Samuel E. Thorne, Latin text of George Woodbine. hlsl.law.harvard.edu/bracton/Common/

Brett, Annabelle. *Liberty, Right and Nature: Individual Rights in Later Scholastic Thought.* Cambridge: Cambridge University Press, 1997.

Bridges, John. *A defence of the Government Established in the Church of England.* London: John Vindet for Thomas Chard, 1587.

Brunner, Emil. *Justice and the Social Order.* London: Lutterworth Press, 1949.

Bullinger, Henry. *The Decades of Henry Bullinger.* Cambridge: Cambridge University Press, 1849–1851.

Calvin, John. *Institutes of the Christian Religion.* Translated by Henry Beveridge. www.ccel.org/c/calvin/institutes/institutes.html

Carleton, George. *Iurisdiction Regall, Episcopall, and Papall.* London: John Norton, 1610.

Carlyle, R.W. and A. J. *History of Medieval Political Theory in the West.* Edinburgh and London: Blackwood, 1903–1936.

Cartwright, Thomas. *Replye to an Answere made of M. Doctor Whitegifte againste the Admonition to Parliament.* Hemel Hemstead: J.Stroud, 1573.

——. *The rest of the second replie of Thomas Cartvuriht* (sic). Basel: Thomas Guarinus, 1577.

——. *The second replie of Thomas Cartwright.* Heidelberg: Michael Schirat, 1575.

Casaubon, Meric. *A Vindication of the Lord's Prayer.* London: Thomas Johnson, 1660.

Case, John. *Sphaera Civitatis.* Francof: Sigifmundi, 1589.

Case, John. *Speculum Moralium Quaestionem in Universam Ethicen Aristotelis.* Oxford: Joseph Barnes, I Barnesti, 1585.

Christopher of St. Germain. *The Dialoges in English between a Doctor of Divinitye and a Student of the Lawes of England.* London: Richard Totell, 1569.

Collinson, Patrick. *The Elizabethan Puritan Movement*. London: Oxford University Press, 1967.

Colman, John. *John Locke's Moral Philosophy*. Edinburgh: Edinburgh University Press, 1983.

Copleston, Frederick. *A History Of Philosophy: vol. II: Medieval Philosophy from Augustine to Scotus*. New York: Image/Doubleday, 1993 (reprint).

——. *A History of Philosophy: vol. III: Late Medieval And Renaissance Philosophy*. London and New York: Continuum, 2003.

Costello, William T. *The Scholastic Curriculum at Early Seventeenth Century Cambridge*. Cambridge, Mass.: Harvard University Press, 1958.

Davies, E. T. *The Political Ideas of Richard Hooker*. London: Society for Promoting Christian Knowledge, 1946.

Davies, Horton, N. J. *Worship and Theology in England from Cranmer to Hooker*. Princeton, N. J.: Princeton University Press, 1970.

D'Entreves, Alexandre Passerin. *The Medieval Contribution to Political Thought: Thomas Aquinas, Marsilius of Padua, Richard Hooker*. Oxford: Oxford University Press, 1939; reprint, New York: Humanities Press, 1959.

D'Holbach, Baron. *Good Sense* (1753). history.hanover.edu/courses/excerpts/347hol .html.

Dickens, A. G. *The English Reformation*. London: B.T. Batsford, 1964.

Diggs, Dudley. *An Answer to a Printed Book*. London: Leonard Lichfield, 1642.

——. *The unlawfulness of subjects taking up arms against their soveraigne*. London: Thomas Mabb, 1664.

Dunn, John. *The Political Thought of John Locke: An Historical Account of the Argument of the Two Treatises of Government*. Cambridge: Cambridge University Press, 1969.

Eccleshall, Robert. *Order and Reason in Politics: Theories of Absolute and Limited Monarchy in Early Modern England*. Oxford: Oxford University Press, 1978.

Elton, G. B. *England under the Tudors*. London: Methuen, 1960; reprint, London: The Folio Society, 1997.

Faulkner, Robert. *Richard Hooker and the Politics of a Christian England*. Berkeley: University of California Press, 1981.

Ferne, Henry. *Conscience Satisfied*. Oxford or London: Leonard Lichfield, 1643.

——. *The Resolving of Conscience*. Oxford: V. V. Webb, 1643.

Field, Richard and Thomas Wilcox? *An Admonition to Parliament*. Hemel Hemstead?: J.Stroud?, 1572.

Filmer, Sir Robert. *Patriarcha and Other Writings*. Edited by Johann P. Sommerville. Cambridge: Cambridge University Press, 1991.

Fortescue, Sir John. *On the Laws and Governance of England*. Edited by Shelley Lockwood. Cambridge: Cambridge University Press, 1997.

Freeman, Ireneus. *The Reasonableness of Divine Service*. London: Tho. Basset, 1661.

Gardiner, Stephen. *De Vera Obedientia*. Translated by John Bale (in 1553). Leeds: Scholar Press, 1966.

Garrigou-Lagrange, Réginald. *The One God*. Translated by Bede Rose. St. Louis, Mo.: Herder Books, 1946.

Gee, Edward. *The Divine Right and Originall of the Civill magistrate from God*. London: George Eversden, 1658.

Gierke, Otto. *Political Theories of the Middle Age.* Translated by Frederick Maitland. Bristol: Thoemmes, 1996.

Giles of Rome. *De Renuntiatione Papae.* Rome, 1555.

Gough, J.W. *John Locke's Political Phillosophy: Eight Studies.* Oxford: Oxford University Press, 1968.

Grant, Ruth W. *John Locke's Liberalism.* Chicago: University of Chicago Press, 1987.

Hallam, Henry. *The Constitutional History of England from the Accession of Henry VII to the Death of George II.* London: Alex, Murray and Son, 1869.

Halverson, James L. *Peter Aureol on Predestination.* Leiden: Brill Press, 1998.

Hamilton, Berenice. *Political Thought in Sixteenth Century Spain. A Study of the Political Ideas of Vitoria, de Soto, Suarez and Molina.* Oxford: Clarendon Press, 1963.

Harris, Ian. *The Mind of John Locke.* Cambridge: Cambridge University Press, 1994.

Harrison, John and Peter Laslett. *The Library of John Locke.* 2d ed. Oxford: Oxford University Press, 1971.

Haugaard, William. *Elizabeth and the Reformation.* London: Jonathan Cape, 1969.

Herle, Charles. *An Answer to Doctor Ferne's Reply.* London: Tho Brudenell, 1643.

Hobbes, Thomas. *Leviathan.* Edited by G. A. B. MacPherson. Harmondsworth: Penguin, 1984.

——. *Leviathan.* Edited by Richard Tuck. Cambridge: Cambridge University Press, 1997.

Hooker, Richard. *Folger Library Edition of the Works of Richard Hooker.* Edited by W. Speed Hill. Binghamton: Center for Medieval and Early Rennaisance Studies, 1993.

——. *Of the Lawes of Ecclesiastical Politie.* London: William Stansby, 1611.

——. *Of the Laws of Ecclesiastical Polity.* Edited by Arthur Stephen McGrade. Cambridge: Cambridge University Press, 1989.

——. *The Works of that Learned and Judicious Divine Mr. Richard Hooker.* Arranged by John Keble. New York: Burt Franklin, 1970 (reprint).

Hughs, Phillip. *The Reformation in England.* London: Burns and Oats, 1963.

Hunton, Phillip. *A Treatise of Monarchie.* London: John Bellamy and Ralph Smith, 1643.

Jewel, Bishop John. *The Works of John Jewel, Bishop of Salisbury.* Edited by John Eyre. Cambridge: Cambridge University Press, 1850.

Kantorowitz, Ernst H. *The King's Two Bodies: A Study in Medieval Political Theology.* Princeton, N. J.: Princeton University Press, 1997.

Keeton, George W. *The Norman Conquest and the Common Law.* London: Barnes and Noble, 1966.

Kelley, J. M. *A Short History of Western Legal Theory.* Oxford: Clarendon Press, 1999.

Kirby, W.J. Torrance. *Richard Hooker's Doctrine of the Royal Supremacy.* Leiden: Brill, 1990.

Kirk, Russell. *The Portable Conservative Reader.* Harmondsworth: Penguin, 1982.

——. *The Roots of the American Order.* Washington, D. C.: Regnery Gateway, 1991.

Kristellar, Paul Oskar. *Renaissance Thought: The Classic, Scholastic, and Humanist Strains.* New York: Harper Torch Books, 1961.

Lake, Peter. *Anglicans and Puritans? Presbyterianism and English Conformist Thought from Whitgift to Hooker.* London: Allen and Unwin, 1988.

Lewis, Bernard. *The Political Language of Islam*. Chicago: University of Chicago Press, 1988.

Locke, John. *Essays on the Law of Nature*. Edited by W. von Leyden. Oxford: Clarendon Press, 1958; reprint, 1988.

———. *Political Writings*. Edited by David Wooton. Harmondsworth: Mentor, 1993.

———. *Questions Concerning the Law of Nature*. Edited, introduction, text, and translated by Robert Horwitz Ithaca, N. Y.: Cornell University Press, 1990.

———. *The Reasonableness of Christianity as Delivered in the Scriptures*. Edited by Victor Nuovo. Bristol: Thoemmes, 1997.

———. *Two Tracts on Government*. Edited by Phillip Abrams. Cambridge: Cambridge University Press, 1967.

———. *The Two Treatises of Government*. Edited by Peter Laslett. Cambridge: Cambridge University Press, 1988.

Long, P. *A Summary Catalogue of the Lovelace Collection of the Papers of John Locke*. Oxford: Oxford University Press, 1959.

MacCulloch, Diarmaid. *Thomas Cranmer: A Life*. New Haven, Conn.: Yale University Press, 1996.

———. *The Reformation: A History*. New York: Viking Press, 2004.

Madison, James. *The Federalist 51*(1788) www.yale.edu/lawweb/avalon/federal/fed 51.htm

Manley, Lawrence. *Convention: 1500–1750*. Cambridge, Mass.: Harvard University Press, 1980.

The Marprelate Tracts: 1588–1589. London: James Clarke and Co., 1911.

Marshall, John. *John Locke: Resistance, Religion, and Responsibility*. Cambridge: Cambridge University Press, 1994.

Marshall, John S. *Hooker and the Anglican Tradition*. London: Adam and Charles Black, 1963.

Marsilius of Padua. *Defensor Pacis*. Translated by A. Gewirth. Toronto: University of Toronto Press, 1967.

Masterson, George. *The Spiritual House in its Foundation*. London: Philemon Stephens, 1661.

Matthew, H. C. G. and Brian Harrison, eds. *Oxford Dictionary of National Biography*, volume IX. Oxford: Oxford University Press, 2004.

Maxwell, John. *Sacro Sancta Regum majestas or, the Sacred and Royal prerogative of Christian Kings*. Oxford: Henry Hall, 1644; London: Tho. Dring, 1689.

McConica, James, ed. *The History of the University of Oxford*. Vol. II. Oxford: Clarendon Press, 1986.

McGinn, D. J. *The Admonition Controversy*. New Brunswick, N. J.: Rutgers University Press, 1949.

McGrath, A. *The Intellectual Origins of the Reformation*. Oxford: Blackwell, 1993.

McGrath, Patrick. *Papists and Puritans under Elizabeth*. London: Blandford Press, 1967.

Melzer, Arthur M. *The Natural Goodness of Man: On the System of Rousseau's Thought*. Chicago: University of Chicago Press, 1990.

Mocket, Richard. *God and the King*. London: John Beale, 1615.

Molina, Luis de. *De Iustitia et Iure Opera Omnia*. Coloniae Allobrogum, 1733.

Morris, Christopher. *Political Thought in England: Tyndale to Hooker*. Oxford: Oxford University Press, 1953.

Muller, Richard A. *God, Creation, and Providence in the Thought of Jacob Arminius*. Grand Rapids, Mich.: Baker Books, 1991.

Muller, Richard. *The Unaccomodated Calvin: Studies in the Foundation of a Theological Tradition*. New York: Oxford University Press, 2000.

Munz, Peter. *The Place of Hooker in the History of Thought*. London: Routledge and Kegan, 1952.

Nalson, John. *The Countermine*. London: Jonathan Edwin, 1678.

Nederman, Cary J. *Community and Consent: The Secular Political Theory of Marsiglio of Padua's Defensor Pacis*. Lanham, Md.: Rowman and Littlefield, 1995.

Novak, Michael. *On Two Wings: Humble Faith and Commonsense in the American Founding*. San Francisco: Encounter Books, 2002.

Novarr, David. *The Making of Walton's Lives*. Ithaca, N. Y.: Cornell University Press, 1958.

Nuovo, Victor. *John Locke: Writings on Religion*. New York: Oxford University Press, 2002.

Oberman, Heiko. *The Harvest of Medieval Theology: Gabriel Biel and Late Medieval Nominalism*. Cambridge, Mass.: Harvard University Press, 1963.

Ott, Ludwig. *Fundamentals of Catholic Dogma*. Rockford, Ill.: Tan Books and Publishers, 1974 (reprint).

Parker, Henry. *Jus Populi*. London: Robert Bostock, 1644.

———. *Natural Law and Introduction to Legal Philosophy*. London: Hutchinson University Library, 1970 (reprint).

———. *Observations upon some of His Majesty's late answers and expresses*. London, 1642.

Pearson, Scott. *Thomas Cartwright and Elizabethan Puritanism*. Cambridge: Cambridge University Press, 1925.

Qutb, Syed. *Milestone*. (Berlin and New York: Globusz Publishing), Cf. www.globusz .com/ebooks/Milestone/00000010.htm also at www.youngmuslims.ca/online_library/ books/milestones/hold/index_2.asp.

Rutherford, Samuel. *Lex, Rex. The Law and the Prince*. London: John Field, 1644.

Sabine, George. *A History of Political Theory*. New York: Holt, Rinehart, and Winston, 1961.

Saravia, Hadrian. *Diversi Tractatus Theologici*. London: Richard Field, 1611.

———. *De Imperandi Authoritate*. London: Christopher Barker, 1593.

Schmitt, Charles. *Aristotle and the Renaissance*. Cambridge, Mass.: Harvard University Press, 1983.

———. *John Case and Aristotelianism in Renaissance England*. Montreal: McGill–Queens University Press, 1983.

Schochet, Gordon. *Patriarchalism in Political Thought: The Authoritarian Family and Political Attitudes Especially in 17th Century England*. London: Transaction, 1988 (reprint).

Secor, Phillip. *Richard Hooker: Prophet of Anglicanism*. Tunbridge Wells: Burnsand Oats, 1999.

Shirley, F. J. *Richard Hooker and Contemporary Political Ideas*. London: SPCK, 1949.

Simmons, John. *The Lockean Theory of Rights*. Princeton, N. J.: Princeton University Press, 1992.

Sisson, C. J. *The Judicious Marriage of Mr. Hooker and the Birth of the Laws of Ecclesiastical Polity*. Cambridge: Cambridge University Press, 1940.

Skinner, Quentin. *The Foundations of Modern Political Thought*. Vol 2. Cambridge: Cambridge University Press, 1978.

Soto, Domingo de. *De Iustitia et Iure Libri Decem*. Antwerp, 1560.

Sparrow, Anthony. *A rationale upon the Book of common-prayer of the Church of England*. London: T. Garthwaite, 1668 (original, 1656).

Spelman, Sir John. *Certain consideration upon the Duties both of prince and people*. Oxford: Leonard Lichfield, 1642.

———. *A View of a Printed Book*. Oxford or London: Leonard Lichfield, 1643.

Stillingfleet, Edward. *Irenicum*. London: Henry Mortlock and John Simmes, 1662.

Strauss, Leo. *Natural Right and History*. Chicago: University of Chicago Press, 2001.

Suarez, Francisco. *De Legibus*. Translated by Luciano Perena. Madrid: Corpus Hispanorum De Pace, 1871 (Spanish/Latin edition).

———. *Tractatus de Legibus Ac Deo Legislatore*. Naples, 1872.

Suttcliffe, Matthew. *A Treatise of Ecclesiastical Discipline*. London: George Bishop and Ralph Newberrie,1590.

Tierney, Brian. *The Idea of Natural Rights: Studies on Natural Rights, Natural Law and Church Law, 1150–1625*. Atlanta: Scholar's Press, 1997.

Tocquevillle, Alexis de. *Democracy in America* (1835). xroads.virginia.edu/~HYPER/DETOC/

Travers, Walter. *A Defense of the Ecclesiastical Discipline Ordayned of God*. Middleburg: Richard Schilders, 1588.

Trevelyan, G.M. *England Under the Stuarts*. London: The Folio Society, 1996.

Trueman, Carl. *Protestant Scholasticism: Essays in Reassessment*. Carlisle: Paternoster Press, 1999.

Tuck, Richard. *Natural Rights Theories: Their Origin and Development*. Cambridge: Cambridge University Press, 1979.

———. *Philosophy and Government: 1572–1651*. Cambridge: Cambridge University Press, 1993.

Tully, James. *A Discourse on Property: John Locke and his Adversaries*. Cambridge: Cambridge University Press, 1980.

Tyrrell, James. *Bibliotheca Politica: An Enquiry into the Ancient Constitution of the English Government*. London: Richard Baldwin, 1694.

———. *Patriarcha Non Monarcha*. London: Richard Janeway, 1681.

Vitoria, Francisco. *Political Writings*. Edited by A. Pagden and J. Lawrence. Cambridge: Cambridge University Press, 1991.

Voak, Nigel. *Richard Hooker and Reformed Theology*. Oxford: Oxford University Press, 2003.

Ward, A.W., ed. *The Cambridge Modern History. Vol. 3, The Wars of Religion*. Cambridge: Cambridge University Press, 1904.

Whitgift, John. *Answere to a certen Libell instituled, An Admonition to the Parliament*. London: Humfrey Toye, 1573.

———. *Defense of the Aunsvvere to the Admonition against the Replie of T.C*. London: Humfrey Toye, 1574.

———. *The Works of John Whitgift*. Edited by John Eyre. Cambridge: Cambridge University Press, 1851–1853.

Wilenius, Reijo. *The Social and Political Theory of Francisco Suárez*. Helsinki: Acta Philosophica Fennica, 1963.

Willet, Andrew. *A Christian Letter of Certaine English Protestants*. Middleburg: Richard Schilders, 1599.

Wilson, James. *Of the General Principles of Law and Obligation*. Indianapolis, Ind.: Liberty Fund, 2007; also at: www.founding.com/library/

Wilson, Timothy. *The Vanity and Falsity of the History of Passive Obedience Detected*. London: George Croom, 1690.

UNPUBLISHED MANUSCRIPTS

Locke, John. Bodleian (Oxford) MSS f 5 (1681).

———. Bodleian (Oxford) MSS f 6 (1682).

———. Bodleian (Oxford) MSS d10 (1682).

ARTICLES AND SHORTER DOCUMENTS APPEARING IN JOURNALS, PROCEEDINGS, OR ONLINE

Adams, John. "To the Grand Jurors of the County of Hampshire, Massachusetts." (1798). In Charles Francis Adams (ed.) *The Works of John Adams. Vol IX*. Boston: Little Brown, 1854: 227.

———. "To the Officers of the Third Division of the Militia of Massachusetts" (1798) in, Charles Francis Adams (ed.)*The Works of John Adams. Vol. IX*. Boston: Little Brown, 1854: 228–229.

Bull, George. "What did Locke borrow from Hooker?" *Thought* 7 (1932): 122–135.

Casey, Lee and David B. Rivkin. "The International Criminal Court vs. The American People." Feb 5, 1999. www.heritage.org/Research/InternationalOrganizations/BG1249.cfm.

Condren, Conel. "The Creation of Richard Hooker's Public authority: Rhetoric, Reputation and Reassesment." *Journal of Religious History* 21 (1997): 25–59.

Cromartie, Alan. "Theology and Politics of Richard Hooker." *History of Political Thought* XXI, Spring (2000): 41–66.

Daniel, William. "The Purely Penal Theory in the Spanish Theologians from Vitoria to Suarez." *Analecta Gregoriana* 164 (1968): 1–218.

Eccleshall, Robert. "Richard Hooker and the Peculiarities of the English: the reception of the 'Ecclesiastical Polity' in the Seventeenth and Eighteenth Centuries." *History of Political Thought* II (1981): 63–117.

Gibbs, Lawrence. "Richard Hooker: Prophet of Anglicanism or English magisterial reformer." *Harvard Theological Review* (2002) 95, 227–235.

Hamilton, Alexander. "A Farmer Refuted." (1775) www.founding.com/library/lbody .cfm?id=148andparent=56.

——. "The Spectacle of Revolutionary France," quoted in Kirk, *The Portable Conservative Reader*. Harmondsworth: Penguin, 1982: 78ff.

Hillerdal, Gunnar. "Reason and Revelation in Richard Hooker." *Acta Universistatis Lundensis* 54 (1962): 9–150.

James, Frank A. "A Late Medieval Parallel in Reformation Thought: *Gemina Praedestinatio* in Gregory of Rimini and Peter Martyr Vermigli." In *Via Augustini: Augustine in the Later Middle Ages, Renaissance, and Reformation*. Edited by Heiko Oberman and Frank A. James. Leiden: Brill, 1991:157–188.

Kearney, H. F. "Richard Hooker: A Reconstruction." The Cambridge Journal V (Oct. 1951–Sept. 1952).

Kelley, Donald R. "History, English Law, and the Renaissance." *Past and Present* 65 (1974).

Kirby, W. J. Torrance. "Richard Hooker's discourse on natural law in the context of the Magisterial Reformation." In *The Theology of Richard Hooker in the Context of the Magisterial Reformation*. Princeton, N. J.: Studies in Reformed Theology and History, Princeton Seminary Press, 1999. Also in www.swgc.mun.ca/animus/ 1998vol3/kirby3.htm (online copy used).

Kraye, Jill. "The Immortality of the Soul in the Renaissance: Between Natural Philosophy and Theology." *Signatures* I (2000): 16–39.

Marshall, John S. "Hooker and the Origins of American Constitutionalism." In *Origins of the Natural Law Tradition*. Edited by Arthur L. Harding. Dallas, Tex.: Southern Methodist University Press, 1954.

McGrade, A.S. "Constitutionalism Late Medieval and Modern-*Lex facit Regem*: Hooker's use of Bracton," from the *Acta Conventus Neo-Latini Bononiensis*. Edited by R.J. Schoek. Binghamton, N.Y., 1985, 116–123.

McNeil, John T. "Natural Law in the Teaching of the Reformers." *The Journal of Religion* 26 (1946): 168–182

Moreno, Angel Facio. "Dos Notas en Tornos A La idea De Derecho Natural En Locke." Revista de Estudios Politicos, 1961: 159–164, www.mtholyoke.edu/acad/ intrel/morg6.htm.

Morgenthau, Hans J. *Politics Among Nations: The Struggle for Power and Peace*, Fifth Edition, Revised. New York: Alfred A. Knopf, 1978: 4–15 (excerpt).

Novak, Michael. "The Faith of the Founding." First Things, 132 (2002): 27–32. Also online www.firstthings.com/ftissues/ft0304/articles/novak.html.

Oakley, Francis. "Christian theology and the Rise of the Concept of the Laws of Nature." *Church History* 30 (1961): 433–455.

——. "Locke, Natural Law and God-Again." *History of Political Thought* 18 (1997): 624–651.

——. "Medieval Theories of Natural Law: William of Ockham and the significance of the Voluntarist Tradition." *Natural Law Forum* 6 (1961).

Prager, Dennis. "If You Believe People are Basically Good." December 31, 2002. www.townhall.com/columnists/dennisprager/dp20021231.shtml.

Previte, C. W. "Marsilius of Padua." *Proceedings of the British Academy* (1935): 163–166.

Robertson, Neil G. "The Closing of the Early Modern Mind: Leo Strauss and Early Modern Political Thought." www.mun.ca/animus/1998vol3/robert3.htm.

Schabel, Charles. "Gregory of Rimini." *Stanford Enyclopedia of Philosophy* (online) plato.stanford.edu/entries/gregory-rimini/

Singh, Raghuveer. "John Locke and the Theory of Natural Law." *Political Studies* 9 (1961): 105–118.

Sirico C. S. P., Robert. "The Sin Tax: Economic and Moral Considerations." www.acton.org/publicat/occasionalpapers/sintax.html.

Sommerville, J. P. "Hadrian Saravia, and the Advent of the Divine Right of Kings." *History of Political Thought* 4 (1983): 229–245.

Stone, Martin. "The Nature and Significance of Law in Early Modern Scholasticsm." In *A History of Philosophy of Law from Ancient Greeks to the Scholastics*. Edited by Fred Miller. Dordrecht: Kluwer Press, 2005.

Thompson, W. D. J. Cargill. "The Philosopher of the Politic Society." In *Studies in the Reformation: Tyndale to Hooker*. Edited by C.W. Dunmore. London: Publisher, 1980:131–191.

Ulm, Wes. "The Defeat of the English Armada and the 16th-Century Spanish Naval Resurgence," Wes Ulm, Harvard University personal website, URL: www.people.fas.harvard.edu/~ulm/history/sp_armada.htm, © 2004.

——. "Top 10 myths and muddles about the Spanish Armada, history's most confused and misunderstood battle," by Wes Ulm, Harvard University personal website, URL: www.people.fas.harvard.edu/~ulm/history/sp_armada.htm, © 2004.

Virginia Declaration of Rights, 1776 (Drafted by George Mason) www.yale.edu/lawweb/avalon/virginia.htm.

Walwyn, William. "Walwyn's just defence." In *The Leveller Tracts 1647–1653*. Edited by W. Haller and G. Davies. Gloucester, Mass.: Peter Smith, 1964: 350–398.

Washington, George. *Farewell Address*. 1796, www.yale.edu/lawweb/avalon/washing.htm.

West, Thomas G. "Alan Bloom and America." Posted June, 2000. www.claremont.org/writings/890101west.html.

Wilson, James. "Of the General Principles of Law and Obligation." 1790–91. www.founding.com/library/lbody.cfm?id=207andparent=61.

Among Encyclopedias I consulted at various points in the course of my research were The Stanford Encyclopedia (plato.stanford.edu/), the Catholic Encyclopedia (www.newadvent.org/cathen/index.html), the New Catholic Encyclopedia (Washington, D.C.: Catholic University of America Press, 1967), and Wikipedia (www.wikipedia.com).

Index

About the Author

Alexander S. Rosenthal lectures on political theory and is program coordinator for the MA in Government at Johns Hopkins University Advanced Academic Programs. He received his bachelor's degree in philosophy from Princeton University, and his PhD in philosophy from the Katholieke Universiteit Leuven in Belgium. He has previously lectured at a number of academic institutions including Loyola College in Maryland and Catholic University of America.